The
PORTABLE
MBA

The
PORTABLE
MBA

FIFTH EDITION

Edited by

Kenneth M. Eades
Lynn A. Isabella
Timothy M. Laseter
Peter L. Rodriguez
Paul J. Simko
Ian Skurnik

WILEY

John Wiley & Sons, Inc.

This book is printed on acid-free paper. ∞

Published by John Wiley & Sons, Inc., Hoboken, New Jersey.
Published simultaneously in Canada.

For general information on our other products and services or for technical support, please contact our Customer Care Department within the United States at (800) 762-2974, outside the United States at (317) 572-3993 or fax (317) 572-4002.

Wiley also publishes its books in a variety of electronic formats. Some content that appears in print may not be available in electronic books. For more information about Wiley products, visit our web site at www.wiley.com.

Library of Congress Cataloging-in-Publication Data:

The portable MBA / Kenneth M. Eades, Lynn A. Isabella, Timothy M. Laseter, Peter L. Rodriguez, Paul J. Simko, and Ian Skurnik. — 5th ed.
    p.   cm.
  ISBN 978-0-470-48129-5 (cloth)
 1. Management. 2. Marketing. 3. Accounting. 4. Personnel management.
I. Eades, Kenneth M.
  HD31.C6134 2010
  658—dc22   2009049299

Printed in the United States of America.

10 9 8 7 6 5 4 3 2 1

Contents

List of Downloadable Materials

Preface

The first edition of *The Portable MBA* was published January 1, 1990. Many changes have occurred across the business landscape over the ensuing two decades, and we have updated our readers about the more salient events with each new edition of this book. In fact, much has happened since 2004 when the fourth edition was published, and we will put those extraordinary events in perspective in the second section of this Preface. Before discussing the past five years of business history, however, there are a number of improvements in this revision that you should know about.

The Fifth Edition

Whether you already have a master of business administration (MBA) degree and are looking for a refresher or you are thinking about entering an MBA program in the near future, you will find this book to be a highly useful resource. To start with, *The Portable MBA* allows you walk the walk of learning the concepts of business. Reading through these chapters and working through the examples provided is the best way for you to get a sneak preview of the feature-length production. Many of the chapters include examples that are available for you to use live on John Wiley & Sons' web site. Simply go to the web site (www.wiley.com/go/portablemba5e) and click the example of interest to see how the numbers were created. Change an assumption for the problem and see how it affects the final answer. True learning comes from the doing, not the watching, and these live examples allow you to experience some of the analytical work required of MBA students. The more you can reinforce concepts by putting them into action, the better you will be able to use those concepts to improve your decision-making skills and to become a more effective leader in the world of business.

While you are on the web site, you will have the opportunity to meet the author team by observing us teach in our classrooms. Our hope is that these videos will serve to give a personal touch to the words we have written in the chapters that follow. Also, you will gain an appreciation for the classroom experience for an MBA program. We will have more to say about the experience of earning an MBA in the next chapter.

As part of our desire to put you in the MBA experience, many of the chapters show how the materials presented relate to specific courses in top-rated programs. For example, Chapter 5, Financial Management, presents the content of a core course in corporate finance, which is part of all MBA programs, albeit under different titles. At the University of Chicago there are two courses, Introductory Finance and Corporation Finance, that cover the theory and practice of finance. At Harvard the courses are called Finance I and Finance II. Stanford's principles course is entitled Managerial Finance, whereas the University of Virginia's Darden School offers Financial Management and Policies as the first course in finance. These same comparisons are provided for accounting, operations, economics, and so on. This information will help you appreciate how business school curricula differ and how they are similar.

And finally, we have provided information about career paths after earning an MBA. Many chapters give a summary of MBA career opportunities to give you a feel for the type of position an MBA might accept as a first job after graduation. For example, there are a host of MBA-level positions in the finance industry, including both the banking and corporate sectors, that provide interesting and rewarding career opportunities. We provide similar information for marketing, strategy, and general management. The final chapter of the book is dedicated to giving hints and guidance about finding a job, which itself is a valued skill taught by the top-ranked programs. We thank Everette Fortner, Executive Director of Corporate Relations, Darden School of Business, University of Virginia, for contributing the final chapter and the various MBA Career sections.

We want to emphasize that every MBA program is unique. There are 463 universities in the United States that offer an MBA degree or the equivalent that are accredited by the Association to Advance Collegiate Schools of Business (AACSB), and each program has its own strengths and particular set of characteristics that make it different. Therefore you should think of this book as the chance to gain a strong appreciation for the knowledge base that serves as the foundation for the value of an MBA degree. We believe that as you read through the book, it will spark within you a curiosity for how this knowledge is communicated within the classroom and how those principles would be enhanced by having a room full of peers involved in a lively discussion about the topic. The interaction and discussion within a classroom as to how the topic relates to the students' own experiences and interests are where much of the value of the MBA degree is realized. To capture that value, you will need to enroll as a student in an MBA program and live the experience. If you make that choice, we will have succeeded in playing a part in a decision that we believe will prove to be one of the best in your life.

2004–2009

Since the previous edition of this book, we have experienced some of the biggest swings in fortune in the history of the industrial age. Individuals and companies alike have seen the best and worst of times. The past five years of the stock market tell much of the story. The Standard & Poor's 500 index is a measure of the performance of the U.S. stock market. This index is composed of 500 stocks of the largest companies in the economy that have their shares traded on public exchanges such that the prices can be observed every day. The S&P 500 index began the period at $1,112 and ended at $909, approximately an 18 percent decline over the five-year period. At its peak value in 2007, the S&P was up 40 percent, from which it plummeted 57 percent to its low point in the fall of 2008 before rebounding 34 percent in the spring of 2009.

The stock market is a window to the economy, and the view that began to emerge in 2008 was particularly dismal. The U.S. economy had been rocked by the bursting of a real estate bubble that was fueled by low interest rates and faulty lending practices in the mortgage market. What happened subsequently has been labeled as the subprime mortgage crisis. The crisis was created by a perfect storm of economic factors that

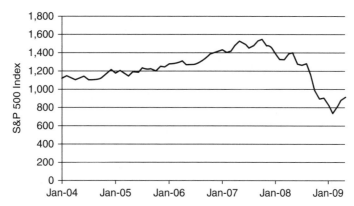

Exhibit P.1   Standard & Poor's 500 Index, January 1, 2004–May 11, 2009

resulted in a domino effect that surprised even the most experienced market analyst. A key factor was the subprime mortgages that were granted to people with substandard credit quality. In other words, they did not have sufficient earning power to reliably make the monthly payments. Many of these mortgages were structured with interest rates that were scheduled to rise over time, making it less likely that the borrowers could consistently make the payments. And finally, the situation was exacerbated by aggressive lending practices that often allowed the borrower to buy a house with little or no down payment; that is, borrowers were given 100 percent of the value of properties. Thus, if homeowners got far enough behind in their payments, they had little or nothing to lose by allowing foreclosure on the house.

The subprime crisis arrived after years of rising real estate prices. MSNBC reported in 2005 that "Despite rising concern about skyrocketing prices—mainly in coastal states— the housing market showed few signs of a slowdown. Sales hit a new record level and prices surged at double-digit rates in many areas."[1] Eventually, however, the housing market ran out of steam and housing prices began to fall. At the same time the economy entered a general slowdown, which put pressure on the subprime borrowers' ability to make their monthly payments. As the default rates began to rise and houses were fore-closed, financial institutions such as banks that held the mortgages began to experience losses.

The fall of the housing market would have by itself created a significant financial crisis. But most of the damage would have been confined to the individuals who borrowed the money and the banks that lent the money. In 2008 it became clear, however, that the crisis was touching a wide range of financial institutions that had nothing to do with the original mortgages. Through financial engineering, mortgages had become a significant investment vehicle for individuals and institutions around the world. Basically this was achieved by bundling lots of mortgages together in portfolios and then selling claims on the portfolios as investment securities for individual and institutional investors.

Because so many Americans had been buying houses over a protracted period of time, there was an astonishing amount of these mortgage-backed securities on the bal-ance sheets for a wide variety of financial institutions, including mutual funds, banks, investment banks, insurance companies, and hedge funds. In addition, the balance sheets of most of these financial institutions had become swollen with debt, much like the individuals' balance sheets were burdened with mortgage debt and credit card debt. Therefore, when the losses on the subprime mortgages began to be realized, it created significant losses for a whole host of financial institutions in the United States and around the world. Banks such as Bear Stearns and Lehman Brothers ultimately failed, while others received financial assistance from the federal government under the Troubled Asset Relief Program (TARP).

The crisis was truly global in nature. Although the U.S. financial industry suffered the largest losses, banks in Europe, Asia, and elsewhere were also affected by the loss in value of their investments. The result was a global decline in wealth as stock markets in Amsterdam, London, Frankfurt, Paris, Tokyo, Singapore, Hong Kong, and Mumbai tumbled to reflect the loss of earning power of the world's corporations. As banks struggled to keep afloat, the credit markets dried up across the globe and corporations as well as individuals found it difficult to borrow money for any purpose. Americans who had become used to routinely accessing credit lines for consumption and investment purposes now had to rely on their savings, much of which had been decimated by the stock and bond market declines.

In the midst of the market crash, the United States became aware of the largest investor fraud every committed by an individual. Bernard Madoff was running a hedge fund with a reported value of $65 billion, when he suddenly admitted that the fund had been operating as a Ponzi scheme for almost 30 years. Rather than investing the funds he collected from investors, he had been using the new funds as payment to existing investors and as money for his family's lavish lifestyle. Madoff's fraud affected a large number of individuals, corporations, and charitable organizations. Many of the individuals lost their entire life savings, and charities were forced to shut down as entire endowments were lost. As we said in the fourth edition, once again we find that "the misdeeds of a few have done great damage to many."

As of the writing of this book, we are well into the recession and the outlook for the economy remains uncertain. Some economists are pointing to signs that the rate of economic decline has begun to slow, meaning that the bottom of the recession is in sight. However, with the unemployment rate at 8.9 percent, the highest point in 26 years, most believe that it will take years before the economy can return to the prerecession unemployment rate of 4.5 percent. Many worry that the heightened role of the government will lead to a decline in innovation and operating efficiency, key ingredients to sustained growth. The national debt has risen to epic levels as the government has embarked on a strategy of investing in the economy to spur overall demand. Neither the short-term nor the long-term effects of this strategy are well understood.

We believe there are, however, good reasons for optimism. Foreclosure rates in many states have fallen. Spending appears to have been stabilized. The weak and volatile stock market has not prevented firms such as Rosetta Stone and Digital Globe from successfully completing their initial public offerings. These IPOs illustrate that there is investment capital available to support companies with promising business plans.

It is within these signs for optimism that we see many of the themes of this book. First and foremost is that business should be about values and value creation. Great companies are those that create and deliver value to customers, shareholders, employees, and the communities in which they do business.

Companies that succeed are those that meet the needs of the marketplace. Strategy begins with an understanding of what those needs are and how to meet them in a better or more distinctive manner than others. Building an enduring business requires innovation to sustain what makes the firm's services or goods distinctive. Executing a business model depends on the active engagement and commitment of employees at all levels of the firm, but more particularly those in the middle, which we refer to as leading from the middle. In these times of uncertainty and upheaval, ensuring that everyone is engaged and involved, working together to move the company in new directions, is the job of those managers in the middle.

That all sounds pretty straightforward, but the lessons of the past few years are based on numerous examples of companies that lost sight of the basics. Clearly, management must have an acute understanding of risk as well as a culture for leading during times of uncertainty. Thus, new to this edition is a chapter dedicated to risk management. Moreover, in a business environment that is turbulent, management is tempted to stray from its core values. One of our major premises is that when a firm encounters turbulence is exactly when it most needs to rely on core values and strengths. If management fails to look to the interests of all the stakeholders and balance the benefits that accrue to each, ultimately this failure will weaken the company.

Much of our attention in this edition, as in previous ones, is focused on the basics. Most of what is in the following chapters represents the core content of a two-year full-time MBA program. One way for you to go beyond the basics is to utilize other books in the Portable MBA series. For a deeper dive into finance, for example, you should get *The Portable MBA in Finance and Accounting*, or for marketing, *The Portable MBA in Marketing*. The next step is to find an MBA program that fits your needs best and "walk the walk" of earning an MBA degree.

The past few years have added credibility to the quote "The only constant in life is change." In fact, each time we revise *The Portable MBA*, we are reminded about the fast pace of change in the business world. It may be that you are reading this book because of the changes in your job that prompt you to have a renewed understanding of business, or perhaps you are considering an MBA degree as a means to change your career. In any case, you should remember that change will always be a part of business and part of your life. You could argue that change is why we need managers, because without change businesses could be run by computers! The principles of business will make you a better decision maker within this complex world and all of its challenges. We congratulate you for investing in yourself by reading this book, and we wish you good fortune on your journey into the new set of uncertain waters.

Note

1. www.msnbc.msn.com/id/10482623/.

About the Authors

Kenneth M. Eades (Charlottesville, VA) is Professor of Business Administration and Area Coordinator of the Finance Department of the Darden Graduate School of Business at the University of Virginia. He has taught a variety of corporate finance topics, including capital structure, dividend policy, risk management, capital investments, and firm valuation. His research interests are in the area of corporate finance, where he has published articles in the *Journal of Finance*, *Journal of Financial Economics*, *Journal of Financial and Quantitative Analysis*, and *Financial Management*. In addition to *Finance Interactive*, a multimedia tutorial software in finance (Irwin/McGraw-Hill, 1997), he has co-authored two books: *Case Studies in Finance* (McGraw-Hill, 2010) and *Case Studies in Financial Decision Making* (Dryden Press, 1994). He has written numerous case studies as well as a Web-based, interactive tutorial on the pricing of financial derivatives. He has received the Wachovia Award for Excellence in Teaching Materials and the Wachovia Award for Excellence in Research. Mr. Eades is active in Executive Education programs at the Darden School and has served as a consultant to a number of corporations and institutions, including many commercial banks and investment banks, Fortune 500 companies, and the Internal Revenue Service. Prior to joining Darden, Professor Eades was a member of the faculties at the University of Michigan and the Kellogg School of Management at Northwestern University. He has a BS from the University of Kentucky and a PhD from Purdue University. His web site is http://faculty.darden.virginia.edu/eadesk/.

Lynn A. Isabella (Charlottesville, VA) is Associate Professor, Business Administration and Area Coordinator of the Leadership and Organizational Behavior area at the Darden School of Business, University of Virginia. She teaches courses in organizational behavior, leadership and change, and teams in Darden's MBA, MBA for Executives, and Executive Education programs. As a researcher, she focuses on questions of developing one's personal leadership expertise, leading change as a middle manager, and the events that shape individual careers and propel organizational change.

She is the co-author of two books (*Alliance Competence* and *Leader and Teams: The Winning Partnership*) and has published numerous articles in both scholarly and practitioner journals. She has also researched and authored over 70 case studies focused on U.S. and international companies and issues. Several pieces of original research as well as an international case study have received recognition (Academy of Management Best Paper Award, Wachovia Award for Research Excellence, and Wachovia Award for Excellence in Teaching Materials). As a management consultant, she has extensive international experience with companies worldwide helping them develop their global leadership talent and organizational effectiveness. She regularly works with companies in Central and Eastern Europe through the Bled School of Management, and has extensive experience in Latin and South America, China, Africa, and Western Europe. Before joining the Darden faculty in 1990, Professor Isabella was on the faculty of the Cox School of Business, Southern Methodist University, and taught at the Harvard Business School. She earned her DBA and MBA from Boston University, an EdM from Harvard University, and a BS in mathematics from Tufts University. Contact Professor Isabella at Isabella@virginia.edu.

Timothy M. Laseter (Charlottesville, VA) serves on the faculty of the Darden Graduate School of Business at the University of Virginia, one of the top-ranked business schools in the country. He also holds adjunct or visiting appointments at IESE in Barcelona, the London Business School, Emory's Goizueta Business School in Atlanta, and the Stern School at New York University. He teaches courses for MBAs and Executive Education programs addressing operations strategy, supply chain management, and product development.

Prior to launching his academic career, Laseter served as a partner with Booz Allen Hamilton. Founder of the firm's global network of sourcing practitioners, he advised senior executives in a variety of industries, including automotive, computers, defense, energy, media, and telecommunications. During his 15 years with the firm, he gained a global perspective by transferring among a variety of Booz Allen offices, working out of Cleveland, London, New York, and McLean, Virginia. Engagements addressed a wide range of issues, including overall business strategy, organization, supply chain management, product development, sourcing, and related topics of operations strategy, and spanned the globe, including the United States, Europe, South America, and Asia. Prior to joining Booz Allen, Laseter worked at Siecor—at the time, a fiber-optics joint venture between Siemens and Corning. Earlier in his career he worked as a management consultant with Arthur Andersen and the McLean Group.

A prolific writer for business executives, he is the author of *Balanced Sourcing* (Jossey-Bass, 1998) and coauthor, with Ron Kerber, of *Strategic Product Creation* (McGraw-Hill, 2006). Additionally he has authored or coauthored dozens of practitioner articles and book chapters plus numerous academic cases and peer-reviewed articles. His research has been cited in a range of publications, including the *Wall Street Journal*, the *New Yorker*, *Purchasing*, and the *Progressive Grocer*. Laseter serves as a contributing editor for *strategy+business* and writes a recurring column on "Operating Strategies."

Laseter earned a bachelor of science degree in industrial management from the Georgia Institute of Technology with high honors. He holds a master of business administration and a PhD in operations management from the Darden Graduate Business School at the University of Virginia and was a recipient of the Faculty Award for Academic Excellence.

Peter L. Rodriguez (Charlottesville, VA) is an Associate Professor of Business at the Darden Graduate School of Business Administration, University of Virginia, where he teaches courses on global macroeconomics and foreign direct investment in emerging economies. At the Darden School he serves as the Associate Dean for International Affairs and the Director of the Tayloe Murphy International Center. His research interests center on the effects and design of international trade and investment policies, economic development, and corruption. He has published articles in numerous peer-reviewed journals in economics and management, including the *Academy of Management Review*, *Academy of Management Executive*, *Journal of Business Ethics*, *Journal of International Business Studies*, *Organization Science*, *Review of International Economics*, and *World Economy*. He is active in Executive Education and has worked with many Fortune 500 companies. He is the recipient of numerous teaching awards from all institutions where he has taught, including Princeton University and Texas A&M University. Prior to his academic career, he worked as an associate in the Global Energy group at JPMorgan Chase. He holds a BS from Texas A&M University and an MA and PhD from Princeton University. His web site is http://faculty.darden.edu/rodriguezp/, and he may be reached via e-mail at Rodriguez@virginia.edu.

Paul J. Simko (Charlottesville, VA) is Associate Dean for the MBA for Executives Program and Associate Professor of Business Administration at the Darden School of Business, the University of Virginia. His research centers on issues related to financial accounting information; he has received numerous national and university recognitions for his work. Professor Simko is particularly interested in topics related to how alternative accounting treatments affect firms' earnings quality. His current research examines the incentives and consequences of earnings management, valuation issues pertaining to intellectual property rights, and the role short sellers serve as information intermediaries. He teaches the core Accounting for Managers course in the MBA and MBA for Executives programs, and elective courses in Financial Statement Analysis. Prior to joining the Darden School faculty in 2002, Professor Simko taught at Emory University, Indiana University, INSEAD, and the Helsinki School of Economics. He has a BS and MAcc from the University of Florida and PhD from the University of Texas at Austin. He has worked as a senior analyst with Citicorp and is a certified public accountant. His web site is at http://faculty.darden.virginia.edu/simkop/.

Ian Skurnik (Charlottesville, VA) is Associate Professor of Business Administration at the Darden School of Business, University of Virginia. His research and teaching focus on marketing, with an emphasis on psychological processes that underlie consumer cognition and behavior. Professor Skurnik is especially interested in how people use information in memory when making judgments and decisions. His research in these areas has been published in journals such as the *Journal of Consumer Research* and *Journal of Personality and Social Psychology*. He has taught the core Marketing Management course, as well as elective courses in Marketing Intelligence and Research, Consumer Behavior, and Research Methods. Prior to joining the Darden School faculty in 2006, Professor Skurnik taught at the Rotman School of Management, University of Toronto. He has a PhD from Princeton University. His web site is at http://faculty.darden.virginia.edu/skurnik/.

The
PORTABLE
MBA

Introduction: The MBA Degree Experience

Ken Eades

Many people with a master of business administration degree say that their MBA education was transformational in its impact on their lives. If you ask them to describe their experience, however, you will hear stories that differ considerably from each other. In fact, no two people have the same experience, because there are 463 accredited MBA programs in the United States and each has a slightly different curriculum, student body demographics, location, specialties, teaching styles, and so on. MBA programs are offered in a number of formats, including one-year programs, part-time programs, and programs offered by distance (i.e., via the Internet). In the United States, however, most of the best-known MBA programs are delivered as full-time two-year programs. We believe the full-time two-year degree offers the best learning experience due to the high concentration of face-to-face learning in the classroom and the resulting intensity of the learning environment.

In the chapters that follow we present a curriculum experience that is typical for most of the full-time two-year MBA programs. Each chapter contains business principles and concepts for a particular business function or topic. This is the content of the MBA program, which is the glue that holds an MBA student's experience together. As an MBA student, you will learn a language of business that will connect you to the university, the business school, the faculty, and fellow students for the rest of your life. We cannot overstate the importance of having a quality curriculum delivered by a first-rate faculty as the key ingredients of an MBA student's experience. However, before we talk about the courses and the curriculum, this Introduction gives you a feel for the overall MBA experience—all the events that surround and contribute to learning, such as the classroom, the community, the career search, and life balance.

The Classroom

The amount of material relevant to developing a business leader has reached epic proportions. While there is a trend toward shortening MBA programs to reduce the time and cost associated with getting the degree, there has also been an explosion of information about business and management practices. Therefore, an MBA curriculum cannot begin to contain all you need to know about business, but rather represents the faculty's careful choice of the most relevant and most impactful topics for a newly minted MBA entering the workforce. Nevertheless, all MBA programs share the trait of "10 pounds of material stuffed into a 5-pound bag." This makes the daily schedule the biggest challenge facing an MBA student. Not surprisingly, much of the daily routine revolves around classes: preparing for classes and attending those classes.

The typical MBA class is fast paced and rich in content. This is where the action is. Whether it's the professor moving the class through a new concept or students engaging in a debate about some aspect of the concept, there is a high degree of engagement and involvement. Teaching styles vary from the classic lecture format to a less structured discussion format. The most common discussion-based classes are those based on a case study.

In a case method class, the discussion is centered on the analysis of a case study that puts the student in the shoes of a manager facing specific challenges at a certain point in time for a particular company or organization. The task of the student is to come to class prepared to make recommendations for courses of action and to explain and defend those recommendations to the professor and the rest of the class. The professor's role is to use various recommendations to facilitate a discussion among the students that brings out the key learning points for the day. In a more traditional lecture class, the professor will build on assigned reading and problems with a lecture and/or discussion about the topic. Every class is a highly valued learning opportunity, and MBA students are not shy about challenging the professor and each other to get the most out of their time together in class. Ultimately, each student is responsible for his or her own education and each student should strive to contribute to the many learning opportunities that arise in each class period.

The learning in the classroom occurs on several levels. There are the theory and the business principles being taught by the professor and presented in the assigned materials. Then there is the exchange of ideas among the students as they seek to explain these principles and put them to use within a business decision context. Ironically, much is learned from mistakes made by others and by yourself. Mistakes are cheap while you are a student, but become very expensive once you enter the workforce. You can learn more by using the classroom as an opportunity to take risks and to test new ideas in a low-cost environment. The classroom is also a unique opportunity to experience a wide range of opinions from a diverse group of individuals. The best MBA programs attract students with a wide variety of experiences from all points of the globe. Business is global, and learning from other cultures is critical to being successful in today's world of international commerce and outsourcing.

In 1977 an acclaimed movie, *The Paper Chase*, portrayed life as a student at the Harvard Law School. Harvard is depicted as a cutthroat environment where students compete intensely to survive. Over the years we have found that MBA students are less focused on the grades they receive and more focused on the value they can gain from the program. Most MBA programs promote a collaborative environment based on teamwork that encourages student interaction and cross-fertilization of ideas. This sort of engagement allows students to develop relationships that are conducive to a tough-minded exchange of opinions inside and outside the classroom. Disagreement is based on facts and logic that ultimately lead to the best-informed decisions. Thus, a lesson learned by MBA students is how to disagree in a productive manner, which makes the classroom discussions safer and more productive.

Students devote a significant amount of time preparing for their MBA classes. Many programs assign students to study groups or learning teams at the outset in order to facilitate the learning process. In fact, it is common for many of the deliverables for courses to be team-based work. Students use these small groups as an important step in the class preparation process. After students work through the assigned materials on their own, they join their learning team to discuss their ideas as a group to learn from each other before attending the class and learning from the professor and the rest of the class. Thus, more time is spent preparing for class than the class itself, and much of the learning occurs during the preparation as well as during formal and informal discussions with students and faculty after class.

The Community

In addition to their academic community, MBA students also have a social community, which encompasses everything outside of academics. There is a natural sense of community among the students, faculty, and staff that develops quickly as a result of the day-to-day interactions of the education process. Becoming a part of the social community may take a little more effort over a slightly longer period of time, but it inevitably becomes an important part of the students' overall experience. For example, MBA students find a number of ways to be involved with the university town or city through the restaurants, entertainment, and involvement with community projects.

In general, an MBA program is not a place for someone who prefers to work alone and avoid interaction with others. The intensity of the educational experience leads to friendships and relationships that endure for a lifetime. To an extent these relationships are an artifact of the many team-based projects utilized in the typical MBA curriculum. Most of the interactions, however, come from the people skills already possessed by the students when they arrive for the program. MBAs typically enjoy each other's company in and out of the classroom. They look for opportunities to work together and socialize together. These are traits of people who typically seek careers in business. MBAs also typically bring a sense of giving back to the community in which they live, and MBA programs provide a variety of clubs and other organizations to facilitate such involvement.

Like any university setting, extracurricular activities are an important facet of an MBA's daily life. Students arrive with a wide variety of interests about their future careers as well as their favorite charities and outreach programs. Most students join a number of clubs and organizations as part of their experience. For starters, there are many clubs based on the student's career focus, such as a finance club, marketing club, consulting club, real estate club, not-for-profit club, and so on. These are natural affinity groups that are particularly useful networking opportunities to support job searches and to facilitate guest speakers or other events. Other clubs and groups are centered around ethnic or other affinities such as the National Association of Women MBAs, the Black Business Student Forum, a military association, an international business society, and others. And finally, students coalesce around common interests such as the outdoors club, the soccer club, or the community outreach society. These clubs and groups often create events that personally touch students, faculty, and staff and serve to enrich the overall experience in the growth and development of the student.

Once in the workplace, the relationships developed outside of class take on the added benefit of a powerful network that enhances careers and supports and creates business opportunities. Business schools have alumni bases that maintain strong ties over time because of the intensity of their shared experience and because of the commonality of their professional interests.

The Career Search

Choosing to leave a job and then pay the necessary tuition to earn an MBA makes it an expensive proposition. For most people, the two years as an MBA student represent the largest investment they will ever make in themselves, and they want the experience to be as rewarding as possible. The good news is that the data show that the benefits of an MBA strongly outweigh the costs. *Forbes* magazine conducts an annual analysis of MBA programs[1] that shows that graduates from the top 20 programs are able to recoup the costs of their degrees within an average of 3.6 years. The costs included tuition plus the salaries forgone during the two years in the program. A higher salary should not be the primary reason for seeking an MBA, but there is no escaping the fact that the MBA degree meets the economic payoff test.

The MBA degree is a vehicle either to accelerate a career or to change careers. Either way there are very few who select a full-time program with the intention of returning to their previous jobs, which makes the selection of the new career path an important decision. The MBA is a pragmatic degree. It is designed to give expertise that is relevant and helps graduates add value to society. Therefore, getting the right job is just as important as getting the skills needed for the job, which makes the search for that first job a significant time commitment.

The competition for MBA talent during buoyant economies is keen. Newly minted MBAs from top-flight programs will be faced with many rewarding opportunities from which to choose. This is both a blessing and a curse, as the range of options creates a need to give time and energy to assessing each alternative. The recruiting process begins almost immediately upon admittance to an MBA program. Large corporations prefer to hire students as interns for the summer following their first year of the program. Therefore, a student is tasked with learning about companies during the first semester with the anticipation of being interviewed by companies during much of the second semester. The process repeats when students return for their second year of studies. With luck, a student will have already received a job offer from his or her summer internship. If not or if the student wants to change companies or career paths, the search for a permanent job offer might be ongoing during the entire second year of study.

During a recession, the job search process is more difficult and more time-consuming. For highly rated programs, the vast majority of students will succeed in finding a job. Unlike during a boom economy, however, they will rarely receive more than one offer and that offer may not align perfectly with their aspirations. This does not mean that the degree is less valued, and in fact the MBA demands premium respect in all economies. However, the pay and terms of the jobs found in a recession are likely to be noticeably less than the norm during a buoyant economy. The time spent finding the job will on average be much longer than when companies are aggressively filling positions to manage their growth objectives.

Regardless of the economic environment, an important part of the career search is learning about oneself. The best career choices come from an understanding of whether you work well in a large organization or prefer a more entrepreneurial environment. How important is the salary? The work hours? Travel? Are you willing to live outside the

United States? Do you ultimately want to run your own company? All of these questions help you discover the best career and the best first job to assist you in reaching your goals.

It is not uncommon for students to return to school with little idea of what they will do next other than that it will be different than what they have done in the past. This is fully understandable, but competition for jobs is intense regardless of the economy, and no one can afford to start their career search too late in the game. In this book we offer descriptions of MBA careers as well as a chapter on what an MBA should do to find a job. We have added this information to this edition because of the importance of the job search in the life of an MBA student. Like anything else, doing the search well pays dividends and doing it poorly or not devoting sufficient time to it will likely result in an undesirable outcome.

A frequent topic of conversation in the halls of an MBA classroom building is the interview experiences of the students. The job search begins with refinement of the student's curriculum vitae, which is the first source of information for companies to find students for their organizations. The campus interview is the key opportunity for students to distinguish themselves with a company and to learn whether the position is feasible for their personal objectives. Following the campus interview will be either a rejection letter or an invitation for a company visit for a round of interviews with management. These recruiting activities can at times be hectic and pose conflicts with studies, but they also provide invaluable experiences and extend the candidate's professional networks. Even if an interview or company visit does not translate into a job offer, they can often provide the groundwork for the next job, which could present itself within a few years of graduation.

Life Balance

Being an MBA student is truly a full-time job. Finding a job is also a full-time job. Getting exercise, seeing your family, having fun, and just simply living your life cannot be put on hold for 21 months. Achieving the right balance among these competing forces is difficult. Most students find that they are constantly fighting to find the right balance and frequently readjusting to get back in sync.

Life balance challenges are not unique to being an MBA student. As business school faculty, we hear these same issues from executives in corporations who have fast-paced and demanding jobs. Therefore, it is a fallacy to think that the balancing act will disappear upon graduation. The key to success is to develop a discipline that recognizes the many demands on your time and makes the most out of the time allocated to studying, to recruiting, and to the rest of your life. Learning is hard work, and it requires a highly disciplined approach to managing your daily schedule. Some hints for success include:

- Leverage your peers: many programs have preassigned learning teams that will serve to make your class preparation as efficient as possible.
- Set a budget of time for class preparation and stick to it; you will rarely feel fully prepared or fully satisfied with an assignment.
- Commit to regular exercise, sensible diet, adequate sleep, and personal downtime.

MBA students find it a constant challenge to balance their professional and personal lives. Most find the first few months of the program to be particularly challenging as they learn the hard way how to make use of every hour of the day. There is no typical day in the life of an MBA, but there are many examples available, such as the following blog written by an MBA student at the Richard Ivey School of Business at the University of Western Ontario:[2]

A Day in the Life . . .

by Chris Green

I am really busy these days. Here's a taste:

6:50 A.M. Alarm goes off, and I slowly wake up from a deep sleep. It is hard to get up when it is so dark and cold outside. As I wait for the coffee machine I check my e-mail and the latest news headlines on Google News.

7:40 A.M. I gather my laptop, papers, and snacks and head out the door.

8:00 A.M. Class begins. Today starts with Leveraging Information Technology. We discuss the Project Manthan case, a huge ERP [enterprise resource planning] implementation at Indian Oil Company. Someone jokes to me that these cases always come down to "hire a consultant." Not quite, but that option is always tempting.

9:30 A.M. We switch to Marketing. Professor Niraj Dawar discusses customer buying behavior by asking us to draw upon our own decision-making process when buying a product. Today he unleashes a sense of humor that we have not seen before. It makes the class quite enjoyable.

11:00 A.M. Our last session with Prof. Dawar focuses on the difficulty of differentiating in the power generation industry. One of his takeaways is "there is no such thing as a commodity"; that is, there are always ways in which you can differentiate yourself as a brand or business. I'd like to see him debate this with an economist.

12:15 P.M. Class ends. We are asked to complete a questionnaire that is part of a GMAC [Graduate Management Admissions Council] research study conducted by another Ivey prof. As we are students, we get $20 and a lunch coupon for the effort. Who said there is no such thing as a free lunch?

12:30 P.M. Grab a quick lunch with classmates down at DK's. Discuss the movie "Slumdog Millionaire," and whether we prefer to read the book before the movie, or never see the movie at all.

1:00 P.M. Meet with my New Venture Project team. We go through major points of the Market Size-up section of our business plan. For homework we will read some marketing reports to get up to speed.

2:00 P.M. Go home and start the Ops [Operations] case for tomorrow. It is only two pages but requires a lot of number crunching.

4:00 P.M. Head back to Spencer and meet with my learning team to discuss the Ops case. Luckily my group is full of engineers and quant people, so we are able to make a lot of progress. We answer about half of the questions before people have to leave to go to other commitments.

6:00 P.M. Go home again. As I wait for Julia to cook dinner I set up the registration for an upcoming mock interview session with Bell. This is part of my Business Technology Club duties. The session is this Thursday so I need to set up the registration on the MBAA [MBA Association] website.

7:00 P.M. Eat dinner and talk with Julia. I barely get to spend any time with her these days.

8:00 P.M. Finish setting up the registration. Send out a few e-mails about miscellaneous items.

8:30 P.M. Read the IT [information technology] case for tomorrow.

10:00 P.M. Take a break, watch whatever Julia is watching on TV (I think it's "The Bachelor").

10:30 P.M. Read market reports on Location-Based Services for my New Venture Project team meeting tomorrow.

12:00 A.M. Turn off the light for some well-deserved sleep.

No matter how crowded, each day of an MBA student's life eventually comes to an end, as does the 21-month experience. There are many ingredients that get mixed together to make the MBA a transformational experience, including the faculty, the curriculum, and the community. A student need only look to left and right while sitting in class to realize that a big reason for getting an MBA is to be immersed in an intense experience with a group of outstanding individuals with a vast diversity of experience and talents. MBA schools attract the best and brightest from all continents and from all races and genders. Consider that if you are sitting in a classroom with 60 students of average age 26, there is approximately 300 years of work experience and 1,500 years of life experience in the room. This is a true opportunity to learn and accelerate one's development as leader and high-performance team member.

If you can immerse yourself into the chapters that follow, you will begin to feel the power of the ideas and concepts offered by the MBA experience. Understanding business principles is a critical first step in becoming a better decision maker and a leader. Whether you are a first-time reader or you are updating your skills with this latest edition of the book, you will find that your business acumen will be sharpened by the pages that follow. Of course, the concepts are only part of the overall MBA degree experience. To get the rest, you will have to take the plunge and walk the walk by enrolling in a program and immersing yourself in the curriculum, the culture, and the community.

Notes

1. "Best Business Schools" by Christina Settimi and Kurt Badenhausen, *Forbes*, August 16, 2007.
2. http://iveymbastudents.blogspot.com/2009/01/guest-entry-chris-green-day-in-life .html.

1

Accounting Principles

Graduate business students will virtually always begin their programs of study with an introduction to accounting principles. The reason for this is simple: Accounting provides quantitative information that enables managers to make informed business decisions. Without a basic understanding of financial statements, accounting methods, and accounting measurement issues, much of the data analysis and interpretation required of business problems would not be possible. Accounting is often called "the language of business," and for good reason. It provides a structural framework and a quantitative vocabulary with which most business issues and their solutions may be expressed. Managers, investors, and countless others would find themselves virtually paralyzed without the information provided by the accounting process. With such information the foundation can be built for understanding most business issues.

The significant demand for relevant, reliable, and timely financial information by capital markets, managers, regulators, and others makes the understanding of the accounting process of critical importance to business. Accounting today is a highly developed field, complete with codified rules, regulatory bodies, and professional certifications that signify degrees of individual expertise. At its core, however, understanding the subject starts with understanding the end objectives of the output it generates: the financial statements. It continues with appreciating the myriad of measurement bases that can exist across accounts included on these statements. Only then can it conclude with the various forms of analysis and decision making that render knowledge of the subject so powerful.

With this in mind, this chapter has five overarching objectives. First, it provides an introduction to the framework of financial accounting. An emphasis on the balance sheet equation is taken, as from this equation the key relationships across the financial statements reported by most companies can be emphasized. Second, the chapter explores the notion of accrual accounting, particularly how the methods, estimates, and assumptions made in the preparation of the financial statements affect interpretation. Third, it offers a step-by-step guide to reading the annual report, the most commonly used document from the accounting process. Fourth, it introduces a systematic approach to analyzing financial statements, including the basics of how to assess the financial health of a company. Finally, it deals with the field of managerial accounting, particularly how variance analysis of a project or business unit can yield valuable insights for the operating manager.

The Framework of Accounting: The Balance Sheet Equation

The foundation, or building block, of accounting rests with this fundamental concept: The resources available to a firm are bound by the claims made on those resources. This concept mirrors what should be economic intuition about the firm: Those providing capital investments to the firm (i.e., investors) have claims equivalent to the assets standing behind those investments. In this sense there must be balance—a balance that can be expressed as assets equal liabilities plus owners' equity.

Consider the basic power of this equation. Increases in a firm's assets must be financed by increases in liabilities (e.g., a bank loan) or in equity (e.g., a sale of stock), or by creating value through operations. Decreases in assets (such as a debt payment or a dividend payment) must be offset with decreases in that corresponding type of capital (e.g., liabilities or owners' equity, respectively). Changes (or Δ) in an element of the accounting system must likewise be balanced out:

$$\Delta\text{Assets} = \Delta\text{Liabilities} + \Delta\text{Owners' Equity}$$

To illustrate, consider what happens when the firm borrows capital from a bank. The cash received represents a new asset to the firm, but there is now a new claim against the firm that must be recorded as a liability. So assets increase by the amount borrowed (i.e., cash), and so do liabilities, and together these changes force a balance of the fundamental accounting equation. As another illustration, consider what happens on the other side of this transaction—that is, from the bank's perspective. The bank has given up cash, but has a new asset that would be labeled as a receivable. The reduction of one asset, cash, is exactly offset by the creation of another, a receivable.

From the balance sheet equation and these two examples, one can readily see that even the simplest transaction must have at least *two sides*, for a minimum of two accounting effects necessary to capture the nature of balancing. Perhaps you have heard of the term *double-entry accounting system*. The previous balancing equation is the basis for that system.

The financial statements are the primary output from the accounting process. How these statements relate to the balancing equation is also not that complex. Consider the context of your own personal financial scorecards. Three very basic questions one would ask about personal wealth would be the following: How much does one have? How much does one earn? How well does one manage one's money? The answer to the first question would come from a balance sheet, the answer to the second from an income statement, and the answer to the third from a statement of cash flows. In a sense, then, these three main statements, found in virtually every firm's financial reports, have as objectives tackling three very fundamental financial scorecard objectives. Here are some more specifics about what each financial statement attempts to capture:

- *Balance sheet.* This financial report presents a snapshot of the assets of the firm, and the claims upon those assets, at a particular point in time (i.e., the end of the fiscal year). The balance sheet is grounded in the balancing equation summarized earlier and attempts to provide detail regarding the firm's assets, liabilities, and owners' equity.

- *Income statement.* This financial report is a measure of the flows of business over a period of time expressed in terms of *profit and loss*. Profits are expressed in terms of total revenue activities of the firm, reduced by the costs incurred to generate those revenues. Some of these flows must be adjusted (or matched) across periods to correspond with other flows that are economically related. The activity captured in an income statement is reflected as certain *changes on the balance sheet*. Because net profit belongs to the owners of the firm, it is in the owners' equity section of the balance sheet that profit will be reported. The individual account capturing profit and loss is commonly referred to as *retained earnings*.

- *Statement of cash flows.* Because the income statement and the balance sheet result from accruals and allocations made by accountants, it can be difficult to tell what really happened to the firm in terms of the actual flows of cash. Did the firm generate more cash this year than last? The statement of cash flows helps answer this question. It recasts the performance of the firm into cash-based accounting and helps the reader understand the changes in cash and the causes. This statement is also often viewed as supplemental, as it merely specifies in detail how the *cash on the balance sheet* changes from period to period. It further segregates these changes as those relating to operations, to investing, and to financing activities.

Contained within each of these statements is a series of *accounts*, into which the transactions within the firm are recorded. Individual accounts therefore only provide additional detail about the fundamental accounting equation that is expressed in terms of assets, liabilities, and owners' equity, as described earlier. Remember this basic use of accounts as we review the financial statements for PepsiCo later in this chapter.

Accrual Accounting

The notion of reporting over distinct periods of time is an important feature of financial accounting. Because financial statement users desire to evaluate performance over time, the accounting process must be closed as of a specific date (quarter- or year-end), and adjustments to some accounts become necessary. Consider that for all practical purposes the accounting process follows predictable mechanical cycles each period. This process entails two distinct activities: the everyday recording of transactions during the period, and adjustments of certain key financial statement accounts after the period has ended. For the former, management sets accounting policies and procedures, and chooses accounting methods consistent with required standards—generally accepted accounting principles (GAAP)—that govern how each identifiable event will be recorded. There are choices here, such as whether to depreciate equipment uniformly or use accelerated depreciation, but the decision should be made with an eye toward accurately reflecting the underlying economics of the activity under measurement. For the latter, the accounting cycle is structured such that many estimates and judgments are adjustments made after a reporting period is complete. There are again choices here, such as how long the remaining life is on that same piece of equipment.

To appreciate the difference in these two activities, note first that the income statements and balance sheets you will see prepared for public U.S. companies are based on the accrual basis of accounting. Loosely speaking, the underlying tenet of accrual accounting is that assets and liabilities can build and shrink over time, with or without an actual exchange of cash. With these changing assets and liabilities come related changes in the net equity of the corporation (i.e., shareholder wealth). Consider a sale made on customer credit with the payment by that customer expected to occur sometime next year. This first activity is a day-to-day transaction that would increase the earnings and asset base of the firm. If the customer's account is still outstanding at the end the quarter when the books must be closed, the second activity, an adjustment, may take place. Specifically, an adjustment for this account *may be necessary* for an estimated amount the manager believes will be uncollectible. For this credit sale event, also note that accrual accounting would dictate that there has been earnings this year, but none next. How? An asset, accounts receivable, will be recorded that reflects an increase in the net earnings of the firm (top-line revenue). Why this year and not next? Because it was this year that the fruits of the firm's effort have been realized. As long as it is reasonably certain that payment will be made, the customer's financing decision should have little to do with communicating to outsiders how well the firm did this year, and likewise what the existing asset base should be.

Most entities of any complexity use the accrual basis of accounting, which recognizes the financial effect of an activity when the activity takes place, without regard to the timing of its cash effects. For its part, the accrual accounting process depends on various allocation and matching decisions. Consider that measuring financial success would be simple if an entity had only to summarize and report its activities at the end of its life. Cash results and accrual results would be exactly the same: We would measure results by simply asking whether the owners of the company had more cash at the end than they had at the start. However, both management and outsiders demand information about an entity's performance during interim periods of its life. Accounting rules and conventions are designed to allocate (or assign) the financial effect of an entity's activities to specific periods of time. Accounting standards and conventions are also designed to comprehensively report all of a transaction's financial effects in the applicable period. The objective of this matching principle is to report revenues in the period in which they are earned and to report all expenses related to those revenues in the same period.

Accounting Discretion and Financial Statement Quality

The recording of most transactions in the accounting process is relatively straightforward and accurately reflect much of the day-to-day activities of the firm. Accrual accounting is designed to provide the most relevant and reliable values relating to assets owned and controlled, liabilities owed, and profits generated. Embedded in virtually every primary account on the financial statement is some amount of preparer discretion, a measurement decision that must be made by management within the bounds of GAAP. Stated differently, to communicate economic activities effectively, managers often must make certain judgments regarding accounting estimates, methods, and assumptions that become part of the measurement of an account. To restrict them in this respect would be to restrict the relevance of information communicated, but of course not to restrict them opens up the opportunity to communicate only in their self-interest. Consider the aforementioned sale on account. What if the average pool of customers tends to pay only 98 percent of the time? If this were truly the case, it would be more informative to record income earned in the year of sale at 98 percent, not the overstated 100 percent. There is clearly some element of judgment in this recording process, even if the company employs controls such as strict aging schedules. But it certainly would convey more valuable information to outsiders to communicate the expected round-trip substance of the sale that occurred that year.

Sales and receivables are not the only accounts subject to reporting discretion. Recorded inventory (and future gross margins) will be dependent on chosen inventory accounting methods and estimates of realizable sales values. Fixed assets are subject to depreciation method choice, estimates of useful lives, and judgments about possible impairments in value. Liabilities recorded (or not) depend on assumptions regarding how likely it would be that amounts will be paid. Unrealized gains or losses on investments held are sometimes dependent on the trading intent in place at the financial reporting date. Deferred taxes may be reduced if there is some reasonable expectation that the tax benefits will never be realized.

So how does one make sense of accounting systems and controls that are abused by unscrupulous managers who manage earnings? How does the accounting system allow firms to keep liabilities off-balance sheet and/or build reserves? The answers lie with both motive and opportunity. Motive has been well chronicled by the financial press. Be it the ability of a manager to cash in on lucrative stock options that indirectly depend on reported earnings, a bonus tied to reported net income, a debt covenant that might be violated, or the mere act of self-preservation through job retention, there are ample motives for why one may choose the path of intentional violation of the accounting system.

Opportunity is a bit more difficult for some to understand. Often it is difficult to appreciate how and why an accounting system that has evolved over time, with significant amounts of time spent by accomplished business professionals evaluating the merits of every proposed accounting rule, can have so many perceived areas for abuse. But consider that the flaw some see in the accounting model is also viewed by most to be its main strength—the reporting discretion described earlier.

Two necessary features of the financial reporting process should mitigate these concerns that intentional fraudulent reporting is pervasive: (1) the required presence of internal controls and (2) the required external verification of financial reports via the independent audit. More specifically, the Sarbanes-Oxley Act of 2002 requires that the CEO and CFO certify, quarterly and annually, to the fairness and accuracy of all financial reports filed. The certifications must state that the reports were reviewed, that they do not omit material facts, that they do not contain untrue statements, and that they fairly present the financial position, earnings, and cash flows of the firm. Further, the CEO and CFO must provide assurance that the company has designed and has in place a system of controls, that any deficiencies in these controls have been disclosed to the board of directors, and that any significant changes to controls are disclosed. The criminal penalties associated with these certifications are quite stiff, with personal fines in the high seven figures and up to 20 years' imprisonment.

The essence of internal control is a system that a company has in place to ensure that actions within the organization are consistent with company financial reporting objectives. From an accounting perspective, these controls include formalized methods and procedures for authorizing transactions, complying with GAAP, and ensuring the accuracy of records. Proper accounting controls would help minimize unintentional errors and outright fraud.

Even with these controls in place, those not intimately familiar with the company who bear some risk of reliance on financial statement information will require some assurance of their validity. The Securities and Exchange Commission (SEC) requires that public companies each year file an audited fiscal year-end financial report. The auditor of the financial statements must be independent, and the accounting profession delineates certain minimum guidelines that must be followed: Procedures used must be designed to detect illegal acts that would have a material effect on the financial statements, identify related-party transactions, and evaluate the company's ability to continue as a going concern. Furthermore, if an illegal act is suspected, including nonconformance with GAAP, the auditor is required to inform the appropriate level of management and assure that the audit committee of the issuer and/or the board of directors is adequately informed.

Even with required internal controls and independent external audits there have been notable breakdowns of the external auditing process. Over the past decade we have been witness to some of the largest corporate financial scandals in history, most of which had at their center financial statements that were grossly misleading by the very management entrusted with their care. WorldCom and Enron come first to mind. The accounting scandal at Enron, in particular, raised public awareness about the pitfalls of compromising auditor independence through relations with management and non-audit-related services. At the extreme, these cases are intentional accounting misstatement and outright fraud motivated by a desire to circumvent the integrity of the accounting process. Investors and other users should have confidence that the financial statements and related disclosures, when the accounting process is properly applied, strike the proper balance between providing information most relevant to decision making and information that is most reliably measured.

A Step-by-Step Guide to Reading Annual Reports

Reading financial statements is one of the best ways to gain an understanding of accounting and its significance to business. The annual report, however, is more than simply a means by which to provide accounting data. Companies often will use this document to communicate their organizational stories, both documenting the company's historical evolution and outlining future strategic plans. The following seven recommended steps illustrate one way to approach getting the most out of reading the typical annual report. The steps are illustrated using PepsiCo's 2008 Annual Report, which covers the entirety of the company's activities in fiscal year 2008, and its financial condition as of December 27, 2008.

Step 1: Pay Attention to the Themes in the Opening Letter to Shareholders

The letter to shareholders is usually the first item in the annual report and is valuable on many dimensions, but mainly for understanding at the start the *strategic intent* of the managers of the firm. The letter usually sums up performance during the past year, and expresses elements of the CEO's goals, values, and vision for the future. As an example, the letter in the 2008 Annual Report from Indra K. Nooyi, Chairman and CEO of PepsiCo, references the new strategic mission rolled out two years earlier, discusses how the company is delivering on objectives while navigating through the current recession, and highlights certain financial trends of importance to shareholders. The letter conveys a sense of practicality while emphasizing to shareholders that the company prevailed during tough times because "our teams of extraordinary people applied their can-do spirit and must-do sense of responsibility to meet the economic and market challenges head on." The letter closes as follows:

> A great company is a place where people come together, with a purpose in common. By defining that purpose, by trying to bottle it, we are bound together. That is the message you see on every page of this report. It is full of stories and portraits that truly demonstrate

the deeply personal, emotional connection our associates have made to Performance with Purpose. In any language, our associates will tell you, "We are Performance with Purpose." Please join us on this trip around the globe, and see for yourself why I'm so inspired by the great things we've accomplished together—and so excited about the many opportunities that still lie ahead.

Through these words, a careful reader would get a hint of the issues to look for in the firm's results for 2008, along with insights about directions to be taken during the next year. For instance, consider the following additional issues and insights gleaned from the letter:

- *Shareholder wealth and growth are key objectives.* The company has grown earnings per share and revenues and has increased dividends and share repurchases, and its stock has performed better than its peers'. A Productivity-for-Growth initiative was begun across all sections of the business.

- *PepsiCo has an international focus.* Significant new investments are highlighted in Brazil, India, Mexico, and China.

- *Sustainability is a corporate priority.* The company recognizes environmental and human capital responsibilities. The PepsiCo brand is a great asset, and with this comes a great responsibility.

In sum, critical thinking prompted by a close reading of the opening letter can lead to better analysis of a firm's financial statements.

Step 2: Check the Auditor's Letter

Investors in companies ordinarily require an annual audit of those companies' financial statements. In fact, as described earlier for publicly traded companies, this is mandatory. The independent annual audit is one of the most basic protections intended to ensure compliance with GAAP. At the end of the financial report, one will find a letter from the firm's independent auditors that explains what they did and what they concluded. Following the PepsiCo 2008 financial statements, the accounting firm KPMG Price Waterhouse wrote:

> In our opinion, the consolidated financial statements referred to above present fairly, in all material respects, the financial position of PepsiCo, Inc. as of December 27, 2008 and December 29, 2007, and the results of its operations and its cash flows for each of the fiscal years in the three-year period ended December 27, 2008, in conformity with U.S. generally accepted accounting principles. Also in our opinion, PepsiCo, Inc. maintained, in all material respects, effective internal control over financial reporting as of December 27, 2008, based on criteria established in *Internal Control—Integrated Framework* issued by COSO.

This is a positive report, as most tend to be. Notably, the report does not just reference the accounting information reported, but also the firm's internal controls designed to help prevent financial fraud from occurring. A negative opinion by an auditor might cite unfair or unacceptable presentation, nonconformance with GAAP, a material misstatement, or deficiencies in controls. In some cases, auditors must explain any material uncertainties affecting the financial statements—these uncertainties depend on the probability of loss due to uncertainty of such things as the "going concern" assumption[1] that underlies the preparation of most financial statements, uncertainty regarding the valuation or realization of assets, or uncertainty due to litigation. The astute reader of an annual report will always check the audit report, because *anything but a positive report should, like a flashing red light, signal a major concern worth further investigation.*

Step 3: Review the Income Statement

The income statement is prepared using accrual accounting and summarizes the operating performance of the firm. It is organized on the principle that what customers buy (e.g., revenues), less what it cost to enable them to buy (e.g., expenses), results in profits. Recognizing this basic notion can help the reader sort out three concerns in looking at the income statement:

1. *The degree of profitability, and why.* Is the company making or losing money?
2. *The trend of profitability, and why.* Are profits increasing or declining over time? Are these due to changes in revenues, expenses, or both?
3. *The composition of profits.* Are the size and trend of profits due to ordinary operations, or to odd events that might distort the true profitability of the firm?

To illustrate, consider PepsiCo's 2006 to 2008 income statements given in Exhibit 1.1. The company had over $5 billion in profits during each year presented, but has experienced a modest decline, to $5,142 during 2008 from $5,658 million during 2007. Earnings per share similarly declined during this period. This trend by itself, all else equal, is not good news for investors. To what can we attribute this? The mathematical answer is simple: Revenues were up, but unfortunately costs went up at a faster rate. Observe that

Exhibit 1.1   PepsiCo Income Statements

Consolidated Income Statement, PepsiCo, Inc. and Subsidiaries (in millions except per share amounts)

Fiscal years ended December 27, 2008, December 29, 2007, and December 30, 2006	2008	2007	2006
Net Revenue	**$43,251**	$39,474	$35,137
Cost of sales	**20,351**	18,038	15,762
Selling, general, and administrative expenses	**15,901**	14,208	12,711
Amortization of intangible assets	**64**	58	162
Operating Profit	**6,935**	7,170	6,502
Bottling equity income	**374**	560	553
Interest expense	**(329)**	(224)	(239)
Interest income	**41**	125	173
Income before Income Taxes	**7,021**	7,631	6,989
Provision for Income Taxes	**1,879**	1,973	1,347
Net Income	**$ 5,142**	$ 5,658	$ 5,642
Net Income per Common Share			
Basic	**3.26**	3.48	3.42
Diluted	**3.21**	3.41	3.34

Source: 2008 PepsiCo, Inc. Annual Report.
Copyright © 2010 by Eades et al. To download this form for your personal use, please visit www.wiley.com/go/portablemba5e.

while top-line revenue grew at a healthy 9.6 percent, PepsiCo's two largest costs grew even faster. Cost of sales, which represents the costs directly associated with creating the vast array of products sold to the end consumer, rose by 12.8 percent. Selling, general, and administrative expenses rose by just under 12 percent. Together these relationships helped drive down PepsiCo's net income.

Step 4: Review the Balance Sheet

For most balance sheets, the major categories of assets are classified and ranked according to their liquidity, with cash, short-term investments, and other current assets (those that should be converted to cash within one year) at the top, and less liquid assets at the bottom.[2] For the remainder of the statement, current liabilities (those due within one year) are listed first. Next come debt and other liabilities, and toward the bottom is shareholders' equity, the residual claim on the firm. For a company such as PepsiCo, most components of the balance sheet are reported at the lower of *historical cost* or *market value*. Not all assets and liabilities of the firm are reported, only those that are *measurable, reasonably certain, and relatively easy to value*. Contingencies (potential assets or liabilities arising from past events such as a lawsuit) can be both difficult to measure and uncertain. The values of some patents, trademarks, and, in PepsiCo's case, its strong brand, are not based on identifiable past transactions and cannot be measured reliably. Thus many are not reported. In reading the balance sheet, one should aim to satisfy four questions:

1. *Is the firm solvent?* Solvency is the ability to pay liabilities as they come due. The back-of-the-envelope test of this is to first observe by how much the value of assets exceeds the value of liabilities.

2. *Are the firm's assets sufficiently liquid?* Liquidity measures the ability to meet near-term cash obligations—these might be liabilities that need to be repaid, or they might be a forthcoming payroll or the need to purchase raw materials in advance of a sudden surge in demand.

3. *What is the mix of assets?* The reader should look for unusual concentrations or categories of assets. Concentration of the firm's resources into a speculative venture would be a cause for concern. Concentration in cash might suggest undue risk aversion or the lack of investment opportunities with attractive return potential. Also, asset categories that seem to have no relevance to the firm's business purpose should raise a red flag.

4. *What is the mix of financing?* Most mature firms finance their businesses with *some* debt. The absence of debt or a very high proportion of debt should raise questions about the outlook of senior management, and/or the bets they are making. Again, odd categories of capital (e.g., exchangeable subordinated bonds) may indicate managerial creativity, or they may indicate desperation on the part of management—either way, they should invite the thoughtful reader of the annual report to dig deeper.

The balance sheet of PepsiCo as of December 27, 2008, is given in Exhibit 1.2. The firm clearly appears to be *solvent* in general terms, since the assets (about $36 billion) handily exceed liabilities (about $24 billion). The firm appears to be *liquid* as well: Current assets (totaling $10.8 billion) exceed current liabilities (accounts payable,

Exhibit 1.2   PepsiCo Balance Sheets

**Consolidated Balance Sheet, PepsiCo, Inc. and Subsidiaries
(in millions except per share amounts)**

Fiscal years ended December 27, 2008, and December 29, 2007	2008	2007
ASSETS		
Current Assets		
Cash and cash equivalents	$ 2,064	$ 910
Short-term investments	213	1,571
Accounts and notes receivable, net	4,683	4,389
Inventories	2,522	2,290
Prepaid expenses and other current assets	1,324	991
Total Current Assets	10,806	10,151
Property, Plant, and Equipment, net	11,663	11,228
Amortizable Intangible Assets, net	732	796
Goodwill	5,124	5,169
Other nonamortizable intangible assets	1,128	1,248
Nonamortizable Intangible Assets	6,252	6,417
Investments in Noncontrolled Affiliates	3,883	4,354
Other Assets	2,658	1,682
Total Assets	$ 35,994	$ 34,628
LIABILITIES AND SHAREHOLDERS' EQUITY		
Current Liabilities		
Short-term obligations	$ 369	$ 0
Accounts payable and other current liabilities	8,273	7,602
Income taxes payable	145	151
Total Current Liabilities	8,787	7,753
Long-Term Debt Obligations	7,858	4,203
Other Liabilities	7,017	4,792
Deferred Income Taxes	226	646
Total Liabilities	$ 23,888	$ 17,394
Commitments and Contingencies		
Preferred Stock, no par value	$ 41	$ 41
Repurchased Preferred Stock	(138)	(132)
Common Shareholders' Equity		
Common stock, par value $1\frac{2}{3}$ per share (authorized 3,600 shares, issued 1,782 shares)	30	30
Capital in excess of par value	351	450
Retained earnings	30,638	28,184
Accumulated other comprehensive loss	(4,694)	(952)
Repurchased common stock, at cost (229 and 177 shares, respectively)	(14,122)	(10,387)
Total Common Shareholders' Equity	$ 12,203	$ 17,325
Total Liabilities and Shareholders' Equity	$ 35,994	$ 34,628

Source: 2008 PepsiCo, Inc. Annual Report.
Copyright © 2010 by Eades, et al. To download this form for your personal use, please visit www.wiley.com/go/portablemba5e.

accruals, and taxes payable, totaling about $8.8 billion). PepsiCo's mix of assets doesn't seem unusual—certainly the concentration in fixed assets is understandable because of the capital intensity of that business. Finally, the financing mix of the firm shows a modest increase in the use of debt financing from 2007 to 2008—long-term debt has increased by $3.6 billion. Overall, the balance sheet raises no red flags.

Step 5: Review the Statement of Cash Flows

The statement of cash flows reports the cash receipts and outflows classified as operating, investing, and financing activities—this breakdown helps the reader determine where changes in cash emerge. The key questions a reader should ask include:

- Was the firm a net user or generator of cash for the year?
- What operational, investing, or financing elements proved to be major drivers of cash flow?
- Are there any major departures in the trends of the cash flow items?

Exhibit 1.3 gives PepsiCo's statement of cash flows from its 2008 Annual Report. This shows that the firm was a net generator of cash from operations in 2008 (about $7.0 billion), which was in line with prior years. Net investing and financing activities are significant uses of cash, totaling $2.7 billion and $3.0 billion, respectively, in 2008. The individual line items suggest a couple of noteworthy points: (1) capital spending has been consistently high, and modestly rising each year, and (2) the company has been increasing the spend rate for both dividends and share repurchases. Both of these dynamics are consistent with the CEO's message of growth and returns to shareholders highlighted earlier. Overall, the statement of cash flows does not give any reason for concern, and in effect shows strong cash management.

Step 6: Read the Footnotes to the Financial Statements

A set of footnotes immediately follows the financial statements, typically spans many pages, and is considered by regulators to be an integral part of the financial statements. The footnotes tend to amplify and clarify information not readily apparent from reference to the statements themselves. For instance, the footnotes to PepsiCo's report offer, among others, the following important information:

- A breakdown of revenue, operating income, capital expenditures, and depreciation expenses by PepsiCo's unique divisions.
- A detailed analysis of a $543 restructuring charge taken in 2008.
- A summary of significant accounting policies adopted by PepsiCo.
- Expanded detail of specific line items contained in the financial statements, including income taxes, fixed assets, and pension obligations.

Footnotes can be very technical and difficult for the novice to understand. But most users of annual reports would tell that they contain many important insights about a company not found elsewhere. At a minimum, footnotes should be referenced as necessary when questions arise in your review of the financial statements.

Exhibit 1.3   PepsiCo Statement of Cash Flows

Consolidated Statement of Cash Flows, PepsiCo, Inc. and Subsidiaries (in millions)

Fiscal years ended December 27, 2008, December 29, 2007, and December 30, 2006	2008	2007	2006
Operating Activities			
Net income	$ 5,142	$ 5,658	$ 5,642
Depreciation and amortization	1,543	1,426	1,406
Other adjustments, net	532	(84)	118
Deferred income taxes and other tax charges and credits	573	118	(510)
Change in net current assets	(424)	25	(569)
Other, net	(367)	(209)	(3)
Net Cash Provided by Operating Activities	$ 6,999	$ 6,934	$ 6,084
Investing Activities			
Capital spending	$ (2,446)	$ (2,430)	$ (2,068)
Sales of property, plant, and equipment	98	47	49
Proceeds from (investment in) finance assets		27	(25)
Acquisitions and investments in noncontrolled affiliates	(1,925)	(1,320)	(522)
Cash restricted for pending acquisitions	(40)		
Cash proceeds from sale of PBG and PAS stock	358	315	318
Divestitures	6		37
Short-term investments	1,282	(383)	2,017
Net Cash Used for Investing Activities	$ (2,667)	$ (3,744)	$ (194)
Financing Activities			
Proceeds from issuances of long-term debt	$ 3,719	$ 2,168	$ 51
Payments of long-term debt	(649)	(579)	(157)
Short-term borrowings, net	445	(395)	(2,341)
Cash dividends paid	(2,541)	(2,204)	(1,854)
Share repurchases	(4,726)	(4,312)	(3,010)
Proceeds from exercises of stock options	620	1,108	1,194
Excess tax benefits from share-based payment arrangements	107	208	134
Net Cash Used for Financing Activities	(3,025)	(4,006)	(5,983)
Effect of exchange rate changes on cash and cash equivalents	(153)	75	28
Net Increase/(Decrease) in Cash and Cash Equivalents	$ 1,154	$ (741)	$ (65)
Cash and Cash Equivalents, Beginning of Year	910	1,651	1,716
Cash and Cash Equivalents, End of Year	$ 2,064	$ 910	$ 1,651

Source: 2008 PepsiCo, Inc. Annual Report.
Copyright © 2010 by Eades, et al. To download this form for your personal use, please visit www.wiley.com/go/portablemba5e.

Step 7: Read Management's Discussion of the Year's Performance

Finally, an annual report will contain a detailed discussion of the year just completed, called the Management Discussion and Analysis (MD&A). The management discussion can reflect management's efforts to influence the reader's assessment of the company, and PepsiCo's MD&A is no exception. For that same reason, however, the MD&A helps the reader cultivate a critical frame of mind necessary for fully understanding the financial statements.

The formal, defined purpose of the MD&A is "to provide to investors and other users information relevant to an assessment of the financial condition and results of operations of the registrant as determined by evaluating the amounts and certainty of cash flows from operations and from outside sources" (SEC Reg S-K, Item 303). Ideally, it should be management's perception of its finances and operations, and it provides an opportunity to disclose known trends and uncertainties, to present detailed analyses of important year-to-year changes that are material to operations, and to clarify and provide context to its operation that are not readily apparent through reference to the financial statements. Many readers of annual reports contend that this is the most important section of the document. As one small example, a review of PepsiCo's MD&A reveals that 2008 profits were adversely impacted by both unfavorable commodity price hedges and higher raw materials costs. While higher costs were observable from the trends in financial statement values, management has now put context around these results that could not be found elsewhere.

Assessing the Financial Health of the Firm

Simply reading an annual report does not always give one the basis to conclude whether a firm is ultimately healthy. Further analysis can reward the reader with fresh insights. Financial analysts and academic researchers have developed an array of ratios found to be particularly useful in providing a deeper understanding of the firm. This collection of ratios includes methods for analyzing operating performance, financial condition, cash flow, liquidity, capital structure, and risk. Although there is no fixed set of such metrics and individual analysts typically will rely on their own personal set of assessment tools, there is a core set commonly used.

In this section, certain key ratios are illustrated in the context of how further information can be extracted from financial reports. As you consider the metrics illustrated, remember that each is just one piece of the mosaic that builds a more complete picture of the firm. A simple piece of data, by itself, does not tell us much. At the end of 2008, for instance, PepsiCo had $36 billion in assets and over $5.1 billion in earnings. Do these magnitudes matter? These numbers seem large, but how large are they really? Only when one analyzes the relative relationships of these amounts, compared to appropriate benchmarks, can one see the whole picture. An astute analyst looks for patterns, changes, unusual relationships, and values that seem to defy explanation.

Examining sets of key ratios, through comparisons of the same firm across time and/or against its peers, can help identify strengths and weaknesses of a company, and where management focuses its efforts. Financial ratios show the performance of the firm in four important areas:

1. *Profitability* is measured both in terms of profit or expense margins and as investment return. Investors typically will focus on *return on assets*, *return on equity*, and *profit margin*.

2. *Leverage* ratios measure the use of short-term and long-term debt financing by the firm. In general, higher usage of debt increases the risk of the firm, and is of particular concern during times of economic recession. Higher ratios of *debt to total capital invested* suggest a company seeking higher net returns, but one also willing to take on higher financial risk. The ratio of *times interest earned* measures the ability of the firm to cover its interest payments; lower levels of this ratio suggest high risk and poor relative operating performance.

3. *Asset efficiency and utilization* ratios measure how well the firm deploys its assets. For instance, the *asset turnover ratio* (sales over assets) indicates how many dollars of sales are generated per dollar of assets in use; a higher figure suggests more efficiency. Over the long term, differences in the *growth rates* of sales and assets can lead to production problems of over- or undercapacity. *Days receivables* and *days inventory* together indicate how quickly the firm converts its manufacturing or purchasing activities to cash from the customer. The longer this process, the less efficient the firm.[3]

4. *Liquidity* ratios measure the resources available to meet short-term financial commitments, should that be required. The *current ratio* answers the question of whether the company has enough current assets to cover all current liabilities. The *quick ratio* is even more restrictive on this dimension, and is the ratio of only cash and short-term investments (i.e., those assets that can be liquidated quickly) to all current liabilities.

Often it can be difficult to assemble a unified view of the firm from these ratios. Fortunately, the *DuPont system of ratios* can help analysts integrate their insights. The DuPont system was developed during World War I when the financial officers of E.I. du Pont de Nemours and Company sought a system to assess the health of their firm, and of the segments within the firm. This system decomposes *return on equity* into several constituent pieces: *profit margin*, which measures the profitability of each dollar of revenue; *sales turnover*, which measures the dollars of sales produced by each dollar of assets; and the ratio of *assets to equity*, which measures the *financial leverage* of the company, or the dollars of assets carried by each dollar of equity. Algebraically, the product of these three components is the return on equity:

$$\text{Return on Equity} = \text{Profit Margin} \times \text{Sales Turnover} \times \text{Financial Leverage}^{[4]}$$
$$(\text{Profit/Equity}) = (\text{Profit/Sales}) \times (\text{Sales/Assets}) \times (\text{Assets/Equity})$$

By examining the DuPont system for comparative years, it is possible to determine the sources of changes in return on equity.

Exhibit 1.4 summarizes example ratios from each of the four broad groupings for PepsiCo. You will observe from this summary particularly strong levels but declining trends in profitability during 2008. The one exception is return on equity, consistent with PepsiCo's stated dividend payout and share repurchase program, activities that reduce the equity base and increase this ratio, on average. The company has expanded its leverage during the year, and also has become slightly less efficient in its use of assets. The increased leverage is certainly no cause for alarm, as the interest coverage ratios indicate that PepsiCo easily has the ability to cover current interest charges. Net liquidity has remained somewhat constant. On the whole, the levels and trends in these ratios indicate a financially strong company, but one impacted by the economic recession that

Exhibit 1.4   PepsiCo Ratio Analysis

Ratio Analysis of Financial Statements, PepsiCo, Inc. and Subsidiaries

Fiscal years ended December 27, 2008, and December 29, 2007	2008	2007	2006
Profitability			
Return on Equity (%) (Net Income/Stockholders' Equity)	42.1%	32.7%	—
Return on Assets (%) (Net Income/Assets)	14.3%	16.3%	—
Return on Net Assets (%) (Net Income/Assets—Payables and Accruals)	18.6%	21.1%	—
Return on Sales (%) (Net Income/Revenues)	11.9%	14.3%	16.1%
Operating Profit Margin (%) (Operating Profit/Revenues)	16.0%	18.2%	18.5%
Leverage			
Debt-to-Equity (%)	67.4%	24.3%	—
Debt-to-Total Capital (%)	22.9%	12.1%	—
Times Interest Earned (EBIT/Interest Expense)	22.3	35.1	30.2
Asset Efficiency and Utilization			
Asset Turnover (Assets/Revenues)	0.83	0.88	—
Revenue Growth (%)	9.6%	12.3%	—
Asset Growth (%)	3.9%	—	—
Days Receivable (365 × Receivables/Revenues)	39.5	40.6	—
Days Inventory (365 × Inventory/Cost of Sales)	45.2	46.3	—
Liquidity			
Current Ratio (Current Assets/Current Liabilities)	1.23	1.31	—
Quick Ratio ((Cash + Short-Term Investments)/Current Liabilities)	0.26	0.32	—

Source of data underlying the ratios: 2008 PepsiCo, Inc. Annual Report.
Source of ratios: Author's analysis.

began in 2007. There appears to be no cause for concern, but net trends have been on the decline. The careful analyst would examine both the *size* and the *trend* of each of these ratios over longer periods and, if possible, compare them to the same ratios for peer firms (the Coca-Cola Company, for instance).

Managerial Accounting: Assessing Performance Against a Plan

The financial accounting process described earlier presents data in a form useful to outsiders such as investors, creditors, analysts, and regulators. The financial statements produced from this process are, unfortunately, often too coarse and too historically based to be of much use to operating managers concerned with driving future performance. The field of study called *managerial accounting* is designed to help provide the data that aids most directly in this task. This section briefly illustrates the application of some managerial accounting concepts frequently used by firms. Note, however, that this field is by its nature one with enormous flexibility and diversity of practice. It is not governed by codified rules and regulations, but rather by established conventions and practices that have evolved over time.

Managerial accounting, broadly speaking, embraces many of the tools and concepts of financial accounting, but the objective is typically to assess *performance against a plan or a standard*. The ultimate goal is to help the operating manager understand his or her division's business dynamics so that improvements, efficiencies, and growth opportunities can be identified. A plan, or budget, is a target or forecast of performance, expected but uncertain. A standard, such as a standard cost, is similar but here suggests an accepted norm against which an actual figure may be compared. For instance, one can assess performance of a project or business in terms of *variance* from the benchmark. A *favorable variance* is either actual revenues higher than expected or actual costs lower than expected. An *unfavorable variance* is the reverse.

Variances in revenues and costs can be decomposed into variances due to price (or cost) changes and variances due to volume changes. Whether a variance arises because of variances in prices or variances in volumes is extremely valuable information for the manager. As one example, this information helps both to remedy problems and to reward certain behaviors. Consider the following simple hypothetical case regarding the DVD release of an animated children's movie by Backyard Production, Inc. (BPI).

Backyard Production, Inc.: DVD Release

At the beginning of 2009, DVD sales for the year of BPI's animated movie were expected to realize revenues of $80 million. This was based on an assumed sale of eight million units at an average price of $10 each. At the core of BPI's sales strategy was a plan to aggressively market the DVD through an array of national discount retailers. The expected $10 per unit revenue was a net "best guess" based on how substantial the concessions demanded by those retailers would be. The DVDs were to be manufactured in Beijing, China, at an expected unit cost of $3.00. The initial production contract specified a production volume of eight million units for the year. Changes in the production volume, up or down, would entail price increases to BPI because of substantial human resource and setup costs incurred by the manufacturer.

At the end of the year, BPI's marketing manager could hardly control her excitement as she reported that revenues on the DVD release would be $85 million. Units sold were 10 million at an average net price of $8.50. She pointed out that the submission of cash rebate coupons had been higher than expected, as had been the concessions made to retailers, but this was more than offset by the increase in sales volume. BPI's purchasing manager was not as happy. He reported that the increased volume had prompted the supplier to impose surcharges on the price to BPI: The average unit cost of the DVDs was $4.00. BPI's president was also disappointed that the project had earned only $45 million, instead of the budgeted $56 million. What had gone wrong and why? What part of this process contributed most to the missed profits? Can this be quantified?

The answers to these questions lie with conventional managerial accounting tools that help illustrate some of the internal processes used by the firm. In this simple case, profits

Exhibit 1.5   BPI Budget versus Actual Profits

	Budget	Actual
Revenue	$80,000,000	$85,000,000
Costs	24,000,000	40,000,000
Net Profit	$56,000,000	$45,000,000

were missed, and by definition this would relate to either revenue or costs, or both. Exhibit 1.5 summarizes the original budget versus actual results.

There are just four levers at work that would describe the profit miss: price received, quantity sold, quantity produced, and manufacturing cost. Intuition should tell you that together they describe the $11 million missed profit. Variance analysis will tell you exactly by how much. These calculations are illustrated as follows:

Total Revenue Variance: Price Received and Volume Sold

Sales Price Variance $=$ (Actual Price $-$ Standard Price) $\times$ (Actual Units Sold)

$$= (\$8.50 - \$10.00) \times (10,000,000) = -\$15,000,000$$

The sales price variance was unfavorable to BPI.

Sales Volume Variance $=$ (Standard Price) $\times$ (Actual Volume $-$ Expected Volume)

$$= \$10.00 \times (10,000,000 - 8,000,000) = \$20,000,000$$

The sales volume variance was favorable to BPI.

Overall, the special price discounts and promotions produced an increase in volume that more than compensated for the lower average price realized. The revenue variance analysis shows that the promotional effort paid off:

Total Revenue Variance $=$ (Volume Variance) $+$ (Price Variance)

$$= \$20,000,000 + -\$15,000,000 = \$5,000,000$$

The pickup in volume had been more than enough to compensate for the decline in price.

Total Cost Variance: Price Paid and Volume Produced

Regarding the cost to BPI of producing the DVDs by the manufacturer, we can analyze variances of actual from budget using similar formulas:

Price (or Cost) Variance $=$ (Actual Unit Cost $-$ Budgeted Unit Cost)

$$\times \text{ (Actual Unit Volume)}$$
$$= (\$4.00 - \$3.00) \times 10,000,000 = \$10,000,000$$

The unit cost variance was unfavorable to BPI, given that it cost more to have the DVDs made than had been originally budgeted. The increase in cost was not unexpected, due to the clause in the supply contract that permitted the supplier to increase prices if the production volume was modified.

$$\textbf{Volume Variance} = (\text{Budgeted Unit Cost}) \times (\text{Actual Volume} - \text{Budgeted Volume})$$
$$= \$3.00 \times (10,000,000 - 8,000,000) = \$6,000,000$$

The volume variance was also unfavorable to BPI. This stands to reason since it had to buy more units than expected, thus paying more in total costs.

Overall, the total cost variance was unfavorable by $16 million:

$$\textbf{Total Cost Variance} = (\text{Price Variance}) + (\text{Volume Variance})$$
$$= \$10,000,000 + \$6,000,000 = \$16,000,000$$

The DVD release project turned out worse for BPI than expected. Putting the variance analysis of sales (revenue) and costs together as in Exhibit 1.6 helps better show the exact contributions of the different levers and highlights the source of BPI's disappointment. Remember that price decreases and cost increases are unfavorable outcomes (U) and that volume increases are favorable outcomes (F) for sales activities but not for production.

The row totals show that the $11 million shortfall in budgeted profits was due to the fact that production costs rose faster than sales revenues. But before we criticize the purchasing manager, consider that part of the rise in costs is due to the fact that BPI simply ordered more units than it had budgeted. Also, look at the column totals. The columns show that the unhappy news originates in the price areas, and that culpability is *shared* between the purchasing manager (who negotiates the supply contracts) and the marketing manager (who handles sales policy): 60 percent of the unfavorable price variance of $25 million originates in sales, and the remainder in production.

A general manager can use analysis such as this to take thoughtful action. One possibility is that BPI should stiffen its spine in negotiations with suppliers and customers. Perhaps the managers of purchasing and marketing should be sent to a negotiation skills workshop. Maybe the purchasing manager should be assisted by a skillful lawyer who could draft an agreement limiting the supplier's ability to hike the unit price. BPI might consider searching for suppliers with more flexible production operations for which a change order is not an expensive proposition. And finally, BPI should reconsider the strategy of selling through discounters—they imposed internal turbulence (in the form of higher-than-expected volume) that rippled backwards through the supply chain, and left BPI earning $11 million less than had been budgeted.

Exhibit 1.6   BPI Variance Analysis of Budget versus Actual

	Price Variances	**Volume Variances**	**Total Variances**
Sales	$15,000,000 (U)	$20,000,000 (F)	$ 5,000,000 (F)
Production	10,000,000 (U)	6,000,000 (U)	16,000,000 (U)
Total	**$25,000,000 (U)**	**$14,000,000 (F)**	**$11,000,000 (U)**

Accounting in MBA Curricula

The field of accounting as taught in MBA programs tends to embrace four distinct areas: (1) financial accounting, (2) managerial accounting, (3) taxation, and (4) financial statement analysis. Introductory courses in financial accounting are virtually always required, although some MBA programs allow course waivers for certified public accountants (CPAs) and others with extensive professional experience. Over the past decade, business school students' interests have tended to shift more toward finance-related career tracks, and with this shift the demand for financial accounting–related electives has grown. These courses most commonly are those related to advanced financial accounting theory.

Managerial accounting is defined by the development of accounting information with a focus on the internal use of that information by managers and executives to operate their businesses. The field is centered on the study of accounting as a tool for managerially relevant decision making within the organization. A managerial curriculum typically includes the topics of strategic and financial planning/budgeting, management control and performance measurement, management incentives, capital expenditure planning, evaluation and budgeting, transfer pricing, and strategic costing. Courses in managerial accounting are required in most MBA programs (but not all). For instance, of the top six programs as ranked by *BusinessWeek* in 2008, four required a specific stand-alone managerial accounting course, one blended both financial and managerial topics in a single course, and one other offered managerial accounting as an elective course.

Taxation is a discipline focused on understanding tax law. While the field itself is quite broad, within the bounds of graduate business education it can be more tightly defined as understanding the motives and managerial strategies related to the imposition of tax law. The curricula of MBA programs typically offer only electives in the field of taxation, with these courses focused on understanding how tax issues are incorporated in general management strategies (e.g., mergers and acquisitions).

Finally, financial statement analysis is a course offered in all MBA programs, in virtually all instances as an elective. The approaches for this course will vary considerably, but the objective is virtually always the same—to develop tools pertaining to how to use external financial reports in the analysis of the firm. Most courses include topics on screening, forecasting, and valuation techniques, with the ultimate goals of assessing firm performance and determining firm value.

Concluding Remarks

A basic mastery of accounting is absolutely essential for the success of the modern manager. Such mastery should include an ability to read financial statements and derive basic insights about the health of the enterprise from them, and to assess the performance of a business or project relative to a budget or standard using variance analysis of prices, costs, and volume.

Perhaps more importantly, a basic mastery of accounting will instill in the manager a general sense of irony about performance measurement. On close examination, one sees that the process of preparing a presentation about the condition of the firm is heavily laden with judgment. Financial accounting is nuanced, and as such requires careful attention to detail and enhance disclosures that help increase transparency. Managers need to recognize and understand the many alternatives they face in presenting financial results, and make faithful, ethical choices in that presentation. Investors and creditors need to read financial statements with thoughtful caution, recognizing that accounting reality is sometimes an abstraction from true economic reality.

Finally, accounting presents an extremely important framework for thinking about the internal workings of the firm. Assets must equal liabilities and owners' equity, and transactions must balance. Relationships across accounts must be understood, and from this an assessment of performance, risk, and overall financial health can begin. Viewed from this standpoint, accounting is not a narrow and technical specialty, but rather an essential tool for corporate renewal and transformation.

Notes

1. The "going concern" assumption holds that the firm will operate for the foreseeable future, and that its assets will not be liquidated hastily in a fire sale. For instance, hasty liquidation of inventory ordinarily realizes lower values than will the regular conduct of business.
2. In the balance sheets of many companies headquartered outside the United States, the order of priority differs greatly. Don't let the differences confuse you. Just remember that Assets = Liabilities + Owners' Equity.
3. *Days receivables* is calculated as the ratio of accounts receivable divided by annual sales, multiplied by 365 days. *Days inventory* is inventory divided by annual cost of sales, multiplied by 365 days.
4. *Financial leverage* generally refers to the use of debt financing. A highly levered firm has a high proportion of debt in its capital structure. There are numerous ratios that measure leverage, but one of the most telling is the ratio of assets to equity. High leverage would be associated with a high ratio.

Downloadable Resources for this chapter available at www.wiley.com/go/portablemba5e

Exhibits 1.1–1.4: PepsiCo Financial Statements and Financial Ratios

2

The Principles of Economics

Economy is the art of making the most of life.

—*George Bernard Shaw*

Economics is a mother discipline of many of the fields most commonly associated with business school: finance, marketing, strategy, and accounting. Each of these fields centers on the decisions made by individuals and the nature of markets, which represent aggregate decisions of individuals and firms. The focus on the behavior of individuals and firms offers fundamental insights that are critical to questions that managers face each and every day. What is the best price to charge for a new product? Should we invest more in research and development (R&D) or advertising? What are the risks of producing in China versus Mexico? How will a recession affect our position in the market and our profitability? Economics informs each of these choices. In fact, it's impossible to think critically about these questions without using economic reasoning.

So, what does it mean to use economic reasoning to think through a business problem? At root, economics is built upon three common assumptions: maximizing behavior, the existence of markets, and stable preferences. These three assumptions form the basis of a powerful system of critical analysis.

The assumption of maximizing behavior embodies the idea that individuals and organizations usually attempt to maximize some measure of value, such as happiness, profits, or public awareness. Maximizing behavior is constrained by all sorts of limitations—time constraints, limited financial resources, limited abilities, and other trade-offs. Nevertheless, economic reasoning begins with an assumption that individuals and firms attempt to maximize behavior given the numerous constraints they face.

The two most important implications of the assumption of maximizing behavior are that individuals seek the least costly path toward their goals and in the process will also seek out all relevant knowledge about how best to improve their situation. Maximizing profit or one's well-being requires knowledge of how best to do so and is always advanced by learning new ways to get more for less. In other words, maximizing behavior implies that individuals and firms constantly seek ways to be more efficient in the pursuit of their goals. This means getting the most value from the resources they employ and getting the most bang for the buck. One way to get the most bang for the buck is to trade with others, particularly those who specialize in the production of items you or your firm does not produce. In other words, maximizing behavior is supported by specialization in production and in seeking out trades with others.

It's easy to see the tie between maximizing behavior and the existence of markets. Markets are venues, physical or virtual, where buyers can come together to buy and sell products and services. Markets don't always magically arise, but economists presume that they do exist or will be developed where there is a sufficient number of buyers and sellers. By assuming that markets for most goods and services exist, an economic approach can center around the contribution of individuals to market outcomes and the incentives that market dynamics and outcomes place on those individuals. The most common manifestation of the assumption of markets is supply and demand analysis, which we cover a bit later in the chapter.

An important implication of the existence of markets is that they ensure mutually consistent behavior. Since trading in markets is voluntary, we can assume that both the buyer and the seller are satisfied with their trade. At least, we can presume that buyers and sellers undertake trades with the expectation that they will be satisfied. This simple idea explains much of the appeal of markets for the delivery of goods and services. Markets are created by people interested in improving their own situation as they see fit and produce trades that both buyers and sellers agree to.

Another key benefit of markets is that they provide strong incentives to minimize the costs of exchange. That is, markets minimize the costs of seeking out products and services by bringing together buyers and sellers in a single location. Through competition, the most efficient producers are the first to sell their goods; thus these producers determine or set the prices in markets. Similarly, producers will sell to those buyers who offer the highest price. Thus, markets ensure that the highest economically valuable trades—those between the producers with the lowest cost and the buyers willing to pay the most—always take place. Alternatively, markets tend to produce the highest net gains for buyers and sellers combined. Last, by rewarding the most efficient producers, markets provide incentives for producers to continually improve the value of their goods and services to their customers. Competitive markets produce strong incentives for innovation and efficiency, which is perhaps their biggest selling point.

The third key assumption of the economic approach is that preferences are stable, or, as some prefer, rational and stable. Preferences are an individual's tastes for a certain good relative to other goods. Simply put, this assumption implies that no one would willingly do something counter to their interest and that their preferences do not change on a whim. If preferences were subject to frequent and substantial changes, voluntary exchanges in markets might not take place, and maximizing behavior would be quite difficult for an individual to undertake. Clearly, people's preferences don't always adhere to the assumptions of rationality and stability, but in some sense, this isn't crucial. A simple economic approach is still valuable as a starting point from which more realistic assumptions can be added and analyzed. And assuming rational and stable preferences allows us to make general predictions about behavior even without an entirely accurate description of reality.

Most of economic analysis proceeds from these three assumptions to investigate decisions made at the firm or individual level. Microeconomics is the general study of decisions, choices, and incentives at the individual and firm level. The next section of this chapter begins with an introduction to microeconomic analysis. Economists also study the economy as a whole, how fast it grows, and the way that changes in individual sectors and industries come together to determine key variables such as unemployment, inflation, exchange rates, and the level of interest rates. The study of a national economy and of the international economy as a whole is called macroeconomics, and it is the subject of the last half of this chapter.

Microeconomics

Microeconomics focuses on understanding individual or firm-level choices and the answers to common but important questions. How much should our firm produce? What price should we charge for our products and services? How profitable will we be? What should we pay our employees? These questions are complex, often fraught with uncertainty and ambiguity, and closely related to each other. Answering these questions is not easy. The answers are affected by literally hundreds and thousands of influences, which we reduce to a few key factors in order to begin our analysis. For example, the pricing decision is affected by those factors affecting the cost of production, the quantity that consumers are willing and able to buy, and the availability of alternative or substitute products. To deal with all these factors and their interactions, economists since Alfred Marshall, the nineteenth-century British economist, have used the framework or tool of supply and demand analysis.

Supply and Demand

Supply and demand graphs, tables, or equations summarize the factors or forces in a market that determine the price and quantity of a particular good, product, or service. Exhibit 2.1 is a representative graph containing a supply curve and a demand curve. Before we begin to look at the details of what factors influence the shapes and positions of the curves, let's first examine some basic facts about their shapes and some immediate conclusions we can draw by examining the intersection of supply and demand curves. This may appear a bit mechanical at first, but we will flesh out the details later.

First, consider the downward slope of the demand curve. Despite all the factors that may influence how much you would pay for a computer, the demand curve simply traces out the quantity of computers that consumers would demand (i.e., be willing to buy) at

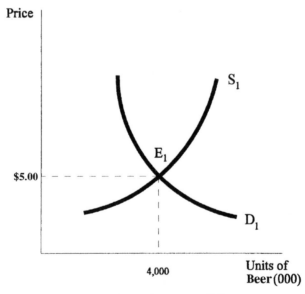

Exhibit 2.1   Supply and Demand for Beer

any given price of computers. At a very high price many consumers would be unwilling, or unable, to buy a computer, whereas many would be willing to buy computers at very low prices. The slope of the demand curve reflects only the relationship between the price of a computer and the quantity of computers that consumers will demand at that price. When we draw the demand curve, we must hold constant all other factors that influence demand. That is, each demand curve reflects the price-quantity relationship for given values of everything else that may influence demand.

Like the demand curve, the supply curve traces out the quantity of computers that producers, or suppliers, of computers will be willing to sell at any given price. The supply curve slopes upward because producers will be willing to sell more when the price they receive is higher. Also like the demand curve, many factors influence how many computers suppliers are willing to sell, and the slope of the supply curve reflects only the relationship between the prices of computers and the quantities that suppliers will be willing to supply to the market. All other relevant factors influencing supply are held constant.

The intersection of the supply and demand curves reflects the interaction of all the forces in the market for the particular good or service being examined. Even though our two curves depict only the relationship between the price and quantity demanded and supplied, the intersection of the two curves reflects the interaction of all the forces in the market for the good or service being examined. In our example, make the product a six-pack of beer. The price of a six-pack of beer is $3.75, and the quantity produced and sold is four million units (remember that this is for the whole market for beer, so that is probably too small a number). That combination of price and quantity represents the market clearing equilibrium (point E_1 on Exhibit 2.1). Those terms are important. *Equilibrium* implies that there are no forces leading to a change in price or quantity. As long as all the factors stay as they are, brewers will continue to produce four million six-packs and consumers will buy them at $3.75 each. We call this the market clearing price because all of the six-packs that are produced are sold, and everyone willing and able to pay $3.75 for a six-pack gets one.

Another important fact about the equilibrium price is that the market will be driven there through the natural, competitive, profit-maximizing behavior. To see why, consider what would happen if producers attempted to set a price different from the equilibrium price, say $4.00 (Exhibit 2.2)? At that price, brewers want to sell more than four million units. They are getting a higher price per six-pack, so, as the supply curve depicts, they produce a higher quantity—4,250,000 units. Yet, at that higher price, consumers, as the demand curve shows, are not willing to buy four million six-packs; in fact, they are willing to buy only 3,750,000 six-packs at this price. What happens to the difference between 4,250,000 and 3,750,000? The market does not clear, and brewers find themselves with unwanted inventories. An excess supply of 500,000 six-packs is generated at the price of $4.00. As the inventories build up, brewers will be motivated to cut their production and their prices. They reduce production because they have too much in stock, and they cut their prices in order to sell off the excess. Holding inventories is not costless, so profits will suffer as inventories grow. As the price falls, the quantity bought will increase, as the demand curve shows, and eventually the market will clear. At what price will the market clear? We know that already: $3.75 per six-pack is the equilibrium price. Ask yourself: What would happen if brewers attempted to set a price of $3.25 per six-pack?

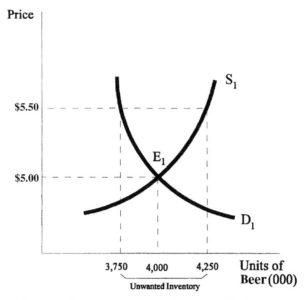

Exhibit 2.2   A Temporary Disequilibrium

Now, imagine how we might use supply and demand curves to examine some change that increases the quantity of six-packs that consumers are willing to purchase at the equilibrium price of $3.75. That is, what if we no longer hold everything else constant and let some factor that influences demand change? To reflect this willingness to demand more beer at any given price, we shift the demand curve outward so that it intersects the supply curve at a higher equilibrium price. Changes in any number of factors could lead to the increased demand and the outward shift: higher income levels, leading consumers to buy more of everything; an increase in the price of a substitute product such as wine and spirits, leading consumers to buy more beer instead of those products; or a decrease in the price of pizza (a complementary product), leading consumers to eat more pizza and, of course, drink more beer along with the pizza.

Let's assume that higher incomes lead consumers to desire more beer at any given price. At the point in time when demand increases, brewers are still producing four million six-packs and selling them at $3.75; but now consumers want 4,250,000 six-packs. Brewers experience a decrease in their inventories, and some consumers are unable to get all they are willing and able to buy. The resulting shortage signals the brewers to do two things: increase prices and production. As prices rise, some of the additional demand for beer on the part of consumers at the old price disappears, and eventually the quantity of beer produced and consumed becomes equal again. That is, the market arrives at a new equilibrium with a price of $3.90 and production of 4,150,000 six-packs. Notice that this new equilibrium has a higher price and quantity than the original equilibrium, because it was caused by an increase in demand. It is a change in equilibrium because demand changed, unlike the temporary changes brought about by the failed efforts of producers to raise prices and output in the face of no changes in the fundamental factors driving the market.

This simple example considers a few of the factors that influence the shape and position of the demand curve. We can summarize four general factors that determine the shape and position of demand curves:

1. The level of income of consumers.
2. The prices of substitute goods or services.
3. The prices of complementary goods or services.
4. Tastes—the broad preference for a particular good or type of good.

In general, as income, the price of substitute goods, and tastes (preferences) for a particular good or service increase, the demand increases and the curve will shift farther to the right because there is a positive relationship between the demand for a good (i.e., the quantity demanded at each price) and those three factors. The relationship is reversed for complementary goods or complements, which are goods that are consumed along with a particular good or service. As the price of a good or service rises, the demand for its complements falls (and vice versa). In the previous example, pizza was a complement to beer, so when the price of pizza fell, the demand for beer increased. Had pizza prices risen, beer demand would have fallen instead.

The shape, position, and factors that shift the supply curve are equally intuitive. The most important factor influencing the supply curve is the cost of production. For firms in many industries, the cost of producing an additional unit eventually increases. Costs may eventually rise with the quantity of production, because more production requires that more resources be bid away from other uses. That is, if it costs a brewer $3.00 to make the millionth six-pack, the millionth and first may cost $3.02. Economists refer to the incremental cost of producing a unit of output as its marginal cost. Because the marginal cost increases as output increases, suppliers are willing and able to produce more only if they obtain higher prices. This relationship between rising marginal costs leads to the upward-sloping supply curve.

Factors that affect suppliers' cost of production determine the shape and position of the supply curve. The prices and availability of labor and materials used in the production process are the key components. Continuing with our beer example, if prices rise for inputs like hops and yeast, brewers will require a higher price for any given quantity of beer that they sell. A subtler factor that affects the supply curve is the opportunity cost of using resources to produce a particular good. The opportunity cost is the cost of the next best available use of those resources. In other words, it is the value you give up when you choose a particular use for some resource. What happens if the resources needed to brew beer could also be used to produce soft drinks and the prices of soft drinks rise? Brewers will look at their alternatives and switch into the soft-drink industry because the higher prices there represent greater profit opportunities. This would shift the beer supply curve upward to the left and reduce the quantity of beer produced. As a result, beer prices would rise (see Exhibit 2.3).

Although we have simplified enormously, the framework that has been outlined here is a very powerful tool. It is an analytical tool that allows decision makers to quickly evaluate the impact of changes that occur in their marketplace. Managers can and do use this tool to think through how to price their products and how changes in the market will affect their profitability. Similarly, policy makers use it to assess the effects of changes in regulation, taxes, subsidies, and tariffs. Moreover, it is an important philosophical

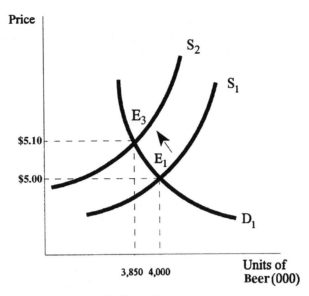

Exhibit 2.3   A Shift in Supply

concept. What we have outlined in terms of the price mechanism and how it reacts to changes in supply and demand is what Adam Smith called "the invisible hand" in his classic book, *The Wealth of Nations*, published in 1776. Resource allocation is determined in a market system by reactions to and changes in prices. While the mechanics are rather simple, the implications for society and the belief that firms and markets are valuable social institutions rest in large part on the ideas embodied in supply and demand analysis.

> *It is not from the benevolence of the butcher, the brewer or the baker that we expect our dinner, but from their regard to their own self interest. . . . [Every individual] intends only his own security, only his own gain. And he is in this led by an invisible hand to promote an end which was no part of his original intention. By pursuing his own interest, he frequently promotes that of society more effectually than when he really intends to promote it.*

—*Adam Smith*

Macroeconomics

Whereas microeconomics focuses on individual and firm-level decisions, macroeconomics focuses on the broad state of the economy. When people ask, "What's the economy doing?" or "What's the state of the stock market?" they are asking about the macroeconomy. Macroeconomics employs tools and concepts that help us to think about and predict the level of unemployment, the rate of inflation, rates of economic growth, the level of interest rates, and the policies governments pursue to influence them. Because ultimately the impact of policies depends on the behavior of individuals and firms, macroeconomics does not ignore microeconomic analysis. Models of macroeconomic behavior are rooted in ideas and evidence of how individuals react to changes in their environment. Macroeconomic models range from the simple to the incredibly complex, and all embody some key relationships that we discuss in the remainder of this chapter.

To begin with, we can represent what goes on in the economy with a supply and demand graph very similar to those used in the microeconomics section. Exhibit 2.4 is

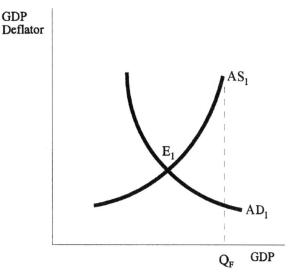

GDP
Deflator

AS₁

E₁

AD₁

Q_F   GDP

**Exhibit 2.4   Aggregate Demand and
Aggregate Supply**

such a graph. Notice that we have appended an A to the D and S to note that we are now dealing with aggregate demand (AD) and aggregate supply (AS). By aggregate, we mean the value of all of the goods and services produced in the economy during a period of time. The more common phrase for this value is the gross domestic product (GDP) of the economy. Since the AD curve represents all goods and services, the price in this analysis is not a single price, but a price index that is representative of the millions of goods and services produced in the economy. The most commonly used index is the GDP deflator.

The AD and AS curves function similarly to individual demand and supply curves, but they also reflect some important differences. One key difference relates to the nature of the AD curve and the relationship between the quantity of goods demanded and the aggregate price level. In our previous beer example, we considered what happened to the demand for beer as its price changed while all other prices were held constant. As beer prices fell, beer became a more attractive good to buy relative to all other goods. But when we consider the AD curve, all prices are reflected at once so we cannot hold any other prices constant. If all prices are changing proportionally as they are when we move up and down the AD curve, how is demand affected? It's not affected by the relative attractiveness of goods as in our beer example, and this is a key difference between the AD curve and demand curves for traditional goods. Instead, the AD curve slopes downward because the buying power of wealth (e.g., your bank account or cash in your pocket) rises and the general price level falls. Likewise, inflation (a general rise in the price level) will erode the buying power of your wealth and reduce your demand for goods and services as a whole.

Like the AD curve, the AS curve is not a perfect analogue to the supply curve we examined in our beer example. Notice that the AS curve becomes almost vertical at some level, Q_F (where the subscript F reflects full employment). That point represents the absolutely highest possible level of production in the economy when all of the resources are fully employed. This characteristic of the AS curve acknowledges that resources are finite and that for a given state of technological capabilities a maximum level of economy-wide production exists. Thus, the *AS* curve reflects what is possible for an economy at a given moment in time and for the existing state of technology.

Two crucial questions are implicit in the construction of the *AD* and *AS* curves in Exhibit 2.4. Is it possible to have an equilibrium in the economy as a whole at some level of GDP lower than the level that will employ almost everyone looking for a job? Also, is it possible to have inflation, a rise in the general price level, at a level of GDP below that which fully employs job seekers and other productive resources? In simplistic terms, those questions characterize key points of contention among economists and policy makers. The first question in particular is the one that John Maynard Keynes addressed in his book, *The General Theory of Employment, Interest and Money*, published in 1936. Before we turn to those questions and related ideas, we first need to introduce a way to measure GDP and account for different important categories of spending. We turn now to the subject of national income accounting and examine in more detail the concept of GDP and the relationships among national economies.

National Income Accounting

To understand the relationship between aggregate demand and aggregate supply and to be able to better evaluate economic policy, economists began to develop the concept of national income accounting in the 1920s. National income accounting attempts to measure the output or production of the economy, how that output is allocated among different uses, and what decisions are made about the income the output generates. The key to analyzing and using the national income accounts is to understand that they are based on an identity—a relationship that, by definition, must be true. In words, that identity, which is shown here, is that the total output, what we have called GDP, is equal to the total income, and that in turn is equal to the total allocation of income among the various forms of expenditure and savings:

$$\text{Output} = \text{Income} = \text{Expenditure}$$

That might appear to be vague at first glance, but once we have expanded the discussion it will become clearer. We have already defined output as the total value of goods and services produced in an economy during some period of time, or GDP. Since the value of something equals its cost plus the profit margin, and the cost and profits represent someone's income, then GDP can be measured from an income or an output perspective. Moreover, since the recipients of the income must either spend that income, save it, or pay taxes, then the total income must equal GDP. And finally, if we look at the various types of expenditures in the economy, they must total the output or GDP as well. Therefore, we can work with the national income identity in the following form:

$$GDP = C + I + G + (X - M) = C + T + S$$

where:
- C = household consumption
- I = business investment
- G = government spending
- X = exports
- M = imports
- T = taxes
- S = savings

Aside from some estimation issues, there is nothing controversial about these relationships. Every economist, regardless of his or her policy views, accepts this identity. The definitions of the categories are largely self-explanatory, except perhaps for the category of business investment, I. Investment usually calls to mind purchases of stocks, bonds, or other financial instruments, but these are not included in I in this identity. Rather, I reflects investment in productive resources like physical production plant, property, and other equipment or ideas that directly contribute to the production process. Purchases of stocks and bonds are vehicles for saving one's income for future use. While one's savings are typically channeled by financial markets to those firms and individuals who purchase things that go into our category I, national income accounts separate the act of saving by buying financial instruments, S, from the expenditures on productive assets, I.

The argument in support of the economy finding itself at or near full employment as an equilibrium is similar to the adjustment process described in the microeconomics section. Start by assuming that the economy is operating below its full employment level. Some productive resources are idle. Plants are running below capacity. Willing workers are unemployed, and raw materials are sufficient to expand production. The unemployed workers begin to despair of getting a job and suffer unsustainable financial distress so they become willing to work for less pay. Similarly, with excess capacity and raw materials available, manufacturing costs drop. As wages and other costs drop, manufacturers are willing to produce more (the supply curve shifts outward), but they need to lower prices to sell the expanded output. That is fine with them because costs have fallen. As prices fall, households, businesses, and government are all willing and able to buy more, so the quantity demanded increases. When does this stop? At full employment! At that level of output, there are no excess resources and no pressure for wages and prices to fall.

For those who believe in the power of markets, it is an elegant and convincing story. And there is no question that it has some empirical validity. When there is excess capacity, prices do fall or at least rise at a slower rate. However, in general the evidence is overwhelming that the economy can and does operate at levels below full employment for sustained periods of time. Considering only the United States, one of the world's most successful economies, at least two significant events highlight the severity of situations when the economy operates below full employment. The first was the Great Depression that persisted for more than a decade from the end of 1929 through the end of 1941. Unemployment reached more than 25 percent of the labor force and remained above any reasonable full employment level throughout the Depression. The second is the profound recession that began as the subprime crisis in late 2007. Unemployment rates nearly doubled from full employment levels in the first 18 months of the recession and continued to rise nearly two years after the onset of the economic contraction. Surely these long, profound departures from full employment aren't merely voluntary episodes or holidays from work. They must reflect some notable inability of markets to operate and clear in the way that classical economists describe.

The counter story to the classical view of market adjustment toward full employment begins with the view that prices and wages, although softer during weak economic periods, seldom fall enough to keep the economy at full employment. The reason the economy reaches an equilibrium below the full employment level is that aggregate demand is insufficient to sustain the full employment level of GDP. Households have lower income because people are unemployed and they spend less. Businesses that already have excess capacity reduce their investment in capital equipment. These reductions lead aggregate demand to shift to the left or downward, and the economy stagnates. In the 1920s in Europe and the 1930s in the United States, the downward spiral reached dramatic proportions as the unemployment rate exceeded 25 percent. Prices, wages, and interest rates did fall to very low levels, but there was so little demand that businesses did not invest even at a rate equal to depreciation, and they had no incentive to increase production.

A typical dynamic in recessions is that as prices fall, individuals and firms hold off on making purchases. Why buy when prices have further to fall? As a result of delayed purchasing, profits fall and even more jobs are lost. The same dynamic paralyzed the housing market in the United States in late 2007 through at least the middle of 2009. Housing prices began to fall, notably in some regions, but sales failed to occur because the expectation was that prices would fall further still. The expectation of falling prices paralyzed the housing market, just as it can paralyze an economy in general.

During the Great Depression many feared for the future of democracy and capitalism because the economic conditions were so dire. Among those most concerned was John Maynard Keynes, who not only identified insufficient demand as the primary problem of the Great Depression but also offered a policy to combat it. Keynes argued that steps needed to be taken to stimulate the economy. There was a need for the government to intervene in such a way as to increase aggregate demand through expansionary fiscal and monetary policy. For reasons beyond the scope of this book, Keynes advocated fiscal policy, but the major contribution he made was that government should and could do something to keep the economy closer to full employment. After the war, that view became the dominant one among economists and policy makers, and governments have tried to maintain stable economies by utilizing fiscal and monetary policy to manage aggregate demand.

Fiscal Policy

Fiscal policy refers to the use of government expenditures and taxation to influence the level of aggregate demand. A government's activities have both direct and indirect effects on aggregate demand. As the government spends money on programs such as defense, education, highways, or space exploration, it is buying goods and services. This shifts aggregate demand upward and to the right, which raises prices and the level of output. In order to meet the new higher level of quantity demanded, firms need to expand production by offering more overtime or hiring new workers. Either way, wages increase and the additional income allows households to increase their spending. That represents an increase in C or consumption. At some point, firms will find themselves short on capacity, so they will buy more manufacturing equipment and build new plants. The increase in C and I leads to an outward shift in aggregate demand that is more than the initial shift brought about by the increase in G, government spending. The total change in output that occurs is a multiple of the initial change in demand, and when economists speak of fiscal policy, they speak of the multiplier effect. The resulting increase in GDP is larger than the initial increase in government spending. This kick-start effect results when recipients of government purchases respend part of the income they receive.

Fiscal policy concerns both government expenditures and tax collections. Reducing taxes instead of increasing expenditures can bring about a similar stimulus to the economy. As the government reduces taxes, households and businesses will have more disposable income, some of which they would choose to spend. That spending shifts aggregate demand outward and sets into action the round of income and spending increases described earlier.

There are a number of programs and policies that have caused fiscal policy to be countercyclical. That is, when the economy is slowing, fiscal policy becomes more expansionary; and when the economy is growing rapidly, fiscal policy turns contractionary. These countercyclical effects are referred to as automatic stabilizers. What are they and how do they work? Basically, they take effect because some government expenditures and tax revenues are directly related to the level of income in the economy.

The two key places where that occurs are the entitlement programs and the progressive tax system. Entitlements are programs that provide some form of government payment based on an individual's income. As incomes rise, fewer people are eligible for the payments, and government expenditures fall. A progressive tax system causes tax collections to rise as incomes rise; as long as the tax schedule is progressive, collections rise at an increasing rate. The impact of the automatic stabilizers is to decrease government expenditures and increase tax collections when incomes rise. This puts a brake on the economy to keep it from overheating. Conversely, when the economy is slowing or enters a recession, incomes fall, government spending increases, tax collections decline, and the economy receives the necessary stimulus.

Fiscal policy, whether discretionary or automatic, cannot by itself keep the economy on an even keel. It takes time for the effects to be felt, and often other issues such as political concerns keep it from being implemented in a timely fashion. The other half of the policy tool kit is monetary policy, which often can be implemented more quickly, and independently of the political arena.

Monetary Policy

The conduct of monetary policy is almost always determined by a nation's central bank. In the United States, monetary policy is determined by its central bank—the Federal Reserve System, more commonly referred to as the Fed. The Fed consists of two major parts, the Board of Governors and the regional Federal Reserve Banks, of which there are 12. The Board of Governors has seven members who are appointed by the president of the United States. Each of the banks has an administrative, policy, and research staff headed by a president who is appointed by the Board of Governors. The seven members of the board and five of the 12 presidents, serving on a rotating basis, make up something called the Federal Open Market Committee (FOMC). This group determines monetary policy for the United States.

How does monetary policy work? That is not such an easy question to answer. It is the source of considerable disagreement among economists. To simplify, we will ignore points of dispute about the mechanisms through which policy operates and focus on the basics. Like fiscal policy, monetary policy has its impact through its ability to affect aggregate demand. It does that through two routes: changes in the level of interest rates in the economy, and changes in the availability of credit to firms and individuals. It's easy to see how lower interest rates would stimulate aggregate demand. Just imagine how lower interest rates would affect your willingness to buy a new home or car. Likewise, firms should be more willing to invest and expand if the costs of borrowing are lower. Higher rates would have the opposite effect of reducing aggregate demand. In a similar way, tightening the availability of credit lowers the ability of firms and individuals to consume and invest, thereby lowering aggregate demand. Thus, the Fed usually lowers interest rates and makes credit more available in recessions and raises interest rates and tightens credits when the economy is overheating.

To see how this happens, assume that the FOMC detects signs that inflation is accelerating. These signals might be that wages are increasing more rapidly than productivity, that commodity prices are rising at an unusually high rate, or that manufacturing plants are operating near capacity. The members of the committee feel that they should act, so they instruct their operating arm, the open market desk at the New York Federal Reserve Bank, to pursue contractionary policies. They might even specify quantitative targets for their policies, but basically what they want is for the open market desk to raise interest rates and slow the growth of the money supply.

The open market desk can push interest rates higher by entering the securities market and selling U.S. Treasury bonds. In order to sell the securities, the open market desk will offer them at a lower price than it had previously demanded. The lower price on a bond causes its yield or interest rate to rise. At the same time, as banks buy the bonds from the Fed, their ability to make loans is reduced. The Federal Reserve actions drain liquidity from the banking system. Banks go along with that and buy the bonds because the interest rate on them is higher. Banks reallocate their funds from loans to government bonds. As the banks reduce their loan volume, the level of deposits decreases and this in turn reduces the money supply.

With interest rates higher, loans less available, and the money supply smaller, aggregate demand will fall. The higher interest rates will lead consumers to put off purchases of durables like homes, automobiles, and appliances. Firms will invest less, because the higher rates make fewer projects pass the net present value hurdle rate. Banks are restrictive in making loans, so credit is not available for discretionary purposes. All of these changes shift the aggregate demand curve to the left, slowing the economy and easing the inflationary pressures. If the Fed wanted to stimulate the economy by increasing aggregate demand, it would lower interest rates and increase the money supply. The appropriate open market operation would be to buy bonds, raising their prices and expanding the reserves in the banking system.

Interest Rates

An important element of the macroeconomy is the level of interest rates. We have already seen that monetary policy works in part through its influence on interest rates. Also, because so many business and personal decisions are influenced by interest rates, they receive a great deal of attention. Interest rates are the price of credit. They are what we pay when we borrow or what we receive when we lend. The general level of interest rates in the economy is determined by the supply and demand for credit and the level of inflation. The specific rate an individual or firm pays depends on the general level plus a premium for credit riskiness of the borrower.

The famous economist Irving Fisher was the first to recognize the importance of inflation in the determination of interest rates. He distinguished between nominal rates and real rates where the nominal rate includes expected inflation.

$$\text{Nominal Rate} = \text{Real Rate} + \text{Expected Inflation}$$

The nominal rate is the interest rate we observe in the market or see reported by the press. The real rate has to be estimated or measured with hindsight, but the key is to realize that interest rates rise when inflation rises. Countries experiencing the highest rates of inflation also have the highest interest rates.

Real rates tend to be influenced by the demand for credit. During periods of economic expansion more people want to borrow because profit opportunities are plentiful. As a consequence, we tend to see higher interest rates during rapid growth periods and lower rates during recessions.

Balance of Payments

The earlier discussions of national income accounting and economic policy making were couched almost entirely in domestic terms. We did not discuss the role of trade and capital flows between countries or consider exports and imports, which are the subject of tremendous interest among firms and governments. But the focus on domestic economic activity is not quite as troubling as you might think. Most nations' economies are still largely domestic. For the United States, only about 14 percent of the GDP consists of exports and imports. Nevertheless, the share of international trade in the U.S. economy is rising and low relative to some economies, particularly in emerging markets. Moreover, trade and capital flow more freely across borders than ever, raising the influence of foreign firms and economic actions over all economies. The relationship of one economy's health to that of its trading partners and financial counterparties is a significant influence on common macroeconomic variables such as the level of interest rates, inflation, and even unemployment. Understanding the international economy is more important than ever.

The first step in understanding the basic relationships among national economies is to understand the financial/capital and goods flows among nations for a given period, typically one quarter or one year. The balance of payments is a statistical record of all the cross-border transactions engaged in by the residents of a country; an importer that brings wine or olive oil into the United States, an exporter that distributes movies overseas, a tourist who travels in China, and an investor who buys Brazilian equities are all engaging in cross-border transactions that show up in the balance of payments.

The range of transactions is broad, so there are a number of measures or definitions of the balance of payments. We are going to focus on one, the current account balance. The current account is commonly used to discuss the relationships among countries as measured by their trade flows, or exports and imports. Specifically, the current account measures all the transactions involving goods and service trades and unilateral transfers (i.e., one-way gifts) or foreign aid. Using the same notation from the national income accounts, the current account balance is:

$$X - M = GDP - (C + I + G)$$

We arrive at this identity for the current account by simply subtracting three categories of domestic expenditure, C, I, and G, from GDP on the left-hand side of the national income identity. An intuitive way to think about the relationship is that the current account equals the difference between the total amount of production in an economy and the total expenditures of its citizens and government. If an economy engages in no international trade, and therefore has no imports or exports, then GDP simply equals $C + I + G$. The current account can be expressed as:

Current Account = Total Production − Total Expenditure

Let's imagine a country where its total production exceeds its total expenditures. For this country, $GDP > (C + I + G)$, so is must be that $X > M$. This is a powerful result to remember. It tells us that countries that produce more than they consume have exports that exceed their imports. We say that countries where exports exceed imports have a current account surplus. Conversely, a country that spends more than it produces—that is, where $GDP < (C + I + G)$—have a current account deficit, meaning that their imports exceed their exports (i.e., $X < M$). Countries such as the United States that have a current account deficit have expenditures greater than production. We can use the current account identity and see how this must be true mechanically, but how does a country go about consuming more than it produces? The answer is that it borrows some of the output of other countries. That is exactly what a current account deficit represents: the borrowing of output beyond the level of a country's current production. Countries with current account surpluses lend to countries like the United States that have current account deficits. The borrowing country gives the lending country a claim on its future output. When people describe a country as a debtor country, what they mean is that the country is running a current account deficit and is issuing goods and services. Surplus countries are those that save. They consume less than they produce and acquire financial assets in exchange for their surplus production.

The relationship between current account items and capital flows, or between savings and investments, is perhaps the most important concept in all of international macroeconomics. It is so fundamental to understanding the interrelationships among economies that it is sometimes referred to as the Big Equation.

Referring back to our national income accounting identity allows us to derive the Big Equation. Recall that $C + I + G + (X - M) = C + S + T$. Through a little rearranging we can see that this identity implies that $(X - M) = (S - I) + (T - G)$. That is, the current account $(X - M)$ must equal the difference between domestic savings and investment plus any government surplus $(T - G)$. For the moment, let's focus on the relationship of the current account to savings and investment by assuming that the government runs a balanced budget, $T = G$. In this case, this identity reduces to: $(X - M) = (S - I)$. We call the right-hand side of this identity the capital account. When either the current account or the capital account reflects inflows into the economy (i.e., when $X > M$ or $S < I$), we say that it is in surplus. Conversely, when either reflects outflows from the economy (i.e., when $X < M$ or $S > I$), we way that it is in deficit. Thus, our identity shows that a current account surplus $(X > M)$ always implies a capital account deficit $(S > I)$, and a current account deficit $(X < M)$ always implies a capital account surplus $(S < I)$. In this sense these payments always balance, hence the term *balance of payments*.

There are numerous factors that influence whether a country runs a current account deficit or surplus. Many of them are related to macroeconomic policies that influence the levels of output, consumption, investment, and government spending. As a country's economy grows more rapidly than those of its trading partners, its consumption increases. Generally, that leads imports to grow more rapidly than exports and results in a deficit. A country with a higher inflation rate than its trading partners have will see its goods become less desirable, and that will also result in a deficit. Policies to correct the deficit are actually policies to influence the levels of aggregate demand (expenditure) and aggregate supply (output). What is important to remember is that countries that run current account deficits borrow from countries that run current account surpluses and that this implies capital flowing from the lending country to the borrowing country.

To conclude this section, it is important to note that a current account deficit is not necessarily bad. At various times, it is desirable for countries to borrow in order to consume more than they produce and therefore to invest more than they save. The key question is what type of consumption or expenditure is taking place. If the borrowing is to build infrastructure and expand manufacturing capabilities, then the deficit is likely to contribute to future growth and the borrowing probably represents a wise choice. The country's future output will grow and allow it to repay the financial claims and improve its overall standard of living. If the borrowed savings is not invested or does not create future production, then the country will have to default on its claims and/or experience a decline in its standard of living. Even among countries, the bills eventually come due.

Savings, Exports, and the Crisis of 2008–2009

For at least 20 years, if not longer, pundits, policy makers, and the general citizenry of the United States have agonized over the poor performance of our export sectors. To many, the causes seemed obvious: Americans just can't compete with the quality and/or prices offered by our trading partners abroad. Specific causes were and still are offered—bloated corporations, poorly trained or poorly motivated workers, unreasonably low wages abroad, and the hollowing-out of our manufacturing sector. Year by year it seems the United States has bequeathed its ability to export to China, Japan, Mexico, and other lower-income markets with which we trade. Our inability to export seems to be our structural weakness and a sure sign of a weakening economy.

Along with endless laments over our inability to export, most in the United States also worry about our reckless consumer culture in which most people seem to live only for today with seeming disregard for any future consequences. We save quite a bit less than our counterparts abroad, as reflected in our low national savings rate. From about 1950 to 1980 workers in the United States saved about 10 percent of their paychecks on average, but this fraction began to slide by the early 1980s. The number slid to about 5 percent by the mid-1990s, all the way to 0 percent by 2004 and even dipped into the negative in 2005. Amazingly, the United States had become a nation where the average savings from current income was zero or less!

And yet, the United States experienced steady and at times superb economic growth from the mid-1980s to the middle of 2007. Far from being a relative laggard in its peer group, the United States shone, growing notably faster and more steadily than Japan and Western European nations. How is this possible? Is there no penalty for a reckless disregard for savings? Are there no consequences for a lack of export prowess? The answers to these questions are conditional, as is so much in economics, but they reveal quite a lot about the profound economic crisis that began in late 2007 and how its resolution will change the U.S. economy and the world.

The starting point for understanding how the United States managed to grow without saving or exporting is our balance of payments identity: $(X - M) = (S - I)$. As our identity shows, the twin concerns of not exporting and not saving are really one and the same, different aspects of the same economic feature. The United States saved very little but was nevertheless able to invest quite a lot because other countries were very willing to lend to us. In other words, savings, S, was very low, but investment, I, remained at a healthy level. The lack of savings in the United States did not result in a lack of investment, because foreigners were happy to lend us the capital to invest. Of course, if I is much larger than S, then M must be much larger than X; hence the United States, in keeping with its position as a capital importer, also ran very large current account deficits.

For decades the United States ran large trade deficits and imported lots of capital for investment, while many nations, such as Japan, China, and South Korea, did precisely the reverse. Remarkably, the flow of funds into the United States was so abundant that interest rates reached historic lows all the while domestic savings had completely evaporated. Long-term growth in the United States was not decidedly threatened so long as investment remained high and foreign nations remained comfortable piling up mountains of investments in U.S. financial instruments and assets.

This simple depiction of a complex story involving the whole of the world economy is the starting point for understanding the end of the housing bubble in the United States and the worst economic collapse since the Great Depression. To see how, ask yourself: What happened to the funds sent to the United States by those foreign nations running current account surpluses? The funds were put to many uses, to be sure, but they also supported very low interest rates and, in places, serious run-ups in the values of particular classes of assets over the years. Following the late 1990s and the end of the so-called tech bubble, a large portion of the funds supported low mortgage rates and easy lending conditions. Complemented by low interest rate policies by the Fed, these historically low mortgage rates fueled an unprecedented boom in housing prices. The boom drew in developers who rapidly expanded home production and buyers who sought the apparently easy financial returns of buying a new and perhaps second or third home.

Banks proved particularly eager to profit from the home buying frenzy and adopted, willfully or merely accidentally, loose lending standards that further fueled the explosion in home prices. Not surprisingly, the boom was unsustainable and the end of the boom crushed the value of billions of dollars in mortgages. The frenzy and poor lending standards were not limited to banks lending into the housing markets, but reflected a national crisis that was supported by the United States' long-standing position in the world economy as the only real capital importer. This lonely position is why the Great Recession of 2008–2009 is often attributed to the problem of global imbalances, meaning the lopsided position of the capital and current accounts in the United States and its major trading partners.

So what's next for the global economy? Will the United States recover from the Great Recession of 2008–2009, and if so, how? No one knows the specifics, but our simple balance of payments identity provides some useful guidance. First, a safer rebalanced world economy with a healthier United States means that the United States must save more than it has in the past and yet continue to invest in assets and resources to support future growth. This means the United States must run a smaller capital account surplus (i.e., $S - I$ must be less negative). But, of course, this means that the United States must also run a smaller current account deficit, meaning that it must export more, import less, or both. Conversely, some economies outside the United States, such as China and Japan, will need to run smaller current account surpluses and capital account deficits. At root, this is what rebalancing means, and it's not likely to be easy. What will the United States export and what will drive its economy if Americans suddenly start to save and stop consuming? Can China and Japan reverse course while adhering to their economic goals?

Are they willing to import from the United States? However it is achieved, the recovery from the worst economic crisis in 80 years will adhere to the constraints imposed by the balance of payments and the complex web of financial and goods flows that define the world economy.

Appendix: Courses in Economics at Top Business Schools

All top MBA programs require some courses on economics and typically offer numerous elective courses as well. Microeconomics is most often the required course in economics, but many top schools require macroeconomics instead and offer elective courses in microeconomics. Microeconomics courses offer a foundation in understanding individual and firm-level decision making and are highly useful in courses on marketing, strategy, and finance. Macroeconomics courses often have a strong connection to international finance and international business. Macroeconomics courses offer a framework for understanding the broad environment of business and the nature of the global economy. In addition to core courses in economics, most top schools offer electives in price theory, managerial economics, and some courses related to international trade and development.

University of Chicago	Microeconomics—one of three Foundation courses from which all students choose one. Analysis of major policy issues. Macroeconomics (elective)—Understanding Central Banks.
University of Virginia (Darden)	Global Economies and Markets—a required course for all students in the first year. Focus is on an open-economy macroeconomic model. Electives focus on exchange rates, international trade, and investment and development economics.
University of Michigan (Ross)	Applied Microeconomics—required in the first year Core Curriculum—The Economics of the Firm. Growth and Stabilization in Macroeconomy—second year elective.
Northwestern University (Kellogg)	Microeconomics—required in the first year Core Curriculum. International Macroeconomics for Managers—second year elective.
University of Pennsylvania (Wharton)	Managerial Economics/Applied Microeconomics—required in the first year Core Curriculum. Macroeconomic Analysis and Public Policy.
Harvard University	Macroeconomics—required in the first year Core Curriculum. Institutions, Macroeconomics and the Global Economy—second year elective.
Dartmouth University (Tuck)	Macroeconomics—Global Economics for Managers, required in the first year Core Curriculum. Managerial Economics, required in the first year Core Curriculum.

Downloadable Resources for this chapter available at www.wiley.com/go/portablemba5e

Demand Curve Exercise at www.how-to-price.com (second paragraph of Supply and Demand section)

Download Economic Report of the President at www.nber.org/erp/2009_erp.pdf (next to discussion of GDP)

See Balance of Payments materials at www.balanceofpayments.net (after discussion of balance of payments in chapter)

Introduction to Business Ethics

3

Despite the Sarbanes-Oxley Act of 2002,[1] it is not unusual to open any major newspaper or turn on the television news anywhere in the world and be greeted by something like the following:

- Bernard Madoff's hedge fund is revealed to be a Ponzi scheme resulting in an estimated $50 billion loss for individual and institutional investors around the world.
- Martha Stewart is found guilty of obstruction of justice related to the investigation of insider trading of ImClone stock.
- Despite receiving billions of federal support dollars, American International Group (AIG) pays over $1 billion to executives as bonuses only months after the bailout.
- Payoffs to officials in countries around the world are alleged.
- Critics claim that executives need to deal with child labor, unsafe working conditions, and environmental degradation.

Each of these issues and countless others that bombard us on a daily basis raise questions in our minds about the relationship between business and ethics. The purpose of this chapter is to explore this connection along a number of dimensions. First, it examines some criteria for determining what makes a business issue an ethical one as well. Along the way it looks at some common myths about the role of ethics in business. It examines the basic moral reasoning tools as they are applied to business, paying particular attention to the role of values and principles. Then it examines a way of understanding business so that ethical issues are endogenous to the way that we think about our companies. It argues that this method, which we call *stakeholder capitalism*, is in keeping with Adam Smith's ideas about business several hundred years ago. Finally, it explores some difficult ethical challenges for business in today's business environment.

What Constitutes an Ethical Issue?

Andrea is negotiating a difficult contract with a supplier. The supplier is responsible for a key manufacturing component for Andrea's company and has driven a hard bargain around terms, conditions, and price. After a tough day of negotiating in a hotel conference room, the supplier team leaves with the deal not yet consummated. After they have left, Andrea notices that a folder has fallen down under the table. She picks up the folder, glances at the inside, and immediately recognizes that it contains what appears to be very

47

important information about the supplier's cost. What should she do? Should she read the folder?[2]

Does Andrea have an ethical issue? Granted, there is no front-page headline issue at stake, but what Andrea does will potentially have large effects on others. There are several arguments to the effect that Andrea needs to see this issue in ethical terms.

The first argument is that the folder is not Andrea's property, and therefore she should not read the folder or use it in any way. Suppose that Andrea had found a wallet under the table instead of the folder. Common morality requires that she should return the wallet without using the contents to her own advantage. The folder case is an ethical issue because it involves making decisions about the legitimate uses of private property. Does Andrea have the right to use other people's property without their permission?

The second argument is about fairness. According to this position, Andrea would be taking unfair advantage of her suppliers by reading this information. She would know something that they don't intend for her to know, and she would not have earned the right to that knowledge. Andrea would not be negotiating from a level playing field, and that would be unfair. An alternative to this position is to see business as a game or institution with its own set of rules: "All's fair in love and war and business" suggests that in a negotiation, you can use whatever tactic is available—from bluffing to getting information nefariously. Note that even in this interpretation, Andrea still has an ethical issue about fairness. The difference in the two interpretations is not the lack of an ethical issue in one of them, but a disagreement about defining fairness.

A third argument involves the consequences of Andrea's action. Will the relationship with the supplier be sustainable? Will others think that Andrea is not a woman of good character? Will using the information lead to a better or worse outcome for Andrea's company? For the supplier company? Andrea has an ethical problem because of the consequences that are possible.

Each of these arguments goes a long way in helping us to identify ethical issues. Ethical issues are usually concerned with (1) rights and duties, (2) principles such as fairness, or (3) harms and benefits. Ethics concerns how we ought to live our lives. It is about how we reason together regarding the effects of our actions on others. We always have an alternative to entering such a conversation—that alternative is violence and coercion. However, we can think of ethics as the substitution of reason for violence as we try to figure out how we can survive and flourish together in spite of our differences.

There are usually two levels of ethical issues. The first is the personal level, and our example of the folder is a good illustration. Andrea must figure out what she believes is the right thing to do—what fits with the way that she is trying to live her life and with her own principles and values. However, ethics doesn't end there. Because others are affected by Andrea's decision, their own interests, indeed the way they are trying to live their lives, are also important. Ethical issues almost always appear at the personal and interpersonal (or social) levels simultaneously.

It is a mistake to think that ethics is only personal. The standard test, "Well, I have to live with myself if I do this," is a good start, but what that test misses is that others have to live with you, too. Being true to your own beliefs—being authentic—is a good starting point for a conversation with others, but it is only a starting point.

The view that each person is the sole arbiter for right and wrong is called ethical relativism, and it prevents us from reasoning together. If the only criterion for the correctness of a particular action is your personal belief, then we don't need to reason about ethics. We just need to check whether a person truly acted on his or her beliefs. Furthermore, if a person or a group of people is trying to solve a difficult ethical issue, it is just a waste of time, because the real measure of correctness, according to ethical relativism, would be personal beliefs.[3]

Needless to say, ethical relativism is a thoroughly discredited view, but it does contain a grain of truth. For the most part, individuals make ethical decisions. Individuals are the locus of decision making. In an individualist culture it would be natural to give individuals a great deal of autonomy. Such individualism, the view that individuals know their interests best and should be left free to pursue them, is different from relativism. You can easily think of ethical rules agreed to by individuals in order to smooth the way for them to pursue their interests.

Almost all major issues that managers face have an ethical component. However, to read the business press or to examine business books, you would think that ethical issues are the exception rather than the rule.

Tell someone that you are worried about business ethics and you'll likely as not get a response like "I didn't know that business had any" or "Isn't that an oxymoron, like jumbo shrimp?" Our common idea of business has evolved into the belief that business and ethics are somehow separate—that managers can think about business without thinking about ethics and vice versa.[4] Such a separation leads to a natural tendency for us to think of business as morally suspect and to joke about business ethics. However, if the arguments in this book are correct—that business is the dominant institution for creating value in today's world—then business must be part and parcel of the very best way that humans can live. We must intertwine business and ethics in a very fundamental way.

It is impossible to determine just how business became separated from ethics in history. If we go back to Adam Smith, we find no such separation. In addition to his famous book on business and capitalism, *The Wealth of Nations*, Adam Smith also wrote *The Theory of Moral Sentiments*, a book about our ethical obligations to one another. It is clear that Smith believed that business and commerce worked well only if people took seriously their obligations and, in particular, their sense of justice.[5]

The early capitalists in the United States, the so-called robber barons, clearly separated business from ethics, but brought back their social responsibility through philanthropy.[6] Andrew Carnegie, in *The Gospel of Wealth*, outlined two principles for businesspeople. The *charity principle* suggested that more fortunate people in society should help those who are less fortunate by contributing to organizations designed to offer assistance. The *stewardship principle*, from the Bible, viewed the wealthy as holding their property in trust for society, with the obligation to use it for any legitimate societal purpose. Acting on these principles, Carnegie and U.S. Steel had an active program of social philanthropy. Over time, these principles became increasingly accepted, as did the idea that power implies the responsibility to use it for at least some common good.

A more modern version of these two principles could be called the *principle of social responsibility*—the view that business has an obligation to act in the interests of society. This principle has been invoked to justify many different business actions, from giving to the arts to rebuilding neighborhoods to contributions to political figures. The idea is that business must see itself as a citizen in the community and do what it can to make the community a better place.

If business did not act in a socially responsible way, many executives realize that government would regulate and force such action. Indeed, one explanation of the extensive regulatory regimes in countries around the world is that business has failed to act in a way that fulfills its social responsibility.

The chief counterview of business as a socially responsible entity was promulgated by Chicago economist Milton Friedman, who is usually identified with the view that the only ethical obligation of a business is to maximize profits. This is sometimes interpreted to mean that capitalism is an anything-goes system without morality or humanity. What Friedman actually said is a bit different.

Friedman recognized that business creates and allocates wealth in society. He suggested that, within certain rules and constraints, the system of shareholder capitalism could efficiently create and allocate such wealth only if managers focused on managerial tasks—efficiently managing the business. Of course, Friedman knew, as did Adam Smith, that the anything-goes philosophy couldn't work, and Friedman believed that profits could be maximized within the constraints of law and ethical custom. In particular, Friedman knew that if people did not tell the truth most of the time, and if they tried to mislead others about the attributes of products and services, that business would not work very well. Capitalism as an anything-goes system is neither Friedman's idea nor a very sound one.

While there are hundreds of articles written to counter Friedman's view, the best suggestion is to think more deeply about ethics in business. What are some ways of understanding ethical rules and customs? How can we analyze ethics and business together? In short, we need to critically examine the tools that we have for ethical or moral reasoning.

Tools of Moral Reasoning

The language of ethics is very rich. We teach our children about values, rights, duties, principles, and the like, and there is no reason to believe that these processes are not relevant to business life.

Values

Much of our thinking about ethical issues in business is based on our *values*. Values represent our desires and can be either good in themselves (*intrinsic values*) or a means to other ends (*instrumental values*). Values provide a framework that serves as both the reasons for and the causes of many of our actions. It is relatively important to know whether a value is intrinsic and worth pursuing for its own sake or instrumental and likely to lead to or be an indicator of something more important.

Some business thinkers (for example, Peter Drucker) have argued that a common mistake that managers make is to make profit an intrinsic value to be pursued in its own right. Drucker suggests that organizations are far more interesting when profit is an instrumental value, pursued for the sake of some other values.

A book by Jim Collins and Jerry Porras (*Built to Last: Successful Habits of Visionary Companies*, HarperBusiness, 1994) reinforces Drucker's idea. They found that great companies that have been "built to last" place achieving their core purpose above profits. Their advice is to focus on the purpose, not the profits.

Merck & Company, a U.S.-based pharmaceutical company, is a good example. First of all, Merck has had a tradition of being very profitable for many years. Yet profit is an instrumental value. At Merck, the intrinsic value is to help the sick. In the words of George Merck, "We try never to forget that medicine is for the people. It is not for the profits. The profits follow, and if we have remembered that, they have never failed to appear. The better we have remembered it, the larger they have been." Being highly profitable allows Merck to pursue other, more important values.[7]

Obviously, individuals have values that determine in part their behavior. Not so obviously, companies also have values. Often these appear to be business-related values such as customer service, quality, and teamwork, but often there are more straightforwardly ethical values such as respect and integrity.

Values serve as an important tool in reasoning about ethical issues in business. There is often a conflict among competing values. For instance, if a company values both customer service and respect, there are certain kinds of behavior expected of its employees to meet customer service requirements. Many companies, such as Johnson & Johnson, try to capture values in a statement or code. Exhibit 3.1 is Johnson & Johnson's corporate values statement or credo.

Values can help an organization and its members clarify what is important in the organization. Values serve to raise interesting and important questions and to reveal difficult trade-offs. It is a mistake to see corporate values statements as mere "warm and fuzzy" statements that make everyone feel good. Rather, they are statements of what an organization stands for—its main purpose for existence.

Corporate values and individual values can often conflict. Many times the statements of the values don't conflict, but the interpretations that bosses and employees put on the values vary widely. If values statements are to be effective in organizations in empowering employees to work for the organizational purpose, then there must be some means to question the values and, more important, to question processes, systems, and behaviors that appear not to be aligned with the values.

Rights, Duties, and Responsibilities

Values form the background against which other moral notions can be applied. Some values are so important and pervasive that they are picked out for special acclaim in the form of rights.[8] Because we value freedom and autonomy so much, we define *rights* as a sphere of autonomy in which everyone can act equally. The right to free speech is a right that everyone has, not just a few. The rights to life, liberty, and the pursuit of happiness are broad categories of permissible actions. However, rarely are rights absolute. The scope of any individual's rights are limited by the rights of others. It is often said that "My right to swing my fist ends at the beginning of your nose."

While there is much talk of rights in our society, there is little talk of a correlative concept—*duties*. Duties are obligations that we incur to take specific steps, or to refrain from taking specific steps, that are connected with the rights of others. For example, if Jack has the right not to be killed, then everyone has the correlative duty not to kill Jack. If Jill has the right to a living wage, then someone (a government, a community, a company) has the obligation/duty to provide or guarantee that wage. Rights without duties are not very useful. And duties without rights are not worth the trouble.

Exhibit 3.1   Johnson & Johnson's Credo

We believe our first responsibility is to the doctors, nurses and patients,
to mothers and fathers and all others who use our products and services.
In meeting their needs everything we do must be of high quality.
We must constantly strive to reduce our costs
in order to maintain reasonable prices.
Customers' orders must be serviced promptly and accurately.
Our suppliers and distributors must have an opportunity
to make a fair profit.
We are responsible to our employees,
the men and women who work with us throughout the world.
Everyone must be considered as an individual.
We must respect their dignity and recognize their merit.
They must have a sense of security in their jobs.
Compensation must be fair and adequate,
and working conditions clean, orderly and safe.
We must be mindful of ways to help our employees fulfill
their family responsibilities.
Employees must feel free to make suggestions and complaints.
There must be equal opportunity for employment,
development and advancement for those qualified.
We must provide competent management,
and their actions must be just and ethical.
We are responsible to the communities in which we live and work
and to the world community as well.
We must be good citizens—support good works and charities
and bear our fair share of taxes.
We must encourage civic improvements and better health and education.
We must maintain in good order
the property we are privileged to use,
protecting the environment and natural resources.
Our final responsibility is to our stockholders.
Business must make a sound profit.
We must experiment with new ideas.
Research must be carried on, innovative programs developed
and mistakes paid for.
New equipment must be purchased, new facilities provided
and new products launched.
Reserves must be created to provide for adverse times.
When we operate according to these principles,
the stockholders should realize a fair return.

Source: http://www.jnj.com/connect/about-jnj/jnj-credo/.

A third idea helps to tie together these abstract notions, and that is *responsibility*. Responsibility is a set of behaviors that we should engage in if a system of rights and duties is to be stable and useful. For instance, while Jack may have the right to free speech, it would be unwise and irresponsible to use that right in a way that constantly harmed others. Indeed, if Jack and others did such a thing, it would undermine the very nature of civil society that gives rise to the rights in the first place. In this sense, responsibility involves the judicious exercising of a set of rights.

Rights, duties, and responsibilities play an important role in analyzing ethical issues in business. What rights do customers have vis-à-vis product performance and safety? What duties do companies have regarding employees? What rights do employees have in terms of basic political freedoms? What does it mean to be a responsible company? A responsible manager? A responsible employee?

Consequences

One of the most critical concepts in ethics is quite familiar to all modes of business analysis—the idea that actions have *consequences*. Most business theories and models assume that all consequences of a business decision can be measured in economic terms and quantified, or at least specified in enough detail to allow a cost-benefit analysis. With ethical issues the consequences are not always so simple.

Consider an issue such as insider trading—buying and selling securities on the basis of material, nonpublic information—a practice that is illegal in the United States. The decision to trade on such information clearly allocates harms and benefits in a certain way. The insider is benefited at the expense of the person on the other side of the trade who is harmed. However, there is a more subtle consequence here. If insider trading were prevalent, then public confidence in the market could well be undermined. It is not clear how to value this consequence economically, but it must be taken into account in a thorough analysis of the ethics of insider trading.

Business ethics issues often focus on harms that have been created by business activity. Too often, benefits are ignored. And, we will argue, business as an institution creates a lot of good things. Computer technology, new life-prolonging drugs, and systems for the spread of knowledge are but a few of the inventions that have made our lives better. If we blame businesses for the harm they create, then we should also give them credit for the good they create. Understanding both harms and benefits of business issues is critical to a balanced view of business ethics.

Principles and Rules

Over time, we have developed a number of generalizations from the judgments that we make about right and wrong. These generalizations are based on our values, our assignment of rights and duties, and our experience with consequences to be desired and those to be avoided. We capture these generalizations in the form of moral rules or principles.[9]

For most ethical problems we have devised a set of rules or principles on which there is widespread agreement. *Common morality* is the set of principles that determine how we live most of the time. Promise keeping, mutual aid, respect for persons, respect for property, and so forth are usually uncontroversial principles that cover a host of daily situations. We learn these principles as children, and they are reinforced in most of our social institutions.

Business is no exception here. Businesspeople keep their promises most of the time, treat others with respect and dignity, and help each other when they can do so at little additional cost. Furthermore, when we find someone not living by these common principles, we call his or her character into question. Business consultant Stephen Covey has gone so far as to suggest that we come to view the idea of leadership as living by moral principles and advocating the same in others.[10]

However, moral dilemmas arise for common morality in several instances. First, new technology makes us unsure of how a principle applies. For instance, we might agree on the right to privacy and the corresponding duty to respect the privacy of others, and we might formulate a principle such as "Unless there is an emergency, you shouldn't interfere in the private affairs of another." (The "unless" clause covers the cases where you could save someone's life by interfering, for example.) Normally, we would agree that personal mail, desk files, and so on are the private affairs of a person. However, the new computer technology may change this definition. E-mail, voice mail, electronic files, and the World Wide Web may force us to rethink the applicability of this principle. There are sure to be a number of meaty dilemmas that get raised.

Principles can also be questioned when we encounter a society or a culture that does things differently or applies the same principle in a different manner. For instance, in many cultures the principle of freedom of the press is not understood in as far-reaching a manner as it is in the United States. We need more conversation and more reasoning to figure out how our principles may or may not apply in those situations.

A third challenge to principles and common morality may come from new groups being empowered in society. Indeed, in today's business world, the empowerment of women and minorities in the workforce has forced a rethinking of the biases that may be present in the workplace. The very idea of respect may be interpreted differently along gender roles. We don't need a new principle, but we do need a new conversation about its interpretation and applicability.

Parallel Cases

When we are faced with a difficult ethical dilemma, one in which principles conflict, where there are uncertain consequences and where values and rights don't clearly help us to find an answer, we need to turn to parallel cases. We need to look for cases that we are clear about and to extrapolate reasoning from those cases to ones that are similar but less clear.

Consider the case of the H.B. Fuller Company, maker of a glue called Resistol. This glue was being abused by young children in Honduras, who were called *Resistoleros*. A parallel case would be someone driving a car while intoxicated. The car is not being used in a manner for which it is intended, and if there is a crash we could hardly blame the car manufacturer. At the other end of the spectrum we find Johnson & Johnson's response to the deaths of Extra Strength Tylenol users that were caused by product tampering. J&J was not to blame, yet the company took the product off the market until it could introduce a tamper-resistant package. H.B. Fuller weighed such parallels and others to find a course consistent with its corporate values and the ethical expectations of both Honduras and the United States. In fact, the company undertook an extensive program of education and social service to try to help those who had been affected and to prevent others from misusing the product. Eventually this meant addressing the formulation of the product itself in an ongoing manner.[11]

A Method for Understanding Capitalism in Ethical Terms

One way to connect business and ethics is to begin by understanding that businesses can affect more than just shareholders.[12] Indeed, customers, suppliers, employees, communities, and shareholders are all affected in major ways by businesses. These groups have come to be known as the *stakeholders* in the firm. The stakeholder concept tries to set forth exactly who is affected by a business and to map the set of relationships that comprise the value-creation enterprise.

The concept of stakeholders was developed in the 1960s through the work of management theorists Eric Rhenman, Igor Ansoff, Russell Ackoff, and their students. The idea is connected to a very old tradition that sees business as an integral part of society rather than as an institution that is separate and purely economic in nature. Identifying and analyzing stakeholders was originally a simple way to acknowledge the existence of multiple constituencies in the corporation. The main insight was that executives must pay some strategic attention to those groups who were important to the success of the corporation.[13]

As the pace of change accelerated in business, these thinkers and others began to advocate more interaction with stakeholders so that they would have some sense of participation in the day-to-day affairs of the corporation. We had the emergence of consumer advisory panels, quality circles, just-in-time inventory teams, community advisory groups, and so on, all designed to get the corporation more in touch with the key relationships that would affect its future. During the 1980s, the idea of "stakeholder management" was articulated as a method for systematically taking into account the interests of "those groups which can affect and are affected by the corporation."[14]

As discussed previously, we have recently seen the emergence of a strong movement concerned with business ethics. Much of the business ethics movement has been in response to perceived corporate wrongs such as financial scandals, excessive executive compensation, business-government collusion, and celebrated cases of whistle-blowing. But a small number of thinkers began to ask questions about the very purpose of the corporation. Should the corporation serve those who own shares of stock, or should it serve those who are affected by its actions? The choice was laid bare: Corporations can be made to serve stockholders or they can be made to serve stakeholders.

Most thoughtful executives know that this choice between stockholders and stakeholders is a false one. Corporations must be profitable at rates determined by global capital markets. No longer can executives ignore the fact that capital flows freely across borders and that rates of return are more complicated than indicated by internally generated financial hurdle rates and payback schemata. Business today is truly global.

Most thoughtful executives also know that great companies are not built by obsessive attention to shareholder value. Great companies arise in part out of a shared sense of purpose among employees and management. This sense of purpose must be important enough for individuals to expend their own human capital to create and deliver products and services that customers are willing to pay for. We need only return to the wisdom of Peter Drucker and W. Edwards Deming to see the importance of meaning and purpose and the destructiveness of fear and alienation in corporate life.

Management thinkers such as Tom Peters, Charles Handy, Jim Collins, and Jerry Porras have produced countless examples of how employees, customers, and suppliers work together to create something that none of them can create alone. And capital is necessary to sustain this process of value creation. From Cadbury to Volvo, Nordstrom to Hewlett-Packard, executives are constantly engaged in intense stakeholder relationships.

In this view, the interests of stockholders and stakeholders are very often in alignment rather than in conflict. Stockholders are a key stakeholder group whose support must be sustained in the same way that customer, supplier, and employee support must be garnered. The issue is one of balancing the interests of these groups, not favoring one at the expense of the others. Furthermore, in a relatively free political system, when executives ignore the interests of one group of stakeholders systematically over time, these stakeholders will use the political process to force regulation or legislation to protect themselves. Witness the emergence of stakeholder rights in the United States in the form of labor legislation, consumer protection legislation, environmental (community) protection legislation, even shareholder protection legislation.

Quite simply, there are many ways to manage a successful company. Management styles of Toyota will be different from those of Ford. Procter & Gamble's methods will differ from Unilever's. However, all will involve the intense interaction of employees—management and nonmanagement alike—with critical stakeholders. The more that stakeholders participate in the decisions that affect them, be they product design decisions or employment contract decisions, the greater the likelihood that they will be committed to the future of the corporate enterprise.

Contrast this commonsense view of the workings of business with the traditional business ideology that we outlined earlier: separating business from ethics and proclaiming that it is amoral, that business ethics is an oxymoron, and that business exists to do only what shareholders require. In this old philosophy, business is seen as warfare, and executives are the lonely soldiers on the battlefield of global markets, playing "shoot 'em up" with competitors. This myth of the primacy of the shareholder and its view of business as so-called cowboy capitalism leads to a profound public mistrust and misunderstanding of the basic processes that make companies successful. We need a new story—one that elevates business to the higher moral ground—and one that smacks of common sense and reality in today's business world.

Stakeholder capitalism, properly formulated, is just the new story that we need. Stakeholder capitalism is based on five principles (see Exhibit 3.2), each of which is important to remember if we are to craft a capitalism that will serve us throughout this century.

First of all, the *principle of stakeholder cooperation* says that value is created because stakeholders can jointly satisfy their needs and desires. Business is not a zero-sum game. Capitalism works because entrepreneurs and managers put together and sustain deals or relationships among customers, suppliers, employees, financiers, and communities. The support of each group is vital to the success of the endeavor. This is the cooperative commonsense part of business that every executive knows, but the myth of primacy of the shareholder tells us that some stakeholders are more important than others. Try building a great company without the support of all stakeholders. It simply cannot be sustained.

Second, the *principle of stakeholder responsibility* applies reciprocally to all stakeholders. If an entrepreneur, manager, or firm has responsibility for the effects of its actions, so too do customers, communities, suppliers, financiers, and employees. Firms are not the sole carriers of responsibility in today's world. Customers have a duty to use products as they were intended, or else take reasonable care, including the burden of responsibility, when they do not. Employees have a responsibility to support their employers within reason. Suppliers have the duty to do their best to make the supply chain work properly

Exhibit 3.2   Principles of Stakeholder Capitalism

Five Principles of Values-Based Capitalism or Stakeholder Capitalism

1. **The principle of stakeholder cooperation**
   Value is created because stakeholders can jointly satisfy their needs and desires.

   (Capitalism works because entrepreneurs and managers put together and sustain deals with stakeholders, rather than becoming agents of the owners of capital.)
2. **The principle of stakeholder responsibility**
   Parties to an agreement must accept responsibility for the consequences of their actions. When third parties are harmed, they must be compensated or a new agreement must be negotiated with all of those parties who are affected.
3. **The principle of complexity**
   Human beings are complex creatures, capable of acting on multidimensional values, some of which are selfish, some of which are altruistic, and many of which are jointly created and shared with others.

   (Capitalism works because of this complexity rather than in spite of it.)
4. **The principle of continuous creation**
   Cooperating with stakeholders and motivated by values, people continuously create new sources of value.

   (Capitalism works because the creative force is primarily continuous rather than primarily destructive.)
5. **The principle of emergent competition**
   In a relatively free and democratic society, people can create alternatives for stakeholders.

   (Capitalism works because competition emerges out of the cooperation among stakeholders, rather than being based on some primal urge of competition.)

---

and be efficient. And shareholders have a responsibility to elect responsible directors who will take seriously their duty of care to manage the affairs of the corporation. For example, sweatshop working conditions in the developing world have raised questions regarding the responsibility of corporations for the actions of their subcontractors as well as those farther removed in the supply chain (sub-subcontractors) both upstream and downstream.

Third, the *principle of complexity* claims that human beings are complex creatures capable of actions based on many different values. We are not just economic maximizers. Sometimes we are selfish and sometimes we are altruistic. Many of our values are jointly determined and shared. Capitalism works because of this complexity rather than in spite of it.

Fourth, the *principle of continuous creation* says that business as an institution is a source of the creation of value. Cooperating with stakeholders and motivated by values, businesspeople continuously create new sources of value. This creative force of humans is the engine of capitalism. The beauty of the modern corporate form is that it can be made to be continuous rather than destructive. One creation doesn't have to destroy another; rather, there is a continuous cycle of value creation that raises the well-being of everyone. People come together to create something, be it a new computer program, a new level of service, a way to heal the sick, or simply greater harmony.

Finally, the *principle of emergent competition* says that competition emerges from a relatively free and democratic society and therefore stakeholders have options. Competition emerges out of the cooperation among stakeholders rather than being based on the primal urge to defeat the other person. Competition is important in stakeholder capitalism, but it is not the primary force. It is in its ability to manage the tension created by simultaneous cooperation and competition that stakeholder capitalism distinguishes itself.

Stakeholder capitalism takes a firm ethical stand: that human beings are required to be at the center of any process of value creation, that common decency and fairness are not to be set aside in the name of playing the game of business, that we should demand the best behavior of business, and that we should enact a story about business that celebrates its triumphs, admonishes its failures, and fully partakes of the moral discourse in society as a routine matter.

Stakeholder capitalism is no panacea. It simply allows the possibility that business may become a fully human institution. There will always be businesspeople who try to take advantage of others, just as there are corrupt government officials, clergy, and professors. Stakeholder capitalism bases our understanding and expectations of business not on the worst that we can do, but on the best. It sets a high moral standard; recognizes the commonsense, practical world of global business today; and asks managers to get on with the task of creating value for all stakeholders.

Ethical Challenges to Business

In the global business environment of today there are a host of ethical issues that managers must learn to deal with. The first group of issues could be called *cross-cultural issues* and is the result of encountering different ways of doing business around the world—in other words, a different set of assumptions about people and their motivations. For instance, one typical cross-cultural issue is bribery. In some countries, such as the United States, bribery paid to officials is not an acceptable social practice (and is illegal), while in other countries, making payments to facilitate officials' complying with a request is standard practice. Gift giving, entertainment of purchasing and marketing executives, and showing favoritism to relatives or to relatives of important clients are all issues that are dealt with differently all over the world. There are vast global differences in employment practices with respect to women and minority groups, minimum wages, and working conditions. Executives need to address these issues in sophisticated ways that can coherently justify corporate policy.

Thomas Donaldson has suggested a heuristic for solving such issues.[15] Suppose that a particular practice, say petty bribery, is not permitted in the home country but is permitted in the host country. Donaldson claims that executives should ask two questions. First, is engaging in the practice a necessary condition for doing business in the host country? If it is not, then the company should not engage in the practice; since it is not ethically permitted in the home country, the company already has a good reason not to engage in it. Second, does the practice violate any important human rights as defined by international treaties that home and host country have both signed? Even in cases where a practice is necessary to do business, companies should not violate important human rights. We might argue that small payments to customs officials to expedite orders are in fact necessary in some countries and violate no important human rights. Donaldson would distinguish such a case from engaging in unsafe working practices and conditions that would indeed violate basic human rights.

A second group of ethical issues could be called *competitiveness issues*. Issues such as restructuring and reengineering, the new social contract with employees, aligning individual and corporate values, outsourcing of work, contract/temporary employees, offshore moves of production, and many more are all ethical issues that are present in the current business environment. To address these issues with "I'm only doing what is best for the business" does not excuse the manager from making ethical justifications. We have suggested that these issues can best be addressed in a stakeholder framework, but regardless, with the information technology available today, they must be addressed in a way that stands the *publicity test*: Can our solution to this problem face the light of day? What happens when what we did is printed in the newspaper? Increasingly, competitiveness issues are public, especially for large multinational companies. Solving issues differently in different countries is a strategy that is increasingly indefensible.

Often the choice is offered between "when in Rome do as the Romans do" and "when in Rome do as we do in Charlottesville." The latter doesn't respect the Romans and leads to a moral imperialism that is increasingly irrelevant. The former doesn't respect our own values and leads to moral relativism and situational ethics that are alien to the moral point of view. Perhaps we should offer an alternative: "When in Rome do as we and the Romans can agree upon." Such a directive places a premium on learning and sharing in an open conversation about the connection between business and ethics.

A final group of ethical issues in business could be called *everyday issues*. Honest performance appraisal and objective setting, openness in communication, employee empowerment, dealing with customer complaints, treating suppliers fairly, representing corporate performance honestly, dealing with troubled employees, family and work issues, sexual harassment, the glass ceiling, racism in hiring and promotion decisions, and affirmative action are but a few of the ethical issues that companies must address on a daily basis. While there are a host of complex issues, the following questions can be used to guide an ethical analysis:

- Who are the stakeholders? Who is affected by this issue and how? What does each party have at stake?
- What are the most important values of each stakeholder? How is each stakeholder harmed or benefited by options that might be considered?
- What rights and duties are at issue?
- What principles and rules are relevant?
- What are some relevant parallel cases?
- What should we do?

These questions offer no more than an analytical start to asking questions about ethics in business. The role of ethics in business is likely to increase, as is the complexity of the issues involved. Today's effective executive must have a keen ability to sense and address issues in both business and ethical terms.

Exhibit 3.3   Ethics Courses for MBA Programs

Business School	First Ethics Course	Required?	Total Ethics Electives
Northwestern University (Kellogg)	Values and Crisis Decision Making	Required	3
Harvard University	Business and the Environment	Not required	3
University of Michigan (Ross)	(Many choices)	Required	12
Stanford University	Ethics in Management	Required	5
Duke University (Fuqua)	Leadership, Ethics, and Organizations	Required	6

Business Ethics in MBA Curricula

The formal study of business ethics has increased in interest and importance in MBA programs. All of the top 20 "General Management" programs as ranked by *Business-Week*'s 2008 poll offer a business ethics course as part of their curriculum or include the content within various courses throughout the program. Exhibit 3.3 summarizes the courses related to ethics for five full-time MBA programs among the highest-ranked "General Management" specialties in *BusinessWeek*'s poll.

Notes

1. The Sarbanes-Oxley Act of 2002 was passed following a series of corporate and accounting scandals. The law covers issues such as auditor independence, corporate governance, internal control assessment, and enhanced financial disclosure that applies to all U.S. public companies and accounting firms. It also imposes new civil penalties for senior executives related to the accuracy and completeness of corporate financial reports.
2. This case has been around the business ethics field for quite some time. Thanks to Michael Josephson, Thomas Donaldson, and Joan Dubinsky for pointing it out to us. We have no idea who originally designed it, but it has been validated as real by hundreds of executives.
3. For a more complete view of relativism and its problems, see R. Edward Freeman and Daniel R. Gilbert Jr., *Corporate Strategy and the Search for Ethics* (Englewood Cliffs, NJ: Prentice Hall, 1987).
4. For a more careful statement of the "separation thesis," see R. Edward Freeman, "The Politics of Stakeholder Theory," *Business Ethics Quarterly* 4, no. 4 (1994).
5. For a clear statement of Smith's view, see Patricia H. Werhane, *Adam Smith's Legacy for Modern Capitalism* (New York: Oxford University Press, 1991).
6. These paragraphs are based on R. Edward Freeman, "A Note on Ethics and Business," Darden School, Charlottesville, VA, UVA-E-0071. Also see William C. Frederick, "Corporate Social Responsibility and Business Ethics," in *Business and Society*, ed. S. Prakash Sethi and Cecilia M. Falbe, 142–161 (Lexington, MA: Lexington Books, 1987).

7. The quote from George Merck is from "Merck & Co., Inc. (A)," *Business Enterprise Trust*, Stanford, California, 1991.

8. We are glossing over the philosophical point that values are about "the good" and rights are about "the right." Any introductory textbook on ethics can provide more details for those interested.

9. We make no distinction between rules and principles here. Some see principles as higher-order rules—indeed, as the justification for rules. For more, see Tom Beauchamp and James Childress, *Principles of Biomedical Ethics*, 3rd ed. (New York: Oxford University Press, 1989).

10. Stephen Covey, *The Seven Habits of Highly Successful People: Restoring the Character Ethic* (New York: Simon & Schuster, 1989).

11. See Norman Bowie and Stephanie Lenway, "H.B. Fuller in Honduras," in *Ethical Issues in Business*, 5th ed., ed. T. Donaldson and P. Werhane, 78–90 (Englewood Cliffs, NJ: Prentice Hall, 1996).

12. This section is based on R. Edward Freeman, "Understanding Stakeholder Capitalism," *Financial Times*, July 19, 1996, and R. Edward Freeman and Jeanne M. Liedtka, "Stakeholder Capitalism and the Value Chain," *European Journal of Management* 16, no. 3 (June 1997). The authors of the present volume are grateful to the editors of both publications for permission to reprint selected paragraphs. Defining *stakeholder capitalism* is an ongoing project. For some preliminary statements, see R. Edward Freeman, "Managing for Stakeholders," in *Ethical Theory and Business*, 5th ed., ed. N. Bowie and T. Beauchamp (Englewood Cliffs: Prentice Hall, 1997), and R. Edward Freeman, "The Politics of Stakeholder Theory," *Business Ethics Quarterly* 4, no. 4 (1994): 409–422.

13. For a more careful history, see R. Edward Freeman, *Strategic Management: A Stakeholder Approach* (Boston: Pitman, 1984), and Thomas Donaldson and Lee Preston, "The Stakeholder Theory of the Corporation: Concepts, Evidence, and Implications," *Academy of Management Review* 20 (1995): 65–91, and more recently still, Ronald K. Mitchell, Bradley R. Agle, and Donna J. Wood, "Toward a Theory of Stakeholder Identification: Defining the Principle of Who and What Really Counts," University of Victoria, Faculty of Business, manuscript.

14. R. Edward Freeman, *Strategic Management: A Stakeholder Approach* (Boston: Pitman, 1984).

15. Thomas Donaldson, *The Ethics of International Business* (New York: Oxford University Press, 1989).

For Further Reading

Beaumont, P. B., *Human Resource Management: Key Concepts and Skills* (London: Sage Publishers, 1993). This is a non-U.S.-oriented text with a comprehensive overview of HR issues.

Beer, M., B. Spector, P. Lawrence, D. Mills, and R. Walton, *Human Resource Management: A General Manager's Perspective* (New York: Free Press, 1985). This classic statement of how HR should be every manager's job has been written by a team of professors from the Harvard Business School.

Business Ethics Quarterly is the source for many scholarly articles, book reviews, and new ideas about business ethics.

The Dictionary of Business Ethics, edited by Patricia H. Werhane and R. Edward Freeman (Blackwell's Publishing, 1997). This is a comprehensive guide to topics in business ethics written by the leading thinkers in business ethics from around the world.

Harzing, A., and J. Van Ruysseveldt, *International Human Resource Management* (London: Sage Publishers, 1995). This is a sourcebook of essays by leading thinkers and practitioners in the HR field, especially dealing with issues of globalization of HR.

Human Resources Management (Society of Human Resource Management and John Wiley & Sons). This journal represents the best new thinking in the field of HR.

Noe, R., J. Hollenbeck, B. Gerhart, and P. Wright, *Human Resources Management: Gaining a Competitive Advantage* (Chicago: Irwin, 1997). This is an encyclopedic textbook that combines the traditional personnel administrative tasks with the new strategic tasks of HR.

The Ruffin Series in Business Ethics, published by Oxford University Press, contains 10 volumes of the latest ideas, theories, and concepts about the connection of ethics to business.

4

Marketing Management

The Walt Disney Company is one of the world's biggest entertainment conglomerates. Walt Disney and his brother started the firm in the 1920s, and Walt personally funded the production of his first hit cartoon, *Steamboat Willie*, which introduced the character Mickey Mouse. Following the instant success of Mickey, the Walt Disney company grew steadily over the next 80 years. In 2008, the Disney empire had grown to $4.4 billion in net income on $37 billion in sales. Disney's holdings include movie studios (e.g., Touchstone Films and Hollywood Pictures); television networks that reach 99 percent of U.S. television households (e.g., ABC, A&E Network, Disney Channel); the Disney Cruise Line; two professional sports teams (the Mighty Ducks hockey team and the Anaheim Angels baseball team); a consumer products company for Disney-themed content; various distribution networks and licensing agreements that make its products widely available; and a number of other entertainment delivery companies.

Probably the best-known division of Disney to Americans is its theme parks and resorts—in particular, Walt Disney World in Florida. This agglomeration of theme parks, hotels, conference centers, restaurants, and golf courses covers an area of 25,000 acres, roughly twice the size of Manhattan. More than 50,000 employees served over 52 million visitors in 2008.[1] According to the company, more than 75 percent of Disney World visitors are repeat guests.[2]

What makes Disney World such an attractive destination? There is no single factor. Guests often cite Disney World as being high on many of the dimensions that are important to them: fun rides, family-friendly atmosphere, excellent service, cleanliness, nostalgia, enjoyable atmosphere, and so on. In many ways, Disney World epitomizes how a company can create value for customers and build loyalty. Disney finds ways to satisfy its customers in a way that is profitable over time. In short, it does an outstanding job of marketing.

The American Marketing Association defines marketing as "the activity, set of institutions, and processes for creating, communicating, delivering, and exchanging offerings that have value for customers, clients, partners, and society at large." Practicing marketers often use less formal definitions, with marketing described as (for example) "creating lasting value for customers" or "where the inside of the firm meets the outside world." These statements all reflect fundamental points about marketing activities. First, marketing refers to an expansive set of business processes and functions; it is not limited to a single functional area within a firm. Second, marketing seeks to build more than single-exchange relationships with customers. Third and most important, marketing is driven by customer needs and desires.

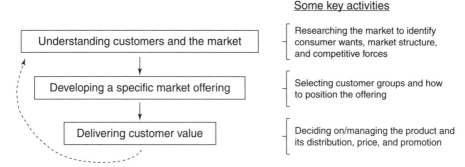

Exhibit 4.1   Overview of the Main Stages of the Marketing Process, with Key Activities at Each Step

Successful marketing efforts focus on satisfying customer needs. Of course a firm that satisfies its customers must also profit in return, but maximal profit need not come with each transaction, and short-term profits should generally be secondary to long-term customer equity. In contrast, people unfamiliar with the practice of marketing sometimes think marketing is synonymous with advertising and sales. These are certainly distinctive activities of marketing, but they are far from its only activities. In fact, most of the marketing process takes place outside of advertising and sales efforts. This is reflected in the marketing truism that the better a firm's marketing efforts are, the less it needs to rely on advertising. (A corollary saying is that nothing kills a bad product faster than good advertising.)

As explored in the remainder of this chapter, marketing—in essence, taking goods or services successfully to market—involves a number of general stages. An overview of these stages is presented in Exhibit 4.1. The first stage occurs far in advance of any advertising and sales activities, often beginning before a final product has been designed. The second stage requires making decisions about how to use the firm's resources to appeal to specific subsets of valuable customers. The third step involves decisions about final versions of the product and its distribution, pricing, and promotion. And as the dotted arrow in Exhibit 4.1 shows, the process continues in cyclical fashion, based on successes and failures in providing value to consumers.

The rest of the chapter expands on these basic steps of marketing planning, roughly in the order depicted in Exhibit 4.1. Bear in mind as you read, however, that the strict order of steps suggested by Exhibit 4.1 is a bit artificial. Marketing decisions involve many interrelated components, and it is often difficult to know which decision should come first. Marketing courses at the MBA level spend significant time developing an understanding of these interrelationships and dependencies.

Understanding Customers and the Market

The first stage of planning marketing activities involves understanding customers and the overall market. For the firm, the operative question is: "How can we add value for customers in the marketplace?" At this stage, strategic and macro-level organizational goals come into play (in fact, "marketing strategy" and "strategy" share many features; see Chapter 9 on strategy for more detail). Planning at the strategic level normally begins with thinking broadly about large-scale and long-term forces that will provide opportunities or challenges for the firm. Strategic planning requires assessing the firm's capabilities and evaluating the firm's place in the larger marketplace.

The broadest drivers of organizational goals are forces outside the control of the firm, such as social, economic, legal, and technological changes in the marketplace. For example, the initial success of Martha Stewart Living Omnimedia (MSLO) has been attributed in part to a coincident trend for working women to stay home after having children, hence forming a core audience of highly educated, affluent women. This social-demographic trend was not under the influence of MSLO, but the company understood and benefited from it.

MBA Concepts in Action: Strategic Response to the Marketing Environment

Consider the Disney World example that opened this chapter. Revenue and net income figures were reported for 2008, which was the first full year of a global economic recession. During recessionary periods, consumer spending on nondurable leisure products and services drops quickly; 2008 was a down year for the travel and leisure industry. If you were part of the Disney World management team, what marketing strategies would you suggest to respond to a recession?

A common reaction when faced with a strong recession is to cut back the firm's marketing spending in anticipation of reduced revenues. But Disney World's strategic response was different. Disney renewed its marketing efforts and focused them on keeping park attendance high, by offering special price discounts for longer-than-average hotel stays (e.g., "seven days for the price of five") and by advertising new promotions with partnering companies. Because the incidence of repeat purchases (visits) is so high, these plans fit with Disney's long-term strategy of gaining market share from competitors, by attracting visitors' dollars away from competing alternatives. A risk of this approach is that it might decrease Disney World's differentiation from lower-cost competitors.

Understanding Customers, Competition, and the Company

If the fundamental purpose of marketing is to deliver value to consumers, then the firm must have a thorough understanding of several groups of consumers—chiefly, consumers it serves, consumers served by its competitors, and competitors it might serve in the future. Understanding consumers in the context of marketing efforts means gaining insight into what will satisfy consumer needs and the reasons for their purchase and usage decisions. Knowing why consumers purchase or decline to purchase is fundamental to knowing how to provide value.

Some basic and common ways of characterizing consumer groups involve demographic information: age, place of residence, income, and so on. While this kind of information can be useful and is fairly easily available, much of consumers' decision making is guided by factors that are internal to the consumer and not directly observable. For instance, individual motivations, attitudes, personalities, and social-cultural backgrounds have enduring effects on purchases, but are harder to discern than is basic demographic information.

In addition to these somewhat stable influences on consumers' decisions, there are many moment-to-moment contextual factors that can change decisions in the moment. The final purchase decision for any given consumer can be influenced by momentary mood, the presence/absence of friends and family, and the range of competitive offerings. For example, suppose that you are trying to choose which of two restaurants you should have dinner at with some friends. One restaurant is more convenient but has lower-quality food and service, while the other is less convenient but has higher quality. This situation is represented in the left panel of Exhibit 4.2 by Option A and Option B, respectively. Which of these two would you choose? Now, suppose you have three options rather than two, with the third option having noticeably greater quality than the other options but even less convenience, as illustrated in the right panel of Exhibit 4.2. Which will you choose now? Often, people who choose Option A in the first situation will instead choose Option B if faced with the second situation, almost as if B is a more reasonable choice now that a more extreme option anchors the consideration set. This phenomenon has been observed in retail settings for products where people make a final choice when confronted by the options on the shelf in front of them.

A firm must develop an understanding of its potential consumers in order to segment the market and select a target (discussed later). In general, successful firms match their offerings with segments of consumers who will get the most value from those offerings; marketing activities are most efficient when directed toward a well-understood segment of customers. Knowledge of consumer behavior should cover not just what products consumers say they want, but also how customers get information, and how they make purchase and usage decisions.

The firm's activities should be oriented toward understanding and capturing value from its customers. (For a more detailed look at understanding consumers, see Chapter 11 on consumer behavior.) Successful strategic planning also requires understanding any competitors to the firm's brands, products, and services. Competitive advantages may be small and fleeting, or may develop into market-leading brand loyalty.

Competition can be classified as direct and indirect. National brands generally have very direct competition: firms with similar products that may be competing for groups of customers that heavily overlap. Crest and Colgate toothpaste, American and Northwest

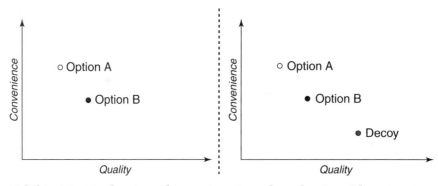

Exhibit 4.2   Evaluating Alternatives Based on the Consideration Set

airlines, and Heinz and Hunt's ketchup compete directly with each other. Such firms are in the same industry and are obvious competitors for consumers' attention and purchases.

In contrast, indirect competition may not be in the same industry, but still has a large influence on your customers' willingness to purchase your product. For a carpet company, other carpet brands and other flooring options (e.g., hardwood floors) are direct competition. But carpeting part of a home can be quite expensive, and consumers may think of the purchase as coming from a general household improvement budget. In such cases, products that have nothing to do with flooring may compete with the carpet company—window and door suppliers, roofers, painters, kitchen cabinet makers, and so on. Firms that market wristwatches have faced significant indirect competition in the past 15 to 20 years from cell phones. For business-to-business relationships, indirect competition for a firm can sometimes come from its own customers, who begin to internalize services that were once outsourced. The challenge in these settings is to provide enough value (in terms of dollars, efficiency gains, distribution reach, etc.) to make the outsourced service more attractive.

A final piece of the strategic marketing planning puzzle is an analysis of the firm itself—an assessment of its capabilities and shortcomings, and its capacities and usable networks. For example, before developing a new product, a firm should project unit sales at different levels—not just for estimating financial returns, but also to plan production capacity use and distribution needs. A heartbreaking scenario for firms with a popular new product is to lose money by having to change production schedules or buy new equipment that the new product revenue may not repay. Similarly, companies that plan to lower prices preemptively in a competitive market should know their cash position well beforehand.

Marketing Research

From the preceding discussion, it should be clear that understanding both customers' needs and the market requires a complex mixture of information—from social and economic trends to customer decision processes, competitor analysis, and reflexive assessment of the firm. The relationships among these types of information are often nonlinear, interactive, unstable, and probabilistic (if they are known at all). In addition, firms often pursue objectives that to some degree are mutually incompatible—for example, quickly producing a car that is more powerful, safer, and also more fuel-efficient. These complex properties of marketing information make a difficult job for strategic marketing decision makers. Marketers rely on information gained from market research to address questions of varying detail and focus. Market research can be useful throughout the marketing process, from developing a firm's future strategy and tactics to assessing existing programs.

At a strategic level of planning, research questions often focus on broad trends and themes in the marketplace in order to identify opportunities and to integrate a firm's goals across multiple time horizons, varying business units, and competitor responses. Marketing research can ask fundamental questions for the firm, such as what aspects of a product or service provide the most value for consumers, and how the firm's offerings are perceived relative to those of the competition. Answers to strategic questions can help the firm set more specific goals, such as those relating to market share, revenue, and profit.

Market research data comes from sources both internal and external to the firm. For example, many chains have an in-house marketing intelligence system (MIS) that collects, for example, databases of customer transactions combined with sales analysis and accounting information. The subfield of marketing intelligence uses publicly available data sources to gain insights that are useful to the firm. Other external sources of marketing information can be provided by market research firms, such as the Nielsen Company, which tracks TV viewership.

Techniques of market research vary widely and draw from a number of different disciplines. Most people are familiar with survey and focus group techniques; marketing research firms also conduct anthropological depth interviews for novel insight into consumer behavior, perform conjoint analyses to assess how consumers trade off desired features of a product and service, or carry out full-blown test markets in towns selected for demographic psychographic profiles of interest to the firm. At the cutting edge of technology, Sands Research combines portable electroencephalograph (EEG) sensors with eye-tracking devices to scan consumers' cortical brain activity as they shop.

The greatest difficulty with market research is often not in collecting information per se, but in sifting through and managing a huge volume of information to draw useful conclusions. In some cases, conducting market research could be beneficial, but may take too long for the firm's decision window, or may cost more than its answers would return. Last, firms have to know when not to take their customers' responses too literally, but to figure out how to satisfy their underlying needs. Henry Ford is reported to have said, "If I'd asked my customers what they wanted, they would have said a faster horse."

MBA Concepts in Action: Marketing Research

Put yourself in the place of management of the biopharmaceutical firm Biopure. The company was developing a blood substitute based on cow hemoglobin (oxygen-carrying red blood cells). Biopure was developing two nearly identical versions of the substitute for use in veterinary and human medicine. There are chronic shortfalls of donated blood in both markets. The veterinary substitute was ready for the market, but the human substitute still had to go through the final stages of rigorous clinical trials before approval for sale. So far, clinical testing had been positive, but there were still several stages to go.

Biopure management had a number of crucial decisions to make as quickly as possible. A major issue was the timing of the market release of the substitutes. Preliminary market research had suggested that the human substitute could command a substantially higher price per unit volume than the veterinary substitute, despite the products being nearly identical. Some managers worried that releasing a lower-priced product to the veterinary market first would limit the price Biopure could eventually charge if it was approved for the human market. Other managers felt that Biopure should capture as much market share and visibility as possible before a competitor beat Biopure to market. What other issues should the firm consider in deciding the type and timing of its marketing efforts? If you were a Biopure executive, what information would you want to help guide your decisions, and what market research questions would you ask?

(Adapted from John T. Gourville, "Biopure Corp.," HBS Case 598150-PDF-ENG.)

Developing a Specific Market Offering

After a firm makes broad strategic marketing decisions, it uses those decisions to guide further decisions about its market offerings. The first of these decisions is to divide the full range of customers into groups based on key variables to the firm. This process is known as market *segmentation*. The second is to select a group or set of groups that the firm can approach and serve best. Each of these groups is a *target* market for the firm. Finally, firms *position* their offerings for consumers, or take them to market in a way that emphasizes their value to consumers over the offerings of the competition.

Market Segmentation

Recall a recent airline trip. If you were fortunate enough to sit in the front of the plane, you were treated better than the travelers in coach by virtue of the cost of the ticket. You may have noticed that certain business-class passengers were treated even better. United Airlines calls these passengers their 1K members, and American and Delta have similar names for their most frequent fliers. These passengers are served first, receive upgrades frequently, and are treated in a manner that is intended to keep them flying on the airline in the future. From the point of view of these firms, not all customers are created equal; in effect, certain customers are more valued and receive greater attention.

These airlines have segmented their market, and provide increased value to a certain subgroup of customers, who in turn are especially profitable for the firm. Note that profitable segments may not come from customers who are willing to pay a premium. Southwest Airlines, for example, intentionally attracts a price-conscious segment of the air travel market, and provides value to this segment in ticket price, efficiency, and level of service.

Sometimes firms operate without trying to segment their market—that is, they function as mass marketers. Companies can approach the market as though all consumers are the same and as though differences in products, or product offerings, are not meaningful to these people. The legendary remark made by Henry Ford is an illustration of this approach. Mr. Ford said, "Customers can have any color car they want, as long as it is black." Mass marketing has obvious limits and may work only in certain industry structures and stages of the product life cycle (discussed later). On this approach to value creation and capture by the firm, the Profit Impact of Market Strategy (PIMS) data are consistently clear: Firms that segment their markets have higher returns than those that do not.[3]

Fundamental to most marketing strategy is the recognition that there are groups of customers who differ from other groups of customers on any one of a number of key dimensions. For telecommunications companies, the work-at-home market has a number of identifiable segments. It is possible to isolate self-employed people and moonlighters who might be more value-driven and seek products and services that offer a strong price and performance relationship, while corporate users might be less price-sensitive because they are less likely to own their equipment and might desire better service and technical support. Both FedEx and United Parcel Service (UPS) differentiate customers by their degree of time urgency—offering, at different rates, a number of options for the delivery of overnight or second-day packages and documents. Similarly, airlines price discriminate, or segment, travelers by their sense of urgency and ability to plan ahead, and the frequency with which they fly.

To the extent that marketers can understand and meet the needs of these different segments, they are able to reap higher returns, although the initial costs associated with segmentation can exceed those of a mass marketer that does not attempt to differentiate among groups of customers. Segmentation strategies are not always visible to customers. For example, over the years the Weather Channel's programming has changed to supplement the weather with content aimed at different audiences. Early morning news is directed at the business traveler and contains travel-related information and stories about the effect of weather on companies. Evening programming contains stories and analysis of weather and is aimed at the 25- to 54-year-old lifetime learner.

The bases for market segmentation cover an enormous range, from simple geographic variables (e.g., customers who live less or more than two miles from a retailer) to complicated perceptions of price-performance ratios. Other common segmentation variables include demographics, such as income, age, and family size; psychographics, such as lifestyle and personality; and behavior, such as usage frequency and loyalty toward a product or brand. Combinations of these variables are also used to form segment groups.

Successful firms segment their markets carefully, because the activity has many implications. First and perhaps most obvious, segmentation allows a firm to match the product or service to the most suitable customer. Marriott, for example, has in its portfolio of hotel chains a number of choices for different customer groups. Residence Inn by Marriott is designed for the business traveler who is on an extended stay away from home, while the Ritz-Carlton is recognized worldwide as a fine luxury hotel. For its major clients Marriott can offer a portfolio of hotel choices for different needs, events, and the like on a national level.

Second, segmentation provides an opportunity for a company to develop alternative channels of distribution to reach different kinds of customers in a more cost-efficient manner. Motorola has experimented with club stores as a viable outlet for its least sophisticated mobile radios in order to reach the low end of the marketplace.

Third, there often exists a segment of the market that is being neglected, or could be better satisfied with a somewhat different offering. Segmentation affords an opportunity for the firm to develop strategies to reach this part of the marketplace. For example, Charles Schwab discount brokers reached out to a segment of investors who objected to relatively high brokerage fees for transactions where no advice was given or was needed. Based on the success of this marketing strategy, the number of discount brokerage houses grew; now investors can trade over the Internet.

Fourth, rather than attempting to compete in a large and highly competitive market, a firm might decide to select one subsegment on which to focus its entire marketing efforts. For example, Paccar competes quite favorably against Ford in the long-haul truck business by concentrating its energies on the high-end, customized part of the truck-buying market. Although Ford enjoys a more favorable cost structure by virtue of its volume, Paccar's Kenworth and Peterbilt brands have a much higher market share in the high end of the independent trucker market. Paccar has decided to focus its efforts and exclusively serve a niche of the market.

Finally, the process of segmentation helps define the customer universe because it enriches a firm's understanding of customer groups. The firm also gets a better understanding of its own competitive position, and how its products and services are perceived in the marketplace. Industrial buyers, for instance, are not found just in large and small firms or across different Standard Industrial Classifications (SICs). Buyers can be adversarial in nature or collaborative; they can be risk averse or risk seeking; they can be leaders or laggards in adopting innovation. Such descriptions allow marketing managers additional insight so they can better provide value to the market through their programs and offerings. The ability to thoroughly define a customer universe also provides an opportunity to track changes in buying behavior over time. For instance, in early-growth markets, buyers might require high levels of service and training as part of the product offering to achieve differentiation in the marketplace.

In business-to-business and industrial settings, companies sometimes segment their markets by business operations, using internal activities as a way to differentiate among different kinds of customers. This segmentation approach is not necessarily wrong, and it does depict what many companies actually do, but it has several inherent weaknesses. First, this approach is internally focused and may not reflect accurately the differences that exist in the marketplace. Second, segments overlap and cannot be bounded easily, given that product functionality can be substituted at certain ranges of performance (e.g., one channel might serve multiple segments). A beneficial complement to the business-operations approach would be segmentation that is customer-based and is derived from factors that more accurately describe the industrial marketplace.

These factors range from more macro, industry-level variables to more micro, individual characteristics. Macro variables are typically easily ascertained and can often be found in trade and government publications. While the SIC code is useful, its applicability is often limited to questions of how big the market is and what the market potential is for a particular product by SIC segment. This SIC data is less useful in helping understand the decision-making processes of a particular segment. At the other extreme, individual and decision-making-unit characteristics bring to life the political realities of the buying process and shed light on the complex interplay among organizational members, each potentially with a personal agenda as well as a stake in the decision outcome. Generally, as the decision becomes more complex and more expensive and as the selling cycle becomes longer, more information is required beyond the typical macro segmentation variables. Bombardier, a North American supplier of subway cars and railcars, must carry its segmentation processes down to the individual level, given the complex interplay of politics involved in a local government's decision to purchase subway cars. This multiyear process entails a number of constituents and, as a result, is probably much more complex than is CSX's decision to buy a comparable number of freight railcars.

No matter how diverse segmentation schemes may be, good ones tend to adhere to a small set of criteria. First, the characteristic that forms the basis for segmentation should be measurable by the firm. Segmenting on eye color is possible, but that information is not among standard demographic marketing variables (DMVs), and DMV records are not public. Second, a segment should be accessible to the firm's marketing efforts. Cumberland Metals developed a money- and time-saving part for construction pile drivers, but faced a difficult time reaching thousands of independent pile driver renters and operators to communicate about its innovation. Third, different segments should differ in response to the firm's marketing efforts. If older and younger people respond in the same ways to a product, then for the firm's purposes they are the same segment.

Targeting and Positioning

Market segmentation allows the firm to clarify its strategic possibilities in the market. The firm's next step in the marketing process is selecting target segments. In general terms, target segments are those that the firm can best satisfy, or, other things being equal, the segments that fit best with the firm's overall strategy, or the segments that will be most profitable in the future. All the strategic decisions that the firm has made so far come into play in narrowing down segments to a handful (or sometimes just one segment).

Target segment choice is far from obvious. The biggest, fastest-growing segment, for example, is not always the most attractive. Big segments in growing markets also attract intense competition, and there may be powerful suppliers in the distribution channel that have undesirable control over pricing and placement. In other cases, the firm might choose to stay out of a growing market because of inadequate production capacity, or because the firm lacks experience or expertise with unfamiliar markets.

The segments that are selected by a firm may not be the only segments that a firm expects to serve. First, some very distinct segments overlap heavily across time. For instance, consumers who are traveling for business will travel for leisure at a later date, and these consumers will have very different needs and desires as they move from one segment (business travelers) to the other (leisure travelers). Second, a firm rarely turns down sales to segments that it hasn't selected as targets of its marketing efforts. Although the firm may have a selected particular target segment, other segments will still purchase its product or service. But the main marketing efforts will be directed toward the firm's target segment instead. In some cases, a firm's marketing plans are frustrated when a product becomes popular with the wrong segment, which can alienate an intended target through reputational effects. If the intended target was selected as part of a strategy to build brand loyalty over many years, then the firm may have to redesign its strategy.

After selecting its target segments, firms are ready for one of the most important decisions they will make: how to position their product for the market. Positioning has been described as "the essence of marketing strategy" and "one of the most important decisions a marketer makes."[4]

Whereas a segmentation scheme reveals a firm's view of its customers, positioning reflects the impression that the target segment has of the firm. Think for a moment about your impressions of automobile brands. Porsche and BMW likely occupy a position in your mental map of the market that emphasizes performance, Volvo has a safety-oriented position, and Honda's reputation trades on the reliability of its cars. There are certainly physical differences among these cars, but the firms' marketing efforts also seek strongly to reinforce their positions. A recent ad campaign for Porsche featured shots of the car's exterior smoothly speeding through curving roads, accompanied by the noise of the car's engine (a highly distinctive sound to Porsche enthusiasts). Volvo's ads, in contrast, often emphasize market-leading safety features. Certainly Porsches are built to be safe, and Volvos perform quite well, but the firms position the cars on attributes that stake out differentiated positions.

A position, then, is a mix of consumer attitudes, background knowledge, and emotions that are part of consumers' psychological market space. Firms generally choose a positioning strategy that will communicate value to customers in a way that differentiates the firm's offering from those of competitors. Positioning may come easily when a firm has a branded product line, and a new product can borrow the positioning of its forebears. Positioning is more difficult in new product categories, where customers don't have a clear idea of the value being offered to them, or in markets with highly concentrated competition. If a firm has no ability to position its offering, then the offering operates in the market like a commodity, and the firm loses control of critical marketing variables such as distribution and price.

Firms can also try to reposition a brand or product in response to changing customer desires or new competition. Consider the positioning map in Exhibit 4.3 of U.S. women's clothing retailers. The relative positions of eight retailers are represented on the dimensions of fashion (forward or traditional) and price/quality (high and low). Such maps are calculated from customer judgments through a procedure called multidimensional scaling (MDS). Marketers use positioning maps to understand customer perceptions of the overall market and the place of individual firms, brands, or products. In the example map, Sears is the most traditional of all the retailers. The empty space surrounding Sears suggests that customers do not perceive other retailers in a similar market position (at least among these eight). Sears stores are also best known not for women's clothes, but for hardware and tools and inexpensive durable household goods. Sears saw the opportunity to reposition its women's clothing lines in a more fashion-forward, higher-quality direction—into open space on the positioning map. For many years, Sears' ads for women's clothes ended with the tagline "Come see the softer side of Sears," in an attempt to reposition its women's clothing in the minds of target customers.

Positioning implicitly refers to positioning against the competition, but sometimes firms intentionally introduce new products whose market positions overlap heavily with their own existing products. This phenomenon is known as *cannibalization*. Firms cannibalize their own positions and revenue most often to prevent an outside competitor from stealing sales and market share. In short, firms say, "Some company in the changing market will provide the best value to our target segment, so it may as well be us."

Positioning via marketing communications is a surprisingly difficult task. Positioning on any unique attribute, or on too many attributes, is typically not effective. Good marketing involves finding just the right combination of attributes and a succinct way of communicating them. A position should turn on benefits that are important to customers, distinct from or better than competitors, and easily communicable to customers.

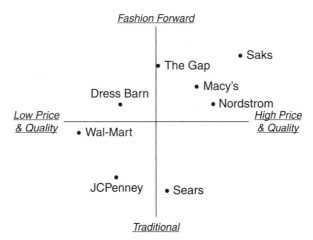

Exhibit 4.3 Positioning Map of Women's Clothing Retailers

Delivering Customer Value

Positioning gives specific focus to a firm's strategic planning, and paves the way for tactical decisions about delivering value to customers. These tactical decisions are referred to collectively as the 4 Ps: product, price, place, and promotion. This section considers each of these areas in turn.

Product

The essence of the marketing process is to deliver value to consumers. For most people, this value takes shape most clearly in the form of a particular product or service offered by a firm. For consumer goods it may seem natural to think of a product as a tangible object, such as a car or a cup of coffee. But from a marketing perspective, the tangible object is part of the overall product being offered. The larger offering, not just the tangible object, is the focus of marketing strategy and tactics in delivering value to customers.

Part of what customers buy when they purchase a car or a cup of coffee is a core benefit: a fundamental need that is satisfied by the purchase. For a car, the core benefit may be a means of transportation or a way to achieve public status. For a cup of coffee, the core benefit may be to wake up or to meet with friends. In addition to the core benefit, a product is associated with peripheral features such as packaging, installation, warranty, or repair services, and sometimes reputation. Many coffee shops understand that their customers want more than just a cup of coffee, and are attentive to the entire experience of a customer's visit. The value that customers appreciate in purchasing coffee includes the layout, design, and atmosphere of the coffee shop.

Marketing decisions can be more difficult when a firm produces more than one product in a category and customer demand for the products is not independent. Instead, changes in the demand for one product can affect demand for the other product. For example, if Apple adds a valued feature to its top-of-the-line iPod, this will reduce demand for the next model in the line. This property is known as cross-elasticity of demand.

Finally, the very design of new product offerings can be driven by other offerings from the firm. Tide laundry detergent, drawing on decades of market leadership, has spawned an entire product line, all of which share the Tide brand name. To take a more complicated example, Disney World and several other theme parks, such as Universal Studios' park in Orlando, Florida, often design new rides by taking into account upcoming movies from the companies' studio divisions, and vice versa. That is, the design of a new park ride might be driven by an upcoming blockbuster movie, and the movie might incorporate scenes that mimic the experience of the upcoming ride. More about marketing decisions based on the product life cycle appears later in this chapter; also see Chapter 12 on new product development.

Price

The price that a customer pays for a product obviously involves its purchase price in monetary units. But from a marketer's point of view, there is more to the notion of a price, such as the cost of the time invested by the customer in the decision, and the opportunity cost of choosing one product over other options. Price occupies a special place among the tactical tools of a marketer; it represents the only direct control over revenues that the firm can wield.

Pricing decisions should mesh with the firm's overall marketing strategy and goals. When firms introduce new products, for example, they generally follow one of two pricing strategies: skimming or penetration. Pricing to skim the market means setting a high price and expecting to capture sales from a smaller market segment that is willing to pay. Firms choose to skim for a number of reasons: They may want to emphasize the high-quality reputation of the product, they may not have production capacity to produce much of a new product, or they may think that the product requires extra marketing and sales support, which drives the price up, to name some examples. The opposite strategy is called penetration pricing: Firms price low and hope to gain the loyalty of as many customers as they can before competitive entries appear. TiVo, the first national market entrant in the digital video recorder (DVR) category, initially priced to skim the market. With Microsoft threatening to enter the market by building a DVR system into its Xbox platform, some experts thought TiVo should have tried to penetrate the market, to build market share before the giant competitor was ready to compete.

The least market-facing pricing strategy is probably target profit pricing, where a firm sets a profit goal and prices accordingly. For example, a firm might decide to price a new product at 15 percent over its costs. Another option is pricing relative to competitors, assuming that costs permit it. A third option is value pricing, which means setting a price according to a product's perceived value by customers. For instance, Gaynor-Minden produced a high-tech ballet shoe that lasts up to five times longer than a traditional ballet shoe. Because professional ballerinas wear out shoes within two or three hours after breaking them in, Gaynor-Minden's shoes could provide substantial savings in money and time. The firm could follow a target profit strategy by ignoring price and performance advantages over traditional shoes, and just try to recoup a target profit or return on investment (ROI). Competitor-based pricing would lead to a price close to a market average, with some adjustment for other strategic concerns such as skimming or penetration. Finally, value-based pricing could support a price of up to five times higher than the competition, to capture the perceived value of the shoes' longevity.

MBA Concepts in Action: Break-Even Points

Breaking even refers to the point at which the firm's sales exactly match its costs—that is, the point at which the firm neither makes nor loses money. Calculating a break-even point for various time frames is a common test for the reasonableness of a pricing plan for the firm. Simple break-even sales volume can be calculated as:

$$\text{Break-Even Unit Volume} = \frac{\text{Fixed Costs}}{\text{Sales Price} - \text{Variable Costs}}$$

Fixed costs are costs incurred by the firm that do not vary with sales volume. For example, rent, management salaries, and advertising are often treated as fixed costs. Note that these costs may change if there is an extreme change in sales volume; however, in most scenarios they don't vary with sales. Variable costs are those that change with sales volume: Increased sales imply increased production,

(continued)

(Continued)

so raw materials and hourly labor costs increase as well. Sales price minus variable costs yields the contribution to the firm per unit sold.

Suppose a winery wants to determine its break-even point for a given year's harvest. Assume the winery's fixed costs are $150,000, it sells a bottle of wine to a distributor for $8, and variable costs per bottle are $2. The break-even sales volume would be $150,000/(8 - 2) = 25,000$ bottles of wine. The winery could use this formula to gauge the impact of price changes on its break-even point, or modify it to calculate sales volume to reach a given goal. For instance, for a profit goal,

$$\text{Volume} = \frac{\text{Fixed Costs} + \text{Total Profit}}{\text{Sales Price} - \text{Variable Costs}}$$

Place (i.e., Distribution)

Firms rarely single-handedly manufacture a good, take it to market, and sell directly to a final consumer. Instead, firms rely on intermediaries in a marketing distribution channel to transport, stock, and redistribute their goods. Wholesalers and retailers are the two most obvious examples of intermediaries for consumer goods. The success of a firm's offerings in the market often depends in part on these channel partners.

Channel partners add value to a firm's offering not just through physical transportation and storage of products. Valuable channel partners can also add value through services such as financing for the firm or customers, creating assortments of products that suit customer needs, and performing market research. Firms try to select channel partners carefully to match with strategic needs. For example, a major marketing decision involves distribution intensity. Intensive distribution means that a firm's product will be widely available to customers. Intensive distribution is a good match with a market penetration strategy, and with certain kinds of goods, such as convenience goods and small impulse purchases. More selective distribution is desirable for more expensive products, or for brands that want to position themselves as higher quality or more exclusive.

Firms would like to treat channel members as partners to the extent possible. But channel conflicts arise due to imbalances in power among channel members. Large national market-leading brands of consumer goods are used to having a say in how their products are stocked and displayed at retailers. But Wal-Mart sells such a high volume of merchandise that it is able to exert more control over product display (not to mention pricing and product assortment).

Sometimes channel members can create or resolve conflicts for customers in discerning value. For instance, one channel might offer superior service and technical assistance, while another channel might carry the product with no service but at a more competitive price. Today's desktop computer marketplace typifies the range of options available. A consumer can buy a computer at Sam's Club, or from a value-added reseller (VAR) who supplements the basic product along with customized software for specific applications, training, on-site repair, and technical assistance. The challenge exists when the same shopper frequents these two channels and begins to comparison shop. To avoid channel conflict, a number of manufacturers offer different products and product lines to different channels. In this manner, price comparisons are less valid and shoppers cannot get a free ride from the full-service retailer, whose role is to provide information and product knowledge, and then buy in the alternative channel that offers little service but low prices.

Promotion

A firm can create a wonderful product, perfectly suited to a target segment of customers, but it will not sell unless the firm can communicate the product's value. A successful promotional strategy involves the use of marketing tools such as advertising and selling. The overarching goal behind promotional efforts is to achieve clear and consistent communication to customers about brands and products, carefully coordinated across channel members and media. Achieving this goal of synchronizing a firm's messages and images is known as integrated marketing communications (IMC).

The precise mix of promotional tools that a firm will use depends on strategy, budget, and timing of promotional needs. Advertising, the most publicly visible feature of the marketing process, has the greatest reach of any format; at the extreme, over 100 million people each year watch TV ads during the Super Bowl football game. For brief messages to a mass audience, advertising is hard to beat. In contrast, personal selling, for example through a sales force, provides face-to-face contact and is very expensive on a per-customer basis. Firms with a sales force find that it is typically their largest promotional expense. Personal selling is especially effective for customers who are forming preferences and attitudes for the future.

Another promotional tool is sales promotion, which can take the form of temporary discounts, coupons, or rewards and incentives related to a purchase. Video game makers provide value to customers by designing enjoyable games. Some firms also make the computer consoles that are needed to play games, and price the consoles very low compared to their manufacturing cost. This promotional discount allows the firms to capture customers for a longer period of time and for more purchases. See the MBA Concepts in Action feature on a way to calculate the amount of discount to offer.

MBA Concepts in Action: A Tool for Calculating the Future Profitability of a Customer

Suppose a firm that provides satellite TV reception wants to acquire customers in a new area. Because customers normally stay with providers for several years, the firm is willing to forgo immediate profits in order to attract new customers. However, the firm must still be profitable over the long run. One attractive promotional offer that the firm could make to entice new customers would be a discounted digital video recorder (DVR). How deep could the discount be, in light of the company's need to make an eventual profit?

The firm can plan a workable discount by calculating customer lifetime value (CLV), which gives an estimate of dollars returned by a customer over a certain period of time. Simplified CLV is given by:

$$CLV = \frac{M}{(1 - r + i) - ACQ}$$

(continued)

(Continued)

where *CLV* is customer lifetime value; *M* is the dollar margin from the customer per period (revenue minus cost to serve); *r* is the likelihood of the customer continuing to purchase the firm's services over the period (retention rate); *i* is an interest rate (the firm's cost of capital, or a discount rate for future revenue); and *ACQ* is the cost to acquire the customer.

Suppose that over a year, the firm's margin per customer is $70; the retention rate is 90 percent (that is, at the end of each year, 90 percent of the existing customers are still with the firm); the interest rate is 10 percent; and the firm can purchase DVRs for $350. If the firm completely subsidizes the DVRs for new customers—that is, it gives the DVRs away for free when customers sign up for service—then the firm breaks even: $70/(1 - .90 + .1) - 350 = 0$. If retention drops, the firm loses money in this scenario. In order to ensure profitability, the firm could try to increase retention, or lower its acquisition cost by charging customers a small amount for the DVR. Which option do you think is better and why? What other options should the firm consider?

Marketers can employ these tools in two types of basic promotional strategies. A *pull* strategy involves communicating directly with customers and convincing them to buy or request a firm's product. In essence, the firm is trying to pull demand through the distribution channel. The other promotional approach is a *push* strategy, where promotional and sales efforts are focused on channel partners, in order to incentivize them to sell further down the channel. In effect, the firm is trying to push demand for its product through the channel.

It should be clear that many marketing decisions are interdependent. For example, exclusive distribution generally suggests a high price. In turn, a high price often carries expectations of additional marketing spending for consumer education and support.

Some general interdependencies can be highlighted by considering the life span of a successful product, from entry into the market to its eventual demise. Although firms develop new products regularly, the hope is that each new product will have a successful place in the market for as long as possible. To this end, marketing efforts are attuned to particular stages of the product life cycle (PLC). The time line of the PLC is illustrated in Exhibit 4.4. Each stage has particular marketing activities and decisions. Here, the word *product* in the PLC refers to a product category—say, four-door sedans—rather than a particular brand or model, such as Toyota or Camry.

The introductory phase marks the debut of the first product in the category. Generally a firm is taking a risk by introducing an unfamiliar product to consumers. The first hybrid cars are an example: Most members of the car-buying public had no idea how the cars worked, or exactly what value they could provide. There tend to be few, if any, competitors during this phase, and firms have some freedom to define the category, at least temporarily. Products in the introductory phase tend to be simple, with fewer features than products that survive to later stages of the PLC. This simplicity of initial products is often a source of competitive advantage for firms that enter the market later. Pricing strategies usual follow either a penetration or a skimming strategy. Distribution generally matches pricing and/or manufacturing strategy, with either wide or exclusive

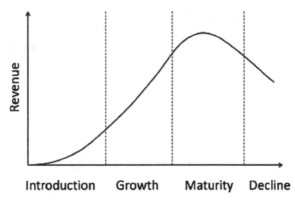

Exhibit 4.4   Stages of the Product Life
Cycle (PLC)

placement. The focus of promotions is to educate consumers about the new product and to motivate trial by new customers.

The growth phase of the PLC is marked by a rapid increase in sales and adoption by consumers, and by entry of competing firms to the category. Apple's iPod was not the first portable MP3 player in the market, but it took over from competitors' products as the product category gained wide popularity. As sales increase, so do manufacturing economies of scale and industry-wide profits. Product design enters a second or third generation, with the addition of features to basic initial models. Prices for new models increase, but for old basic models prices tend to decrease. The market begins to diversify enough to support several segments of customers, which may drive pricing, feature selection, and distribution decisions. Marketing communications focus less on educating consumers about the product class and more on differentiating a particular brand's value.

Established products with long lives make it to the maturity phase of the PLC. For example, Procter & Gamble's Tide laundry detergent has been a market leader for over 50 years. Growth of the category stops as the market becomes saturated. Firms are less likely to enter the market unless they can capture a niche, and some competitors withdraw from the category altogether. Product development concentrates on smaller quality improvements, and on extending the brand through a product line. All firms in the category are subject to price pressure, as a few firms try to capture customers with price decreases. Distribution power can shift away from firms as channel members stop stocking products with reduced customer demand. Promotions and communications tend to emphasize brand value, while at the same time spurring short-term sales (e.g., through coupons).

The final, and perhaps most difficult PLC stage is decline. VCRs are late in the decline stage, with little consumer interest or channel support. Industry margins are at their lowest since the early introduction phase, and remaining firms compete for a shrinking market. A firm may decide to simply delete a product from its offerings, or to gradually reduce investment in a strategy known as *harvesting*. Price pressure continues in the category, combined with high production costs for the firm. Fewer channel members are willing to carry the firm's product. Promotion and communications efforts tend to focus on price and availability information.

Exhibit 4.5   Marketing Courses in MBA Curricula

Business School	Core Course in First Year
University of Pennsylvania (Wharton)	Marketing Management: Program Design Marketing Management: Strategy
University of Chicago (Booth)	Marketing Strategy I Marketing Strategy II
Columbia University	Marketing Strategy Managing Marketing Programs
Northwestern University (Kellogg)	Marketing Management
Harvard University	Marketing
University of Virginia (Darden)	Marketing Management

Marketing in MBA Curricula

Almost every MBA program requires at least an introductory course in marketing. These programs also offer a range of elective courses in marketing, and some marketing courses are cross-listed in strategy areas. Exhibit 4.5 lists example courses—all required—from six leading MBA programs.

MBA Careers in Marketing

At the center of almost any enterprise is the customer. Nearly every definition of marketing, either explicitly or implicitly, has at its core the customer (or consumer). The most simplistic is "the right product, in the right place, at the right time, at the right price."

Most marketing careers follow the general conception of marketing, outlined in this chapter, as a discipline that focuses on understanding and providing customer value. For example, brand or product management, market research, sales, advertising and media, public relations, pricing analysis, and direct marketing all represent possible marketing careers. If your job focus is driving revenue or customer value, then chances are you are in a marketing function. Similarly, if you like getting up close and personal with your customers, chances are you'll be successful in marketing.

MBAs tend to gravitate toward companies that are driven by marketing—that is, companies that use brands and marketing as the primary tool in driving shareholder value. Many of these companies employ a brand or product management structure in which the brand manager is at the center of the business process—essentially the general manager of the business or brand. Brand managers have responsibility for brand strategy and delivering on three core deliverables: revenue growth, market share growth, and profit growth. Brand managers oversee all elements of the marketing mix: product strategy, positioning, marketing spending, promotion, pricing, distribution, advertising, and Internet strategy.

Brand or product managers tend to have the skills of a general manager: keen ability to lead, manage, and work in teams; broad, strategic perspective; analytical, yet creative in solving problems; results orientation; excellent oral and written communication; ability to multitask; and flexibility and adaptability to new or changing situations. MBAs generally are well suited and required for brand management roles because of the broad range of skills needed.

Traditional brand management companies include Colgate, General Mills, Kraft, PepsiCo, and Procter & Gamble. In addition, companies in consumer health like Johnson & Johnson also have traditional brand management structures in their consumer divisions. These companies have many large, prominent, and well-supported brands, any of which will provide excellent experience running the brand. In addition, these companies are known for their marketing training and their broad exposure to many different types of business: mature, new, large, small, and advertising versus price driven.

A marketing career, however, does not have to deal with consumer categories like soap or food. Every company has a marketing function, even if not formally named that; many outside consumer packaged goods are marketing driven. Pharmaceutical, media, entertainment, retail, and high tech are increasingly marketing-driven industries. In pharmaceuticals the product development cycle is long and arduous, and marketers spend a great deal of time involved with research and regulatory issues. In high tech the product life cycle may be short and innovation at a premium, so marketing must be close to the consumer or even ahead of the curve. In these industries, reaching the end consumer is different; therefore the marketing focus is different. Understanding how your consumer relates to your product may be different as well.

Advertising and public relations are two less common but still important destinations for marketing-focused MBAs. Generally, MBAs in these two industries work in account management. Like the brand manager, the account manager focuses on the customer's (in this case, the client's) needs. An account manager (or account executive or account director) acts as the liaison between the client and the agency. Account managers marshal the resources of the agency to address the client's marketing problem. These advertising resources might include creative, strategy, research, media, or planning. Good account executives have skills similar to brand managers: Project management, teamwork, ability to influence, and multitasking are at a premium.

Marketing consulting and brand identity consulting are also common career paths for MBAs. While the consulting skill set and lifestyle are generally quite different from typical marketing career paths, the focus on customer/consumer value is still at the core. Large strategy firms like McKinsey and Monitor have strong marketing practices. Specialized consulting firms like Marketbridge focus exclusively on marketing consulting. For more details, see "MBA Careers in Strategy" in Chapter 9.

Is a marketing career for you? Answer the following questions.

- Do you like to multitask?
- Do you enjoy pop culture?
- Do you like dealing with ambiguity and change?
- Do you love communications?
- Do you want a job in analysis?
- Are you good at problem solving?
- Do you consider yourself creative (but can't draw a thing)?
- Do you like (no, need) to lead?
- Are you easily bored?

- Do you like to watch TV or read tons of magazines?
- Do you like linear career paths with regularly changing assignments?
- Do you work best in teams?
- Are you driven by results?
- Do you want to be a general manager?

These are the common themes in marketing careers. If you answered yes to most of these questions, then a marketing career may be in your future.

Notes

1. Dow Jones Factiva.
2. Charles Passy, "Some Ask If the Disney Magic Is Slipping," *New York Times*, July 31, 2005.
3. R. Buzzell and B. Gale, *The PIMS Principle* (New York: Free Press, 1987).
4. Marian Moore and Richard Helstein, "Positioning," technical note, Darden Graduate School of Business, University of Virginia, 2007.

For Further Reading

Aaker, D. A., V. Kumar, G. S. Day, & R. Leone, *Marketing Research*, 10th ed. (Hoboken, NJ: John Wiley & Sons, 2009).

Bazerman, M. H., & D. A. Moore, *Judgment in Managerial Decision Making*, 7th ed. (Hoboken, NJ: John Wiley & Sons, 2008).

Cialdini, R. B., *Influence: The Psychology of Persuasion*, rev. ed. (New York: Harper Paperbacks, 2006).

Farris, P. W., N. T. Bendle, P. P. Pfeifer, & D. J. Reibstein, *Marketing Metrics: 50+ Metrics Every Executive Should Master* (Philadelphia: Wharton School Publishing, 2006).

Kotler, P., & K. Keller, *Marketing Management*, 13th ed. (Upper Saddle River, NJ: Prentice Hall, 2008).

Kotler, P., N. Roberto, & N. Lee, *Social Marketing: Improving the Quality of Life*, 2nd ed. (Thousand Oaks, CA: Sage Publications, 2002).

Porter, M. E., *Competitive Strategy: Techniques for Analyzing Industries and Competitors* (New York: Free Press, 1998).

Wells, W. D., & S. Moriarty, *Advertising: Principles and Practice*, 7th ed. (Upper Saddle River, NJ: Prentice Hall, 2005).

Zaltman, G., *How Customers Think: Essential Insights into the Mind of the Market* (Boston: Harvard Business School Press, 2003).

Downloadable Resources for this chapter available at www.wiley.com/go/portablemba5e

Break-Even Template

Customer Lifetime Value Template

5

Financial Management

Financial management is concerned with *raising* and *investing* money by a publicly owned company. The underlying goal of a financial manager should be to *create value* for the stakeholders of the company via the decisions made about raising and investing money. The field has an elaborate underpinning of economic theory and empirical research, all of which boils down to this piece of well-known advice:

Buy low, sell high.

Despite its simplicity, this aphorism has two profound implications for decision makers. First, it directs them to think about value (what *low* and *high* mean). Second, it directs their gaze outside the firm, to the capital markets, as the ultimate test of their thinking.

The field of finance is devoted to estimating *intrinsic values* as a foundation for action taking. This is equivalent to taking the point of view of the buyers and sellers in the capital markets; that is, the market prices that investors pay should approximate the intrinsic value of the stock or bond or other financial security being traded. Hence, *valuation analysis* is the core skill used in this field. How a financial manager buys low and sells high is guided by the following five principles:

1. Think like an investor.
2. Invest when the intrinsic value of an asset equals or exceeds its cost.
3. Sell securities (raise funds) when the cash received equals or exceeds the value of securities sold.
4. Ignore options at your peril: They are pervasive and can strongly influence a decision.
5. If you get confused, see Principle #1.

Principle #1: Think Like an Investor

The study of corporate finance covers the thinking of three sets of decision-makers: investors, intermediaries, and issuers (sellers) of securities. These players are inextricably linked through the *capital markets*, the markets where such financial instruments as stocks, bonds, options, currencies, and futures are traded. Exhibit 5.1 shows that intermediaries facilitate the flow of funds by standing between issuers and investors in the capital markets.

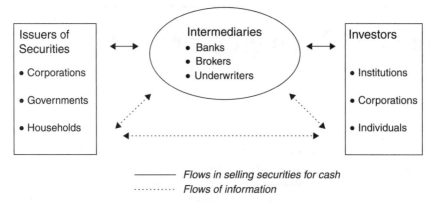

Flows in selling securities for cash
.... Flows of information

Exhibit 5.1   Major Players in Capital Markets

The capital markets allow buyers and sellers to come together in an efficient (low-cost) manner. An important by-product of the transactions in these public markets is the conveyance of *information* regarding the value of corporations. In particular, a stock price reflects information obtained from annual reports and press releases from issuers, recommendations and hot tips from brokers, and in-depth analysis by professional analysts. Thus, the market serves as a critical source of information as an input for decisions by financial managers.

Examples of Areas in Which Firms Should Think Like an Investor

Investing	Raising Capital
Capital budgeting	Bank borrowing
New products	Selling bonds
Market expansion	Selling equity
New technology	Leasing
Plant closing	Employee stock ownership plan (ESOP)
Merger/acquisition	Leveraged buyout (LBO)
Divestiture	Bankruptcy

Corporations as Issuers of Securities

Most MBAs choose to concentrate on corporations because that is where most jobs are, and where the most interesting dilemmas for intermediaries and investors originate. Corporations are huge investors and raisers of capital, accounting for around $1 trillion in new investment each year.

Being a financial manager inside a corporation does not alleviate the responsibility of the manager to think like an investor. When a corporation issues common stock, the buyers of the stock are investing in the company with the expectation that management can find investment opportunities that will ultimately increase the value of the outstanding shares of stock. In making investment decisions, financial managers are acting as *agents* of the owners of the firm and should take into account the wishes of the owners. Similarly, one can argue that as issuers of securities, corporations need to anticipate the wishes of investors as they design and price those securities.

Intermediaries

As the word *intermediary* suggests, these players stand between issuers and investors, and help make the market in securities. To *make the market* means simply to help connect buyers with sellers. Intermediaries earn a fee with the completion of each transaction. Examples of intermediaries are banks that link depositors (sources of lendable funds) with borrowers (users of lendable funds). Another example would be investment banks, which link issuers of long-term securities (such as corporations) with investors. A final example would be insurance companies, which *pool* the exposures of many risk-averse persons to more efficiently manage their risks.

Intermediaries are large in absolute terms and in their significance to the national and global economy. For instance, Goldman Sachs, a leading American investment bank, has an asset base of approximately $900 billion. Fidelity Management and Research, a mutual fund management company, manages funds totaling $1.25 trillion. In addition to their size, these firms are *opinion leaders* or lead steers in the valuation of investments—they help frame standards for investment in the United States and worldwide.

Because intermediaries earn their fees from deals that others make, they have an interest in growth and in the smooth functioning of capital markets. But most important, intermediaries must act in their clients' interests: Issuers need to obtain capital at fair prices, and investors need to earn fair rates of return.

Investors

Even though all eyes are (or should be) turned toward investors, it is stunning to find the conventional thinking that investors are sleepy, ignorant, and indifferent to corporations' performance. In fact, the reality is quite the opposite. It is true that individual investors are major holders of securities—around half of American households today own equities or bonds. But individuals tend to buy and hold their securities and to look toward professional analysts and advisors for recommendations. In 1980 only 5.7 percent of households owned mutual funds; today, around 44 percent own mutual funds.[1] The *thought leaders* in the pricing of securities are sophisticated institutional investors who today account for over 90 percent of the trading volume on major securities exchanges. These are large players who spend a great deal of money on obtaining the best analysis and obtaining it sooner than others do.

How Do Investors Think?

Principle #1 tells us to think like an investor. A considerable amount of academic theory and research is devoted to modeling how investors think. Here are eight attributes of the investor mind-set:

1. Focuses on economic reality, not accounting reality.
2. Accounts for the cost of the lost opportunity.
3. Looks forward and accounts for the time value of money.
4. Understands that diversification of portfolios is good.

5. Knows that required return follows risk.

6. Focuses on wealth creation.

7. Invests on the basis of information and analysis, assuming that the market is generally efficient.

8. Knows that the alignment of management and owners is beneficial to firm value.

Fortunately, the behavior of the most successful investors (such as Warren Buffett[2] and Peter Lynch[3]) convey many of the same attributes.

Focus on Economic Reality, Not Accounting Reality

Financial statements prepared by accountants might not adequately represent the *economic* reality of a business. Accounting reality is conservative, backward-looking, and governed by generally accepted accounting principles (GAAP).[4] Investment decisions, in contrast, should be based on the economic reality of a business. In economic reality, intangible assets such as patents, trademarks, special managerial know-how, and reputation might be very valuable, yet under GAAP they would be carried at little or no value. GAAP measures results in terms of net profit; in economic reality, the results of a business are its *flows of cash*. Warren Buffett has written:

> [B]ecause of the limitations of conventional accounting, consolidated reported earnings may reveal relatively little about our true economic performance . . . . [B]oth as owners and managers, [we] virtually ignore such consolidated numbers . . . . Accounting consequences do not influence our operating or capital-allocation process.[5]

Account for the Cost of the Lost Opportunity

The concept of the *opportunity cost* is one of the most important in finance, and marks finance as a sibling of economics: Economics encourages decision makers to think not in terms of simple yes/no decisions, but rather in terms of either/or decisions. In almost all business decisions there is an explicit or implicit *alternative opportunity*—in the case of investing, it is to buy another asset with similar attributes to the one you are considering. In investment decisions, for instance, one should compare the attractiveness of an asset against an alternative investment that would be forgone (or lost) if you proceed to invest in the first asset. This is nothing more than common sense: *Test any course of action against your next best alternative.* Warren Buffett demonstrated that he accounts for opportunity costs when he said that an important standard of comparison in testing the attractiveness of an acquisition is the potential rate of return from investing in common stocks of similar companies. Economists call this the minimum required rate of return on equity or the cost of equity capital. Another important opportunity cost is the weighted average cost of capital (WACC), which represents the minimum required rate of return for use of a corporation's funds for capital investments such as expansion projects or efficiency-enhancing investments. WACC is measured as the blended cost of capital for the company (i.e., the weighted average of the cost of debt and the cost of equity).

Look Forward and Account for the Time Value of Money

To look forward means that one should not consider any *sunk costs*, expenses that have already incurred or events that have happened in the past. It is only the cash flows expected to be realized or to be spent in the future that matter to the prudent decision maker. For example, Buffett holds that intrinsic value is the *present value* of future expected performance.

> [All other methods fall short in determining whether] an investor is indeed buying something for what it is worth and is therefore truly operating on the principle of obtaining value for his investments. . . . Irrespective of whether a business grows or doesn't, displays volatility or smoothness in earnings, or carries a high price or low in relation to its current earnings and book value, the investment shown by the discounted-flows-of-cash calculation to be the cheapest is the one that the investor should purchase.[6]

Enlarging on his discussion of intrinsic value, Buffett has said:

> We define intrinsic value as the discounted value of the cash that can be taken out of a business during its remaining life. Anyone calculating intrinsic value necessarily comes up with a highly subjective figure that will change both as estimates of future cash flows are revised and as interest rates move. Despite its fuzziness, however, intrinsic value is all-important and is the only logical way to evaluate the relative attractiveness of investments and businesses.[7]

Diversification of Investments Is Good

As the old wisdom says, "Don't put all your eggs in one basket." Peter Lynch has written that "it isn't safe to own just one stock, because in spite of your best efforts, the one you choose might be the victim of unforeseen circumstances."[8] Also, as Buffett has said, "Diversification is protection against ignorance."[9] This is one of the most important ideas in finance and is sometimes referred to as portfolio mathematics, which shows analytically that diversification is good because it spreads (and thus reduces) the risk of loss. This principle is widely illustrated by banks, which seek to minimize the impact of credit loss by diversifying their portfolios of loans, and by insurance companies, which seek to reduce the impact of insurance loss by diversifying their portfolios of insured exposures.

Required Return Follows Risk

Common sense tells us that the more risk one takes, the more one should get paid. Thus, we must always be careful to judge future cash flows that are risky against a higher required return than a set of lower-risk cash flows. The principle of matching risk and return is very important when determining intrinsic values. The risk and return paradigm is illustrated daily in the behavior of traders and investors in the capital markets. Consider, for instance, the rates of return available on bonds of different levels of credit risk (credit risk refers to risk of default by the borrower).

Exhibit 5.2 shows that the riskier the bond, the higher the rate of return demanded by investors. Indeed, the table illustrates that the logic of bond investors in determining required rates of return on assets is to add a risk premium to the long-term risk-free rate of return (such as the yield of the 10-year U.S. Treasury bond).

Intuitively, the required return on equity for a company is always higher than the required return for its debt, because equity investors always face more risk than the debt holders. From the company's point of view this means that the opportunity cost of borrowing money equals the market's required rate of return on debt, and the opportunity cost of using equity funding (either retained earnings or proceeds from issuing new common stock) equals the market's required rate of return on the company's equity. This reminds us that when funds are spent within a company the opportunity cost equals the company's weighted average cost of capital (WACC), since on average those funds come from both debt and equity sources.

Exhibit 5.2 Bond Quality Grades and Yields

Bond Quality Grade	Annual Yield to Maturity
U.S. Treasuries (commonly regarded as the least risky bond investment; 10-year bond yield)	2.7%
AAA "Capacity to meet its financial commitment on the obligation is extremely strong."	5.4%
AA "Capacity to meet its financial commitment on the obligation is very strong."	5.8%
A "[These bonds are] somewhat more susceptible to the adverse effects of changes in circumstances and economic conditions than obligations in higher-rated categories. However, the obligor's capacity to meet its financial commitment on the obligation is still strong."	6.4%
BBB "[These bonds are] adequate protection parameters. However, adverse economic conditions or changing circumstances are more likely to lead to a weakened capacity of the obligor to meet its financial commitment on the obligation."	8.4%
BB and B "[These bonds are] regarded as having significant speculative characteristics.... While such obligations will likely have some quality and protective characteristics, these may be outweighed by large uncertainties or major exposures to adverse conditions."	11.5%–14.4%

Source: Bloomberg Financial Services. Rating definitions are quoted from Standard & Poor's web site (www2.standardandpoors.com/portal).

This intuitive relationship between risk and return offers one other profound guidance to managers: *Risk is in everything—the point should not be to eliminate it, but rather to price it properly, and to manage it carefully.* Walter Wriston[10] has written,

> Our American economic system, like our political system, is untidy—it offends those people who love tidy, predictable societies. We make a lot of mistakes in this country, we have a lot of failures. Some people see only the failures; they cannot seem to grasp the fact that the failures are the price we pay for the successes. It's as though they wanted to have "up" without "down," or "hot" without "cold." We read in our newspapers, and even in our business magazines, solemn words about "risky investments" and "risky loans" from writers who do not seem to realize that these phrases are as redundant as talking about a one-story bungalow. All investments and all loans are risky because they are based on educated guesses about the future, rather than certain knowledge of what will happen.[11]

Measure Wealth Creation by the Gain in Intrinsic Value, Not Accounting Profit
Warren Buffett has written:

> Our long-term economic goal ... is to maximize the average annual rate of gain in intrinsic business value on a per-share basis. We do not measure the economic significance or performance of Berkshire by its size; we measure by per-share progress.[12]

The gain in *intrinsic value* within a corporation can be measured in many ways. For example, one way is to compare the market value of a company's stock to its book value. The market-to-book ratio compares the value assigned by the capital market to the amount of money invested to achieve that value. A ratio greater than 1.0 confirms that the management of the company has created wealth for its shareholders. A second method to measure the gain in intrinsic value is to compare a realized rate of return with an appropriate cost of capital. For example, if a firm's return on equity (ROE) exceeds its cost of equity (K_E), the company is succeeding in creating value due to the positive ROE spread:

$$\text{Return on Equity Spread} = \frac{\text{Net Income}}{\text{Equity}} - K_E$$

The return on equity is measured as net income divided by equity such that the ROE spread is simply ROE less the required return on the company's equity capital. Alternatively, we could compare the company's return on capital to its WACC to assess whether the investment returns within the company have achieved a positive spread over the company's overall cost of capital:

$$\text{Return on Capital Spread} = \frac{\text{NOPAT}}{\text{Debt} + \text{Equity}} - \text{WACC}$$

Net operating profit after tax (NOPAT) is operating profit times 1 minus the tax rate. NOPAT is divided by the sum of debt and equity capital on the company's books to get the rate of return earned on the capital employed (ROC). From this is deducted the firm's weighted average cost of capital (WACC). When the ROC spread is positive, value has been created. When the ROC spread is negative, value has been destroyed. Analysts in leading corporations use yardsticks such as this to assess financial performance of corporations, and of units within corporations. The appeal of economic profit is that it gives simple and clear guidelines to operating managers about how to create or avoid destroying value:

- *Increase sales.* Holding other factors constant (like costs and capital), an increase in sales will increase NOPAT, which increases the return on capital (ROC) spread.

- *Cut costs.* Holding other factors constant (like sales and capital), a decrease in costs will increase NOPAT and the ROC spread.

- *Reduce capital employed.* Holding other factors constant (like sales and costs), reducing the capital employed in a business will increase the return on capital and the ROC spread.

- *Minimize the weighted average cost of capital (WACC).* It may be possible to lower WACC through sensible management of the firm's capital structure (more is said about this under Principle #3). But be careful in the way you think about WACC: The cost of capital is determined by investors, not managers. In competitive markets there is only one reliable way to reduce the cost of capital: take less risk. But investors want managers to take sensible risks in pursuit of premium rates of return. For a manager to try to lower the cost of capital beyond sensibly trying to mix debt and equity capital would be wrongheaded.

Invest on the Basis of Information and Analysis, Presuming That the Market Is Efficient

Experience shows that it is extremely difficult for an investor in the stock market to beat the market consistently over time. One explanation for this is that the stock market is very *efficient* in incorporating news and analysis into current stock prices. If the capital market is efficient in absorbing news into security prices, then securities will be *fairly priced* on average and over time. Clearly there are exceptions to market efficiency, and it is to these exceptions that the great investors flock. Warren Buffett has repeatedly emphasized "awareness" and information as the foundation for investing, and is fond of repeating a parable told him by Benjamin Graham:

> There was a small private business and one of the owners was a man named Market. Every day Mr. Market had a new opinion of what the business was worth, and at that price stood ready to buy your interest or sell you his. As excitable as he was opinionated, Mr. Market presented a constant distraction to his fellow owners. "What does he know?" they would wonder, as he bid them an extraordinarily high price or a depressingly low one. Actually, the gentleman knew little or nothing. You may be happy to sell out to him when he quotes you a ridiculously high price, and equally happy to buy from him when his price is low. But the rest of the time you will be wiser to form your own ideas of the value of your holdings, based on full reports from the company about its operations and financial position.[13]

Graham believed that an investor's worst enemy was not the stock market, but oneself. Superior training could not compensate for the absence of the requisite temperament for investing. Over the long term, stock prices should have a strong relationship with the economic progress of the business. Indeed, a reasonably large mass of research suggests that stock prices impound economic news rapidly and without bias—this is the phenomenon of *capital market efficiency*.

Few people believe that the market is perfectly efficient, which academics refer to as *strong form* efficiency. Most, however, would ascribe to the so-called *semistrong form* of efficiency, which states that on average stock prices react quickly and in an unbiased fashion to new public information about a company. No one can know everything that is relevant about a company at every point in time. And, in fact, investors could overvalue or undervalue a share of stock as Graham recognized, but it would be difficult to rush in and out of stocks with every new tidbit of news and consistently earn a profitable rate of return.

Alignment of Agents and Owners Is Beneficial to Firm Value

When managers think like investors, the goals of managers and investors are said to be *aligned*. Usually the point of agreement is on creating value. Explaining his significant ownership interest in Berkshire Hathaway, Buffett said,

> I am a better businessman because I am an investor. And I am a better investor because I am a businessman.[14]

As if to illustrate this sentiment, he said,

> A managerial "wish list" will not be filled at shareholder expense. We will not diversify by purchasing entire businesses at control prices that ignore long-term economic consequences to our shareholders. We will only do with your money what we would do with our own, weighing fully the values you can obtain by diversifying your own portfolios through direct purchases in the stock market.[15]

Managers are aligned with the interests of owners through the creation of effective corporate governance systems (beginning with the Board of Directors) and with the implementation of good incentives. To that end, Berkshire's Corporate Governance Guidelines state that the company seeks directors "who have very substantial personal and family ownership stakes in the Company's stock." Thus, a primary reward to Berkshire's directors comes in the form of stock price appreciation, the same reward reaped by the stockholders of the company.

There are examples of other companies, however, that have arguably implemented compensation systems that created the incentives to take excessive risks. American International Group (AIG), for example, paid large bonuses to managers who were able to book a large amount of credit default swap business. A credit default swap is a complex financial instrument called a derivative that has significant downside risks. When the global financial crisis occurred in 2008, AIG found itself overly exposed to the dramatic decline in corporate bond prices such that the stock price of AIG plummeted and the company was forced to accept loans and investment capital from the U.S. government.

Principle #2: Invest When the Intrinsic Value of an Asset Equals or Exceeds its Cost

Thinking like an investor when you work inside a corporation can be a challenge since you aren't necessarily managing your own money, and since the investment decisions you face generally don't involve financial securities such as stocks and bonds, but rather physical assets such as a new plant or equipment. Principle #2 can help focus your thinking like an investor when you face these sorts of corporate investment decisions.

Time Value of Money

"Time is money," said Benjamin Franklin. Our intuition tells us this is true because a dollar we receive today could be invested for the next year to return the dollar plus some added value. Thus, receiving a dollar today is worth more than receiving a dollar one year from now.

Future Values

To find out what a dollar invested today would be worth one year from now—that is, to find the future value (FV)—consider that at the end of the year we will receive the dollar back, plus a profit or return. The return is calculated by multiplying r, the interest rate if we invest in bonds, for example, times the invested amount. At the end of the year, we will receive back $(1 + r)$ times our initial investment.

This logic can be extended to more than one year. Over two years, we receive $(1 + r)$ times the investment at the end of the first year—*and then turn right around and reinvest it at the same rate for the second year*. This means that at the end of two years, we have a future value (FV) worth our investment times $(1 + r)(1 + r)$. The pattern continues for three years and longer. Fortunately, the use of exponents simplifies what could otherwise become a lengthy equation; the following equations show the future value of our dollar invested today at the rate of return r.

$$FV, year 1 = \$1.00 \times (1+r) = \$1(1+r)$$
$$FY, year 2 = \$1.00 \times (1+r)(1+r) = \$1(1+r)^2$$
$$FY, year 3 = \$1.00 \times (1+r)(1+r)(1+r) = \$1(1+r)^3$$

Present Values

Of more interest to most decision makers is today's value of some future value. Because of the hidden opportunity cost in virtually all investments one makes, it is necessary to recognize the time value of money. Instead of just waiting for the future value to arrive, perhaps there is an alternative course of action that would give us some present value, which, if invested, would yield a future value larger than the one we foresee. Only by discounting all future values to the present can we compare them on an apples-to-apples basis.

Arithmetically, the process of discounting is just the reverse of compounding—we divide the future value by the compound interest factor:

$$\text{PV of FV, year } 1 = \frac{\$1.00}{(1+r)} = \frac{\$1.00}{(1+r)}$$

$$\text{PV of FV, year } 2 = \frac{\$1.00}{(1+r)(1+r)} = \frac{\$1.00}{(1+r)^2}$$

$$\text{PV of FV, year } 3 = \frac{\$1.00}{(1+r)(1+r)(1+r)} = \frac{\$1.00}{(1+r)^3}$$

Free Cash Flows

When analyzing an investment opportunity within a corporation, the value of the investment equals the discounted value of the expected future cash flows less the outlay amount. This is called the *net present value* (NPV). Whenever cash flows are discounted, it is critical that the cash flows and discount rates are matched with respect to risk. To value a capital investment opportunity within a company, the cash flows should be calculated as *free cash flows* and the discount rate should be computed as the weighted average cost of capital. Free cash flow has a specific definition in corporate finance:

$$\text{Free Cash Flow} = \text{NOPAT} + \text{Depreciation} - \Delta\text{Net Working Capital} - \text{Capital Expenditures}$$

NOPAT was defined earlier as the after-tax operating profit. Note that the taxes computed for NOPAT will rarely match the actual taxes paid because the computation ignores the benefit of interest expense on taxes. In essence, free cash flow is computed as the cash flow that would have occurred if the company had no financing costs: no interest payments and no dividend payments. This makes the cash flow estimates free of any financing effects, which will be accounted for when we use WACC as the discount rate.

Depreciation expense is a noncash expense that was deducted to compute operating profit. To recognize the fact that we deducted a noncash expense, we have to add it back to NOPAT. The next two terms represent cash outflows that are not captured on the income statement, but do show up on the balance sheet. Net working capital is the difference between current assets such as accounts receivable and inventory and current liabilities such as accounts payable. These accounts tend to vary directly with sales volume and generally represent a net use of funds. Therefore, when net working capital increases, it represents a use of cash and should be subtracted from free cash flow. Capital expenditures are also cash outflows, but these are recorded as increases to one of the long-term asset accounts such as property, plant, and equipment.

Weighted Average Cost of Capital

The WACC is a straightforward calculation:

$$\text{WACC} = \text{Debt\%} \times K_D \times (1 - \text{Tax Rate}) + \text{Equity\%} \times K_E$$

The cost of debt, K_D, equals the interest cost a company must pay to borrow new funds, which also equals the rate of return required by investors to buy the company's bonds. The cost of equity, K_E, equals the rate of return required by investors to be enticed to buy the company's common stock. Thus, whenever management decides to invest in a project within the company, it is on behalf of the bondholders and stockholders, and the return earned on that investment should be sufficient to satisfy the required rates of returns for both sets of claimants. We can estimate that cost as the weighted average of the cost of debt and the cost of equity for which the weight assigned to the debt equals the percentage that debt represents of the capital structure; that is, Debt% is the ratio of debt to debt plus equity, and Equity% is the ratio of equity to debt plus equity.

The final component of WACC occurs because interest payments are a deductible expense for tax purposes. When a company borrows money, it must pay whatever interest rate is required by the markets. The cost to the company, however, is reduced because the interest payments reduce the company's tax liability. No such benefit is available for the cost of equity, because dividends are not deductible for corporate tax purposes. Therefore, the cost of debt is reduced by the tax effect; that is, we use the after-tax cost of debt, computed as $K_D \times (1 - \text{Tax Rate})$, to calculate WACC.

An Example

To illustrate the calculation of free cash flow and net present value, consider the following example of the kind of investment decisions operating managers face. Suppose that you manage a manufacturing plant. An important machine in your plant has reached the end of its useful life and must be replaced. One of your analysts suggests two alternatives. The first alternative is to put in a new machine costing $1 million that is just like the old one. The second alternative is to put in an upgraded machine that costs $200,000 more to buy, but will save $50,000 per year in labor costs, will free up $25,000 in work-in-process inventory on the plant floor, and can be sold at the end of its useful life for $30,000 (after taxes). The company's WACC is 10 percent; that is, the required rate of return for an investment in either machine is 10 percent. This is a classic choice between saving on an investment outlay today versus saving on operating expenses in the future. Which should you choose?

First, to think like an investor means to focus on the free cash flows for each that are *relevant* to your decision. Therefore, we must identify components of free cash flow that change as a direct result of the investment decision, and we do not focus on the accounting profits or losses as these are only part of the cash flow story. The relevant cash flows in this decision are the additional investment outlay, the after-tax labor savings each year, the additional depreciation, the release of inventory, and the salvage value. These are presented in Exhibit 5.3.

The net present value of investing in the upgraded machine *relative to a standard replacement machine* is $17,626. The NPV has a very important interpretation: It is the amount by which the value of the firm will increase (or decrease if negative) if the upgraded machine is chosen over the standard machine. We can also measure value

Exhibit 5.3 Estimate of the Value-Added of Replacing a Standard Machine with an Upgraded Machine

Upgraded Replacement Machine

	Now	Year 1	Year 2	Year 3	Year 4	Year 5
Labor Cost		($150,000)	($150,000)	($150,000)	($150,000)	($150,000)
Depreciation		(240,000)	(240,000)	(240,000)	(240,000)	(240,000)
Pretax Cost		(390,000)	(390,000)	(390,000)	(390,000)	(390,000)
Taxes		136,500	136,500	136,500	136,500	136,500
After-Tax Cost		($253,500)	($253,500)	($253,500)	($253,500)	($253,500)
+ Depreciation		240,000	240,000	240,000	240,000	240,000
Inventory Reduction		25,000				
Salvage Value						30,000
− Investment Outlay	($1,200,000)	0	0	0	0	0
Free Cash Flow	($1,200,000)	$ 11,500	($ 13,500)	($ 13,500)	($ 13,500)	$ 16,500

Standard Replacement Machine

	Now	Year 1	Year 2	Year 3	Year 4	Year 5
Labor Cost		($200,000)	($200,000)	($200,000)	($200,000)	($200,000)
Depreciation		(200,000)	(200,000)	(200,000)	(200,000)	(200,000)
Pretax Cost		($400,000)	($400,000)	($400,000)	($400,000)	($400,000)
Taxes		140,000	140,000	140,000	140,000	140,000
After-tax Cost		($260,000)	($260,000)	($260,000)	($260,000)	($260,000)
+ Depreciation		200,000	200,000	200,000	200,000	200,000
Inventory Reduction		0				
Salvage Value					0	0
− Investment Outlay	($1,000,000)	0	0	0	0	0
Free Cash Flow	($1,000,000)	($ 60,000)	($ 60,000)	($ 60,000)	($ 60,000)	($ 60,000)

	Now	Year 1	Year 2	Year 3	Year 4	Year 5
Upgraded Cash Flow	(1,200,000)	11,500	(13,500)	(13,500)	(13,500)	16,500
Standard Cash Flow	($1,000,000)	($ 60,000)	($ 60,000)	($ 60,000)	($ 60,000)	($ 60,000)
Incremental Free Cash Flow	$ (200,000)	$ 71,500	$ 46,500	$ 46,500	$ 46,500	$ 76,500

Discounted Cash Flow Value of Free Cash Flows at 10% Discount Rate	$17,626
Internal rate of return	13.4%

Note: See this table as an interactive exercise at www.wiley.com.
Source: Author's analysis.
Copyright © 2010 by Eades et al. To download this form for your personal use, please visit www.wiley.com/go/portablemba5e.

creation by comparing the internal rate of return (IRR) to the cost of capital. In the example, the project's rate of return is 13.4 percent, which is 3.4 percent higher than the WACC of 10 percent. Note that NPV is reported as a dollar value whereas the spread over WACC is reported as annual percentage, but both are positive when value is being created and both are negative when value is being destroyed. Therefore, regardless of whether we use NPV or the spread over WACC, when we are thinking like an investor, we would choose the new machine. This gives us two rules of thumb that provide the same result:

1. When the NPV is positive, make the investment.
2. When the internal rate of return exceeds WACC, make the investment.

Drivers of Value Creation

The positive NPV in the machine-investment example raises the question about the source of the value creation. Four factors determine the extent to which an investment creates or destroys value:

1. The internal rate of return on investment.
2. The investors' required rate of return.
3. The reinvestment in the project: what percent of the cash thrown off you plow back into the project each year.
4. The length of the project's life.

To illustrate how these factors interact to create or destroy value, consider the hypothetical case presented in Exhibit 5.4. Suppose a company has the opportunity to invest $100 million in the assets of a business—this is its cost or book value. This business will throw off cash at the rate of 20 percent of its investment base each year; that is, the return on capital is 20 percent. Suppose that instead of paying out the cash to investors, the buyer decides to reinvest all cash flow back into the business such that the book value or investment value of the business will grow at 20 percent per year.

Suppose further that the investor plans to sell the business for its accumulated investment value at the end of the fifth year. Does this investment create value for the individual? One determines this by discounting the future free cash flows to the present at the investment's opportunity cost. The opportunity cost is the required return that could have been earned elsewhere at comparable risk, which is the company's WACC that we are assuming equals 15 percent. Dividing the present value of future cash flows (i.e., Buffett's "intrinsic value") by the cost of the investment (i.e., Buffett's "book value") indicates that every dollar invested creates intrinsic value of $1.24. Value is created.

Consider an opposing case, summarized in Exhibit 5.5. The example is similar in all respects except for one key difference: The annual return on the investment is 10 percent. The result is that every dollar invested creates intrinsic value of $0.80. Value is destroyed.

Comparing the two cases in Exhibits 5.4 and 5.5, the difference in value creation and destruction is driven entirely by the relationship between the expected returns and the discount rate (i.e., the required return). In the first case, the spread is positive and value is created. In the second case, the spread is negative and value is destroyed. Only in the instance where expected returns equal the discount rate will value be neither created

Exhibit 5.4 Hypothetical Example of Value Creation

Assumptions							
Life of investment	5 years						
Initial investment	$100						
Reinvestment proportion	100%						
Return on capital (ROC)	20%						
Required return on capital (WACC)	15%						
ROC − WACC	+5%						

Year	Now	1	2	3	4	5
Accumulated Investment Value	$ 100	$120	$144	$173	$207	$249
Investment	−100	—	—	—	—	—
Returns		20	24	29	35	41
Reinvestment		−20	−24	−29	−35	−41
Liquidation Proceeds		—	—	—	—	249
Total Cash Flow	−$ 100	$ 0	$ 0	$ 0	$ 0	$249
Net Present Value =	$23.7					
Market or Intrinsic Value =	$ 124					
Book Value =	$ 100					
Market-to-Book Ratio =	1.24					

Value created: $1.00 invested becomes $1.24 in market value.

Note: See this table as an interactive exercise at www.wiley.com.
Source: Author's analysis.
Copyright © 2010 by Eades et al. To download this form for your personal use, please visit www.wiley.com/go/portablemba5e.

nor destroyed. The capital markets demonstrate this relationship between spreads and value creation each day. Exhibit 5.6 presents the distribution of the 30 companies in the Dow Jones Industrial Average[16] by the spread between their cost of equity and their expected return on equity on the horizontal axis, and the market-to-book value ratio on the vertical axis. Immediately, one is struck by the positive slope of the cloud of companies: Positive spreads are generally associated with value creation; negative spreads are generally associated with value destruction.

Exhibit 5.7 varies the *reinvestment proportion* for the project. In Exhibits 5.4 and 5.5 we assumed implicitly that all cash generated was simply plowed back into the project (i.e., 100 percent reinvestment). If the reinvestment proportion assumption is scaled back, investors get some cash earlier, but the lump sum at the end is smaller. Exhibit 5.7 shows what happens to the NPV and market-to-book ratio if the reinvestment proportion varies between 100 and zero percent.

With positive-spread projects, the investor is worse off with a lower reinvestment proportion. This is because the cash coming out of the project is implicitly assumed to be invested at the discount rate, which is lower than the rate of return being earned on the project. With negative-spread projects, the investor is better off with a lower reinvestment proportion. This is because the investor can earn a higher rate of return by

Exhibit 5.5 Hypothetical Example of Value Destruction

Assumptions						
Life of investment	5 years					
Initial investment	$100					
Reinvestment proportion	100%					
Return on capital (ROC)	10%					
Required return on capital (WACC)	15%					
ROC − WACC	−5%					

Year	Now	1	2	3	4	5
Accumulated Investment Value	$ 100	$110	$121	$133	$146	$161
Investment	−100	—	—	—	—	—
Returns		10	11	12	13	15
Reinvestment		−10	−11	−12	−13	−15
Liquidation Proceeds						161
Total Cash Flow	−$ 100	$ 0	$ 0	$ 0	$ 0	$161
Net Present Value =	($19.9)					
Market or Intrinsic Value =	$ 80					
Book Value =	$ 100					
Market-to-Book Ratio =	0.80					

Value destroyed: $1.00 invested becomes $0.80 in market value.

Note: See this table as an interactive exercise at www.wiley.com.
Source: Author's analysis.
Copyright © 2010 by Eades et al. To download this form for your personal use, please visit www.wiley.com/go/portablemba5e.

redeploying the cash in the capital markets (and earning the 10 percent opportunity rate) than by plowing it back into the project. The conclusion is that *a higher reinvestment proportion amplifies the creation or destruction of value, and a lower reinvestment proportion dampens it.*

Exhibit 5.8 varies the lifetime of the project. In Exhibits 5.4, 5.5, and 5.6, we assumed a five-year life of the project. But what if managers can take actions to extend or shorten the life of the project? The life of machinery can be extended by quality maintenance, careful use, and tinkering. The life of profitable consumer products can be extended by reformulations, repackagings, and repositionings in the markets. Alternatively, money-losing plants can be shut down. Value-destroying product lines can be discontinued. Exhibit 5.8 shows that *longer life amplifies the creation or destruction of value; shorter life dampens it.*

In summary, value is created by positive spreads and destroyed by negative spreads. Lengthening the project life and increasing the proportion of cash flows reinvested in the project amplify the creation or destruction of value. Shortening the life and disinvesting dampen the value effect. Understanding the value drivers of an investment and their managerial implications is an enormously important contribution of finance to the work of general managers. With the help of this framework, one can not only think like an investor, but also act like an investor.

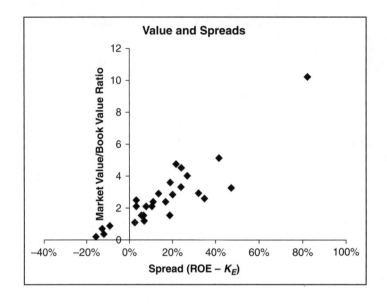

Ticker Symbol	Company Name	ROE − K_E	Market/ Book	Ticker Symbol	Company Name	ROE − K_E	Market/ Book
MMM	3M Co.	27%	4.03	INTC	Intel Corporation	3%	2.14
AA	Alcoa Inc.	−13%	0.71	IBM	International Business Machines	82%	10.17
AXP	American Express Co.	11%	2.39				
T	AT&T Inc.	5%	1.57	JNJ	Johnson & Johnson	24%	3.31
BAC	Bank of America Corp.	−12%	0.37	JPM	JPMorgan Chase & Co.	−9%	0.9
CAT	Caterpillar Inc.	47%	3.24	KFT	Kraft Foods Inc.	6%	1.51
CVS	Chevron Corp.	18%	1.53	MCD	McDonald's Corp.	24%	4.54
C	Citigroup, Inc.	−16%	0.22	MRK	Merck & Co., Inc.	35%	2.6
KO	Coca-Cola Co.	22%	4.78	MSFT	Microsoft Corp.	42%	5.14
DD	E.I. du Pont de Nemours Co.	19%	3.61	PFE	Pfizer Inc.	6%	1.57
XOM	Exxon Mobil Corp.	32%	2.93	PG	Procter & Gamble Co.	16%	2.38
GE	General Electric Co.	7%	1.21	UTX	United Technologies Corp.	20%	2.84
HPQ	Hewlett-Packard Co.	10%	2.14	VZ	Verizon Communications	8%	2.11
HD	Home Depot, Inc.	3%	2.49	WMT	Wal-Mart Stores, Inc.	13%	2.91
				DIS	Walt Disney Co.	2%	1.11

Exhibit 5.6   Illustration of Value Creation and Destruction: Value and Spreads

Exhibit 5.7 Illustration of Value Creation and Destruction: Market-to-Book Ratios as the Reinvestment Proportion and Return on Capital Spread Vary

ROC – WACC	ROC	Reinvestment Proportion				
		0%	25%	50%	75%	100%
5%	20%	1.17	1.18	1.20	1.22	1.24
0%	15%	1.00	1.00	1.00	1.00	1.00
−5%	10%	0.83	0.83	0.82	0.81	0.80

This table presents the market-to-book ratios associated with projects offering three different returns on capital (ROCs) and five different reinvestment proportions. The required rate of return (the weighted average cost of capital, WACC) is constant across all cases at 15 percent. Therefore, where ROC is 20 percent, the project offers a *positive spread* of 5 percent over the required rate of return and all the market-to-book ratios are greater than 1.0. Where ROC is only 10 percent, however, the spread over the required return is negative and the projects destroy value; their market-to-book value ratios are less than 1.0. Where ROC is 15 percent, the spread is zero, and the project neither creates nor destroys value; the ratios are equal to 1.0.

The table shows that as the reinvestment proportion increases, the creation or destruction of value is amplified; as the reinvestment proportion decreases, the creation or destruction of value is dampened.

Note: See this table as an interactive exercise at www.wiley.com.

Source: Author's analysis.

Copyright © 2010 by Eades et al. To download this form for your personal use, please visit www.wiley.com/go/portablemba5e.

Principle #3: Sell Securities (Raise Funds) When the Cash Received Equals or Exceeds the Value of Securities Sold

The field of finance also sheds light on how the firm should raise its capital. The orientation to thinking like an investor and to the value creation framework is relevant here, too. The main difference one encounters here is that the firm *takes the perspective of a seller* rather than of a buyer, because in financing itself the firm is selling securities[17] and receiving cash. Principle #3 invites us to compare the "gives" and "gets" (similar to Principle #2), and proceed with the financing if the "gets" are greater than, or equal to, the "gives." This decision can be reduced to a problem of valuation.

An Example: Valuing an Issue of Debt

Suppose that you manage a hospital that needs $1 million with which to build a new wing. You hire a financial advisor and an underwriter, who recommend that your hospital issue bonds with repayment in a lump sum at the end of five years. The bond rating agencies[18] give this issue a single-A rating. Your financial advisor tells you that an 8 percent coupon[19] should be offered. But your underwriter thinks she can place the bond issue with some investors who believe that the bond and your hospital are really worth a *double-A* rating. The yield on other single-A-rated hospital issues is currently 8.5 percent; on other double-A issues it is 7.75 percent. Should you proceed to issue this debt?

Exhibit 5.8   Illustration of Value Creation and Destruction: Market-to-Book Ratios as the Life of the Project and Its Return on Capital Spread Vary

		Project Life (Years)		
ROC − WACC	ROC	5	10	15
5%	20%	1.24	1.53	1.89
0%	15%	1.00	1.00	1.00
−5%	10%	0.80	0.64	0.51

This table presents the market-to-book ratios associated with projects offering three different returns on capital (ROCs) and three different lives. The required rate of return (the weighted average cost of capital, WACC) is constant across all cases at 15 percent. Therefore, where ROC is 20 percent, the project offers a *positive spread* of 5 percent over the required rate of return. Note that all of these positive-spread projects create value; that is, their market-to-book value ratios are greater than 1.0. Where ROC is only 10 percent, the spread over WACC is negative—these projects destroy value; their market-to-book value ratios are less than 1.0. Where the return is 15 percent, the spread is zero, and the project neither creates nor destroys value (the ratios are equal to 1.0).

The table shows that as the lifetime lengthens, the creation or destruction of value is amplified; as it is shortened, the creation or destruction of value is dampened.

Note: See this table as an interactive exercise at www.wiley.com.

Source: Author's analysis.

Exhibit 5.9 gives the net present value calculation of this bond. The proceeds of the issue are $1 million, which represents a positive inflow. Outflows are the annual interest payments and the principal payment at the end. Because you agree with the single-A rating, you discount these cash flows at 8.5 percent, and estimate the net present value to be $19,703. This financing creates value for the hospital because the proceeds ($1,000,000) exceed the present value of the liability incurred ($980,297). In this example, the source of value is the underwriter's ability to place the securities with investors who disagree with you about the risk (and required return) of the issue. Frankly, these sorts of disagreements are rare, so creating value by issuing debt or equity is very difficult to achieve in an efficient capital market. Creating value by putting the proceeds of the bond issue to work, however, is the key to creating wealth for the shareholders of a corporation. Investing in real assts such as the example of replacing an old machine with a new one is a process of putting money from investors to a higher-valued use. If managers cannot find projects with positive NPVs, they should return the funds to investors by retiring outstanding bonds or repurchasing outstanding shares.

Finding the Optimal Mix of Debt and Equity

The bond example ignores how the tax savings on the interest payments would influence the NPV from the hospital's viewpoint. As a for-profit hospital, its interest payments are a tax-deductible expense, which means that the government is subsidizing the cost to

Exhibit 5.9　Net Present Value Calculation of a Bond's Cash Flows from the Standpoint of the Issuer

Assumptions

Principal amount =　$1,000,000
Coupon rate =　　　　8.0%
Required return =　　8.5%
Term (years) =　　　　5

	Now	Year 1	Year 2	Year 3	Year 4	Year 5
Market Value	$1,000,000					
Principal						$(1,000,000)
Interest		$(80,000)	$(80,000)	$(80,000)	$(80,000)	(80,000)
Cash Flow	$1,000,000	$(80,000)	$(80,000)	$(80,000)	$(80,000)	$(1,080,000)
NPV @ 8.5%	$　19,703					

Note: See this table as an interactive exercise at www.wiley.com.
Source: Author's analysis.
Copyright © 2010 by Eades et al. To download this form for your personal use, please visit www.wiley.com/go/portablemba5e.

your hospital of this bond issue. The benefit of this subsidy should also be reflected in your decision.

Exhibit 5.10 recomputes the NPV of the bond issue, reflecting the *tax shield* of the interest expense. This reduces the cost of the issue dramatically as the NPV increases to $130,041.

As the bond valuation example shows, the tax deductibility of interest payments creates an enormous incentive to borrow. Shareholders reap the gain of the government

Exhibit 5.10　Net Present Value Valuation of a Bond's Cash Flows, Reflecting Corporate Tax Deduction of Interest Expense

Assumptions

Principal amount =　$1,000,000
Coupon rate =　　　　8.0%
Required return =　　8.5%
Term (years) =　　　　5
Corporate tax rate =　35%

	Now	Year 1	Year 2	Year 3	Year 4	Year 5
Market Value	$1,000,000					
Principal						$(1,000,000)
Interest		$(80,000)	$(80,000)	$(80,000)	$(80,000)	(80,000)
Tax Shield	—	28,000	28,000	28,000	28,000	28,000
Cash Flow	$1,000,000	$(52,000)	$(52,000)	$(52,000)	$(52,000)	$(1,052,000)
NPV @ 8.5%	$　130,041					

Note: See this table as an interactive exercise at www.wiley.com.
Source: Author's analysis.
Copyright © 2010 by Eades et al. To download this form for your personal use, please visit www.wiley.com/go/portablemba5e.

subsidy of debt costs. The naive conclusion under the "think like an investor" principle would be that the firm should borrow to the hilt, since more borrowing means more positive NPV.

The problem with this naive conclusion is that more borrowing increases the risk that the firm will default on its debt payments (to default means to be unable to pay interest or principal on schedule). The operating earnings of almost all firms are uncertain. They expand and contract with the regular cycle of the national economy, with changes in technology, with the entrance or exit of competitors in the industry, with changes in consumer sentiment, and so on. Unfortunately, debt payments are fixed by legal contract; they do not increase or decrease as the firm's capacity to pay increases or decreases. Lenders and investors in firms are quite conscious of this risk of default, and set their required returns in reference to that risk. Beyond some reasonable level of indebtedness, lenders and investors will sense that the firm is assuming more and more default risk, and *will raise the required returns (the interest rates) on their loans and on their equity investments*.

The Five C's of Credit

Cash flow: Is the firm's expected cash flow large enough to meet the debt payments?

Collateral: If we have to foreclose on the loan, are there sufficient assets in the firm that we could sell to repay the loan?

Conditions: Do the current economic conditions favor timely debt payments?

Course: Is the use to which these funds will be put appropriate? Is the general strategy of this firm on course?

Character: Are the people involved not only sufficiently intelligent and skilled, but also *morally inclined* to honor the repayment commitment?

For instance, bond investors make an assessment of the firm's creditworthiness through a process of credit analysis. Credit analysis could be as simple as making qualitative judgments on a set of standard criteria such as "The Five C's of Credit," or as complicated as a highly technical computer simulation of the probability of default. For many long-term bonds, creditworthiness is summarized in a bond rating. As the firm borrows more, the rating will decline. As the rating declines, the return that investors require will rise.

As required returns are increased, the NPVs of the bonds will fall—this is the simple result of the time value of money: The higher the discount rate, the lower the present value. As the borrowing of the firm increases, the effect of default risk will *reduce* the value created by borrowing. At some point in the range between all-equity and all-debt financing of the firm, the impact of default risk will begin to more than offset the benefits of debt tax shields. That point is the optimum mix of debt and equity financing for the firm. Cast in graphical terms, Exhibit 5.11 illustrates this effect. The value of the firm rises as the firm goes from no debt to a moderate amount; this is because of the beneficial effects of the debt tax shields. Then the effect of default risk begins to be felt: As leverage increases beyond the optimum, the value of the firm begins to decline. Increasing the mix of debt beyond the optimum destroys value—it is equivalent to accepting financing whose cash received is less than the present value of future debt payments. Destroying value is the opposite of Principle #3. *To "think like an investor" in financing the firm is to choose the mix of debt and equity that maximizes the value of the firm.*

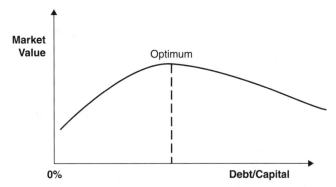

Exhibit 5.11   Finding the Optimal Mix of Debt and Equity

Principle #4: Ignore Options at Your Peril: They Are Pervasive and Can Strongly Influence a Decision

Principles #2 and #3 are presented in terms of discounted cash flow (DCF) valuation; but DCF does not tell the whole story of finance. DCF is based on fixed, "point estimate" forecasts, which may ignore contingent choices that the firm may have today or in the future. Contingent choices are rights to take actions that are sensible only if other things happen. For example:

- The right to abandon a nuclear power plant *if* it loses money.
- The right to hand over the reconstruction cost of a burned-out plant *if* you have a fire.
- The right to exploit a mineral deposit *if* exploration proves the existence of the deposit.
- The right to call a loan (demand immediate repayment) *if* the borrower defaults.

Options are rights (not obligations) to take action. Options permeate the business economy. For instance, all insurance policies are options. Any time a manager says, "I have the flexibility to . . .," she is expressing the fact that she has a right or an option.

All options are valuable, even if it seems unlikely that they would ever be exercised. In the financial pages of the newspaper you can find traded options that are deeply out-of-the-money (i.e., to exercise the option would not be profitable)—yet these options trade at a positive price. The reason all options are valuable is that there remains some chance (however small) that the option will be in-the-money (i.e., profitable to exercise) in the future.

A great deal of research in universities and in the financial community has modeled how options should be valued. The modeling is highly mathematical but boils down to the provocative insight that *an option is more valuable the greater the uncertainty and the longer the life of the option*. This is because more uncertainty and longer life increase the chance that it will be profitable to exercise the option at some point in the future.

Discounted cash flow, with its foundation in fixed forecasts, takes a very static view of the world. For example, it does not consider that if a manager learns that his estimates of cash flows are proving to have been highly optimistic, the manager can choose to abandon the project and escape some or all of the value-destroying cash flows in the future. Similarly, DCF does not consider that a manager might add capacity to a project that proves to be much more profitable than originally estimated. To "think like an investor" means to incorporate the value of options into your estimate of the intrinsic value of an asset.

Decisions by managers and firms frequently demonstrate the significant hidden value of options. For example:

- A manager approves an investment proposal in research and development (R&D) to reengineer an aging product. The proposal has a negative NPV. But the manager believes that the R&D may lead to profitable product extensions or entirely new products. This investment consists of an unattractive fixed portion, as well as a valuable call option on new discoveries.

- XYZ Company must choose between two communities, Sparta and Corinth, in locating a new plant. The communities are equally attractive on all counts except that Sparta has higher taxes but grants companies more flexibility to trade pollution liabilities than Corinth does. XYZ chooses Sparta because even though the DCF value is worse, the option value there is greater, and sufficient to overcome the comparatively negative DCF.

In summary, options are pervasive and potentially highly valuable. DCF, the standard valuation approach, ignores option value; yet, to "think like an investor," managers should incorporate options into their assessment of business opportunities and problems.

Conclusion: Principle #5 Says If You Get Confused, See Principle #1

Business problems are rich and complex, and the use of economic models and advanced quantitative methods appears to deepen the complexity. It is easy to become confused. Finance argues that thinking like an investor is an excellent point of departure for sorting out financial problems. Of course, investors themselves rarely agree precisely.[20] But no fields in business offer strictly right answers—they merely help us avoid the wrong ones. Making financial decisions when you are ignorant of the demands and perspective of investors is a formula for calamity. By thinking like an investor, one increases the likelihood of success.

MBA Concepts in Action

Over the past several decades there has been a steady march by corporate America to adapt modern finance techniques described in this chapter. For example, a survey of recognized leaders in corporate finance, finance textbooks, and consulting firms revealed a high degree of alignment between finance theory and practice.[21] For example, 96 percent of the corporations surveyed reported that they did use discounted cash flow to evaluate investment opportunities, and 96 percent also reported that they used some form of a cost of capital for discounting cash flows. Target Corporation provides a specific example of a company that utilizes MBA concepts in its capital investment process.

Target Corporation

The Dayton Company opened the doors of the first Target store in 1962, in Roseville, Minnesota.[22] The Target name had intentionally been chosen to differentiate the new discount retailer from the Dayton Company's more upscale stores. The Target concept flourished. In 1995, the first SuperTarget store opened in Omaha, Nebraska, and in 1999, the Target.com web site was launched. In 2000, the parent company, Dayton Hudson, officially changed its name to Target Corporation.[23]

By 2008, Target was among the elite of retailing with $65 billion in revenues from 1,682 stores in all 50 states. With sales of $47 billion in 2004, the company had realized a 9.1 percent annual growth rate in sales through 2008.

In contrast with Wal-Mart's focus on low prices, Target's strategy was to consider the customer's shopping experience as a whole. Target referred to its customers as guests and consistently strived to support the slogan "Expect more. Pay less." Target focused on creating a shopping experience that appealed to the profile of its "core guest": a college-educated woman with children at home who was more affluent than the typical Wal-Mart customer. This shopping experience was created by emphasizing a store decor that gave just the right shopping ambience. The company had been highly successful at promoting its brand awareness with large advertising campaigns. This consistent advertising spending resulted in the Target bull's-eye logo being ranked among the most recognized corporate logos in the United States, ahead of the Nike swoosh.

Although the recent recession had curtailed much of Target's aggressive growth plans, the company was actively engaged in strategically assessing sites for new stores and other sites for remodeling. It did consider possibly closing one of its retail stores. Capital expenditures for 2008 were $3.5 billion, 74 percent of which was spent on retail stores and the remaining 26 percent on information technology and other purposes.

The key element of Target's capital expenditure approval process is the Capital Expenditure Committee (CEC). The CEC is composed of a team of top executives who meet monthly to review all capital project requests (CPRs) in excess of $100,000. Either CPRs are approved by the CEC or, in the case of projects larger than $50 million, approval is required from the board of directors. Historically, project proposals have varied widely and included remodeling, relocating, rebuilding, and closing an existing store to building a new store.[24] A typical CEC meeting would involve the review of 10 to 15 CPRs. Prior to being considered by the CEC, each proposal is analyzed by the discounted cash flow technique to assess its net present value (NPV) and internal rate of return (IRR). Only CPRs with positive NPVs and IRRs greater than the company's weighted average cost of capital are passed along for the CEC's evaluation. In the rare instance that a project with a negative NPV has reached the CEC, the committee was asked to consider the project in light of its strategic importance to the company.

The committee considers several factors in determining whether to accept or reject a project. In particular a CPR needs to provide a suitable financial return as measured by discounted cash flow metrics: NPV and IRR. Other financial considerations include projected profit and earnings per share impacts, total investment size, impact on sales of other nearby Target stores, and sensitivity of NPV and IRR to sales variations. Projected sales are determined based on economic trends and demographic shifts, but also considered are the risks involved with the entrance of new competitors and competition from online retailers.

The committee members are provided with a capital-project request dashboard for each project that summarizes the critical inputs and assumptions used for the NPV and IRR calculations. The template represents the summary sheet for an elaborate discounted cash flow model. For example, the analysis of a new store includes incremental cash flow projections for 60 years, over which time the model includes a remodeling of the store every 10 years. Each dashboard includes detailed explanations regarding store sensitivities, where analysts report how much the NPV and IRR changed with 10 percent variation in sales and other value-driving variables. Another important sensitivity feature is the comparison of the project's NPV and IRR to the prototype NPV and IRR. These sensitivity calculations answer the question of how much a certain cost or revenue item needs to change in order for the project to achieve the same NPV or IRR that would be experienced for the typical Target store.

Financial Management in MBA Curricula

A financial management course is a mainstay of virtually all MBA curriculums. All of the top 20 programs as ranked by *BusinessWeek*'s 2008 poll have a financial management or some other finance principles course as part of the required curriculum. For example, the top six full-time MBA programs in *BusinessWeek*'s poll with the highest-ranked finance specialty list the courses shown in Exhibit 5.12 as their first finance courses.

The first courses have a focus on value creation, and they all take an investor's point of view (i.e., a market point of view). As shown in the right-hand column, there is a wide range of finance courses that extend and apply the fundamental concepts beyond the principles courses. Most MBA programs offer a large number of finance electives to satisfy student demand in the area.

MBA Careers in Finance

If you find you enjoy analysis and the concept of valuation and if you are fascinated by the markets, then perhaps you should consider a career in finance. Finance careers are

Exhibit 5.12 Finance Courses in MBA Curricula

Business School	First Finance Course	Required?	Total Finance Electives
University of Pennsylvania (Wharton)	Financial Analysis	Required	52
University of Chicago (Booth)	Introductory Finance Corporation Finance	Not required	12
Columbia University	Corporation Finance	Required	30
Northwestern University (Kellogg)	Finance I	Not required	62
Harvard University	Finance I and II	Required	20
University of Virginia (Darden)	Financial Management Principles	Required	22

as varied as the market is complicated. A common division of finance careers is corporate (client) side versus banking (service) side. Although the skills employed are similar, the environments in which the skills are used are quite different. A second common division on the service side is *sell side* versus *buy side*.

First let's look at corporate, industry-based positions. Corporate finance is generally the internal company management of its finances, particularly its balance sheet. Corporate financial managers tend to the company's assets, liabilities, and shareholders' equity. Identifying trends in data, projecting different scenarios, and building pro forma models based on management assumptions to value different investment options are all skills that are used in corporate finance. Of course, working in corporate finance in a major Fortune 500 company brings with it a relatively steady, predictable career path and work/life balance. Typical corporate career paths might include stints in division (product) finance, treasury, and corporate development/mergers and acquisitions. In addition to technical skills, leadership, management, and team-building skills are critical for MBAs to be promoted in corporate finance. Geographically, corporate finance positions can be found just about anywhere; overseas assignments are relatively common as part of a career in corporate finance.

Service-industry finance jobs, in contrast, are highly unpredictable and subject to the vagaries of the market. Within this market, there are sell-side firms (those that focus on creating and selling financial instruments on behalf of clients) and buy-side firms (those that invest in these instruments). First, let's explore the sell side. Most closely related to industry corporate finance is investment banking. The skills used are similar—only performed by the investment banker as a service for a major corporate customer. Investment banking usually focuses on determining the worth of a company or security in order to buy or sell that security or a target firm for a company. Investment bankers earn their keep by taking a percentage of completed transactions. Since the stakes in investment banking can generally be very high and the timing of transactions critical, investment banking tends to be high pressure, high stress, and high reward. The recent developments in the marketplace probably will not change the stress level; compensation schemes, however, are under great scrutiny.

Investment banking jobs also come in many shapes and sizes; many new products have created new career paths for MBAs to pursue. Within investment banking, one can perform the corporate finance role—in essence, a financial consultant to industry, primarily on issues of shareholders' equity. Two completely different roles in investment banking are sales and trading. Sales associates are responsible for selling the new investment vehicle created by the corporate finance group on behalf of the client. Trading roles are those that literally trade the securities on the stock exchange, thus setting the market prices for these securities. The roles in sales and trading are more predictable than those in the corporate finance side in their hours and compensation, but job security relies solely on the market and profit/loss of a group or an individual.

Two other ways to segment investment banking roles are by the bank's size or by the types of products represented—more specialization, if you will. The large, full-service investment banks are called the *bulge bracket* firms; these banks typically hire dozens of undergraduates and MBAs each year into analysts and associates roles. At the other end of the spectrum are the boutique firms that are small and generally focus by industry segment, geography, or product line. Careers in restructuring, hedge funds, and private equity are common examples of these for MBAs, but typically only after working in a large investment bank first.

Now, the buy side. Buy-side firms are in the business of investing money to make money, usually on behalf of their clients or shareholders. The skills needed in these asset management roles are similar to investment banking—strong quantitative and analytical skills and an intense interest in the market. Even within buy-side firms, there are a variety of different roles. Researchers pore through financial data looking for anomalies or value opportunities. Analysts use the data from researchers to begin to build models and predict the value of certain investment options. Fund managers assemble the optimal mix of investment options to meet clients' risk and reward requirements and then determine when to buy and sell. As you can imagine, buy-side career opportunities are highly dependent on the market. When the market is moving up, firms expand rapidly. When the market falls, costs are cut just as quickly.

A variation of buy-side asset management is private wealth management (PWM), also known as wealth management, private client services, and private banking. Private wealth management is highly personalized management of the finances and investments of high-net-worth individuals. While strong analytical skills are relatively important in PWM, client management skills are more important. Careers in PWM require a broad range of duties, from acquiring new clients (selling) to analyzing security options. While many investment banks have PWM divisions to manage individual portfolios of their large corporate client executives, small boutiques are also common in the PWM business.

Buy side or sell side, client or service, large firm or one-person shop—careers in finance offer variety, flexibility, career progression, challenge, and a high risk/reward trade-off. But in almost all positions, your career is partially at the mercy of the market or how you perform in the market. The closer to the Street, the more likely it will be that your career success will depend on the market's success. If you thrive in this type of environment and if one of your core skills is quantitative analysis, then perhaps a career in finance is for you.

Notes

1. 2008 Investment Company Fact Book (www.icifactbook.org).
2. Warren Buffett is one of the most successful investors in history. Growth in book value per share of Berkshire Hathaway, Buffett's public holding company, has averaged 20.3 percent annually from 1965 to 2008, handily beating the 8.9 percent annual change in the value of the S&P 500 index (including dividends) over the same time period. (*Source:* Berkshire Hathaway 2008 Annual Report.)
3. Peter Lynch was the legendary manager of the Fidelity Magellan Fund. During his 13 years of fund management (from 1977 to 1990) the average annual return on the Magellan Fund significantly beat the average market returns. "Around Fidelity, Peter Lynch was God," remarked one observer.
4. In 2008, the U.S. Securities and Exchange Commission proposed that international financial reporting standards (IFRS) replace U.S. GAAP for U.S. public companies starting in 2010.
5. Berkshire Hathaway, Inc., Annual Report, 1994, 2.
6. Berkshire Hathaway, Inc., Annual Report, 1992, 14.
7. Berkshire Hathaway, Inc., Annual Report, 1994, 7.

8. Peter Lynch, *One Up on Wall Street: How to Use What You Already Know to Make Money in the Market* (New York: Simon & Schuster, 1989), 242.

9. Quoted in *Forbes*, October 19, 1993, and republished in Andrew Kilpatrick, *Of Permanent Value: The Story of Warren Buffett* (Birmingham, AL: AKPE, 1994), 574.

10. Walter Wriston was the CEO of Citicorp, one of the premier banks and financial services institutions in the United States, during its era of rapid expansion in the 1970s and early 1980s.

11. Walter B. Wriston, *Risk and Other Four-Letter Words* (New York: Harper & Row, 1986), 222–223.

12. Berkshire Hathaway, Inc., Annual Report, 1994, 2.

13. Originally published in Berkshire Hathaway Annual Report, 1987. This quotation was paraphrased from James Grant, *Minding Mr. Market* (New York: Times Books, 1993), xxi.

14. Quoted in *Forbes*, October 19, 1993, and republished in Kilpatrick, *Of Permanent Value*, 574.

15. "Owner-Related Business Principles," in Berkshire Hathaway Annual Report, 1994, 3.

16. Only 28 of the 30 companies are included because two of the companies have negative equity values and therefore do not have meaningful ROE or market-to-book ratios.

17. The injunction "sell securities" applies most readily to corporations. But when you think about it, it is equally applicable to individuals. For instance, any homeowner who has borrowed to finance the purchase of a house has "sold" a mortgage.

18. Bonds are rated by independent rating agencies for their likelihood of default. The bond ratings can run from high quality (AAA) to low quality (B). See Exhibit 5.2 for a listing of rating definitions.

19. A coupon was a chit that the investor literally snipped off the bond certificate and sent in to the company to receive an interest payment. In common business parlance, the coupon of a bond is the annual interest payment of the bond, expressed usually as a percentage rate of return. After the advent of an electronic business economy, actual paper coupons have become a rarity.

20. If they did, there would be no trading of stocks and bonds, and no market. On every trade there is a pessimistic seller and an optimistic buyer.

21. See Robert Bruner, Kenneth Eades, Robert Harris, and Robert Higgins, "Best Practices in Estimating the Cost of Capital Survey and Synthesis," *Financial Practice and Education* (Spring/Summer 1998): 13–28.

22. See "Target Corporation" case study (UVA-F-1563), University of Virginia Darden School Foundation, 2008, sales@dardenbusinesspublishing.com.

23. The Dayton Company merged with J.L. Hudson Company in 1969. After changing its name to Target, the company renamed the Dayton-Hudson stores as Marshall Field's. In 2004, Marshall Field's was sold to May Department Stores, which was acquired by Federated Department Stores in 2006; all May stores were given the Macy's name that same year.

24. Target expected to allocate 65 percent of capital expenditures to new stores, 12 percent to remodels and expansions, and 28 percent to information technology, distribution, and other.

For Further Reading

Bernstein, Peter L., *Against the Gods: The Remarkable Story of Risk* (New York: John Wiley & Sons, 1996).

Bernstein, Peter L., *Capital Ideas: The Improbable Origins of Modern Wall Street* (New York: Maxwell Macmillan, 1992).

Bierman, Harold, and Seymour Smidt, *The Capital Budgeting Decision: Economic Analysis of Investment Projects*, 9th ed. (New York: Routledge, 2007).

Brealey, Richard A., Stewart C. Myers, and Franklin Allen, *Principles of Corporate Finance*, 9th ed. (New York: McGraw-Hill Irwin, 2008).

Bruner, Robert F., *Deals from Hell: M&A Lessons That Rise Above the Ashes* (Hoboken, NJ: John Wiley & Sons, 2005).

Copeland, Thomas, Michael Koller, and Timothy Murrin, *Valuation*, 3rd ed. (New York: John Wiley & Sons, 2000).

Higgins, Robert C., *Analysis for Financial Management*, 9th ed. (New York: McGraw-Hill Irwin, 2009).

Homer, Sidney, and Martin L. Liebowitz, *Inside the Yield Book: New Tools for Bond Marketing Strategy* (Englewood Cliffs, NJ: Prentice-Hall, 1972).

Lewis, Michael, *Liar's Poker* (New York: W.W. Norton, 1989).

Lowenstein, Roger, *When Genius Failed: The Rise and Fall of Long-Term Capital Management* (New York: Random House, 2001).

Lynch, Peter, *One Up on Wall Street: How to Use What You Already Know to Make Money in the Market* (New York: Simon & Schuster, 1989).

Malkiel, Burton G., *A Random Walk Down Wall Street: The Time-Tested Strategy for Successful Investing* (New York: W.W. Norton, 2003).

Downloadable Resources for this chapter available at www.wiley.com/go/portablemba5e

Exhibit 5.3: Estimate of the Value-Added of Replacing a Standard Machine with an Upgraded Machine

Exhibit 5.4: Hypothetical Example of Value Creation

Exhibit 5.5: Hypothetical Example of Value Destruction

Exhibit 5.7: Illustration of Value Creation and Destruction: Market-to-Book Ratios as the Reinvestment Proportion and Return on Capital Spread Vary

Exhibit 5.8: Illustration of Value Creation and Destruction: Market-to-Book Ratios as the Life of the Project and Its Return on Capital Spread Vary

Exhibit 5.9: Net Present Value Calculation of a Bond's Cash Flows from the Standpoint of the Issuer

Exhibit 5.10: Net Present Value Valuation of a Bond's Cash Flows, Reflecting Corporate Tax Deduction of Interest Expense

6

Operations Management

Firms exist to create and deliver value to customers, shareholders, employees, and society. Operations management encompasses the activities and processes by which the firm creates and delivers value. These processes embody the firm's capabilities, which determine its future options. Key capabilities—that is, the activities and processes the firm does better than its competitors—critically affect how successfully the firm competes and how effectively it improves and renews itself.

An operations manager oversees the organization's processes that transform inputs into outputs of greater value. This includes service operations as well as manufacturing. A typical operations manager spends most of his or her time on day-to-day issues concerning operations effectiveness. Those concerns generally span a broad scope, including customer service, production, technology, procurement, distribution, and innovation. As such, the operations function offers the primary path into general management at many companies.

Operations strategy entails the set of long-term decisions regarding investments in physical assets as well as critical capabilities. Firms fail to explicitly articulate strategic guidance for the long-term operations decisions at their peril, as many of those decisions prove critical to creating—or destroying—competitive advantage. This chapter covers the contents of a typical foundational course in operations by covering the key principles behind operational effectiveness as well as providing a framework for articulating a firm's operations strategy.

Defining Operations Effectiveness

Improving operational effectiveness may take many forms, such as enhancing quality in products or processes, reducing defects, developing better products faster, implementing improved production processes, employing new capital equipment, expanding capacity, improving testing, increasing on-time delivery, streamlining purchasing, outsourcing nonstrategic activities, eliminating waste, employing more advanced technology, motivating employees better, reducing absenteeism, improving workplace health and safety, improving customer satisfaction, or empowering organizational learning. Achieving and sustaining operational excellence requires vigilant analysis and willingness to change as parts of a continual and relentless effort to improve the firm's processes. It also requires integration with the other functions of the firm so that improvement efforts throughout the firm reinforce each other and so that the functions work together to create and enhance value for customers.

111

Operational effectiveness is critical to a firm's competitiveness; it enables a firm to get more from its inputs or to use less of them to produce high-quality output (or to provide better service). A firm that lags behind competitors' operational effectiveness will face higher costs or offer an inferior product, or both. For example, in the 1980s many Japanese companies achieved operational effectiveness so far above their Western rivals that the Japanese firms were able to offer customers both lower cost and superior quality. Over time, the frontier of productivity continues to shift outward as new technologies, processes, and management methods are developed. This section looks at some of the key concepts that continue to drive ongoing improvements in operations effectiveness.

Career Profile

1993 MBA

Jeffrey A. Wilke

Senior Vice President,

North America Retail

Amazon.com Incorporated

Education:

BSE, Chemical Engineering, Princeton University

MS, Chemical Engineering, Massachusetts Institute of Technology

MBA, MIT Sloan School of Management

Mr. Wilke has served as Senior Vice President, North American Retail, since January 2007. From January 2002 until December 2006, he was Senior Vice President, Worldwide Operations. Jeff Wilke joined Amazon.com as Vice President and General Manager, Operations, in September 1999. He left AlliedSignal (now Honeywell) where he was Vice President and General Manager, Pharmaceutical Fine Chemicals, a $200 million global business. Jeff spent the preceding five years in a variety of operations leadership assignments in the chemical, polymer, and electronics industries. Jeff did his graduate work (MBA and MS in Chemical Engineering) at MIT's Leaders for Manufacturing program, where he focused on Total Quality and Process Improvement techniques.

Source: Amazon.com Inc.

Measuring Productivity

The Goal, by Eliyahu Goldratt and Jeff Cox, has guided millions of operations managers with its simple but compelling logic. Written as a novel, the book engages the reader with the story of a turnaround program at a small manufacturing concern. The plant manager seeks guidance from a former professor cum operations guru who starts the quest with the critical insight that typical efficiency measures are flawed. In response to a claim that the plant's new robots have improved productivity, the guru asks three simple questions:

1. Have revenues increased?
2. Are expenses down?
3. Do you have less inventory?

When the protagonist answers "no" to each question, the guru explains that productivity has obviously *not* improved. Instead, the manager has been focused on the flawed metric of efficiency of production output divided by input. Though the robots produce more parts in less time, they have not helped in the primary goal of the plant: to make money.

The measures that a manager uses are critical. What is measured and how it is measured set very strong incentives for the company's employees. The old adage that "what you measure will improve" is true. Indeed, many argue that the adage is understated because it may be extremely difficult to effect change on aspects of a process that have not been measured and so are not worked into the practices and culture of the workplace.

Capacity Utilization

Capacity measures the maximum output a process can generate over a given period of time. It affects the revenue side of long-run profitability by determining how many customers can be served or how many products can be produced. It affects costs in that people must be hired and plant and equipment purchased or rented. These costs may include large capital investments in plants, machines, buildings, or new technologies.

Utilization measures the actual level of output from a process. The calculation of utilization is simple in concept but difficult in practice. The formula yields a percentage value by dividing actual output over a period of time by the maximum output over that period of time. One practical challenge is that capacity changes over time with changes in the inputs, the mix of outputs, labor, and managerial decisions about the process. For example, imagine a call center that answers consumer questions about a product. The capacity, logically measured in customer calls processed per hour, would be very different if the call center was handling complex technical questions for a computer company than it would be if it were simply helping an online retailer. In a production context, the batch size affects capacity. Taking an everyday example, mixing the dough for a double batch of cookies does not require twice the mixing time as a single batch. So, the capacity of the mixer depends on the amount of dough produced in a given batch.

The biggest challenge often turns upon the definition of *maximum* in a given context. If a hospital schedules its five operating rooms eight hours per day, five days per week, and the average procedure requires half an hour, what is the weekly capacity? Based on the current schedule, the operating room capacity could be defined as 400 operations per week (5 rooms × 8 hours per day × 5 days per week × 2 surgeries per hour). But what if the hospital extended the surgery schedule to 10 hours per day and included Saturdays as well? Would that offer a better measure of capacity?

Another lesson from *The Goal* is that the bottleneck operation defines the capacity of an integrated or multistep process. If the hospital has only enough nurse anesthetists to prepare six patients per hour for surgery, the hospital cannot fully utilize the operating rooms that collectively could process 10 patients per hour (5 rooms × 2 surgeries per hour). Thus identification and relief of bottlenecks proves critical in process improvement.

Classic Teaching Case: Shouldice Hospital

The case on Shouldice Hospital describes an unusual hospital focused exclusively on hernia repair and the unique experience the hospital offers to both its patients and its staff. The hospital charges a lower fee and helps patients recover faster while simultaneously achieving a lower incidence of reoccurrence than does a traditional full-service hospital. The case highlights the reasons for this superior performance, which include its hernia operation technique, careful design of the facility, patient screening, and exercise routine.

The case challenges the student to explore expansion options as demand begins to outstrip the capacity at Shouldice Hospital. The case provides the opportunity for students to explore the technical topic of capacity utilization and bottleneck processes in a service context. It also illustrates the advantage of focus and the importance of aligning the many components of an organization's operations to a clear, common goal. As is typical, the case also forces the student to think beyond the technical aspects of operations to include people and culture.

Source: James Heskett, "Shouldice Hospital Limited," Harvard Business School Case 9-683-068.

Quality Measurement

Quality can be defined on many dimensions, but it boils down to the following: Quality is meeting the customers' requirements. It is what the customer values and pays for. Quality can affect both the cost and the revenue sides of long-run profitability. Poor quality output will immediately or eventually reduce the market value of products or services as well as increase costs of repair, customer service, and handling complaints. These costs may be magnified by reputational spillovers affecting the value of the firm's other products or brands. In addition, poor process quality can increase scrap and rework, reduce effective capacity, and decrease customer satisfaction with service processes. The point is that poor quality can create other problems that require time, resources, and managerial effort to resolve. In general, prevention of quality problems costs less than inspection and correction.

Most laypeople focus on the features of the product or service when considering quality. A Ritz-Carlton provides higher quality than a Marriott Courtyard hotel. The Ritz has fancier furnishings, a wider array of services, and more attentive staff. But consistency or "quality *to* specification" offers an equally important dimension of quality, and on that dimension the Marriott Courtyard generally delivers as well as the Ritz. It simply targets a lower "quality *of* specification."

In product development, techniques such as quality function deployment focus on identifying customer desires and translating them into product specifications for design to best meet customer needs, thereby ensuring that the "quality of spec" is on target for the market served.

Process quality addresses the "quality to spec," and accordingly process controls ensure higher-quality output. Firms may measure such things as missed promises, customer complaints, or on-time deliveries. Service processes and customer interactions may be monitored. Firms may also monitor the settings, temperatures, or force used by machines to ensure proper and consistent operation. Statistical process control measures tend to look at two dimensions: (1) whether the process is *in control* and thus stable and predictable, and (2) whether the process is *in compliance* or within the specifications required for the product or by the customer.

Service Time

Speed of delivery may affect the revenue contribution to long-run profitability. The ability of a firm to provide dependable (i.e., on-time) or fast delivery of a product or service may allow it to command a premium price or to sell more units at the standard price. Speed of delivery may also occur in the development cycle, enabling a firm to benefit by offering the first product or the best revision of a product, or to spend less on the upstream product development activities.

Delivery of existing products and services can be measured as the lead time from order to market. Shorter is generally better, but shortening process lead times can adversely affect input costs, quality, or capacity, and thus benefits can be outweighed by new costs. Often, meeting the schedule (providing *dependable, on-time delivery*) is more important than the lead time itself.

In service businesses, waiting lines or queues may form when customers arrive faster than service is delivered. The length of the queue and the speed at which customers move through it are important measures of the process performance. Long waits may result in lost or disgruntled customers, affecting profitability by reducing the number of current customers, decreasing the rate of repeat customers, and undermining the firm's reputation for quality service.

Principles of Operations Effectiveness

Principle 1: Since the limiting resource defines the capacity, efforts to increase output must focus on this bottleneck resource.

The tendency of managers to be concerned with the efficiency of every machine or person involved in a process is misplaced. The capacity of a system is not determined by the number of idle resource hours. It depends directly on the capacity of the weakest (or least productive) link in the chain. Once this is recognized, a number of managerial insights follow.

First, since bottlenecks determine capacity, identification and alleviation of bottlenecks is the top priority for increasing capacity. Five ways to identify bottlenecks are shown in Exhibit 6.1. To alleviate bottlenecks, resource allocations should be ranked by the project's contribution to the scarce or limiting resource.

Second, balancing the flow of work through a process will maximize capacity. Maximizing the capacity of individual machines or processes is ineffective since the bottleneck will constrain the system.

Third, downtime is very expensive because an hour lost on a bottleneck is lost on the entire system. Idle machines or workers in nonbottleneck activities may not have any

Exhibit 6.1 Five Ways to Identify Bottlenecks

- *Least capacity:* Output of a process is limited by the capacity of the bottleneck.
- *Most utilization:* Activities with the highest rates of use are prime bottleneck suspects. If there is variability in the flow, these areas will sometimes have insufficient capacity.
- *No slack:* Bottlenecks tend to be busy all of the available time.
- *Worker complaints:* There tend to be large numbers of worker complaints about a bottleneck operation.
- *Piled-up inventory:* Inventories (or waiting lines) accumulate upstream of a bottleneck.

adverse effect on capacity. Thus, idle time per se need not be viewed as a problem, but idle time *at the bottleneck* reduces output of the entire process.

Fourth, aggregate measures of capacity, utilization, or throughput provide little actionable information. Problem diagnosis and prescriptions for improvement require that analysis be broken down for individual resources. For example, one way to increase capacity is to reduce the time spent on setup of the processes or machines, but this is effective only when setup is reduced on the bottleneck. Reducing setup in other parts of the system will increase the capacity of individual pieces of the system, but not of the process as a whole. Moreover, the bottleneck may be the capacity of machines or of labor, so the analysis should be separated on that dimension as well. As noted earlier, a hospital may have plenty of operating rooms for its surgeries, but if there are not enough nurses to staff them, the number of surgeries will be limited by the nursing capacity, not by the physical facilities.

Finally, if there is variability, excess capacity is needed at the bottleneck to keep the flow balanced. If the system has barely adequate capacity on average, then variations above the average will result in shortfalls, creating long waits for output or expensive work-in-process inventory, or both. This raises the question of how much excess capacity is reasonable. The answer depends on variability and the relative cost of capacity versus lost sales, but few processes can produce consistently at full capacity for sustained periods of time.

Principle 2: The process should match the needs of the product or service produced.

Different types of processes are appropriate for different types of services or products, for different types of customer requirements, and for achieving different bases of competitive advantage. In their 1979 *Harvard Business Review* article, "Link Manufacturing Process and Product Life Cycles", Robert Hayes and Steven Wheelwright identified five process types with corresponding appropriate product types:

1. Management of unique projects is generally appropriate for one-of-a-kind products such as a communications satellite or custom-made houses.

2. Job shops that produce small batches of a number of different products are appropriate for product lines with high variety and relatively low volume.

3. Disconnected line-flow (or batch) processes produce moderate volumes of several products requiring somewhat similar tasks.

4. Assembly line (or connected line-flow) processes may be machine-paced or operator-paced, using uniform production paths to produce relatively large volumes of products, usually to inventory.

5. Continuous-flow processes involve high-volume, automated, capital-intensive production, usually of commodity-type products.

Generally, firms tend to operate along the diagonal of the product-process matrix, shown in Exhibit 6.2. A firm would not want to be off diagonal *unintentionally*. Unintentional moves off the diagonal occur, for example, when managers bow to competitive pressures by increasing product variety without adjusting operations to the expanding product line.

Increasingly, companies have begun to challenge the logic of the matrix and note that leading manufacturers like Toyota *intentionally* operate off the diagonal. These leading practitioners of lean manufacturing have pushed their assembly operations to accommodate a far greater breadth than thought possible when the product-process matrix was defined. These firms now operate economically below the diagonal on the matrix. As

Exhibit 6.2   Product-Process Matrix

	PRODUCT STRUCTURE			
PROCESS STRUCTURE	**I** Low Volume, Low Standardization, One of a Kind	**II** Multiple Products, Low Volume	**III** Few Major Products, Higher Volume	**IV** High Volume, High Standardization, Commodity Products
I Jumbled flow (job stop)	Commercial Printer			
II Disconnected line flow (batch)		Heavy Equipment		
III Connected line flow (assembly line)	Lean Manufacturing / Cellular Manufacturing		Auto Assembly	
IV Continuous flow				Sugar Refinery

Source: Adapted from Robert Hayes, Gary Pisano, David Upton, and Steven Wheelwright, *Operations, Strategy & Technology: Pursuing the Competitive Edge* (Hoboken, NJ: John Wiley & Sons, 2005).

another example, a firm may also choose to differentiate its product by handcrafting when competitors use automated processes. Steuben Glass is a good example of differentiation by handcrafting. Finally, a firm may move to automation in anticipation of growth before there is really enough volume to justify the automation. As with any framework, the product-process matrix should not be viewed as a fixed template but merely a way to help managers think about the problem of product structure and process technology choice.

Principle 3: Service businesses must resolve a unique set of challenges driven by labor intensity and the expected degree of interaction and customization.

Services represent an increasing share of the economy in all developed nations, and accordingly service operations now garner more executive attention than manufacturing in many parts of the world. The direct interaction with customers demanded in most service businesses presents one of the key challenges along with the amount of customization and the degree of labor intensity.

As shown in Exhibit 6.3, Roger Schemenner developed a useful framework for classifying different types of services, resulting in four basic types: professional service, mass service, service shop, and service factory. Each faces a different mix of challenges that must be resolved to perform successfully.

Professional service businesses face high labor intensity plus a high degree of customization in the work, which demands tight attention to attracting and retaining qualified people who can meet the desired quality standards. These businesses have always depended on the class of employees described as knowledge workers, who often show greater commitment to their profession than to their employer. Scheduling processes must ensure high utilization without inhibiting the ability to respond to new opportunities given the variability of demand as well as the uncertainty of the execution process for customized services.

A *service shop* also faces the challenges of customization but has lower labor intensity. A hospital employs a wider mix of staff than an independent physician practice and also tends to have a greater investment in equipment and technology. As such, attracting and

Degree of Interaction and Customization

		Low	High
Degree of Labor Intensity	**Low**	**Service Factory** • *Airlines* • *Trucking* • *Hotels* • *Resorts/recreation*	**Service Shop** • *Hospital* • *Auto repair* • *Other repair services*
	High	**Mass Service** • *Retailing* • *Wholesaling* • *Schools* • *Retail Banking*	**Professional Service** • *Physicians* • *Lawyers* • *Accountants* • *Architects*

Exhibit 6.3   Service-Process Matrix

Source: Roger W. Schemenner, "How Can Service Businesses Survive and Prosper?" *Sloan Management Review* 27, no. 3 (Spring 1986): 25.

developing people becomes less critical but decisions regarding technology investments become even more critical. In a hospital, this ranges from specialized equipment in the operating rooms to multimillion-dollar magnetic resonance imaging (MRI) machines.

Shifting to the top-left quadrant, the *service factory* captures the businesses that have scaled their service offerings to a more common offering, which also requires less interaction with customers. For example, a hotel offers some of the same duties as a hospital: check-in and check-out, food service, and room cleaning. Obviously, these are secondary activities at a hospital and also require more highly trained staff due to the more complex, nonstandard needs of patients. Service factories also have far more physical assets that either of the other two types, and accordingly focus on asset utilization since the labor is less costly and critical.

Similarly, *mass services* tend to have common service offerings without customization but also to be far more labor intensive than service factories. These businesses generally employ large numbers of less skilled employees and tend to suffer from high employee attrition. As such, these companies must have effective, low-cost processes for attracting and training employees. They also invest considerable resources in developing standard operating procedures that can be easily adopted by the lower-skilled staff to minimize the need for extensive training.

As these examples highlight, service businesses come in many types and forms and face a variety of challenges. Interestingly, many of these challenges apply in the more traditional realm of operations management: manufacturing plants. As such, service businesses can and do draw lessons from manufacturing concerns.

Classic Teaching Case: Deutsche Allegemeinversicherung

This case explores how the head of operations development at Deutsche Allegemeinversicherung (DAV), one of the largest insurance companies in Europe, used lessons from manufacturing to drive process improvement. Facing rising price-based competition, DAV struggled to retain good employees and assure its quality reputation. To avoid commoditization of its insurance services, DAV launched a quality initiative to further enhance customer service and defend its leadership position. This initiative involved improving information accuracy and quality through the use of statistical process control (SPC).

The case describes the pilot project implemented at DAV and highlights the challenges in managing an SPC implementation by addressing issues such as determining appropriate sample sizes, precisely defining errors, resolving measurement difficulties, and achieving senior management cooperation. The case highlights both technical and managerial challenges. Students receive an introduction to SPC tools and charts and explore various possible applications. By taking on the role of the program manager, students develop an appreciation of the benefits as well as the managerial challenges of implementing a quality initiative in a services context.

Source: David Upton, *Deutsche Allgemeinversicherung*, Harvard Business School Case 9-696-084.

Principle 4: Customer waiting lines (queues) should be managed to balance the direct and indirect costs of making customers wait versus idle server time.

All businesses must manage the arrival and potential backlog of customer orders. In service businesses dealing directly with customers, queues (or waiting lines) form, and those customers can also choose to go elsewhere rather than wait. Queues inevitably form when service provided to customers varies in time or complexity and customers arrive at random (unscheduled) times. A long waiting line reduces the value of the product or service for customers and thus the revenues that the firm can earn. The idle time of the server is also costly to the firm since an idle worker waiting to provide service must still be paid. Given uncertainty in both service times and arrival times, a manager should seek to minimize the sum of the costs of poor service and idle servers.

Combining waiting lines, like the single line for multiple cash registers at many fast-food restaurants, can reduce customer waiting and server idle time simultaneously. Combining multiple queues helps to ensure that one server is not idle while another has customers waiting. Sometimes this is as simple as forming a snake line at the airport ticket counter. In other situations, cross-training servers and combining service locations may be necessary to combine queues.

Simulation Exercise: Littlefield Technologies

This simulation exercise from Response Learning offers students a chance to develop an intuitive understanding of queuing theory and the impact of capacity utilization. Students take responsibility for running a high-tech factory comprised of multiple processing stages. Customers demand short lead times from the factory, and accordingly students need to manage the capacity wisely to avoid long waiting times between processes.

_____

Source: Response Learning.

Queuing theory helps quantify the waiting time for a given service configuration. As shown in Exhibit 6.4, for a given number of servers, waiting times increase as server utilization increases—and the times increase dramatically as utilization approaches 100 percent. (*Note: If the servers are utilized 100 percent or more, the waiting time extends to infinity!*) In this example, three different regional call centers serve separate customers and some have higher utilization than others, leading to variable waiting times across the regions. By combining the three regions into a single call center, the average waiting time goes down because of the pooling effect of the random arrival of customers as well as the single entity operating at an average utilization on the flatter part of the curve.

Waiting time and idle server time can be managed in a number of other ways as well. The number of servers can be adjusted, using more servers at peak times and fewer at slower times. The rate at which service is provided can be sped up with training, process analysis and redesign, or investment in technology. The pattern of customer arrivals can sometimes be altered with incentives for customers to arrive at nonpeak times or by extending available service hours to weekends and evenings or with 24-hour telephone services. Arrival rates can also be managed by moving to appointments rather than a first-come, first-served queue.

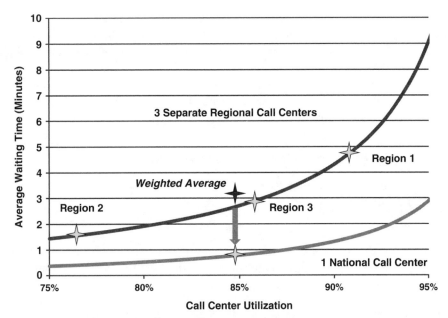

Exhibit 6.4   Server Utilization and Wait Times

Source: Unpublished Darden School teaching materials.

As these choices are considered, it is important to keep in mind the relative costs. Idle time is not necessarily bad. It may be preferable to have a clerk idle in the stockroom part of the day than to have a queue of highly paid engineers or mechanics regularly standing idle while they wait for parts at the stockroom window.

Principle 5: High quality may not be free, but it can be a good investment.

Successful quality management programs pursue quality, not for its own sake, but to enhance the net value delivered to customers. In 1979, quality guru Phil Crosby asserted that "Quality is free" because often quality management programs return financial benefits well in excess of the cost. For example, efforts to improve quality directly may reduce costs by lowering the number of defects or by reducing scrap or rework by doing things right the first time. Investments that raise quality management costs can sometimes result in products or services sufficiently differentiated that customers pay a premium above the costs of quality management.

Other times, quality management increases costs without an accompanying current price premium. Although quality is not free in that situation, it is a good investment if managers anticipate less measurable qualitative benefits such as more loyal customers, higher demand, or a future price premium based on the record of high quality. Unfortunately, the costs of poor quality often go unobserved. To identify these hidden costs, companies should examine the four major categories of cost of quality: prevention, appraisal, internal failure, and external failure. The point is not that managers should try to quantify precisely all of the benefits (which may be difficult to measure), but that the value of pursuing quality should be considered relative to its costs. Quality efforts that reduce the sum of these four costs can offer an excellent return on investment.

Given the costs of poor quality, an effective quality management program must span departmental and even organizational boundaries. Quality programs may include measuring product defects or service problems, establishing systems to prevent quality problems, redefining supplier relationships to encourage collaborative problem solving, improving the customer interface to better understand and deliver what the customer values, developing new products to better meet customer needs, changing employee incentives and compensation schemes, and changing business paradigms when necessary to improve processes.

Principle 6: Prevention costs less than inspection and correction.

"I worry that whoever thought up the term quality control *believed that if we didn't control it, quality would get out of hand."*

—Lily Tomlin

Six sigma represents the latest overarching methodology for systematically reducing the cost of poor quality. An earlier framework dubbed Total Quality Management (TQM) emerged in the 1980s as a synthesis of the practices of leading Japanese manufacturers such as Toyota. Regardless of the specific title, the essence of quality management combines analysis and corrective action to improve profitability. The analysis is critical because it provides the understanding that is the basis of prevention and improvement. The alternative to prevention is inspection followed by correction of problems or selection of which goods to sell and which to scrap.

Prevention starts with analysis of the root causes. W. Edwards Deming, the statistician and eventual quality guru credited with Japan's quality revolution, identified two basic sources of problems: *common causes* of quality problems due to management or process design and *special causes* of quality problems due to individual workers or machines. Common causes are *systemic* and due to deficiencies or oversights in process design or management such as poor product design, machines out of order or in poor repair, inadequate training programs, poor quality or scheduling of incoming materials, improper bills of materials, inappropriate incentives for workers, poor working conditions, or other problems shared by numerous operators, service providers, or machines. Special causes are attributable to particular workers or equipment, such as lack of skill, inattention, one machine operating outside of specification, or one bad lot of incoming material.

As part of the post–World War II efforts to revive the Japanese economy, Deming trained Japanese managers to use statistical process control to distinguish between the two types of problems, followed by action to redesign the system to address common causes and attention to specific workers or activities to correct special causes. He offered a simple framework—Plan, Do, Check, Act (PDCA)—as a recurring cycle for continuous quality improvement.

Six sigma programs build on this foundation but employ more advanced statistical tools—and critically put greater emphasis on change management by broadly engaging the organization in improvement efforts. Motorola coined the name for this new approach, which is based on a goal of near-perfect quality: a probability of only three failures out of a million events. This has become the new standard of process capability.

The six sigma standard captures two important concepts from process control: precision and accuracy. Precision measures the consistency of output from a process—for example, the amount of time to handle a customer call. Accuracy measures against some standard. Continuing with the same example, a customer service representative might consistently complete calls in one minute (including 30 seconds of holding time) with high predictability; however, if 45 seconds is our goal, the accuracy would be low. The actions required to improve precision tend to be different from those required to improve accuracy. In this case, the call center manager might be able to improve precision by training the customer service representatives but may need to add staff to improve the accuracy due to the holding time. A process that can meet six sigma standards must have high precision and accuracy.

Classic Teaching Case:
Toyota Motor Manufacturing USA

This case introduces students to Toyota's famous operations philosophy—the Toyota Production System (TPS). It explains some of TPS's key principles and tools, including just in time (JIT), *jidoka*, *hiejunka*, *andon*, and *kanban*. The case illustrates that TPS comprises more than a collection of tools and techniques, but instead a philosophy ingrained in the culture that ensures thoughtful rather than mindless application of the tools. The case offers a historical account of Toyota's initial foray into manufacturing in the United States, shedding light on the challenges of replicating its famous production system at the facility. It challenges students to resolve a specific problem the plant faces—a growing number of cars with defective or missing seats accumulating outside the assembly plant.

Students analyze the application of TPS to address the problem and suggest actions to solve it. Thus this case allows students to integrate various aspects of operations management, including quality control, scheduling, supplier relationships, and human resource management. Discussion of this case encourages students to think about the different facets of solving this challenging problem and highlights the distinction between technical and managerial problem solving.

Source: Kazuhiro Mishina, "Toyota Motor Manufacturing, U.S.A., Inc.," Harvard Business School Case 9-693-019.

Operations Strategy versus Effectiveness

Following the principles for continuous improvement of operations effectiveness consumes much of the time of a typical operations manager.[1] But a solely tactical focus puts the manager on the frustrating treadmill described by the Red Queen in *Alice in Wonderland*: "Now, here, I see, it takes all the running you can do, to keep in the same place. If you want to get somewhere else, you must run at least twice as fast as that!"

In the fall of 1996, Michael Porter published a *Harvard Business Review* article with the provocative title "What Is Strategy?" Porter, creator of the famed Five Forces model, applied by corporations worldwide (and covered in Chapter 9 on strategy), feared that companies had lost sight of the importance of strategy. A decade of unrelenting pursuit of operational effectiveness to close the cost and quality gap with an array of Japanese competitors had set many industries on a path of competitive convergence. For Porter, this single-minded pursuit of operational effectiveness would lead to mutual destruction, culminating in industry consolidation where the survivors were companies who merely "outlasted others, not companies with real advantage."

So concerned about this trend, Porter opened his article with a statement intended to grab the attention of his readers: "Operational effectiveness is not strategy." He explained that operational effectiveness efforts tended to move a company closer to the "productivity frontier." Dismissing the ongoing pursuit of best practices, Porter defined strategy as "the creation of a unique and valuable position, involving a different set of activities." He also noted that "strategy is making trade-offs in competing," including "choosing what *not* to do." Finally, he emphasized the importance of fit among a company's activities: "The success of a strategy depends on doing many things well—not just a few—and integrating among them."

Though operations practitioners and academics bristled at Porter's trivializing of operations, a closer examination of his arguments actually suggests that strategy and operations have more in common than either side was willing to admit. Effective overall strategy, by Porter's own definition, reinforces the critical need for an operations strategy. Porter dismissed the Japanese focus on cost and quality improvement, but he failed to appreciate the richness of the operations strategy of a company like Toyota in creating a differentiated position, the essence of strategy in Porter's model. Admittedly, Toyota's *product* positioning may not be distinctive from that of the rest of the industry. But the Toyota Production System stems from a revolutionary view of the function of a supply chain: It could produce the car a customer wanted *just in time* rather than push cars onto dealer lots and count on dealer financing and haggling to convince customers to take them. That vision led to the series of operational innovations that allowed Toyota to easily respond to changing customer demands. Creating self-reinforcing systems of activities that display good strategic positioning is the essence of an effective operations strategy that supports the corporate strategy.

From Manufacturing Strategy to Operations Strategy

In fairness to Porter, he is not alone in trivializing operations. Strategists have been dismissing the function for decades. Another Harvard professor, Wickham Skinner, attempted to make business practitioners aware that the manufacturing function warranted more executive attention in a 1969 *Harvard Business Review* article. Titled "Manufacturing, the Missing Link in Corporate Strategy," the article anticipated Porter's argument by more than 25 years, noting that "a production system inevitably involves trade-offs and compromises." But rather than focusing on strategic positioning, Skinner highlighted a number of "decision areas" where the operations arena needed to resolve important trade-offs.

Other academics built upon Skinner's foundation as the concept of a manufacturing strategy evolved into a framework for a broader operations strategy. In the late 1970s, Steven Wheelwright highlighted the importance of decisions regarding the "manufacturing infrastructure," which led over time to the distinction between *structural* decision areas (such as plant location and capacity) and the increasingly pervasive computer systems like manufacturing resource planning (MRP) used to manage the facilities. As information technology investments began to rival investments in production equipment, the scope of an operations strategy clearly needed to expand to encompass these *infrastructural* decisions.

Ultimately, this focus on the strategic decisions regarding operations systems and processes found support in a competing strategy framework, the resource-based view (RBV) of the firm. Porter's industrial organization economics school examines the structure of an industry and considers the choice of industry to be paramount. In contrast, the RBV school offers an opposing school of thought that focuses on capabilities as the central precept of strategy. The resource-based view of strategy dates back 50 years to a provocative book entitled *The Theory of the Growth of the Firm* by Edith Penrose (Oxford University Press, 1959). This strategy school, popularized by Jay Barney in the early 1990s, applies a bottom-up perspective focusing on the firm rather than the industry. Its proponents highlight the need to build capabilities over time and note that "path dependencies" can limit a firm's options as it invests in different strategic activities over time.

Porter's argument that a company must choose a unique set of activities to support its competitive position gives short shrift to the difficulty of building capabilities. His perspective tends to imply that a company need only select among a Chinese menu of activity options, just as a conglomerate can choose among a set of industries. As such, the strategist thoughtfully decides upon the activities that will produce a competitive advantage . . . and the operations executive merely executes. In reality, operations strategy must explicitly consider what capabilities to build and refine over time.

Merging Porter's positioning perspective with Skinner's manufacturing decision areas and Barney's capabilities-based strategy offers a richer perspective on the appropriate contents of an operations strategy. Simply put, an operations strategy should encompass structural decisions as well as the operational capabilities needed to support a distinct competitive position.

Structural Decisions

Practitioners and academics alike admit that the operations strategy at most companies can only be inferred by the pattern of past decisions. Rarely does a company formally document a separate operations strategy: At best, guidance on a few key operations decision areas might be found in an overall corporate strategy. Looking at a few case examples of past decisions, however, can highlight both good and bad operations strategies.

Structural decisions define the what, when, where, and how for investing in operations bricks and mortar. Though the original logic of operations strategy focused on manufacturing plants, the same issues need to be addressed for distribution plants or call centers. Four interrelated decision areas ultimately influence the size and scope of a company's operational footprint: vertical integration, facility capacity, facility location, and process technology. Each of the four should be addressed explicitly and collectively in light of the company's competitive positioning.

Vertical Integration

The logical starting point is to consider what activities (to use Porter's terms) should be conducted in-house versus outside. Henry Ford's original River Rouge complex in Detroit was the epitome of vertical integration in the days when Ford revolutionized the automobile business with the Model T and Model A. Barge loads of raw iron ore fed the plant steel mills, which supplied virtually all of the individual parts for the assembly plants, which produced hundreds of cars a day. Strategically, Ford was competing on low cost using the new paradigm of mass production and scale economies to break out of the pack of a still nascent industry composed of dozens of smaller companies.

More recently, at its formation in the mid-1990s, Amazon.com went against the general trend of outsourcing and the dominant pattern among Internet retailing start-ups by building a vertically integrated network of fulfillment centers that assemble and ship the orders customers submit over the Web. Amazon invented and continues to perfect the operating model for Internet fulfillment, and outsourcing would put its competitive advantage at risk. "We would be the teacher and then they would offer those services to our competitors," explained a senior operations executive in the early days.

Facility Capacity

Assuming a company envisions a sufficient competitive advantage from some degree of vertical integration, the specifications for the facility come to the forefront. Should a company aggressively build capacity ahead of demand or take a more conservative path of only adding capacity in smaller increments once market uncertainty subsides? Consider two case examples, which produced opposite results from the same strategy. In 1987 Copeland, a division of Emerson Electric, introduced the scroll compressor, a fundamentally new design concept for initial application in residential air-conditioning. Copeland built capacity ahead of demand and even continued with a capacity expansion in 1989 despite initial demand falling short of forecasts. The company was convinced—correctly, as history showed—that new regulatory efficiency standards would favor the new technology, and built a competitive advantage that it retains today. Today, the scroll technology dominates the market and Copeland's design leads the industry, giving the company unmatched scale economies.

Webvan took a similarly aggressive stance during the height of the Internet bubble but unfortunately ended up in bankruptcy and the poster child of Internet excess. Webvan faced far more uncertainty than Copeland did. No pressing need was driving individual consumers to adopt Webvan's fundamentally new model of grocery retailing. Webvan, a start-up with no previous operating experience to draw upon, added additional risk by designing a network comprised of $30 million, technology-intensive facilities containing literally *miles* of conveyors even though fulfillment operations typically offer fairly limited scale economies. Rather than dominating the market like Copeland, Webvan ran out of money building new fulfillment centers before it could reach break-even utilization at its first facility in Oakland, California.

Even in mature markets, the capacity for an individual facility represents a strategic operations decision that should reflect the company's competitive positioning. For example, the retailer Zara competes by offering high-fashion knock-offs at a discount price. Because its competitive position demands fast fulfillment as new fashion trends emerge, Zara purposely maintains excess capacity in its distribution center in A Coruña, Spain. By contrast, Wal-Mart, which competes on cost, seeks to maximize the capacity utilization of its distribution facilities.

Facility Location

Facility location also requires trade-offs in designing the operations footprint regardless of whether the facility is in-house or outsourced. Using Zara as an example again, it maintains scale-intensive pattern-cutting operations in-house and subcontracts the labor-intensive sewing to small mom-and-pop facilities in the surrounding region. Most fashion retailers outsource cut-and-sew operations to Asia to tap into the low labor cost but face long supply chains requiring early design decisions and advanced volume commitments. Zara's more responsive supply chain fits its strategy, and in-house cutting offers enhanced control and helps offset some of the labor cost disadvantage of the geographic location of its sewing plants.

Plant location decisions must also trade off intellectual property risk and the cost of transportation. Accordingly, Intel builds most of its high-tech wafer fabrication facilities in the developed world to protect its intellectual property, and Chinese appliance maker Haier built a refrigerator plant in South Carolina to avoid the prohibitive shipping cost for big refrigerators across the Pacific to the U.S. market.

Process Technology

Finally, the structural footprint decision should address the process technology used in the facility. Reinforcing the interaction among these four structural decision areas and the evolving nature of an operations strategy, consider the case of Copeland's scroll compressors again. A dozen years after the introduction of its scroll design, Copeland felt compelled to add a Chinese plant to its operations footprint; many customers were now producing in China, and the labor cost advantage of the region could offset some of Copeland's scale advantage if it ceded China to Asian competitors. Accordingly, Emerson opened a new scroll compressor plant in Suzhou in June 2000. But Copeland made distinctly different decisions regarding process technology at this new plant. Concerns over intellectual property protection led the company to exclude proprietary process technology and import the critical scroll plates from its U.S. plants. Furthermore, though Copeland had been a stickler for precisely replicating plant layout and technology as it added facilities, in China the company realized that more labor-intensive process technology would be appropriate, given the vast difference in wage rates.

Operations Capabilities

While the structure of a company's operations footprint represents a critical set of strategic decisions, increasingly management focuses attention on the activities that can create competitive advantage. While Porter properly dismissed the pursuit of "operational effectiveness" without a clear linkage to the company's competitive differentiation, he tended to underestimate the importance of building operational capabilities.

In Porter's defense, many operations executives do not think about building unique capabilities but mindlessly pursue so-called best practices. The concept of best practices, in fact, reinforces the flawed mind-set that triggered Porter's attack on operations effectiveness. There are no universally superior methods that should be applied by all industry participants. Such a model yields competitive convergence and the often destructive model of pure cost-based competition. Instead, capabilities should be nurtured with a clear focus on the company's desired, differentiated position in the marketplace. But where does one start? Ideally, the operations strategist should identify the key operations processes for the specific industry in which the company competes. To illustrate the concept, however, consider the following six processes that provide reasonably comprehensive coverage of most operational contexts.

Innovation/Product Development

To generate a competitive advantage, an operations capability must support the firm's competitive position. Consider again Zara, which competes by quickly copying ideas from the Paris and Milan catwalks as well as the nightclubs of New York and Tokyo. Unlike the fashion leaders, Zara has not built an innovation and product development capability around big-name designers who create the next fashion trend. Zara's approach of using teams of designers does not represent a general best practice, but it provides a competitive advantage, given Zara's positioning. These teams work collaboratively, gathering insight from over 500 Zara store managers who report daily on what is selling in over 40 countries from Austria to Uruguay. They may lack the creative inspiration of the next design sensation, but they get product to the market and quickly tweak designs to avoid the markdown headaches of the competition.

Career Profile

1989 MBA

Eileen Auen

Chairman & CEO,

PMSI

Education:

BA, Economics and Finance, Towson University

MBA, Darden Graduate School of Business Administration, University of Virginia

Eileen O. Auen is a recognized leader in the health care, workers' compensation, and financial services industries. She currently serves as chairman and CEO of PMSI, one of the nation's largest providers of specialty managed care services and products for workers' compensation and liability markets. Prior to joining PMSI, Ms. Auen served as head of health care management for Aetna, the nation's third largest health insurance carrier. While at Aetna, she was responsible for managing more than $35 billion of health care spending, as well as the company's network management, care management, and informatics organizations. Earlier in her career, Ms. Auen developed her expertise in health care management as an operations consultant at Booz Allen Hamilton.

Source: PMSI.

Customer Service Management

Or consider Progressive Insurance, which has built its reputation through the way it manages claims processing. Progressive has built a competitive advantage through on-the-spot claims settlement by its ubiquitous fleet of white SUVs. More recently, in select markets, Progressive has taken its customer service a step further. Rather than issuing a check quickly, it now offers to take care of the repair. Customers drop their vehicle off at a Progressive Customer Service Center and the company returns it with repairs guaranteed for as long as you own the car. In both cases Progressive didn't raise prices to cover the increased service level. Instead it built the capabilities in a self-funding way. Progressive gets the best prices from a certified set of repair shops, whereas an individual, typically interacting with a repair shop for the first time, might be overcharged or be willing to accept a premium price for an expedited repair since the insurance company is paying for it.

Operations Planning and Control

As discussed earlier, Amazon.com made a strategic decision to vertically integrate into fulfillment. To leverage that structural investment, Amazon has invested to build a competitively advantaged capability under the generic banner of operations planning and control. For example, Amazon informs the customer of the precise cutoff time for ordering to receive a delivery the next day. No competitor manages such a broad product range with such precision. To leverage its scale and strengthen its operational competitive advantage, Amazon continues to pursue some of the most daunting Internet retailing challenges. Amazon Fresh attacks the delivery of groceries that bankrupted Webvan, and the recent acquisition of Zappos will force Amazon to tackle the pernicious problem of returns, the bane of online shoe retailing. If anyone can conquer these headaches, it will be Amazon. And if Amazon does, it will reinforce its competitive advantage as the preeminent Web retailer.

Purchasing and Supplier Development

Over the past 20 years, Honda of America has invested heavily to develop its local supply base, leveraging a capability in purchasing and supplier development inherited from its parent in Japan. Given a strategic need to localize and a domestic supply base incapable of meeting its quality standards, Honda had little choice initially but over time reaped huge rewards in its continual pursuit of affordable, mass-produced cars like the Accord. By contrast, Liz Claiborne chose to completely outsource its purchasing and supplier development activities to the global supply chain management company Li & Fung. In fact, over 700 companies, ranging from Toys 'R' Us to Sanrio (the Japanese company behind the "Hello Kitty" brand of products) depend on Li & Fung rather than an in-house capability to manage its supply network. Different competitive priorities demand different operations strategies.

Quality Management

A company's approach to quality management also represents an opportunity to build a capability to support a differentiated competitive position. For example, the Palm Restaurant and McDonald's both have strong quality management capabilities, but each focuses on a different quality positioning. The Palm Restaurant chain, with nearly 30 locations from London to Los Angeles, has built its reputation on ample servings of hand-cut, aged steaks cooked to the individual tastes of the customers. McDonald's quality management process focuses on delivering consistent meals in 31,000 restaurants in over 100 countries worldwide. In quality management parlance, the Palm competes on "quality *of* spec" (short for specification) and McDonald's compete on "quality *to* spec." Rather than mindlessly pursuing best practices, each company has tailored its quality management capability to support its quality positioning.

Attracting and Developing People

Many companies proclaim that people are their most important asset (though few behave as such). All of the operations capabilities depend on people, and accordingly a comprehensive operations strategy must explicitly address how the company will attract, develop, and retain the right people. Management gurus laud General Electric's Crotonville learning center and its succession planning process for developing executives. GE's scale and diverse businesses justify its investment in managers who can move around the company to provide fresh energy and perspective. Few competitors can match its ability to develop great executives. Google, in contrast, has built a capability for efficiently screening candidates. After three years of doubling head count from 2004 to 2007, the company developed an algorithm to screen the 100,000 applications it receives each month. Given the growth and dynamic nature of the company, Google appropriately focuses on identifying the right people more than developing them like GE does.

From Theory to Practice

We now have a clearer view of the day-to-day principles of operations management as well as operations strategy's contribution to an overall corporate strategy. An operations strategy offers guidance for the decisions related to structural investments as well as investments in capability building. The consistency or fit among these decisions determines the effectiveness in achieving the desired positioning.

Porter used Southwest Airlines as a prototypical case example. Southwest developed its business model to support a low price positioning, prices so low that people could afford to fly rather than take a bus. To succeed, Southwest made a number of reinforcing structural and capability-building decisions. For example, the company explicitly chose a point-to-point model from secondary airports over the industry standard hub-and-spoke model to avoid congestion and keep flights predictably on schedule. Southwest sent ground crews to observe Indy pit stops to build the capability for fast aircraft turnaround times to maximize utilization of the fleet. Similarly, Southwest chose to standardize on Boeing 737s for its process technology to speed the turnaround and simplify maintenance. The company pays higher-than-industry-average pay but demands flexibility from its unions to ensure that everyone pitches in to get the planes airborne again.

In short, most of what Porter highlights as the critical elements of Southwest's strategy fall within the domain of an operations strategy. Though admittedly most companies do not explicitly articulate an operations strategy, the decisions made by operating executives ultimately produce—or erode—competitive advantage.

Operations Management in MBA Curricula

As shown in Exhibit 6.5, most top business schools offer multiple courses in operations management, generally with one as a required core course. Some offer further electives in core operations tools, such as the vaunted six sigma quality method pioneered by Motorola and adopted by many Fortune 500 companies. Given the growth of the service sector—in developed economies particularly—many schools also have offerings focused on service operations and in some case more narrowly on retail services operations. A growing emphasis on global operations reflects another curriculum trend driven by

Exhibit 6.5 Operations Management Course Offerings

Business School	Course Name	Type
Carnegie Mellon University (Tepper)	Production and Operations Management	Core
	Manufacturing Strategy	Elective
Columbia University	Operations Management	Core
	Operations Strategy	Core
	Service Operations Management	Elective
	Quality Management	Elective
	Operations Consulting	Elective
	Retailing Strategy and Operations	Elective
Cornell University (Johnson)	Managing Operations	Core
Dartmouth College (Tuck)	Operations Management	Core
	Management of Service Operations	Elective
Duke University (Fuqua)	Operations Management	Core
	Operations Strategy	Elective
	Service Operations Management	Elective
	Global Operations	Elective
	Quality and Six Sigma	Elective
Harvard University	Technology and Operations Management	Core
	Operations Strategy	Elective
	Managing Service Operations	Elective
INSEAD	Process and Operations Management	Core
	Management of Services	Elective
London Business School	Operations and Technology Management	Core
MIT (Sloan)	Introduction to Operations Management	Elective
	Management of Services: Concepts, Design, and Delivery	Elective
	Operations Strategy	Elective
	Theory of Operations Management	Elective
Northwestern University (Kellogg)	Operations Management	Core
	Operations Strategy	Elective
	Service Operations	Elective
	Inventory Management	Elective
NYU (Stern)	Competitive Advantage from Operations	Core
	Business Process Design and Implementation	Elective
	Operations Strategy	Elective
	Service Operations and Strategy	Elective
Stanford University	Operations	Core
	Business Process Design	Elective
	Global Operations	Elective
UC Berkeley (Hass)	Operations	Core

Exhibit 6.5 (*Continued*)

Business School	Course Name	Type
UCLA (Anderson)	Operations Technology Management	Core
	Managing Service Operations	Elective
	Global Operations Strategy	Elective
University of Chicago (Booth)	Operations Strategy and Performance Analysis	Elective
	Managing Service Operations	Elective
University of Michigan (Ross)	Operations Management	Core
	Sustainable Operations	Elective
	Topics in Global Operations	Elective
University of Navarra (IESE)	Operations Management	Core
	Operations Strategy	Core
	Analytic Tools in Operations Management	Elective
University of North Carolina–Chapel Hill (Kenan-Flagler)	Operations	Core
	Service Operations Management	Elective
	Retail Operations	Elective
	Operations Management Models	Elective
University of Pennsylvania (Wharton)	Operations Management: Quality and Productivity	Core
University of Toronto (Rotman)	Operations Management	Core
	Operations Management Strategy	Elective
	Service Operations Management	Elective
University of Virginia (Darden)	Operations Management	Core
	General Management and Operations Consulting	Elective
	Emerging Topics in Technology and Operations Management	Elective
	Operations Strategy	Elective
Yale University	Operations Engine	Core
	Operations Analysis and Strategy	Elective
	Service Operations Management	Elective

Source: School web sites, accessed October 2009.

growing offshoring in both manufacturing and services. Several schools offer courses on operations consulting, which continues to be a mainstay service of the large consulting firms. Even those firms known more for strategy than for operations, such as McKinsey and the Boston Consulting Group, actually do a significant amount of operational consulting. The operations faculties at many business schools also offer courses in supply chain management and new product creation, but those courses are described in Chapters 8 and 12, respectively.

Note

1. With permission, this section draws heavily on the *strategy+business* article entitled "An Essential Step for Corporate Strategy" by Tim Laseter from the Winter 2009 issue.

For Further Reading

Garvin, G. A., "Competing on the Eight Dimensions of Quality," *Harvard Business Review*, November 1987.

Goldratt, Eliyahu M., and Jeff Cox, *The Goal* (Great Barrington, MA: North River Press, 1992).

Hayes, Robert, Gary Pisano, David Upton, and Steven Wheelwright, *Operations, Strategy & Technology: Pursuing the Competitive Edge* (Hoboken, NJ: John Wiley & Sons, 2005).

Laseter, Tim, and Eric Johnson, "Reframing Your Business Equation," *strategy+business* 55 (Summer 2009): 18–23.

McClain, John O., L. Joseph Thomas, and Joseph B. Mazzola, *Operations Management: Production of Goods and Services* (Englewood Cliffs, NJ: Prentice Hall, 1992).

Porter, Michael E., "What Is Strategy?" *Harvard Business Review*, November–December 1996, 62.

Stalk, George, Philip Evans, and Lawrence E. Shulman, "Competing on Capabilities: The New Rules of Corporate Strategy," *Harvard Business Review*, March–April 1992.

Downloadable Resources for this chapter available at www.wiley.com/go/portablemba5e

Scale Curve Exercise

7

Managing People

"I tell them what to do and they do it."

—Casey, MBA student, on answering the question "What does it take to manage people?"

Introduction

If only it were that easy! Strong managers understand either intuitively or through experience what Casey had yet to learn: that managing people is just plain hard and solutions to people issues are neither easy nor obvious. Managing is an interdependent activity, complicated today by the diversity of the workforce, the global nature of our companies, and the complexity of the work (i.e., products and services) offered by our modern corporations. Newly minted managers often equate managing well with managing the numbers. Seasoned managers quickly understand that no work gets done unless it is done by or through people. Knowledge of finance, accounting, marketing, or operations might get an MBA his or her first job, but the ability to work with, inspire, and manage others has a much stronger impact on that same individual's subsequent promotions.

Managing others is exactly what confronted Lauren, a new director of marketing at a major services company. Suddenly she had a variety of different kinds of people she needed to interact with: internal staff, employees who reported directly to her, clients outside the firm—a virtual web of relationships. James, an older and longtime employee, was the most challenging. He was the second choice for the job opening that had been given recently to Lauren. While his marketing expertise and knowledge of the customers were impressive and noteworthy, so were his many e-mails to Lauren's boss and to others in his informal network that were critical of her decisions and seemed to undermine her authority. She encouraged him and others, as members of her team, to coach and support one another, share knowledge, and pitch in when the going was tough. James was not interested in sharing his knowledge with anyone, and Lauren found herself having to answer the most detailed questions from him on numerous occasions. He never seemed to be able to see the bigger picture. Lauren found James to be moody, often depressed, definitely cynical, and less than fully committed to the production of world-class service that was the firm's and Lauren's main mission. Her worries that she might be neglecting other team members were soon borne out when she learned that her best performer, Jason, was quietly making inquiries to switch to another area; he wasn't feeling challenged enough by her. Jason was a young high-potential employee that Lauren had fought hard to put on her team. He was everything that James was not—upbeat, tech savvy, open to new ideas, and totally engaged. His team was the best in her department. Secretly Lauren wished she had a team of people like Jason. She disliked confrontation and seemed to work best with self-motivated individuals to whom she could give broad instructions and they'd know what to do. Every day brought something new, and she wondered whether she was really cut out to be a manager.

Lauren is not alone in her uncertainty. Management is not for everyone. It is a job that involves collaborating vigorously with others, balancing business activities (e.g., meeting goals and objectives) with relationship activities (e.g., listening, empathizing, resolving conflicts), and weighing equally the results with how one gets those results.

Any managerial action, especially dealing with people issues, requires three separate but interrelated abilities. First, a manager must learn how to clearly identify the problem or problems, which may be different from the presenting symptoms. The problem Lauren sees first is a string of critical e-mails. However, there might be other underlying issues as well, such as James's lack of technical sophistication, Lauren's relationship with him and her relationship with Jason, the behavior the company culture has reinforced over the years of James's tenure, or merely who James is. Second, a manager must analyze the root causes for the behavior observed, understanding fully that those problems have origins in both the person and the situation. So for Lauren, the problem could be arising because of her relationship with James and her failure to adequately supply him with the level of detail he requires. It could be that his behavior has been like this in the past and in fact may have been reinforced by the company. Or it might be that Lauren herself holds a belief that she should be respected as the boss—always. Finally, it could just be that James failed to win the cortical lottery on happiness.[1] Exploring each area and balancing all factors avoids making incorrect attributions.

A manager must generate and implement actions to address a problem. Unfortunately, there is not an action template that Lauren, or any other manager, can pull out of her desk drawer. It takes learning the lessons of experience to accumulate a tool kit of options, perspectives, and ideas that can inform action. While "it depends" is often a mantra associated with people issues, there are skills and competencies—a tool kit of abilities—that any manager can develop.

Any manager, like Lauren, must realize that to manage requires a diverse set of competencies and approaches. First, there is the ability to understand herself, to be aware of her own values and beliefs, her own preferences and style, her own way of putting together the world. The second is an understanding that what others see and value may be different. Not only must Lauren understand herself, but she must understand what makes Jason or James behave as they do, as well as understand the issues with and within the relationship between herself and James and why and how that is different from her relationship with Jason. The third level is that of the group or work team, collaborating to accomplish definite tasks. The final level is the organization as a whole: its culture, processes, and ways of doing things that impact their relationships and the small group in which they work.

The purpose of this chapter is to begin the process of developing a set of concepts for understanding why people behave the way they do in an organizational setting. Today's managers must develop a sophisticated and personalized understanding of individuals (including themselves); their relationships with others; the dynamics of people in groups; and larger enterprise-level factors of culture, systems, and processes.

This chapter starts at the individual level and moves through each of these levels: understanding individuals, then relationships, then groups; finally, it raises some current challenges posed at the organizational level.

Understanding Ourselves and Others

As a manager, how do you begin to grasp who someone is, what is important to that individual, and what will motivate the person to deliver extraordinary results or turn him or her off from working hard? Employees' resumes can tell you the string of accomplishments they have and their educational background and expertise, and more informal conversations can tell you something about their likes and dislikes or family status or where they like to take vacations. However, how they think, what they value and believe, and what assumptions they bring—these are all the seeds of what makes understanding people so fascinating and unique.

The first fascinating and unique person to understand is oneself. Because managing and leading start at home, clichéd as it may sound, knowing who you are and how others might be the same or different is the foundation for successfully managing others. So what ideas or theories are available that can help us understand ourselves and increase our self-awareness? The answer is many—many more than can be documented in this chapter. But here are some that often help managers understand something about what makes them and others tick.

Theories about Individual Preferences and Thinking Styles

Carl Jung identified three preference pairs that became the basis for a very well-known personality instrument crafted by Myers and Briggs.[2] These preferences can help us individually understand what is important to us and how we make decisions, but also can help us understand the variety of cognitive differences we must manage in our companies. There is a classic psychological image called "Young Lady/Old Lady." Some folks see an old lady; others see a young lady. We all have preferences for what we perceive and for how we put the world together. Being a strong manager of people means that you understand your preferences first and then try to see and understand the preferences of others.

According to Myers and Briggs, individuals have preferences for:

- How they get energy or channel their energy.
- How they gather information to make a decision.
- How they evaluate that information when making a decision.
- How they like the world to be organized.

The goal here is not to provide an exhaustive window into the intricacies of an instrument like the Myers-Briggs Type Indicator (MBTI), but to provide a sense of how different and challenging these preferences can be in our companies.

Drawing and Channeling Energy

There are two preferences here. One has either a preference for extroversion, which means one draws energy from interacting with others, or a preference for introversion, which means that one draws energy from oneself and/or a few other people. Managers with an extroversion preference like to call meetings, tend to interrupt people during their work, and are generally talkative and gregarious. They finish others' sentences, often talk out loud when no one is around, and can get impatient with silence. Managers with a preference for introversion, in contrast, can find meetings and other interactions to be tedious and draining. They don't call meetings, won't interrupt work in progress, and won't necessarily ask you how you are doing. When asked a question, it can take a manager with a preference for introversion a full eight seconds to respond, during which time extrovert colleagues are going nuts! Both are valid preferences, but together one can quickly see the potential conflicts and misunderstandings. Imagine your preference is extroversion and you have a boss with the opposite preference. You want to keep him or her apprised regularly in person, whereas the boss may prefer that you send progress reports via e-mail. Alternatively, imagine your preference is introversion and you have subordinates who desire more face-to-face time than you are comfortable providing.

Gathering Information

One can have a preference for gathering information through sensing or through intuition. A preference for sensing means that data are real only if it comes through the five senses. Real data are data that can be touched, felt, tasted, heard, or seen. Managers with a sensing preference would respond immediately to financial performance measures, market share indicators, consumer surveys, and so on, especially if they were visually displayed in charts, graphs, or PowerPoint presentations. Managers with a preference for intuition, however, see possibilities and hunches as real data. Data that comes through their sixth sense is considered as valid as, or in fact more valid and primary than, other kinds of information. Imagine a management meeting between individuals with these preferences:

N: I think there is a market here.

S: What is the size of the market? I need to see the data.

N: We don't need the analysis. I'm telling you there is a market here.

S: Well, I need to be convinced with the numbers.

N can be frustrated by S's lack of vision or ability to see potential, and S can be frustrated by N's unwillingness to convincingly present the opportunity. There is value in both preferences for gathering information, but a natural tension between them.

Evaluating Data

In evaluating data, again there are two preferences: thinking or feeling. Individuals who prefer thinking evaluate information in a logical and systematic manner *in their heads*, carefully weighing the pros and cons against a set of standards or objectives. Individuals who prefer feeling, in contrast, evaluate information *in their hearts* (emotionally) through a subjective set of personal values and beliefs. Both are very rational, but use a different set of criteria, and both have value in any management decision. The manager who prefers thinking would have a spreadsheet showing the cost savings associated with closing a plant, and the funds secured from leasing the property to another user or selling it off completely; the manager whose preference is feeling would be concerned about the people losing their jobs, and the fact that the plant has been in the town for over 50 years and has employed multiple generations.

Individuals with a preference for feeling often get a bad rap in business where logic and objectivity prevail. However, there is nothing touchy-feely about a feeling preference. It is merely a preference that invites managers to consider values and beliefs as well as the objective decision.

How the World Is Organized

Myers and Briggs introduced this dimension to augment the prior pairs first proposed by Jung. Individuals have a preference for either J, judging, or P, perceiving. Individuals with a preference for judging like the world organized and predictable; they prefer closure and completion. Individuals with a preference for perceiving are more spontaneous; they like to keep options open and see what develops. This is an interesting management preference dichotomy for managers. J managers make decisions easily with limited information. P managers want to keep the discussion going while they explore all possible alternatives. P managers are comfortable with ambiguity and uncertainty, while J managers are not, craving more routine and certainty.

Given the complexities of business and the unpredictability of the business environment currently, a preference for P has some advantages. It is easier for an individual with a preference for P to learn to adjust to a J environment than it is for a manager with a preference for J to adjust to be a P environment.

Instruments like MBTI can help managers understand their own preferences as well as the preferences of those around them. Although we are often more comfortable with those who share our preferences, we learn from those who are different. A good manager will find a way to harness the strengths of each individual's natural preferences. Employees will find ways to support their boss's preference, even if it is not their own.

Why People Behave as They Do

Preferences are one thing, but managers also must account for their own behavior and the behavior of those around them. Understanding why people behave as they do means having an internal model for thinking about the origins of the behavior observed. Why is James acting as he is? Why does Lauren respond positively to Jason's behavior? To understand behavior, a manager must interpret the origins of that behavior. Each individual holds a complex set of values, attitudes, beliefs, and expectations (VABEs) that are connected to our behavior.[3] A manager must understand his or her own VABEs as well as how those VABEs differ from others in his organization. A good manager might always keep these questions in mind:

- What assumptions am I making about the situation, about the individual, and about myself?
- What do I see happening?
- How does that make me feel? How is the other person feeling?

Studies of emotional quotient (EQ)[4] demonstrate that success in life and career is more intimately tied to our EQ than to our IQ. Being smart—that is, having significant intellectual horsepower—is one thing, but being able to understand ourselves, understand others, and respond appropriately is far more important.

The Problem of Motivation

Simply knowing oneself and understanding others, however, does not ensure that those being managed will be motivated to work in the interest of the organization. As our companies become increasingly complex with multiple stakeholders and goals, ensuring that each individual works toward the same organizational goals and objectives becomes a *problem of motivation*. In one sense motivation is not problematic. A basic psychological premise is that behavior that is rewarded is repeated. While that statement seems simple on the surface, it is far more complicated. The complication rests in the fact that it is not often clear what behavior is desired, what behavior is being rewarded, and what the individual considers rewarding. A lot of energy is expended in most organizations trying to understand how to motivate people. Two predominant sets of ideas, one based on satisfying needs, the other based on comparing to others, offer managers guidance.

At its core, needs theory suggests that every individual is motivated to satisfy his or her individual needs. What those needs are and how to classify them have many variations, however. Abraham Maslow identified a pyramid of five needs, from basic survival and safety through self-actualization. Clay Alderfer offered a fresh spin by identifying three primary needs as essential.[5] Is an individual motivated by a desire for adequate physical comfort (Existence); a need to affiliate with others and to have interpersonal relationships (Relatedness); or a need to be creative, to express ourselves through our work, and to be productive (Growth)? David McClelland identified needs for achievement (success), power (control), and affiliation (caring relationships).[6]

The motivational dilemma that managers face is that needs motivate people differently from situation to situation. Multiple needs may operate at the same time, complicating the understanding of what individuals actually need in the workplace. Individuals might be motivated as well by needs generated by where they are in their careers.[7] Finding out just what is motivating an employee's behavior can make a detective out of any manager. But it is an essential aspect of management.

More important, motivation is not occurring in a vacuum. Employees are constantly comparing their contributions to work and the results they achieve to the perceived contribution and results of others, and that comparison directly affects their own motivation.[8] We are motivated by fair treatment, which means that we desire our efforts to be rewarded the same as the efforts of others. We are demotivated when we see others getting more for the same contribution or for doing less.

The problem a manager faces is that each employee may have a different "other" that they are comparing themselves against. Managers must understand that organizational members are constantly performing mental calculations regarding what they are doing against what they are getting and how that matches up with others on their equity radar screen. The managerial task is to focus on perceived fairness and to communicate about the distribution of rewards as related to efforts.

Engaging with Others One-on-One

With a solid understanding of one's own strengths and weaknesses, as well as an understanding of why others behave as they do (and why we behave as we do), managers engage with others one-on-one. Their ability to build, maintain, and repair relationships up, down, and across is the basis of managerial work. Most managers find attending to business goals and objectives to be relatively easy and straightforward. In fact, our companies make it easy with the metrics in place to measure progress and goal achievement. However, attending to relationship activities is equally important and is often overlooked or underestimated in managing others. Relationships get into conflict when the balance of business and relationship is decidedly out of proportion.[9] So how does a manager build relationships and build trust, which is the core of any strong relationship?

Building Relationships and Trust

The relationships that managers develop with others in their organization take work. The principles of building effective working relationships really are not mysterious.[10] They are, above all, fundamental to achieving strong collaborations at work. They start, as mentioned earlier, with self-insight, patience (providing the time it takes to nurture relationships), and a conviction that issues can be resolved. This collaborative mindset means that a manager is willing and able to do what it takes to create positive and effective relationships with others. This does not mean that managers will not need to make tough calls, be decisive about dealing with personnel issues, and reprimand or fire underperformers. It does mean that how those actions are carried out is done with an eye toward maintaining a positive relationship stance and respect for each individual.

In addition, effective working relationships require managers to maintain personal flexibility and be willing to adjust and adapt approaches as needed, have strong negotiation skills to explore differences creatively and constructively, as well as have relationship repair skills at the ready. Because people are involved, misunderstandings and missteps happen; so knowing how to mend damaged relationships becomes a necessary skill.[11]

Relationships are complicated by the diversity of individuals who populate our companies. Therefore, managers need cross-cultural sensitivity, meaning the ability to decipher the values of others, as well as a sense of cultural humility, especially in global environments, to understand that one's own values are no better than someone else's. Finally, relationship management skills involve cross-cultural sensitivity and tact—that is, the ability to work with others diplomatically, fairly, and honestly.

Issues of Advocacy versus Inquiry

One set of relationship management skills that helps managers to work more effectively with others are the skills of inquiry over advocacy. Peter Senge has told us that managers spend too much time advocating and not enough time inquiring. In fact, an interesting article in the *Harvard Business Review* by Pfeffer and Sutton suggests that what we teach in MBA programs is smart talk.[12] MBA students learn how to analyze, discuss, and argue any case in the abstract, but not necessarily how to implement those decisions and deal with the consequences. One way to avoid this knowing-doing gap is to practice inquiry skills. Inquiry means asking questions, listening—really listening—to the responses of others, and learning about others' thoughts and points of view. In fact, strong collaborative leaders ask questions rather than answer them. Learning how to inquire and listen is an essential skill in relationship building and managing others.

Managing the Boss

One's relationship with the boss bears special attention. When we talk about managing people, we immediately focus on subordinates, those under us. However, the ability to manage one's relationship with the boss, managing up, is an even more critical managing people challenge. The formula is quite simple: understand the boss's world and preferences and react accordingly.[13] Sometimes we can become overly concerned with our own world, our issues, or our challenges and forget that our bosses are facing stresses and pressures, too. Knowing how to support and help them and how to provide them with information in the form they prefer can make for a smooth boss-subordinate relationship. One manager in a large manufacturing firm said that her boss just wanted the information in no more than a sentence or two. She learned this the hard way by watching him lose focus and herself lose power to make her point with long, intricate explanations. Some bosses like lots of contact and interaction, others less. Know your boss's preferences and adjust accordingly.

Collaborating with Others

Working with others collaboratively in groups or teams is an essential dimension of business and managerial life, and more so today than ever before. No manager works alone. He or she works with individuals, but increasingly with groups of others. Some of those groups are his or her work team; others are cross-functional project groups, and still others are loosely coupled folks from other parts of the company. In fact, the number one skill of global leaders is their ability to work collaboratively with others and create high-performing teams.[14] And building a team is one of the skills that first-time managers often fail to have.[15]

There are three fundamental notions of team development that are critical for managers to know: Teams pass through predictable stages, teams develop norms that influence members' behavior, and individuals fall into certain roles within those teams. Chapter 17, Managing Teams, more fully develops these basic team notions. However, as a start here are the basics any MBA needs to know.

Stages of Group Development

Most students of management can rattle off the easily remembered phases of group development: *forming, storming, norming,* and *performing.*[16] This idea has become entrenched in management literature and is an important starting point for understanding group process. Initially, when a group forms, members test out what kinds of behavior are acceptable and set up working rules (both formal and informal rules) as the members get to know each other's styles and expectations and learn to trust other group members. As the group becomes more comfortable with one another, conflict inevitably sets in as individuals become more aware of differing expectations, priorities, or commitments. Tensions rise, emotions are high, and listening falls aside. This so-called storming period lasts until group members can agree on ways to interact that ameliorate the conflicts. If the group is to function well, all members of the group, not just the stormy personalities, must agree to the norms.

It is hoped that a group can move through these first three stages quickly, and by paying deft attention to process concerns as well as task concerns, a well-facilitated group can get on with the performing aspect of group work. The group can begin to work positively together as a whole, dividing tasks and sharing ideas to do the work of the group.

Recently, Lencioni refreshed our understanding of successful group development by identifying the five dysfunctions of a team that prohibit a team from developing to its fullest potential: lack of trust, fear of conflict, little or no commitment, lack of accountability, and no focus on results.[17] Strong team development starts with a foundation of trust, which allows members to work through their differences successfully, which results in increased commitment to the team's efforts, which allows members to hold each other accountable for what they say they will do and accomplish, which turns into results that matter. Many times as managers we drive for results without considering the foundations of trust, conflict resolution, commitment, and accountability needed to ensure those results are the best possible.

Group Norms

Every group develops a set of norms or expectations for what is appropriate behavior in the group. Oftentimes, as managers, we forget that it is important to be explicit about what norms are important. Most often norms are formed implicitly and quickly and only recognized when they are broken. Some norms are core, meaning adherence to those norms is essential to group membership and the functioning of the team. Other norms can be peripheral, meaning that it is okay for some to adhere to those norms and others not. Norms influence behavior of group members, so it behooves managers to understand the norms that are developing with their teams or groups. Strong norms can be hard to change but powerful in their impact.

Group Roles

Every team or group needs all individuals working together, though each individual may do different activities that help the team achieve its goals. Meredith Belbin has suggested there are nine roles that teams need in order to be successful.[18] Exhibit 7.1 outlines each of these roles, its contribution to the team, and the problems this role might cause on a team. Each of these roles offers something unique to the team. While we tend to see many shapers, coordinators, and implementers on our management teams, there are three other roles that we need to see more of, those of plant (meaning idea generator), resource investigator, and teamworker (meaning internal facilitator). Working collaboratively is not just about getting the job done; it is also about how the team works together.

The Organizational Level

So far we've discussed the importance of self-awareness, building effective individual one-to-one relationships, and working collaboratively with others in a team as essential aspects of managing people. However, managers must also be aware of the impact of organizational factors on their ability to manage. Three factors included in this chapter are organizational culture, organizational alignment, and talent management. Although any given manager may not manage these directly, their impact creates the context in which managing occurs.

Exhibit 7.1   Belbin Team Roles

Team Role	Benefits of This Role to the Team	Difficulties of This Role in a Team
Plant	Idea generator. Creative, imaginative, unorthodox. Solves difficult problems.	Ignores details. Can overwhelm the group with one idea after another.
Resource Investigator	Outgoing, enthusiastic, communicative. Explores opportunities. Develops contacts.	Overly optimistic at times. Can lose interest once initial enthusiasm has passed.
Coordinator	Confident chairperson. Clarifies goals. Brings other people together to promote team discussions.	Can be seen as manipulative. Sometimes dumps work onto others.
Shaper	Strives to shape the tone and direction for the group. Challenging, dynamic, courageous.	Often initiates arguments for the sake of argument. Ignores people's feelings in pursuit of desired direction.
Monitor Evaluator	Serious-minded, strategic, and discerning. Sees all options. Judges accurately.	Can lack the drive to inspire and motivate others.
Teamworker	Internal facilitator. Cooperative, even-tempered, perceptive, and diplomatic. Listens, builds, reduces friction.	Can be seen as indecisive in crunch situations.
Implementer	Disciplined, reliable, conservative, efficient, practical. Turns ideas into actions.	Can be a bit inflexible. Slow to change. Often seen as resistant to new possibilities.
Completer Finisher	A detailed, on-time person. Conscientious, anxious. Searches out errors and omissions.	Inclined to worry a lot. Reluctant to delegate.
Specialist	Single-minded, self-starting, dedicated. Provides knowledge and skills in rare supply.	Contributes on only a limited front. Dwells on specialized personal interests.

Source: This chart has been adapted from the chart that appears on the Belbin web site (www. belbin.com/content/page/1950/Belbin_Team_Role_Desciptions.pdf).

Impact of Organizational Culture

Companies have organizational cultures that are powerful determinants of behavior. Organizational culture is defined simply as "the way we do things here." It is a set of values, beliefs, and expectations that help guide the behavior of people in organizations. Organizational culture is a strong and pervasive dynamic that can overtly or subtly affect what people in companies do, both for the good and for the not so good. Wal-Mart,

Southwest Airlines, and Starbucks are companies that have strong corporate cultures. So were Enron and WorldCom. While the culture at Southwest Airlines encourages going the extra mile for the customer, the culture at Enron encouraged going the extra mile for personal gain and some would say avarice. Culture directs people's behavior without management intervention, which is why it is such a powerful force. Sometimes those forces can have more impact than a manager's directive or decisions. Managers need to be aware of the organizational forces at work in their companies. Those cultural forces can be helpful and they can equally make change difficult. Not sure what your company culture is? Ask employees new to the company, and they will tell you what is important and what is not.

The values and beliefs that underpin the culture are embedded in the leader's philosophy. Certainly companies like Southwest Airlines, Wal-Mart, and Starbucks have or have had legendary leaders in Herb Kelleher, Sam Walton, and Howard Schultz who infused what they believed to be important into the fabric of each of their companies. Although the CEO is the leader whom we often associate with the values and beliefs of a company, *every manager in a leadership position* must be aware of his or her philosophy and how through everyday decisions a culture is created within that manager's work unit. What you stand for as a leader and what you wish to see become the foundation for your interactions with your team, your unit, or your company. Knowing what you value and what you stand for provides your "true north,"[19] the compass point that constantly and consistently ensures that your actions and interactions are headed where they need to go. This kind of authentic leadership comes from within as you find the principles to guide your managerial actions and create an authentic organization.

Impact of Organizational Alignment

Companies work best when their structure, strategy, systems, and processes are in alignment. Southwest Airlines has a strategy of low-cost air travel with fun service in the air; consequently it has a structure that is lean; systems and processes, such as one kind of plane, to minimize parts and turnaround times; and people processes that attend to the personal characteristics of friendliness that will deliver that fun experience in the air. When there is organizational alignment, profits follow. When there is no alignment, employees can be confused about what is required of them. Companies want internal collaboration but are organized in functional silos based on expertise, which minimizes the contact points for collaboration. Or companies want employees to work in teams but reward individual performance. Misalignments make the job of managing people much more complex. A manager must be aware of how the alignment or misalignment of structures and processes affects the behavior of subordinates as well as the manager's ability to create the environment needed. A manager needs to be cognizant of how decisions made will affect or be affected by what is already in place.

Challenges of Managing Talent

Human resources management (HRM) is the name given to managing the value chain of human capital, specifically managing (1) how individuals are brought into the company (or exit it), (2) how employees are developed, (3) how employees are rewarded and recognized, as well as (4) the total organizational climate for how people are treated. While the human resources department in a company may take the lead role in orchestrating this system, it is also a process that every manager contributes to and is responsible for.

Jim Collins admonishes managers to put people first, then process.[20] Putting people in the right jobs that accentuate their skills and abilities, and having them doing what they do best, is a natural motivator and part of a manager's responsibility. The issues that complicate a manager's role in developing talent are discussed next.

Psychological Contracts Are Changing

When individuals join companies, they form a *psychological contract*, an implicit understanding of the "give and get" that will occur between the company and employee. The company provides challenging work, for example, at competitive wages with regular promotions, and the individual expects in return to be treated well and be rewarded for good performance and loyalty to the company. Such a psychological contract has long been the foundation of businesses over the past half century. Employees who excelled at their jobs could expect upward promotion. Those who were average could expect continued employment with more gradual increases in pay, but still increases. Nonmanagement employees could expect few layoffs and a job for life through adequate performance.

No longer does the psychological contract hold, especially since the financial crisis of 2009. No employee is without risk these days. In an attempt to make organizations more customer/market focused as well as flexible and responsive, many organizations have eliminated excess layers of management in the hope that decisions can be made more quickly with better information and fewer obstacles along the way. Unfortunately, in an attempt to create lean organizations, people are getting let go not because they are bad performers, but because the company's costs are too high, employees being one of those substantial costs. "Doing more with less" is a pervasive theme as managers are asked to increase work output with fewer resources, especially people resources, than ever before. While some companies like General Electric treat their top employees as assets, most companies see their personnel as expendable resources.

Whereas in the past a company may have been able to count on loyalty, hard work, and lifelong employees almost independent of its actions and decisions, that allegiance is no longer a contract that employees want. Today's employees want flexibility, freedom, and a work/life balance that does not necessarily include giving one's all to the company. This does not mean that those managed will not work hard or be loyal. It does mean that managers need to really appreciate and acknowledge the very different contracts that individuals may have created around their view of work.

Workforce Demographics Are Changing

One of the most talked-about issues of the 1990s was *diversity*, an issue still salient almost 20 years later. Leading up to the 1990s, diversity discussions explored a traditionally white male workforce and more specifically the need to increase the presence of nonwhite males (e.g., women, people of color) in the workforce, especially in the managerial ranks. Although great strides have been made (for example, witness the election in 2008 of the first black president of the United States), there is still much diversity work to be done as our definition of diversity shifts to discussions of difference. Today's workforce is different from past workforces, and those differences consequently make a difference. Age, gender, race, sexual orientation, physical abilities, cultural heritage, and ethnicity are just some of the differences that form a manager's world.

Old versus young is one issue that repeats itself in both MBA and executive education classrooms. As the baby boomers begin to leave the workforce (or don't because they are forced to work longer than they expected), our companies will face challenges of engaging these individuals while making room for new talent. Younger managers will need to learn how to respect and value older workers who may not have up-to-date technological sophistication, but who have years of wisdom and experience. Older workers will need to learn to help younger managers learn to appreciate what they have to offer as well as be open to new ways of conducting the work of the company. Every worker and manager, both young and old, will need to figure out new ways of *interacting and learning together*.

Traditionally, work has been organized along the lines that suited the one-wage-earner (typically male) family. With the rise of different lifestyles, many companies have been forced to rethink the very definitions of work, a typical workday, and the people who do that job. For example, with two-career couples increasingly the norm, companies have had to rethink their policies about transferring fast-track employees from assignment to assignment. International postings become more difficult if the trailing spouse can't find employment or the children are not mobile because of school and community involvement. Many companies have opened or begun to sponsor day-care and elder-care centers. Some companies are even offering health and other benefits to same-sex partners. There has been a dramatic increase in the use of technology to encourage telecommuting. Managers find themselves having to account for work that they cannot see, because the worker is at home in the same city or even in a very different part of the world. All of these issues represent an incredible contextual change for managers, as managers need to manage a different set of employees with very different backgrounds, needs, and desires.

One particular concern remains, however. Despite all the progress our companies have made, we are not seeing a proportionate number of women CEOs. As of March 2009, there were only 12 Fortune 500 companies with a female CEO. In the Fortune 501–1,000, there were only 10 more. Yet, according to statistics assembled by Catalyst in 2009,[21] just over 46 percent of the U.S. workforce is female and just over 50 percent of these women are in managerial, professional, or related occupations. Is there still a *glass ceiling* that seems to prevent women from reaching the very top managerial levels? This is a question that tomorrow's managers will need to embrace.

Growing without Promoting

Finding good talent is one issue, but ensuring that talent in place is developing strongly is much more critical. Fewer middle-management positions means that a continual stream of promotions is no longer a reasonable developmental tool. Dual-career ladders, where an employee is promoted based on technical expertise but not necessarily given managerial authority, have allowed some individuals to achieve salary and level success without becoming managers. However, finding ways to give people the skills they need for the future is not easy. Many jobs we hire for today did not exist 20 or even 10 years ago, so how can employees be groomed for jobs not yet on the radar screen? The key is not to focus on growing talent for particular jobs per se, but finding ways to keep work interesting and demanding while affording employees a chance to expand their transportable skill set.

To meet the challenges that we have discussed, some companies like Motorola create their own "universities," such that education becomes a strategic tool to manage the growth and development of employees. Motorola claims that for every dollar it spends on education, it receives a $30 return. For example, rather than laying off an employee,

Motorola offers retraining. The resulting loyalty far outweighs the cost of the training, and the company retains an employee who is oriented, is socialized, and knows the Motorola culture. When markets change, the company uses the ability of its *employees to learn new skills* as a platform for entering new markets.

Smaller companies, such as the Johnsonville Sausage Company in Wisconsin, have found ways to leverage learning without a corporate university infrastructure. At Johnsonville, employees are rewarded for learning, and they receive raises when they learn new skills such as budgeting or production planning, take on new learning challenges such as leading their work team, or even attend a course in basic economics. The atmosphere is one of constant improvement, both in the sausages that they make and in the people who make them. It has been said that learning is the only sustainable competitive advantage. Part of managing is helping others learn.

Evaluating Performance Can't Be One Size Fits All

Performance appraisal has also changed in the new business environment. A number of companies are moving from the traditional boss-subordinate models of performance appraisal to *360-degree feedback*, which is a process whereby employees receive input from a sample of the people with whom they work directly and whom they affect in the course of executing their job responsibilities. Customer satisfaction data, employees in other departments, peers, teammates, and bosses all provide input into a comprehensive assessment of performance. With the new emphasis on competitiveness, many companies have tried to turn their performance appraisal processes into more effective tools for performance improvement.

Also, by distinguishing between kinds of rewards, managers can use the compensation system to encourage corporate or subunit goals like teamwork and customer satisfaction. All employees—not just a few top executives with large stock option packages—become engaged in the success of the organization.

In addition to meeting the demands of a changing workforce, more companies are moving to *flexible benefits* or *cafeteria benefits*. Under these arrangements, employees can design their own package of benefits to meet their individual needs. For example, one employee may well need a benefits package with child care and medical care paid for in pretax dollars, whereas another employee may prefer more catastrophic coverage or life insurance. The basic idea behind strategic pay is to design a compensation system that best meets both the employees' and the company's needs for success.

Putting the Pieces Together

Professors James Heskett and Leonard Schlesinger have studied so-called high-performance or high-capability organizations for a number of years.[22] Leading such high-performance organizations as Wal-Mart, Taco Bell, Southwest Airlines, and ServiceMaster means that the senior managers, including the CEO, are intimately involved in the human resources management process. High-performance cultures are usually based on values and vision that are shared throughout all levels of the organization. Since the values are important in their own right, employees will go to great lengths to realize those values, especially when they are given the latitude and permission to do what it takes to get the job done. High-performance leaders are involved in the entry and exit decisions because they believe that these are some of the most crucial decisions that the organization makes. In these strong-culture companies, people almost self-select into and out of the organization. The growth and development of people are based in part on instilling a sense of pride in employees and pride in what they do—without the arrogance that usually accompanies it. To instill this pride, executives must constantly articulate, communicate, and embody the corporate values while setting the performance bar at a very high level.

In all of these high-performance workplaces, we find the idea that employees are not there merely to put in time and do a job. Rather, work is engaging to them; their teams and tasks matter because the organization plays an important role in their lives. Work has the connotation of joy and imagination and fun rather than drudgery and something to be sharply distinguished from play. The business challenges of the next century will involve more attention to the processes of innovation, creativity, and fun, while continuing to find creative ways to do the administrative tasks that are a vital part of a firm's success.

Some Practical Principles

Although there is no concise formula or model for managing people, there are eight principles from which to build:

1. *Leadership starts at home.* Self-awareness—knowing who you are and what you value—creates a strong foundation for managerial success. Your ability to learn is just as important as your ability to lead.[23] Find ways to learn, be open to the feedback from others, and create a work environment that fosters everyone's best. Managing and leading are collaborative activities that require learning from others.

2. *Communication with employees is central to the effective manager's job.* In the absence of information, people will make up their own information. What a manager takes for granted may be new information to someone underneath. And because each individual is different, the style of that communication needs to be different. Managing is a time-intensive activity: one person at a time, one interaction at a time, all over time.

3. *Effective managers know their personal managerial values and philosophy.* What works to motivate employees also works to motivate managers. Many successful organizations simply start with some theory Y assumptions like "People really can be great and want to win." They don't differentiate between levels of employees in terms of their motivations. They drive a sense of ownership and egalitarianism about the company throughout the organization with the result that the company can become a means to meeting the needs of all employees in a fair and evenhanded manner.

4. *Effective managers foster an environment that brings out the best in others.* Seasoned managers know that you cannot make someone change or do something. However, you can change the context to increase the probability that you will get the behavior that you want. Think of ways to bring out the best, not the worst, in others.

5. *Effective managers are willing to engage in difficult conversations about difference.* They foster an environment where everyone can fulfill their potential and seek to address issues such as gender, race, sexual orientation, ethnicity, age, and language. At Inland Steel, a number of African-American employees were frustrated and thinking of leaving the firm. They worked together and found someone to be a

champion of starting a conversation about diversity. As a result, the company was singled out for a national award for its attention to creating a supportive and diverse workplace.

6. *Effective managers understand how groups and teams work, and they focus on creating a culture of performance through teamwork and collaboration.* With most of a company's work being done in teams, managers need to be aware of team dynamics and become more facilitators of team process than team leaders.

7. *Effective managers are change leaders.* Today, managers are not expected to administer—to follow bureaucratic and systematic processes that mean business as usual. Managers are expected to lead change—to propose ways to make the organization more competitive and more effective and then to marshal the resources to bring about that change.

8. *Effective managers take time out to learn and reflect on the job.* Performance and learning are both needed for success. Unfortunately, managers can spend most of their time performing and requiring performance from others when what is really needed is some time spent reflecting and learning.

One Final Word

Managing people is complex, and you will develop your own methods and skills. There is a story about a lion keeper in the Dublin zoo named Mr. Flood who was quite adept at breeding lions in captivity (which is difficult).[24] When asked his secret, Mr. Flood replied, "Understanding lions." When asked how he did that, he responded, "Every lion is different." So it is with managing people. In striving to develop a deep understanding of human nature and what makes people tick, we need not lose sight of the individual uniqueness that sets each of us apart. For a manager, that uniqueness is an asset and managing those assets a requirement. The goal of this chapter is to provoke some insights for your future managerial effectiveness.

MBA Concepts in Action

Managing people may be one of the most important skills that get side-tracked throughout our careers. We never seem to have enough time to pay attention to all the details at work; yet how we, and those we work with, behave has a huge impact on our own and our organization's success. Take, for example, Jan Gronski and Ivo Raznjevic, who drew extensively on their ability to manage people to build a new business for Cisco Systems in China.

Cisco Switches in China: The Year of the Manager

With buy-in from the top of Cisco Systems' San Jose–based executive team, Jan Gronski, managing director of the Cisco China Research and Development Center (CRDC), and Ivo Raznjevic, engineering director, set out to establish a new R&D organization in Shanghai, China. The initial development plan was to focus on technologies and products targeting service providers and consumer networking sectors. Cisco had committed to invest U.S. $32 million in the center. The process of building the business included securing an appropriate building, assembling a workforce, seeking appropriate projects, developing managers, building teams, evaluating performance, protecting intellectual property, and continuing to grow. Not intending it to be an overseas R&D center for internal outsourcing of Cisco projects, the CRDC leadership team had pushed for innovation and independence from corporate headquarters.

The resource pool for engineering talent in China was immense, and so was the competition for engineers. Recruiting, interviewing, and evaluating candidates was a huge task that the CRDC team took seriously. They advertised for engineers domestically—targeting groups of people within the industry and those at universities. The initial search generated over 4,000 resumes. As a first step in identifying the best candidates, applicants were invited to take a multiple-choice test. The 200 top-performing candidates were then invited to face-to-face interviews to check their English language skills, among other things. "We wanted candidates to be able to explain engineering notions in English," said Jan Gronski.

Hiring local senior engineers with managerial potential for the CRDC, however, was more difficult than hiring engineers with technical expertise. Although there were highly skilled and capable managers who were Chinese, their managerial approach was authoritative, whereas Cisco was a collaborative environment. "We interviewed some of them, but we knew right away that they wouldn't pass on the culture that we wanted," Raznjevic said.

Problems started at 7:00 A.M. and ended at 9:00 P.M. every day, seven days a week. The Chinese tendency to think hierarchically affected the manner in which employees worked and interacted with their bosses. In China, specific work hours were defined, and when the clock struck quitting time, most engineers felt compelled to promptly leave. "In China, my boss is waiting for me to leave," Jerry Chen said, explaining the difference. "In San Jose, you work to get things done, so I need to stay until I finish regardless of the boss." And unlike the United States, where people would jump at an opportunity to spend some time with a boss three or four positions above them, CRDC employees felt uncomfortable being around Ivo Raznjevic and the rest of the senior management team. When Raznjevic first tried to sit with employees in the cafeteria, they disappeared! On another occasion, Raznjevic got an e-mail from an engineer who was unhappy. Raznjevic sent one back: "Why don't you come to my office?" The dissatisfied employee was surprised and answered, "Well, you have more important things to do."

Attempting to bridge those differences, CRDC executives came up with various ways of interacting with employees in a non-work-related manner. Jan Gronski began organizing breakfasts with several employees each day. As the workforce size increased, he moved to lunches and then birthday lunches. Raznjevic felt less comfortable with the dining experience and chose sports as a way to engage employees. On each floor of the CHJ building was a common recreational area where Raznjevic started playing ping-pong:

> At first they would be playing and see me coming along and stop. "You go ahead and play—we can play later." "No, I can wait," I'd say. And of course I would lose all the time! But ping-pong is extremely popular, and they still don't really trust you, but it only took about nine months to reach a comfort level.

The CRDC group started weekly meetings with its engineers that involved design review discussions. Those sessions were eventually nicknamed the Kindergarten Class. Part of its purpose was to cultivate leaders by increasing their decision-making responsibilities. That approach took some time. For example, one of the senior engineers would say little in the meeting and then approach his manager afterward to say, "This is wrong. It will not work, and this is what we should be doing." And although the engineer was right, he would not say it in the meeting. Raznjevic believed that behavior could be changed if Chinese employees were put in a position to make decisions about engineering and the employees reporting to them. This way they would develop as managers and learn to express stronger opinions.

Within a year, the organization had top-notch local engineers who built relationships with U.S. engineers and provided early delivery on the CRDC's first few projects. By the fall of 2007, $100 million had been received, and the CRDC team was proud of its success; but certain personal issues were a constant reminder of how important people skills were to the success of the organization. For example, the Chinese concept of losing face in the eyes of others was something the non-Chinese managers thought they knew about, but a particular e-mail incident suggested to Raznjevic that intellectual understanding went only so far. One of the senior CRDC engineers sent out an e-mail with an idea, a practice that Raznjevic encouraged, and immediately one of the United Kingdom–based managers replied, copying everyone, and said, "You are completely incorrect and false in this area." Within minutes of the e-mail coming out there was an audible silence that Raznjevic could detect from his office. He watched as people looked around the cubicles trying to understand why this had happened. All the junior engineers who worked with the CRDC engineer felt he had lost face.

Another problem arose over the once timid and deferential Jasmine Zhou, who had developed into a strong test manager with advancement potential. They were proud of her development and she was being considered for a lateral move to a managerial position on the development side—a potential move that was arousing controversy. First, there was a natural rivalry between the test and development side of research and development. Although both developers and testers generally had similar educational backgrounds and were highly skilled and trained, there was tension between them. There was a perception in China that testers were not as qualified as developers. Developers often thought testers were failed developers, while testers, who spent a lot of time ensuring that the product worked, frequently felt their quality assurance was crucial but unappreciated.

Zhou, who held a master's degree in computer science and had started her career as a developer for Nortel Canada in southern China, quickly had transferred to another department as a tester. She had worked on wireless technology at Nortel for a year and a half before joining Cisco as a test engineer in January 2005. Moving her from testing to development management would likely pose a potential problem. The situation was further complicated by a development engineer who wanted—and felt he deserved—the position. Raznjevic and his team selected Zhou, and although they exercised great tact when informing the other engineer, he quit.

And then there was Ehud Oentung. He was an American of Chinese origin raised in Indonesia, who had earned his electrical engineering degree at the University of Maryland and had worked for Verizon, Bell Atlantic, and Cisco in Herndon, Virginia. From there, he transferred to the CRDC and became a software manager on the development side. During the most recent performance review cycle, Oentung had one engineer who ranked the lowest, which meant that this individual would not get a bonus. Cisco's ranking system was uncomfortable for Oentung. "Even if you are the bottom it doesn't mean you haven't been doing good work," he said. "Every six months we have to pick someone to do better." Raznjevic recalled Oentung saying, "I didn't want to do it." Raznjevic coached Oentung to deliver his employee a difficult message.

Managing People in MBA Curricula

Courses focusing on managing people reside in the academic discipline of Organizational Behavior (OB), which is broadly concerned with how people and organizations behave. At the micro level, OB focuses on issues of understanding individuals, on the opportunities for and challenges of building effective relationships, and on the theories and concepts behind interacting within groups and teams. At a macro level, OB is concerned with how companies are structured, as well as the effects of different types of structures on individuals, structures, and systems, especially reward systems and human resources systems, issues of organizational culture, and the challenges of individual and organizational change.

All MBA programs have students take at least one required course in Organizational Behavior, the goal of which is to survey the micro and macro landscape of managing and leading. For additional bench strength, students turn to elective courses, such as those highlighted in Exhibit 7.2,[25] which provide students with more depth and focus in a particular area of interest.

MBA Careers in General Management

When most people think of managing people as a career, they think of general managers. The MBA degree, at one time in history, was synonymous with general management. Employers recruited at business schools to find the future leaders of their organizations and placed the recruits in general management roles, running small divisions of corporate conglomerates. The environment has changed, though. In the past 20 years many large companies have centralized management of smaller divisions so that the entry-level general manager position is less common. "Functional excellence" is the mantra of the MBA now, with many programs specializing in functions and even industries.

However, some companies have created a fast track to general management. These leadership or management development programs take many forms and names. A common format is a rotation program, in which the trainee rotates through either different functions in the company or different divisions of the company, in order to get broad exposure and experience. Employees are then placed within the company after the rotations based on their interests and on employer needs.

The upside to these development programs for the employee is broad visibility and exposure and a senior management view of the business. The downside is the inability to own something during the rotation period. Because the rotations are generally short (six months or less), the employee has little time to accomplish much. With four rotations, this purgatory can extend one's MBA-type training another two years. To get value from the time invested, the employee needs to commit to the company for a few years beyond the end of the training period.

For the prospective employee, finding a good fit in a rotation program is important. In general, a successful rotation program has:

- Senior management support.
- Graduates of the program currently in senior management.
- A formal mentoring program to help the employee place upon completion of the program.

Exhibit 7.2 Managing People

Business School	Course Required	Sample of Electives
University of Michigan (Ross)	Human Behavior and Organization	Interpersonal Dynamics in Management Leading and Leveraging Difference Managing Professional Relationships Leadership Development: Self-Awareness, Skills, and Strategies
Northwestern University (Kellogg)	Leadership in Organizations	Managing People for Competitive Advantage Managing with Professionals Behavioral Issues in Strategy Implementation Gender in Management Managing Workforce Diversity
Harvard Business School	Leadership and Organizational Behavior	Authentic Leadership Development Leading Professional Service Firms Managing Human Capital
University of California–Berkeley (Haas)	Leading People	Human Resource Management Power and Politics in Organizations Global Management Skills
Stanford Graduate School of Business	Organizational Behavior	Working with Diversity Leadership Perspectives Interpersonal Dynamics The Paths to Power Lives of Consequence Leading Diverse Organizations Acting with Power
University of Virginia (Darden)	Leading Organizations	Leadership, Values, and Ethics Tactical Leadership Strategic Leadership Crisis Leadership Leadership and Diversity through Literature Managerial Psychology

Recruiters from leadership development programs generally seek candidates with more experience than the average MBA student, typically five to seven years. Relevant industry experience is many times a prerequisite. The primary skill sought is leadership—both people leadership and idea leadership. A candidate's resume should demonstrate a consistent track record of leadership positions.

Companies with highly sought programs include PepsiCo, McGraw-Hill, DuPont, United Technologies Corporation, Danaher, Shell, Ford, Emerson, and Eaton. Many of these companies recruit exclusively at top schools, particularly those whose students have the requisite experience and a stated interest in general management.

Notes

1. Jonathan Haidt, *The Happiness Hypothesis* (New York: Basic Books, 2006).
2. There are many books available on MBTI. Start with the MBTI web site (www.myersbriggs.org/) or do an Internet search using MBTI as a keyword.
3. This terminology was pioneered by a Darden colleague, Jim Clawson. See J. Clawson, *Level 3 Leadership: Getting Below the Surface* (Upper Saddle River, NJ: Prentice Hall, 2008).
4. Daniel Goleman, *Emotional Intelligence: Why It Can Matter More Than IQ* (New York: Bantam, 1995).
5. For a discussion of needs theory, see Richard Steers and Lyman Porter, *Motivation and Work Behavior*, 2nd ed. (New York: McGraw-Hill, 1979).
6. David McClelland, *Human Motivation* (New York: Cambridge University Press, 1988).
7. See L. A. Isabella, "The Effect of Career Stage on the Interpretation of Key Organizational Events," *Journal of Organizational Behavior* (1988).
8. Equity is identified as the "ratio of an individual's inputs (such as level of effort on the job) to outcomes (such as pay) as compared with a similar ratio for a relevant 'other.'"
9. See L. A. Isabella, "Managing an Alliance Is Nothing Like Business as Usual," *Organizational Dynamics* (2002).
10. See E. Schein, "Improving Face to Face Relationships," *Sloan Management Review* 22, no. 2 (Winter 1981): 43–52.
11. For more discussion on having difficult conversations, consult *Difficult Conversations: How to Discuss What Matters Most*, by Douglas Stone, Bruce Patton, and Sheila Heen (New York: Penguin, 1999).
12. See J. Pfeffer and R. Sutton, "The Smart Talk Trap," *Harvard Business Review* 77, no. 3 (May–June 1999): 134–142, 211.
13. This classic article was first published in 1980 by J. Gabarro and J. Kotter, "Managing Your Boss," *Harvard Business Review* (www.slmgtgroup.com/protected/Archives/Harvard%20Leadership%20Articles/Managing%20Your%20Boss.pdf).
14. See M. McCall, *High Flyers: Developing the Next Generation of Leaders* (Boston: Harvard Business School Press, 1998).
15. See L. Hill, *Becoming a Manager: How New Managers Master the Challenges of Leadership*, 2nd ed. (Boston: Harvard Business School Press, 2003).
16. This idea is attributed to Bruce Tuckman.
17. See P. Lencioni, *The Five Dysfunctions of a Team: A Leadership Fable* (San Francisco: Jossey-Bass, 2002).
18. For a more in-depth discussion of Belbin's nine team roles, see www.belbin.com/.
19. See B. George, *True North: Discover Your Authentic Leadership* (San Francisco: Jossey-Bass, 2007).

20. See J. Collins, *Good to Great: Why Some Companies Make the Leap . . . and Others Don't* (New York: HarperCollins, 2001).

21. www.womenonbusiness.com/new-us-women-in-business-statistics-released-by-catalyst/.

22. This paragraph is based on James L. Heskett and Leonard A. Schlesinger, "Leading the High-Capability Organization: Challenges for the Twenty-First Century," *Human Resource Management* 36, no. 1 (Spring 1997): 105–113.

23. Drawn from the dimensions of Prospector, a 360-degree leadership instrument from the Center for Creative Leadership (www.ccl.org/leadership/pdf/assessments/prospector.pdf).

24. John Wisdom, *Philosophy and Psychoanalysis* (Berkeley: University of California Press, 1969).

25. Elective courses focusing on teams and groups are included in the chapter on Managing Teams.

Downloadable Resources for this chapter available at www.wiley.com/go/portablemba5e

Practical Principles of Managing People

8

Supply Chain Management

Supply chain management (SCM) has grown in scope and importance over the past 30 years. The term, coined by global consulting firm Booz & Company, first appeared in print in a 1982 article by Arnold Kransdorff in the *Financial Times*. The term originally referred to the narrow goal of "tearing down the functional silos that separated production, marketing, distribution, sales, and finance to generate a step-function reduction in inventory and a simultaneous improvement in customer service" within a single company. As described in a retrospective 2003 *strategy+business* article "When Will Supply Chain Management Grow Up?" coauthored by Keith Oliver, the originator of the concept of supply chain management, the term now encompasses the extended enterprise spanning a company's in-house operations and an increasingly global supply base. While the original premise of SCM sought to avoid suboptimal tactical decisions within a company, today SCM executives seek to improve the strategic deployment of *capabilities* to manage the inherent conflicts within and among companies.

Companies now have executives managing this broad responsibility ranging from procurement to logistics to customer service. For example, IBM formed an Integrated Supply Chain business unit in 2003. By integrating the separate supply chains supporting its 13 business units, the new group achieved the lowest inventory in 30 years while reducing cycle times and increasing sales productivity by 25 percent. Within two years the group achieved $6 billion in cost reduction and freed up $580 million in cash from the balance sheet.

Given the evolving and increasingly wide scope, the key principles embodied by supply chain management range from the tactical to the truly strategic. At the most fundamental level, tracing back to the original focus of the concept, SCM examines the root causes for holding inventory to ensure appropriate deployment of the firm's resources. Capturing the recent, broader definition, SCM addresses the strategic relationships companies have with their suppliers.

The broad, global scope of supply chain management offers the MBA student a career path in either industry or consulting with deep exposure to both the internal and external workings of a company and a unique opportunity to have a real impact on firm performance. This chapter discusses the key principles covered in a typical course or course module focused on supply chain management covering both the tactical and strategic issues of the topic.

Career Profile

1974 MBA

H. J. Markley

EVP Worldwide Parts Services, Global Supply Management and Logistics, Enterprise Information Technology, and Corporate Communications

Deere & Company

Education:

BA, Economics, College of Wooster

MBA, Tuck School of Business at Dartmouth College

In his role as Executive Vice President, a position he has held since September 2007, Markley is responsible for four enterprise-wide global functions: parts, supply management and logistics, information technology, and communications.

Markley joined Deere & Company in 1974 as a factory auditor. Since then he has held a number of management positions at various John Deere facilities. In 1996, Markley was appointed Senior Vice President, Manufacturing, for the Worldwide Construction Equipment Division. He was named Senior VP, Worldwide Human Resources, in February 2000. In August 2001 Markley was named President, Agricultural Division—North America, Australia, Asia, and Global Tractor and Implement Sourcing. In January 2006, Markley was named President, Agricultural Division—Europe, Africa, South America, and Global Harvesting Equipment Sourcing.

Source: Deere & Company.

Inventory: Root Causes

Principle 1: Reducing inventory levels starts with understanding the root causes for holding the inventory.

In accounting and finance, inventory is often described as raw materials, work in process, or finished goods. That categorization tells *what* is in inventory, but not *why*. For operational decisions about how much inventory to hold or how to reduce the amount of inventory, it is more useful to classify inventory by the reasons for which it is held. *Cycle stock* is inventory held to take advantage of batch economies. Larger order sizes reduce setup costs but increase the average inventory between orders. *Safety stock* is inventory held in case of a disruption in supply or an unanticipated surge in demand. It is intended to cover variability in supply or demand without stock-outs or service disruptions. *Pipeline stock* includes inventory in transit between locations. A growing proportion of total inventory among companies operating global supply chains, pipeline stock depends on the transit time between the two locations. *Leveling stock* occurs when companies decide to maintain level production despite seasonal demand. For example, though most textbooks are sold at the beginning of the school year, a printer may choose to produce the books throughout the year to avoid the cost of hiring and firing staff and holding excess capacity for the peak season. Finally, firms may hold *speculative stock* of raw materials or finished goods in anticipation of changes in availability or prices.

All inventory incurs costs. The costs to firms of holding inventory include warehousing and insurance costs as well as the financial opportunity cost of capital tied up in inventory. In addition, for firms with global operations, the cost and risk of holding inventory may depend on where the inventory is held. For example, inventory held in Brazil faces greater risk of currency fluctuation than stock held in Canada. However, if the firm experiences a shortfall, it faces the cost of a shortage or service problem as well as the setup costs or ordering costs for resupply. In addition, inventory enables a firm to fill customer orders faster than the actual production lead time.

Companies increasingly strive to reduce inventory because it masks production problems in addition to its measurable financial cost. A useful analogy is to think of inventory as the water in a river and process problems as rocks. As the water level is lowered, rocks appear that can impede the flow if not removed through continuous improvement efforts. Once the problem rocks are removed, the water runs more freely, and the company can again lower the water level to expose more rocks. Repeating the cycle over time, the river flows freely with a much lower level of water—that is, much less inventory. The message delivered by this analogy is that the cycle of improving the process and reducing inventory must be *repeated* for continuous improvement and the full benefit of skillful inventory management.

Inventory: More versus Less

Principle 2: Inventory decisions hinge on the tradeoff between the cost of holding more inventory and the cost of holding less.

The management of inventory trade-offs is often thought of in terms of order quantities, but actually also involves a much richer array of decisions, as shown in Exhibit 8.1. For example, the choice of how much cycle stock to hold depends on the trade-off between holding costs and setup or ordering costs. Larger batches require more inventory to be held, but may enable the firm to take advantage of bulk pricing in purchasing and to reduce setup costs by producing the product less often. Shorter setup times enable a firm to produce smaller lots more economically and thus hold less inventory. Similarly, a colocated supplier can deliver economically in small batch sizes. Traditionally companies sought to find the optimal order quantity given the batch-related costs for setups or transportation. Increasingly companies seek to lower setup time and travel distances to enable smaller batch sizes, which reduce waste, shorten lead time, and provide faster identification of quality problems.

Decisions for one type of inventory can also affect other types. As indicated earlier, colocated suppliers can lower ordering costs and thereby reduce cycle stock. Shorter delivery times also reduce pipeline stock directly and safety stock indirectly. Safety stock protects for uncertainty over the lead time from order to delivery of the goods. Faster delivery times leave the company exposed to uncertain demand for a shorter period of time and accordingly reduce the need for safety stock. The need for safety stock can be reduced by improving forecasts so that production can track demand better. Many levers can be pulled to reduce the required investment in inventory.

Exhibit 8.1   Inventory Types

Reasons for Inventory	Trade-Offs	Decisions
Pipeline (distance)	Cost of inventory versus Cost of reducing lead times	Manage lead times Set mode of transit Invest in materials-handling equipment Backward-integrate Improve scheduling and loading practices
Cycle (lot size)	Setup cost versus Holding cost	Determine lot size Define warehouse procedures Reduce setup time Invest in technology Affect demand
Safety (operational uncertainty)	Cost of inventory versus Cost of downtime or Cost of shortfall	Minimize variability Improve quality Change customer service requirements Reduce forecast errors Manage lead time
Leveling (seasonality)	Holding cost versus Cost of capacity and overtime	Change amount of inventory Add counter-season products Use subcontractors Smooth out changes in demand
Speculative (macroeconomic uncertainty)	Holding cost versus Price fluctuations, shortages	Change vendors Hedge financially Hedge operationally

Source: Adapted from James Freeland, "Managing Inventories," Darden Graduate Business School Case UVA-OM-0623, 1987.

Forecasts

Principle 3: Forecasts are always wrong, but some more than others.

Companies often turn to improved forecasting to reduce the need for inventory but fail to appreciate the three rules of forecasting. The first and most important rule of forecasting is that the only thing we know for certain about the future is that we cannot predict it: Forecasts are always wrong. Given the certainty of this, one of the most important things to know about a forecast is how far from reality our estimate is likely to be. Can we predict with a confidence of plus to minus 5 percent, or is it more likely to range from minus 50 percent to plus 300 percent? If we know the range of error, we can design the supply chain to absorb some of this error with safety stock or extra capacity.

The second rule of forecasting is that we can predict in aggregate better than at the detail level. Hewlett-Packard can predict its overall unit sales for a month with far greater accuracy than it can predict the monthly sales for a particular model. This observation led the company to introduce the concept of postponement, which delays the differentiation of a product to its final model as late in the process as possible. For example, Hewlett-Packard employs a common design for its computers and printers despite different power specifications and outlet designs across countries. The distribution center in Europe then customizes the generic products with a different power cord and instruction manual to fit the needs of a particular country as orders arrive. This flexibility allows the company to focus on the total demand for a product across all of Europe rather than having to predict demand accurately for each individual country.

The third rule of forecasting states that we can predict near-term demand better than future demand. Mrs. Fields cookies can predict sales for the next day with reasonable accuracy using simple inputs such as the current day's sales, the day of the week being predicted, and the expected temperature and weather conditions. Predicting the sales for a single day two months into the future, however, is much more difficult due to the uncertainty around the input variables. This observation also motivates companies to design supply chains with faster responses. Mrs. Fields faces far more risk if it has to place orders for key ingredients two months in advance than if it can wait to order only two days in advance.

Bullwhip Effect

Principle 4: Without thoughtful management, variability and uncertainty propagate along a supply chain, creating a bullwhip effect of increasing impact along the chain.

Jay Forrester, a systems dynamics professor at the Massachusetts Institute of Technology, coined the term *bullwhip effect* to describe the phenomenon of increased variability along a supply chain. Forrester observed that a slight change in demand at a retailer would often translate into a bigger volume shift at the wholesaler. In turn, the wholesaler variability drove an even larger volume fluctuation at the next link in the chain, such as the original equipment manufacturer.

Simulation Exercise: The Beer Game

This simulation exercise provides students with the opportunity to experience the bullwhip effect firsthand. In the simulation, teams of students make ordering decisions for companies along a four-tier supply chain much like the beer industry (hence the name). Retailers place orders with wholesalers, which in turn order from distributors, which order from the beer manufacturer. Despite their best efforts, teams inevitably produce the bullwhip effect in the initial run. Typically, students complete the exercise a second time with a new set of operating conditions, including shorter lead times, better information visibility, and the chance to collaborate with their supply chain partners.

Source: Darden School Publishing.

A wide variety of factors cause the bullwhip effect. First, retailers often generate variability in demand through promotions that encourage customers to stock up on a sale item one week and skip purchasing it the next week when the sale ends. Batching also contributes to variability along the chain. A company ordering a large quantity that represents many weeks of supply produces a more variable demand pattern than one that orders small batches daily. Similarly, a supplier that chooses to deliver in large batches also produces greater variability. Long lead times magnify the bullwhip effect, since uncertainty is magnified the further into the future we must predict. The longer it takes for a supplier to fill a customer order, the more uncertainty the supply chain must absorb. Couple this problem with poor communication along the chain, and even slight variations get magnified to extremes.

Wal-Mart and Procter & Gamble work in partnership to minimize the bullwhip effect. Wal-Mart employs an "everyday low prices" policy to avoid inducing needless demand variation on staple products with stable demand such as Tide detergent. Wal-Mart also shares sales information across its vast network of stores each day to ensure that Procter & Gamble can observe demand fluctuations as they occur. Collaborative efforts between the two companies strive for ever shorter lead times through techniques such as cross-docking. Though implementation has been slower than anticipated due to supplier resistance to the required investment, Wal-Mart leads in encouraging adoption of radio frequency identification (RFID) throughout the supply chain in hopes of achieving nearly instantaneous visibility.

Competitive Positioning

Principle 5: Set supply chain policies strategically based on competitive positioning.

Keith Oliver, the father of supply chain management, continues to highlight this principle even 30 years after coining the term. There are inherent tensions in setting supply policies. For example, sales and marketing wants to offer a wide array of products and short lead times, whereas operations prefers fewer stock-keeping units (SKUs) and adequate time to respond.

To manage this conflict, Marshall Fisher of the Wharton School at the University of Pennsylvania challenged managers to first clarify the strategic role of the supply chain. Fisher noted that products can be characterized as *functional* or *innovative* and accordingly require an *efficient* or a *responsive* supply chain. Companies need to design a supply chain aligned to the correct objectives.

For example, Campbell's Soup represents a functional supply chain. It has highly predictable demand based on stable products, including the ubiquitous can of tomato soup found in virtually every pantry in the United States. Its supply chain appropriately focuses on efficiency. By contrast, Sport Obermeyer, Ltd., the maker of ski apparel, needs a highly responsive supply chain to support its innovative product. The vast bulk of its product line changes each year, and it must sell its products during a very short winter ski season. Sport Obermeyer must manage unpredictable demand, which produces a high risk of both stock-outs and markdowns.

Fisher's framework expands the thinking beyond the simplistic "best practices" model of supply chain management, but Oliver pushes further. He challenges managers to "break constraints" rather than merely set priorities. The Toyota Production System offers a great example. To make Taichi Ohno's vision of a *pull* rather than *push* system of supply, Ohno needed to produce in small batches without incurring a big cost penalty. So, he sent Shigeo Shingo and a team of industrial engineers on a quest to achieve "single-minute exchange of die," that is, quick changeovers so that large batch sizes no longer mattered. Toyota broke the constraint of large batches in mass production and ushered in a new era of mass customization.

Classic Teaching Case: Sport Obermeyer

This case examines some of the challenges in production planning in the apparel industry. Sport Obermeyer, Ltd, a fashion skiwear manufacturer, was facing problems in making accurate forecasts of retailer demand. Every year it had to start production well in advance of the selling season, being fully aware of the fact that the market trends might change in the meantime. Greater product variety and intense competition made making demand predictions very challenging, and hence inaccurate production forecasting was a growing problem at the company. In order to make appropriate production commitments for the coming year's line, the firm was considering a new approach of statistically analyzing the data of retailer demand forecasts made independently by each member of the buying committee, rather than making a decision with committee consensus. In addition, it also had to decide where to source each product and allocate production between factories in Hong Kong and China.

This case engages students in exploring some of the challenges in the apparel industry and the factors to be considered in making decisions regarding production planning and outsourcing, like demand patterns, production quality, productivity, and lead times. It also introduces students to the use of statistical tools in production planning. Additionally, it illustrates an example of the challenges managers face in the real world, like dealing with ambiguity and making decisions in uncertain environments. The new production forecasting approach also demonstrates creativity and thinking out of the box in problem solving.

Source: Janice H. Hammond and Ananth Raman, "Sport Obermeyer, Ltd," Harvard Business School Case 9-695-022.

Making Tactical Trade-Offs

Principle 6: Analyze trade-offs holistically with the help of cross-functional support systems.

Even after setting clear strategy and policies, managers must still continuously make tactical trade-off decisions. Typically this is achieved within a company through a weekly or monthly cross-functional session variously referred to as sales and operations planning (S&OP) or production, sales, and inventory (PSI) meetings. In these meetings managers within a company make decisions to increase or lower production rates to accommodate the latest demand forecast, drawing on deep insight into the cost of such actions versus the risk of guessing wrong on the demand side.

Increasingly, companies are extending this process across the supply chain by employing collaborative planning, forecasting, and replenishment (CPFR). This basically expands the logic of the S&OP/PSI meeting across the extended enterprise. But it also demands better information systems as well as appropriate incentives. The emerging concept of federated planning encourages companies to collaborate strategically while maintaining a clear focus on individual company goals, much like the original colonies did in forming the United States' federal government model.

While systems enable better decision making, people must engage in the process. Do not let computer systems evolve into so-called black boxes lacking clear transparency into the underlying logic. For example, a manufacturer of pots, pans, and other cooking utensils installed an enterprise resource planning (ERP) system to manage its supply chain supporting retailers like Wal-Mart, Williams-Sonoma, Cooking.com, and others. After months and millions invested in the new system, it failed to produce the supply chain performance improvement promised by the software company and the consultants who installed it. Upon investigation, the company discovered that the original system implementers had assigned default planning parameters throughout the system rather than values based on the unique characteristics of the company's supply chain. Simply changing the order sizes to reflect economic order quantities (EOQs) and calculating appropriate safety stock levels dramatically improved service levels while simultaneously lowering inventory levels.

Classic Teaching Case: Zara

This case describes Zara, the leading brand of fast-growing Spanish apparel retailer Inditex. Zara has developed a supply chain with the unique ability to translate the latest fashion trends into 10,000 new designs each year arriving on store shelves less than 15 days after the point of creation. By producing limited quantities and constantly changing the product mix with the latest trends, Zara encourages customers to shop more frequently, making stock-outs desirable. Unlike the typical apparel retailer, Zara does not rely on low-cost producers in Asia but instead sources 87 percent of its products from Europe, mostly from a local collection of subcontractors, to make its supply chain more responsive. It also seeks input from store managers on both replenishment orders and new products through biweekly orders from stores across the globe. As a result, Zara marks down fewer items and with less of a discount than its competitors.

This case illustrates an example of an integrated supply chain focused on a unique competitive positioning in the apparel industry. The case highlights the key elements of the strategy and challenges the students to consider how to continue Zara's phenomenal growth. In the five years prior to the case setting, Zara had grown from 180 stores, mainly in Spain, to over 1,000 stores in 33 countries and on three continents. As the company considers its further expansion plans, management faces the challenge of deciding whether to continue with the same supply chain design or adopt a new one.

Source: Guillermo D'Andrea and David Arnold, "Zara," Harvard Business School Case 9-503-050.

Balancing Cooperative Relationships with Competitive Pricing

Principle 7: Structuring the network of suppliers demands an appropriate balance between a focus on cooperative relationships and competitive pricing.

Research conducted by the global management consulting firm Booz & Company demonstrated the challenges of maintaining supplier partnerships and simultaneously ensuring competitive pricing. A single-minded focus on competitive pricing—sometimes employing reverse auctions over the Internet—tends to drive a Darwinian rivalry among suppliers. Desperate suppliers may bid down prices to marginal costs to avoid losing sales in the short run but ultimately find themselves unable to reinvest in the business for the long run. Over time, these suppliers become increasingly less viable and often fail. Furthermore, this focus on supplier competition fails to tap the potential for waste reduction possible from combining the knowledge of customer and supplier. For example, the U.S. government insists on competitive bidding among an ever dwindling defense supply base. The focus on price fails to address the key driver of weapon system overruns—gold-plated performance specifications.

Career Profile

1995 MBA

Patrick Houston

Partner,

Booz & Company

Education:

BS, Chemical Engineering, University of Southern California

Masters, Manufacturing Management, McCormick School of Engineering and Applied Sciences

MBA, Northwestern University, Kellogg School of Management

Based in New York, Pat Houston is a partner at Booz & Company focused on the consumer and media industries. He specializes in operational and organizational transformation with particular emphasis on sourcing and supply chain initiatives. Mr. Houston has over 14 years of global consulting experience and is the leader of the firm's strategic sourcing functional offering in North America.

Prior to committing to a long-term career in consulting, Mr. Houston worked in strategic planning for automotive manufacturer Eaton and served as a drummer in a rock band.

Source: Booz & Company and author correspondence.

Alternatively, some companies have aggressively pursued supplier partnerships with a reduced base of suppliers. While such partnerships enable the companies to collaborate on specifications and eliminate waste in their interactions, many companies fail to capture their share of the benefits. Worse yet, many that mindlessly pursue a misguided program of supply base reduction find themselves dependent on complacent suppliers that now wield increased negotiation leverage since the company has eliminated competitive options in its quest for strategic relationships with fewer suppliers.

Honda and Toyota exemplify an emerging model of a balanced commitment to cooperative supplier relationships coupled with a clear expectation of competitive pricing. Suppliers to both companies highlight that the two companies rank among their most demanding customers. Unlike most companies, however, these Japanese automotive manufacturers do not drive price improvement by simply squeezing supplier margins. Instead, Toyota and Honda collaborate with a stable base of long-term suppliers to eliminate the waste that drives up cost. Though Honda and Toyota tend to work with a small base of suppliers, they rarely sole-source and instead maintain multiple suppliers and award a shifting proportion of business over time based upon the suppliers' efforts at continuous improvement. Cost competitiveness results less from the competitive pressure but more from the fact that Toyota and Honda understand the product cost and constantly seek to eliminate waste.

As explained in the book by Timothy Laseter, *Balanced Sourcing: Cooperation and Competition in Supplier Relationships*, companies need to develop a set of organizational capabilities to achieve the appropriate balance, including total cost modeling, creating sourcing strategies, and leveraging supplier innovation. Though companies should adopt the philosophical mind-set of long-term, cooperative supplier relationships, that mind-set is a necessary but not sufficient condition of success. Finding the right balance demands strategic thinking supported by detailed cost insight, as discussed next.

Classic Teaching Case: Tork Corporation

This case explores a possible strategic response by an air-conditioning original equipment manufacturer (OEM) that received an outsourcing proposal from Korean electronics and appliance giant LG. Tork, a pseudonym for a U.S. manufacturer, initiates a competitive cost analysis of its low-end model versus LG after the latter offered to manufacture low-end air-conditioner units for Tork at a price significantly below Tork's current in-house cost. Tork seeks to confirm that LG's price reflects an underlying cost advantage and not anticompetitive dumping. Students face the task of extrapolating the competitive cost, modeling results across the full product range, and then recommending action based on those findings.

The case introduces the concept of product teardown—deconstructing and scrutinizing competitor units—and explains the process of carrying it out by constructing a cost model. It also introduces a framework for cost-driver analysis considering design, geography, facility, and execution, which allows for the organization of cost differences according to the strategic levers necessary that drive the costs. The case discussion builds on a strong fact base and inevitably leads the students to consider the long-term implications of global outsourcing.

Source: James Hammer and Tim Laseter, "Tork Corporation: Competitive Cost Analysis," Darden School Publishing Case UVA-OM-1171.

Global Outsourcing

Principle 8: Global outsourcing demands a strategic perspective coupled with a deep understanding of supplier cost and competencies.

Outsourcing has become common in the increasingly "flat" world described by business journalist Thomas Friedman. Improved transportation economics and better information systems have allowed companies to build ever more complex global supply chains. Over the past two decades, the default assumption that a company should be vertically integrated to maximize control of its supply chain has been replaced by the assumption that everything except core knowledge-based work should be outsourced to low-cost specialists around the world. And, with the lower cost and speed of Internet-enabled global communications, even knowledge work faces the risk of outsourcing to the highly educated engineers and computer specialists in developing regions of Asia and Eastern Europe.

Designing a supply chain with the proper degree of vertical integration requires a strategic perspective and a clear understanding of the risks and rewards of global outsourcing. Consider the electronics industry, which employs very different strategies across its supply chain.

Starting upstream in the electronics supply chain, the leading silicon chip manufacturer, Intel, has succeeded through a tenacious pursuit of Moore's law: the adage coined by one of its two cofounders in 1965. Gordon Moore observed that the processing capacity of the computer chip doubled consistently every 18 months, driving a constant improvement in performance versus cost. Intel has sustained that progression for nearly 50 years by investing in constant improvement in wafer fabrication technology. Intel regularly invests several billion dollars to build or upgrade a single wafer fab in the constant pursuit of finer circuitry that allows the designers to pack more functionality into the same or less silicon, thereby further enhancing the lightning-fast processing speeds of these miracles of human ingenuity.

Recognizing the critical need to protect its intellectual property and the relatively minor role of labor cost in a multibillion-dollar wafer plant, Intel continues to fabricate the wafers in developed regions such as the United States and Europe despite the higher labor cost. For the packaging manufacturing process, Intel operates plants in developing countries like China and Vietnam for a variety of reasons. This more labor-intensive stage of the manufacturing chain involves far less proprietary technology and also benefits from being closer to the electronic contract assembly plants that use Intel chips in computers, telephones, and MP3 devices—often located in Asia as well. Software development for these devices, however, continues to migrate to India.

The global appliance industry offers a different model, however. Electronics, which have a very high value-to-size ratio, can be air-freighted around the globe at relatively low transportation cost. Appliances reflect a wide variation in relative transportation cost, however. Companies like Whirlpool, General Electric, LG, and Haier produce many of the small appliances such as microwave ovens and room air conditioners in Asia for import into the U.S. market. The large refrigerators demanded by U.S. households face significant transportation penalties, however, and accordingly, even the China-based appliance company Haier produces refrigerators for the American market in the United States. Local production also gives Haier a shorter supply chain, which allows it to operate more responsively and compete on innovation, not just cost.

Managing a Global Supply Chain

In our increasingly "flat" world, MBAs will inevitably face a global supply chain. Though the same principles apply regardless, a global reach adds complexity and multiplies the risk. The bullwhip is more severe, total accumulated costs less transparent, potential problems less predictable, and communications more challenging. As such, global supply chain managers must heed the advice of John Le Carré, who noted, "A desk is a dangerous place from which to view the world." Instead, follow one of the key principles embedded in the culture of Toyota, "*Genchi genbutsu*," which loosely translated implores the manager to "Go and see." Firsthand observation of your global supply chain provides a level of understanding that cannot be gleaned from a desktop computer. Unfortunately, this critical advice also implies that today's global supply chain manager will live the old gypsy curse: "May you wander over the face of the earth forever, never sleep twice in the same bed, never drink water twice from the same well, and never cross the same river twice in a year." If you aspire to manage a global supply chain, you had better pack your travel bag.

Supply Chain Management in MBA Curricula

Most top business schools offer a course in supply chain management, though generally an elective option. A few of the schools known for their manufacturing orientation, such as the Sloan School at the Massachusetts Institute of Technology and the Ross School at the University of Michigan, offer multiple electives, as shown in Exhibit 8.2. These elective courses tend to focus on subtopics such as logistics and strategic sourcing and/or emphasize key issues such as globalization and information technology. Regardless of your desired career path, a course covering the key issues in supply chain management offers an important knowledge base for all students expecting to ultimately find themselves in general management positions.

For Further Reading

Feitzinger, Edward, and Hau L. Lee, "Mass Customization at Hewlett-Packard: The Power of Postponement," *Harvard Business Review*, January–February 1997.

Fisher, Marshall L., "What Is the Right Supply Chain for Your Product?" *Harvard Business Review*, March–April 1997.

Freeland, James, "Managing Inventories," Darden Graduate Business School Case UVA-OM-0623, 1987.

Laseter, Tim, and Keith Oliver, "When Will Supply Chain Management Grow Up?" *strategy+business* 32 (Fall 2003): 20–25.

Laseter, Timothy M., *Balanced Sourcing: Cooperation and Competition in Supplier Relationships* (San Francisco: Jossey-Bass, 1998).

Lee, Hau L., "The Triple A Supply Chain," *Harvard Business Review*, October 2004.

Downloadable Resources for this chapter available at www.wiley.com/go/portablemba5e

Boxer World Packaging Exercise

Exhibit 8.2   Supply Chain Management Course Offerings

Business School	Course Name	Type
Carnegie Mellon University (Tepper)	JIT Manufacturing and Supply Chain Management	Elective
	Optimization Models for Logistics	Elective
Columbia University	Supply Chain Management	Elective
Cornell University (Johnson)	Business Logistics Management	Elective
Duke University (Fuqua)	Supply Chain Management	Elective
Harvard University	Coordinating and Managing Supply Chains	Elective
INSEAD	Competitive Supply Chains	Elective
London Business School	Global Supply Chain Management and Leadership	Elective
MIT (Sloan)	Case Studies in Logistics and Supply Chain Management	Elective
	International Supply Chain Management	Elective
	Logistics Systems	Elective
	Manufacturing System and Supply Chain Design	Elective
	Supply Chain Planning	Elective
Northwestern University (Kellogg)	Logistics and Supply Chain Management	Elective
NYU (Stern)	Global Outsourcing Strategy	Elective
	Supply Chain Management	Elective
Stanford University	Supply Chain Management and Technology	Elective
UCLA (Anderson)	Supply Chain Management	Elective
University of Chicago (Booth)	Supply Chain Strategy and Practice	Elective
University of Michigan (Ross)	Manufacturing and Supply Operations	Elective
	Supply Chain Analytics	Elective
	Supply Chain Management	Elective
	Logistics	Elective
	Information Technology Strategy in Supply Chain and Logistics	Elective
	Strategic Sourcing	Elective
	Special Topics in Supply Chain Management	Elective
University of Navarra (IESE)	Logistics	Elective
	Procurement Management	Elective
University of North Carolina– Chapel Hill (Kenan-Flagler)	Supply Chain Management	Elective
University of Pennsylvania (Wharton)	Operations Management: Supply Chain Management	Core
University of Toronto (Rotman)	Supply Chain Management	Elective
University of Virginia (Darden)	Supply Chain Management	Elective

Source: School web sites, accessed October 2009.

9

Strategy—Defining and Developing Competitive Advantage

The purpose of business is to create value for people, including customers, shareholders, employees, and communities. Strategy defines the purpose, intent, and mission of the firm—how it aims to create value. Sustained superior returns require a clear and well-communicated vision of how the firm creates value. Leaders have a critical role in defining and clearly communicating these goals and in demonstrating commitment, courage, and resolve.

Jim Collins's study of firms with extraordinary performance over a sustained period of time found that leadership is critical, but perhaps not in the ways that are usually assumed. Superb leadership is characterized not by power and charisma, but by humility and firm resolve. Consistent with this finding, strategy development requires the firm's leaders, at all levels, to understand the firm's core values and to continually look hard at how to be ever more unique and valuable and how to stay true to not only to the firm's mission, but to what the firm does *not* do.

This chapter looks at the strategy development process, which provides frameworks and questions that leaders throughout the firm can use to design and improve strategy and performance. Strategy overlaps well with marketing; see also Chapter 4 on marketing management.

What Is Strategy?

Firms strive for sustained, superior return on investment. *Superior* returns, relative to other competitors in the industry, require a sustainable competitive advantage (that is, a way of providing value to customers that is unmatched by competitors). *Sustained* profits require investment in capabilities that enable the advantage to improve, renew, and change. *Strategy*, therefore, is concerned with the definition of competitive advantage and the development of activities, resources, and capabilities that enable the firm to sustain advantage in a changing world. (See Exhibits 9.1 and 9.2.)

Essentially, strategy is the definition of how a firm competes: its values, its commitments, and the opportunities it creates. Strategy defines the firm's competitive position

Exhibit 9.1   What Is Strategy?

In his classic article "What Is Strategy?" Michael Porter defines strategy as creating a company's position, making trade-offs, and forging fit among activities:

- "Strategy is the creation of a unique and valuable position, involving a different set of activities."
- "Strategy is making tradeoffs in competing. The essence of strategy is deciding what not to do."
- "Strategy is creating fit among a company's activities."

Source: Michael E. Porter, "What Is Strategy?" *Harvard Business Review*, November–December 1996, 62.

in an industry and develops consistency of purpose among the firm's activities to achieve that position. Strategy is not a detailed plan describing what the firm will do; instead, it provides direction for making significant choices and strong guidance about what the firm will *not* do. Strategy is most powerful when its core is clearly understood values that guide and motivate choices and actions. In highly successful firms, strategy often has the feel of a shared cause.

Exhibit 9.2   Three Levels of Strategy: Corporate—Competitive—Functional

A firm's strategy is often discussed at three levels: corporate, or multi business strategy, competitive or business unit strategy, and functional strategy within a business. This chapter focuses on competitive strategy. Functional strategies are also discussed in Chapter 6 on operations.

Corporate strategy is the definition of the firm's values, and its financial and nonfinancial goals. It centers on the identification and building or acquisition of key resources and capabilities, and entails the decisions of which industries the firm will compete in and how the businesses will be linked. Corporate strategy determines how resources will be allocated among the businesses of the firm, and thus the constraints on what the firm will do and will not do.

Competitive strategy defines how a firm competes in a given industry. A firm's competitive strategy is how the firm creates a valuable position in the industry. This involves a vision (explicit or implicit) of what customers the firm serves and how it delivers value for them. But competitive strategy is more than vision; it is the combination of specific activities and processes throughout the firm's operations that enable a firm to create unique value for customers. Thus, strategy also entails the fit among the firm's activities so that efforts throughout the firm consistently reinforce the potential advantage in the firm's competitive positioning.

Functional strategies, such as financial strategy, research strategy, and operations strategy, reinforce the firm's competitive strategy and define activities and processes to enable the firm to achieve the benefit of its competitive position. Articulating and analyzing functional strategies clarify whether and how the firm's functions each fit with the competitive strategy and focus explicit attention to the coordination among functions.

The strategy development process creates insight about how to create and enhance uniqueness and sustainable competitive advantage. The challenge of strategic thinking is to open the minds of managers, provide new perspectives on threats and opportunities, challenge conventional wisdom, and develop a vision of the firm's uniqueness.

The Strategy Development Process

Strategy is *not* making plans.

Plans are worthless; planning is priceless.

—Dwight David Eisenhower

A variety of strategy development approaches are used in practice, such as frameworks for analyzing industry profitability, competitive positioning, core competencies, capabilities, resources, strategic intent, and future scenarios. Each of these frameworks provides a guide for thinking through critical questions; none provides definitive answers. The answers come in the form of the insights generated by the process. Using any of the frameworks well is an art, so different managers may find they are more effective in developing insights with different frameworks.[1]

Think of a framework as a box. The box limits vision if you step into it and close the lid and think "inside the box." But throwing the frameworks away can be just as limiting; without any frameworks, managers tend to overlook critical considerations or put great effort into reinventing well-understood ideas. So getting "out of the box" is only part of the challenge. The trick is to *use* the box without getting trapped in it! Instead, use the framework (or box) as a foundation for developing insight; then stand on top of the box to expand your view of the horizons ahead. Thus, the value of a strategy framework can be seriously limited by the person using it. Be skeptical when someone says that a given framework is useless; the statement may simply mean that the person has other frameworks in mind for the same purpose, or it may mean that person does not know how to use the framework to develop insight. Frameworks used only to validate old views are much less useful. Frameworks must be used to gain insight and inspire vision, to see new perspectives and develop new ideas.

Also be alert to the allure of the latest and greatest frameworks and buzzwords. Although new approaches for thinking about strategy can help managers to perceive new opportunities, the danger is that popular strategy fads encourage rivals to compete in similar ways and thus undermine the firm's attention to competing differently from other firms. Competing *differently*—with unique positioning, special target customers, or innovative ways of performing combinations of activities—is the essence of competitive advantage.

A complete strategy development process usually includes using several frameworks and doing a lot of creative thinking about the implications of the analysis. The seven-step process outlined here covers the critical strategy questions from a variety of perspectives. (See Exhibit 9.3.) Each step is considered in turn.

Step 1: Industry Analysis—Industry Profitability Today and Tomorrow

One of the fundamental insights of competitive strategy is that average profitability varies among industries. Average return on investment in the pharmaceutical industry in the late 1980s and early 1990s was about 25 percent, whereas the trucking industry achieved only

Exhibit 9.3   The Strategy Development Process

The Seven Steps of the Strategy Development Process

1. Industry analysis—industry profitability today and tomorrow.
2. Positioning—sources of competitive advantage.
3. Competitor analysis—past and predicted.
4. Current strategy assessment—relative position and sustainability.
5. Option generation—a creative look at new customers and positions.
6. Development of capabilities—positioning for future opportunities.
7. Choosing or improving a strategy—uniqueness, trade-offs, fit.

about 5 percent on average, and grocery stores even less. Those differences in averages are due to structural differences in the industries; the key for a firm in these industries is to outperform the average and achieve superior returns relative to its competitors.

Industry analysis is critical for several reasons.

- First, the success of the firm is indicated by its *return relative to other firms in the industry*. A 15 percent rate of return in trucking in the early 1990s was impressive, but a 15 percent rate of return in pharmaceuticals indicated serious underperformance.

- Second, industry analysis allows managers to *understand the drivers of industry profitability* and thus how it may change in the future. A common mistake is to analyze only the current profitability, but much of the power of the analysis is in using it to consider potential future changes and their implications for the firm's strategy.

- Third, different segments of the industry may have different profit potentials. Industry analysis can help to identify the *attractive and unattractive segments*.

- Fourth, the current level of industry average profitability should not be taken for granted. Firms may have significant opportunities to *improve industry structure* or to prevent its deterioration. These opportunities may apply throughout the industry, or in a specific industry segment.

- Fifth, industry analysis provides a good first *test on the rigor of new strategy frameworks and approaches*. Frequently, the examples that are claimed to prove the validity of the latest strategy fad can be entirely explained by differences in industry average profitability, leaving the additional insight of the current fad in question.

Determinants of Industry Profitability

Industry profitability (or attractiveness) can be analyzed by considering *five forces*: buyer power, supplier power, intra-industry rivalry, the threat of substitutes, and the threat of new entry.[2]

Exhibit 9.4 displays the five forces and the drivers of their power. By assessing the strength of each of these forces, one can understand and predict industry average profitability. So, for example, the high average profitability of the pharmaceutical industry in the 1980s and early 1990s was explained by industry structure and the confluence of the five forces. Buyer power was low because patients did not shop based on price. Doctors chose products with little reason to consider price; patients paid. The threat of substitution was low because substitutes of other types of therapy or doing without

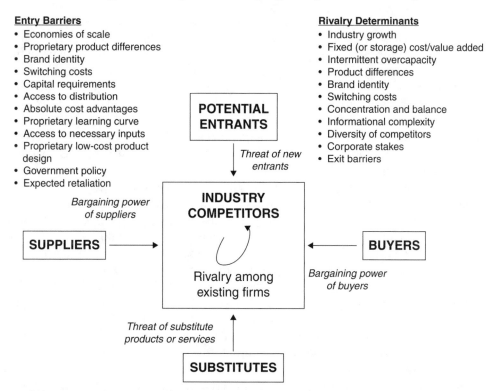

Exhibit 9.4   The Five Competitive Forces That Determine Industry Profitability

Source: Michael E. Porter, *Competitive Advantage* (New York: Free Press, 1985).

treatment usually offered little value compared to effective pharmaceuticals. Supplier power was low because the inputs tended to be available from multiple sources. Rivalry was limited by firms competing in different niches with patent protection. The threat of new entry was blocked not only by patents, but also by the complicated regulatory process for new drug approval and the difficulty of establishing sales forces and distribution systems. Even a firm with a new biotech drug might need to ally with a major drug company to produce, market, and distribute its product.

Conversely, the trucking industry faced large, powerful, price-sensitive buyers who could easily switch to other truckers. Suppliers included large automakers as well as powerful unionized labor. Substitutes such as rail and airfreight provided real alternatives. Rivalry was intense because many competitors were vying for the same business without distinct strategic positions. Entry was as easy as leasing a truck, although given the other industry forces, one would not expect to make much money doing that.

In general, to do an industry analysis one must gather data and make observations about the considerations listed in Exhibit 9.4. Although the examples of pharmaceuticals and trucking are unambiguous, the picture is often less clear. Frequently, some forces are positive and others negative, so one must assess the strength of the forces and qualitatively weigh the overall picture to make a judgment about industry average profitability. Often one can also gather profitability data about some firms in the industry and use that to help calibrate current profitability.

It is critical, however, not to stop the analysis with a judgment about current industry average profitability. Much of the power of the analysis is in the view of the future that it can provide. So, the next step is to consider trends and drivers of possible changes in the industry and then analyze how these changes would affect profitability. For example, if current buyer power is moderate and supplier power is low but both are increasing, the industry can be expected to be less profitable in the future. As a result, rivalry is likely to become more intense unless the firm can alter the drivers of change or position itself to compete in an industry segment where competitors are unlikely to venture or succeed.

The pharmaceutical industry provides an example of industry structural change under way. Buyer power is increasing as buyers consolidate. Large government payers and health maintenance organizations (HMOs) are covering drugs and becoming price sensitive to a degree that individual patients never were. Rivalry is increasing as generics become increasingly common and as price pressure fuels competition. The threat of substitute products is increasing in markets where over-the-counter alternatives are available. And the threat of new entry by biotech companies is increasing. A few biotech firms have even managed to develop their own marketing and distribution channels.

Industry analysis of separate industry segments can be used to consider which segments are most profitable or are likely to be more profitable in the future. For example, proprietary drugs have a much more profitable industry structure than generics. Similarly, future industry analysis can sound a critical warning about industry segments that are likely to experience serious declines in profits, or provide critical insight about how to provide unique value in a changing world.

Analysis of future industry structure is a tough step to perform, because change is difficult to predict. Established firms often get trapped in conventional wisdom and lulled by widely shared forecasts, making them less able to see the problems and opportunities presented by possible future change. Accounting firms lobbied vigorously (and unsuccessfully) against the Sarbanes-Oxley Act of 2002, a provision of which requires public companies formally to vouch for internal financial records. As a result of Sarbanes-Oxley, privately held accounting firms gained significant business through audit fees.

Free-ranging brainstorming about the future and challenges to conventional wisdom about the industry should be encouraged in this process. It is often useful to ask what the competitors might predict, what technologies might leapfrog those currently used, and how a seemingly very unlikely future might be explained if it came to pass. It is also important to ask how a better future can be created. Used in this manner, industry analysis is a powerful tool for developing insights about strategy for future success.

MBA Concepts in Action: Strategic Planning for the Future

The scope of the future in strategic planning varies widely. In some cases, future planning applies to the following year within a narrow industry. In others, the future may be so far away as to seem speculative in terms of industry planning and business cycles.

Consider the issues surrounding the idea of global warming induced by human activities such as fossil fuel use. On one hand, global warming represents a threat to some businesses. For instance, growing seasons are gradually getting longer, and growing regions are spreading northward, introducing new competition to the agricultural industry. Or mid- to low-elevation ski areas in the United States are receiving less snow during winters, and hence fewer visitors. Many other firms would be directly affected by measures to control greenhouse gases released to the atmosphere (e.g., taxation, cap-and-trade programs, etc.), or to alter land use patterns. If greenhouse gas release is no longer an externality to firms, then some competitive advantages will no longer be—so to speak— sustainable.

On the other hand, many of the problems associated with greenhouse gas release could present strategic opportunities. For example, take the long residence time of carbon dioxide in the atmosphere (70 to 85 percent of any emitted quantity will affect the atmosphere over the following 100 years; the rest for much longer). This time scale yields a large procrastination penalty for taking action to reduce emissions, and presents strong incentives to reduce the source of the problem. Carbon capture technology and alternative energy sources all present enormous opportunities for innovation and for capturing value from a worldwide market. Predicting the nature and timing of these opportunities is far from certain, but that is the starting point for good strategic planning.

Step 2: Positioning—Sources of Competitive Advantage

Positioning analysis is about uniqueness. It addresses the question of why some firms outperform industry average profitability and others fail to achieve it. Superior performance demands that a firm has a sustainable competitive advantage and invests in the development of capabilities that will enable it to renew that advantage as the future unfolds.

Fundamentally, competitive advantage stems from superior value creation for customers. Value in this context is the way a consumer thinks when shopping; it is enhanced either by a lower price for the same good, or by qualities or features that are superior for a given customer. An inferior product may not be a good value, even at a low price. Conversely, a superior product at too high a price is not a good value.

In strategy, the two sources of superior value creation for customers are known as lower cost and differentiation. In both cases, competitive advantage stems from offering more value to customers than competitors offer. This additional value is delivered by performing activities and processes differently from competitors in ways that reinforce or accentuate the value.

Analysis of positioning is often facilitated with a diagram such as a value chain or business system map. These diagrams picture all of the firm's activities and processes from procurement to after-sales service, including also research and development and overhead activities (see Exhibit 9.5). They are used to enable or encourage a thorough analysis of how each activity throughout the firm affects costs and differentiation. They

Firm Infrastructure				
Human Resource Management				
Technology Development				
Procurement				
Inbound Logistics	Operations	Outbound Logistics	Marketing and Sales	Service

Exhibit 9.5   The Value Chain

Source: Michael E. Porter, *Competitive Advantage* (New York: Free Press, 1985).

may also be used to identify important processes or linkages among activities that span several functions or are performed through alliances or by suppliers.

Increasingly, competition takes the form of a network (a loose alliance of a firm with its suppliers and distributors) competing with other firms or other networks.[3] A firm may perform activities differently and increase value for its customers by the way it manages the linkages among its own activities or by the way it manages the linkages with other firms in its network. This underscores the potential benefit of coordination among firms in a network to lower the overall cost for customers or enhance the noncost elements of value delivered, such as shorter lead times or better service. Rather than focus on appropriating value from buyers and suppliers in the firm's network, the cooperative mind-set of network management needs to consider how the network as a whole can create the most value. Relationships need to be built and managed so that each player in the network profits by advancing the network's strategic position.

Cost Leadership—Equal Quality at Lower Costs

Cost leadership stems from performing activities and processes (or groups of activities) in less expensive ways than competitors. It is not a matter of providing inferior products or services; indeed, matching (or exceeding) the quality of competing products or services is critical for providing greater value to customers. Above-average returns result from being able to charge a higher margin than competitors charge for equal-quality products without charging a higher price (as pictured in Exhibit 9.6), or from selling an equal-quality product with the same margins as competitors, but at a lower price and thus commanding a bigger market share. Sometimes the firm can achieve cost advantage by offering a lower price to a focused group of customers who are happy to forgo certain product features or service attributes. Because these customers do not care about the additional features, they view an inherently less costly product as having equal quality, and they benefit from its lower price.

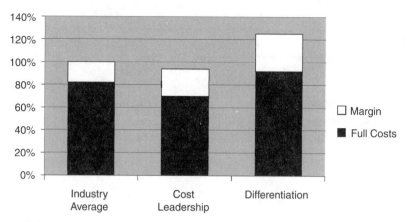

Exhibit 9.6   Types of Competitive Advantage

Note: Vertical axis represents percent of industry average revenue and cost. "Full costs" includes capital costs.

MBA Concepts in Action: Cost Leadership

Brilliant examples of cost leadership, such as Crown Cork and Seal in tin cans, have strong consistency of purpose throughout the firm's functions. Crown Cork and Seal's "no-waste, no-nonsense" approach to cost saving included relentless attention to detail. Its tile floors and metal desks left no doubt about its attention to cost reduction. Research and development (R&D) did not focus on innovation, since the fast follower approach was cheaper. But not all R&D expenses were pruned. R&D expertise was available to customers with problems on their canning lines. Superior customer service built loyalty, reduced marketing costs, and increased economies of scale; thus it was not a frill but a savvy approach to implementing the low-cost strategy.

Gallo Wines' successful cost leadership includes economical purchasing of grapes, specially developed blending technology, low-cost bottling operations, and distribution through supermarkets. National advertising may sound like an expensive practice for a cost leader, but it reinforces the cost advantages of volume production and supermarket distribution.

Differentiation—Value Above and Beyond the Premium Price

Differentiation is a matter of delivering nonprice value for which customers are willing to pay. Thus, differentiation is much more than simply offering a different or better product. The key to success is making additional (costly) expenditures only on activities or features that cost the firm less than the value they add for customers. Diligent cost cutting remains important in all areas that do not affect the differentiation for which customers will pay a premium price. The result is usually a premium-priced product or service, but it is still a good value (or even a bargain) to customers who desire the additional benefit of convenience, customization, special service, durability, or other dimension of nonprice

Exhibit 9.7 Cost Drivers and Differentiation Drivers

Cost Drivers	Differentiation Drivers
• Scale	**Intrinsic**
• Learning	• Product quality
• Capacity utilization	• Product variety
• Linkages within the value chain	• Bundled services
• Interrelationships across business	• Timing and delivery
• Levels of integration	**Signals of Value**
• Timing	• Reputation or image
• Location	• Cumulative advertising
• Institutional factors	• Product appearance
	• Installed base
	• Price

Source: Michael E. Porter, *Competitive Advantage* (New York: Free Press, 1985).

value. As this suggests, differentiation often involves choosing a defined customer base and not trying to serve other customers who value different attributes than the company's target market.

As in a well-executed low-cost strategy, well-executed differentiation shows up in many processes or activities performed differently from competitors. For example, Sony achieves differentiation in high-quality consumer electronics with extensive R&D into new consumer applications, minimal defects in manufacturing, an authorized sales and service network, and responsive after-sales service. Many of these activities entail extra expense to achieve the quality that differentiates Sony. However, Sony reduces costs with efficient scale facilities and tight cost control.

Drivers of Competitive Advantage

While discussions of competitive advantage often focus on the value perceived by customers, the firm must understand the sources of advantage in terms of specific activities or processes that it performs throughout the company to reduce costs or increase nonprice value. This is where the functional strategies within the firm come into play. Excellence in the implementation of each function is critical to achieving advantage, but the functions must be well coordinated or they may undermine each other's efforts. One role of strategy is to guide the fit among the various functions and coordinate efforts toward a common, clearly communicated vision. Clear goals and values enable managers, and indeed all employees in a firm, to enhance the firm's success consistently.

Failure to understand actual costs is a common pitfall for both low-cost and differentiation strategies. It helps to consider each function of the firm (including support activities as well as line operations) and attempt to compare costs of that function with competitors' costs. This analysis should then be followed by a hard look at possible ways to reduce costs further or enhance the nonprice value added for customers. Careful thinking through how, why, and when the product or service is used often adds ideas for ways to accentuate value that were not initially obvious. In addition, the drivers of low cost and differentiation listed in Exhibit 9.7 may spark other ideas for sources of improvement.

Step 3: Competitor Analysis—Past and Predicted

Although common sense points to the importance of analyzing competitors before deciding how to compete, ignoring competitors is a frequent mistake.

- Clorox should have predicted that a new product offering combining bleach and detergent would be swiftly matched by Procter & Gamble, but it did not anticipate that response when it entered the detergent market in 1988. Clorox might even have predicted that the marketing muscle of P&G and the strength of the Tide brand would have the net effect of reducing the bleach market, yet Clorox faced that outcome as an unpleasant surprise.

- Epson may have predicted that offering a low-priced laser printer in 1989 would hasten the decline of the dot-matrix printer market. But it appears to have assumed that the decline would not matter because loyal Epson customers would buy Epson laser printers. Epson failed to foresee that Hewlett-Packard, the leader in laser printers, would notice the competitive entry and be able to match the entry product's lower prices. The unfortunate result for Epson was the accelerated decline of its dot-matrix market combined with rapid growth in Hewlett-Packard's laser printer sales.

The moral of these all-too-common stories is that a vital step in strategy development is viewing the issues and opportunities from the perspective of specific competitors. One should consider not only how competitors may react, but also what strategic initiatives competitors may pursue. Although managers often mistakenly assume that competitors are caught in a state of inertia, one should instead assume that competitors are pushing ahead at full speed. Ongoing analysis of the competitors' perspective is important for avoiding unpleasant surprises that one later realizes were predictable.

Beyond improving prediction of competitors' moves, competitor analysis may enable a firm to influence those moves. Again, rather than stopping with an improved understanding of the situation a firm faces, managers can use strategic analysis to spur thinking about ways to reshape the future. In addition, competitor analysis provides a new perspective on one's own business and on relative sources of competitive advantage.

Considerations for Competitor Analysis

Competitors' moves and reactions are often consistent with their stated goals, their past assumptions, their known strengths and weaknesses, and their leaders' public statements. Thus, to do a competitor analysis, one should assess for each competitor:

- Current strategy (uniqueness and source of advantage).
- Leadership (recent or anticipated changes).
- Capabilities (cost position, value provided to customers, exclusive relationships, proprietary skills or processes, intangible assets, etc.).
- Future goals (what, when, and why).
- Assumptions (their view of the future market and of their own competitors).
- Stakes (economic, strategic, and emotional).
- Signals they have sent to other firms.

A surprisingly clear picture of competitors' future intentions can be developed from public sources and customer and supplier comments. The trick is to develop the

Exhibit 9.8   Competitive Dynamics: Good Moves and Poor Tactics

Good Moves	Poor Tactics
• Hard for your competitors to match: —Would cost their firms more. • Have commitment value: —Are costly to reverse. —Intentions will be believed. • Fit with the firm's capabilities.	• Simply raising advertising spend: —Easy to match. —Has little commitment value. • Price cuts by a higher-cost firm: —Give lower-cost competitor an advantage. —Intensify rivalry; provoke price wars. • Provoke competitors.

competitor's profile rather than to get caught in the trap of just collecting data that validates current assumptions about the competitor.

Step 4: Current Strategy Assessment—Relative Position and Sustainability

Assessment of the firm's competitive position in the industry integrates the insights from analysis of the industry, the firm's position, and the competitors. At this point it is critical to clearly identify the firm's current position in the industry, both in terms of its financial results and in terms of its strategy. The insights from the previous stages of the strategy process may provide a new perspective on the firm's strengths and weaknesses relative to others in the industry. (See Exhibit 9.8.)

The trend toward networks of alliances among firms means that a firm may need to assess the position of its network relative to other networks. A cooperative mind-set is then required to consider how the weaknesses in a network can be corrected by combined efforts such as working more closely together, sharing information, or changing processes to improve coordination or reduce costs.

It is also critical at this stage to go beyond the analysis of the present to consider the sustainability of the firm's (or network's) competitive advantage in the future. Even stunning current success does not guarantee the future. Examples abound of leaders assailed, such as Fairchild in semiconductors, Kodak in film, or Caterpillar in earth-moving equipment. Over time, new products and services become more commonplace, easier to copy, or less valuable relative to more recent innovations. Without investment and improvement, a firm's profitability will fall as other firms invest and improve.

Generally, threats to sustainability fall into four categories: imitation, substitution, appropriation of value by firms upstream or downstream, and shrinkage in profits due to rising costs of salaries, discretionary expenditures, or changes in the division of revenues among partners.[4]

Step 5: Option Generation—A Creative Look at New Customers and Positions

Change, often viewed as a threat to profitability, is the most powerful source of new opportunities. The insights from strategic analysis can help firms to identify new needs, new customers, new distribution channels, promising new technologies, and new sources of uniqueness.

To generate options, one wants to think in an entrepreneurial mind-set, adopt the perspective of industry outsiders, and challenge conventional wisdom about how to compete. The goal is to generate a broad, creative list of truly different strategies. New strategic positions are not obvious; they rely on inspiration, vision, and insight. However, the quality of the brainstorming of future strategic possibilities can be greatly enhanced by a solid understanding of the industry, customers, competitors, and the firm's own strengths. The trick is to avoid narrow thinking about traditional ways of competing.

Remember that a strategic position defines how a firm creates value for its customers. New strategies stem from new ways to create value, serving new sets of customers, or finding better ways to provide the real value the customer seeks. Unserved customer groups and empty or previously unimagined strategic positions can present important opportunities. Thus significant insight is uncovered by a focus on the customers' goals and values. When the customer is a business, insight is gained by looking for ways to improve how that business serves its customers. Copying only increases competition without adding new value.

One of the most common strategic errors, however, is to match competitors or copy their positions. Many hospitals in the United States in the 1990s and early 2000s have illustrated this mistake by frantic efforts to match their rivals and become increasingly alike and increasingly broad, rather than focusing on becoming uniquely excellent. Conventional wisdom often supports the mentality that rivals must be matched, but in truth, that mentality undermines uniqueness and success.

Step 6: Development of Capabilities—Positioning for Future Opportunities

Future success of the firm depends critically on the capabilities the firm develops. New strategic positions usually require additional capabilities that cannot be acquired or built overnight. Thus, the options under consideration must be analyzed from the perspective of required future capabilities. Developing those capabilities will involve a series of investments and changes in activities or processes. The direction and vision can be specified, but the precise steps cannot.

MBA Concepts in Action: Positioning for the Future

All of the strategic options under consideration may have different implications for development of capabilities, because different capabilities support different sources of competitive advantage. The difficulty of developing the required capabilities and the potential payoffs from the capabilities should be explored, and goals that cause the firm to stretch and learn need to be encouraged.

Komatsu's strategy in earth-moving equipment shows a progression of capability development. Threatened by Caterpillar in Japan in the 1960s, Komatsu first developed improved quality; then it undertook serious cost reductions. Critical capabilities were product and process excellence to defend its home market. Komatsu next developed export markets, and then in the 1970s it launched significant efforts in new product development. Future success required more; it required innovation to shape the new product offerings and lead the market.

Although some argue that developing capabilities is an implementation issue, it is important to consider future capabilities and the investments they require in the strategy development process for three reasons. First, a strategic position is a path, not a point. The dynamic development of the path should not be taken for granted. Analyzing required capabilities focuses the decision makers on the future, on the creation of opportunity, and on learning. Second, the development of future capabilities may require significant current investments. Analysis of these investments is an important aspect of choosing a strategy. Third, some capabilities can be gained effectively through network relationships among firms, but others will be less expensive or more effective if the firm develops them itself.

Investing to develop capabilities is risky in the usual (financial) sense of investing capital for uncertain returns. *Not* investing, however, is at least as risky, but in the strategic sense of falling behind or failing to sustain profits. Compromised capabilities lead to lost opportunities. Lost opportunities, however, lead to failing to improve capabilities. A vicious cycle of failure may result.

Step 7: Choosing or Improving Strategy—Uniqueness, Trade-Offs, Fit

Competitive advantage stems from difference: serving different needs, different customers, or different geographic locations, or providing different access, different products, or different dimensions of value. The point is to find a way of creating value that customers will not get from other sources. The most common error in choosing strategy is *imitation.* Successful strategy requires choices *not* to follow competitors.

Another common error is to try to eliminate the trade-offs between firms' different competitive positions. Superficially, it may seem advantageous to be able to match the competitor, but one must remember that eliminating trade-offs also makes it easier for someone to challenge your position. Strategy should aim to sharpen the trade-offs between positions, not to eliminate the trade-offs. In addition to making competitive advantage more sustainable, very distinctive positions can improve industry structure.

Strong leadership is necessary to define the firm's different, unique position and delineate directions in which the firm will *not* go. Strong leadership is also necessary to communicate the firm's values and strategy clearly so that choices made by managers throughout the firm will be consistent with the firm's intent. That consistency is critical to the successful implementation of strategy; without it, decisions made at the functional level (i.e., in operations or finance) may work against each other, or even against the source of competitive advantage that the firm seeks.[5]

With increasingly global competition, part of the challenge of creating fit among activities and consistency with strategic goals is deciding where to configure activities around the globe and how to coordinate dispersed activities.[6] Generally, large economies of scale, steep learning curves, and tough coordination issues push toward the decision to concentrate activities rather than disperse them around the globe. Dispersion is increasingly attractive when local market needs or governments require local presence, transportation costs are high, learning is country-specific, or a single site has significant risks that can be hedged with multiple locations.

When activities are dispersed, the challenge of creating fit and consistency among activities is accentuated. Information, knowledge, and technology from diverse locations must be effectively integrated. And strategic goals and choices must be clearly communicated throughout the worldwide functions of the firm. Because these challenges make an effective global configuration difficult to copy, well-executed coordination can make appropriately dispersed activities a significant source of competitive advantage.

Characteristics of Good Strategy

Evaluating a strategy is not a simple matter of looking at results. Because the goal is sustained, superior return on investment, short-term profits are not a sufficient indicator of success. Indeed, some firms that achieved brilliant success began with five or more years of negative cash flows. So how does one know if a strategy is good?

- A good strategy is built on values and purpose.
- A good strategy has at its center a specific understanding of competitive advantage. This understanding should be clear enough to state its essence in a single sentence.
- A good strategy is consistent. It is pursued consistently through combinations of activities that create a whole that is strongly reinforced and much more than the parts.
- A good strategy does not flip-flop over time. It defines a dynamic path that clearly bounds the firm's choices, but does not constrain the firm from adjusting to the uncertain future.

Strategy—Commitment or Flexibility?

There is a long-standing debate about whether the essence of strategy is commitment or flexibility. One side argues that strategy requires commitment (in the economic sense, meaning fixed investments), so place your bets wisely. Strategy does require commitment, but this advice is about as useful as "buy low, sell high." It doesn't tell one how to choose wise bets. The other side argues that in a changing world, strategy requires flexibility, so keep your options open. Strategy does require flexibility given the world's uncertainty, but this advice is about as useful as "do nothing risky." One cannot keep all options open, and this advice does not tell which options to foreclose.

Strategy actually requires *both* commitment and flexibility. The two are not in conflict when one recognizes that a firm must make investments now (commitments) in order to develop the capabilities (flexibility) that will enable it to succeed in the changing and uncertain future. Strategy defines the types of capabilities to invest in and the types of investments to forgo. Commitment to core values and to a vision of the essence of the firm's competitive advantage is critical. Those values and that vision point to a strategic path that is not fully defined or planned in advance. Choices along the way are guided by consistency with the values and vision. This means that the vision has to be explicit about how the firm differs from competitors, rather than simply stressing high quality, leadership, or other laudable but vague goals.

Flexibility does not mean simple opportunism. Flexibility is developed through investments in building capabilities that other firms will not have without similar advance investments.[7] For example, prior investments in a product line create the option to expand the line. Prior investments in new technologies enable the firm to use these technologies or to apply them better (or less expensively) than competitors as the future unfolds. Prior investments in processes and organizational knowledge enable the firm to perform its activities in ways that competitors cannot easily match.

Flexibility is not a strategic position, but an outcome of strategic thinking. Investments in developing capabilities provide flexibility to implement a strategy successfully in a changing world. These investments define the firm's future opportunities that sustain competitive advantage. Thus, while it is not reasonable or even desirable to keep *all* options open, successful strategy must develop the capabilities required to create value for future customers. The choices of which capabilities to develop and which types of future opportunity to create must be driven by the core values and future vision at the heart of the firm's strategy. Thus commitment in the sense of purpose, values, and mission *is* critical because commitment in this sense is the compass that guides the firm's future direction.

Strategy in MBA Curricula

Most MBA programs offer at least one first-year introductory course in strategic management, although many are offered late in the year, after students build their familiarity with other core disciplines such as marketing, accounting, and finance. These programs also offer elective courses in strategy, and some strategy courses are cross-listed in marketing areas. Exhibit 9.9 lists example courses from six leading MBA programs.

MBA Careers in Strategy

Every organization has someone who does strategy. It may be the CEO alone, or it may be an entire strategy department, but strategy is imperative to a firm's success. Three common careers with significant strategy components are corporate strategy, business development, and management consulting.

Corporate strategy is a function in many large organizations that is responsible for assisting the senior leadership of the organization in creating and implementing strategic plans. The corporate strategy group explores macro issues affecting the company and will analyze business unit performance versus competitors on a macro level. Which businesses to compete in and how to best leverage company assets are frequently the purview of corporate strategy. Many of these roles require strong analytical skills (similar to corporate finance skills), critical strategic thinking, and project management skills.

Exhibit 9.9   Strategy Course Offerings in MBA Curricula

Business School	First-Year Course
University of Pennsylvania (Wharton)	Competitive Strategy/Global Strategic Management
University of Chicago (Booth)	Strategy
Columbia University	Strategy Formulation
Northwestern University (Kellogg)	Business Strategy
Harvard University	Strategy
University of Virginia (Darden)	Strategy

Often the corporate strategy department reports to the chief financial officer of the company. Many times corporate strategy positions are filled internally with employees that have line experience in the company. Some companies, though, have created entry-level associate roles or rotational programs that start in strategy.

Business development (discussed more thoroughly in Chapter 4 on marketing) is also an area in the company where strategy is often created. Business development may be less "blue sky" than corporate strategy, but business development associates will work on strategic issues of how to leverage a company's assets or how to best compete in certain categories.

The most common way to pursue a career in strategy from a top business school is via management consulting. Consulting companies in general are one of the largest employers of MBAs. Basically, consultants advise management on key issues and provide solutions to a company's problems. Strategy consulting is a subset of the field of management consultants and focuses squarely on the companies' broad strategies. A typical engagement is with the CEO of the company and consists of a defining phase, a research phase, and a recommendation phase. Seldom are strategy consultants involved in the implementation of their recommendations. In addition to strong analytical skills, strategy consultants must demonstrate an ability to analyze patterns in data and connect the dots from different sources of data. Interviews with clients, customers, and suppliers are a frequent way that consultants gather data, so inquisitiveness is a highly valued skill. Finally, consultants always work in teams, so they must have a strong ability to work well with others, particularly team members at multiple levels in their own and their clients' organizations. The strategy consulting industry is dominated by a few large firms like Bain, Booz, Boston Consulting, and McKinsey, but many small specialists thrive as well.

Notes

1. For more on profitability and competitive positioning, see Michael E. Porter, *Competitive Advantage* (New York: Free Press, 1985). For more on core competencies, see C. K. Prahalad and G. Hamel, "The Core Competence of the Corporation," *Harvard Business Review*, May–June 1990. For more on capabilities, see George Stalk, Philip Evans, and Lawrence E. Shulman, "Competing on Capabilities: The New Rules of Corporate Strategy," *Harvard Business Review*, March–April 1992. For more on strategic intent, see G. Hamel and C. K. Prahalad, "Strategic Intent," *Harvard Business Review*, May 1989. For more on future scenarios, see Elizabeth Teisberg, "Strategic Response to Uncertainty," Harvard Business School Note 9-391-192, 1991.
2. Michael E. Porter developed the five forces framework for analyzing industry attractiveness in his book *Competitive Strategy* (New York: Free Press, 1980).
3. See the related discussion of supply chain management in Chapter 6, Operations Management.
4. Ghemawat, Pankaj, *Commitment: The Dynamic of Strategy* (New York: Free Press, 1991).
5. Discussion of this point, with examples, can be found in the corresponding chapters of this volume.
6. For detailed discussion of these challenges, see Michael E. Porter, "The Competitive Advantage of Nations," *Harvard Business Review*, March–April 1990.
7. Such investments are known in economics as *real options*.

For Further Reading

Collins, James C., *Good to Great: Why Some Companies Make the Leap ... And Others Don't* (New York: HarperBusiness, 2001).

Dess, G. G., G. T. Lumpkin, and A. B. Eisner, *Strategic Management: Creating Competitive Advantages* (New York: McGraw-Hill, 2007).

Eisenhardt, Kathleen M., Jean L. Kahwajy, and L. J. Bourgeois III, "How Teams Have a Good Fight," *Harvard Business Review*, 1997.

Ghemawat, Pankaj, *Commitment: The Dynamic of Strategy* (New York: Free Press, 1991).

Grove, Andy, *Only the Paranoid Survive: How to Exploit the Crisis Points That Challenge Every Company* (New York: Broadway Business, 1999).

Hamel, G., and C. K. Prahalad, "Strategic Intent," *Harvard Business Review*, May 1989.

Kim, W. C., and R. Mauborgne, *Blue Ocean Strategy: How to Create Uncontested Market Space and Make Competition Irrelevant* (Boston: Harvard Business School Press, 2005).

Liedtka, Jeanne M., "Strategy Making and the Search of Authenticity," *Journal of Business Ethics* 80, no. 2 (June 2008): 237–248.

Liedtka, Jeanne M., and R. Friedel, "Possibility Thinking: Lessons from Breakthrough Engineering," *Journal of Business Strategy* 28, no. 4 (2007): 30–37.

Porter, Michael E., *Competitive Advantage* (New York: Free Press, 1985).

Porter, Michael E., "The Competitive Advantage of Nations," *Harvard Business Review* (March–April 1990).

Porter, Michael E., "What Is Strategy?" *Harvard Business Review* (November–December 1996).

Stalk, George, Philip Evans, and Lawrence E. Shulman, "Competing on Capabilities: The New Rules of Corporate Strategy," *Harvard Business Review*, March–April 1992.

Teisberg, Elizabeth, "Methods for Evaluating Capital Investment Decisions under Uncertainty," in *Real Options in Capital Investment: Models, Strategies, and Applications*, ed. Lenos Trigeorgis (Westport, CT: Praeger, 1995).

Teisberg, Elizabeth, "Strategic Response to Uncertainty," Harvard Business School Note 9-391-192, 1991.

10

Financial Analysis
and Firm Valuation

Earlier chapters described the framework of financial accounting and the financial considerations the manager must make when allocating capital. The intersection of these two broad topics occurs most tangibly in financial analysis activities that ultimately translate into estimates of firm value. Perhaps no single estimation both intrigues and mystifies more than the valuation of the corporate entity. The objective of this chapter is to describe this process by introducing the basic concepts of financial analysis and its relationship to corporate valuation.[1]

There can be no exact prescription for how the analysis and valuation of a company will unfold, because so few companies are actually alike. However, a general approach can be offered that will help answer most fundamental questions about a firm. No matter what your motivation may be to understand a company, your objective will always be satisfied if you understand three characteristics of that company: how it has performed in the past, where it is headed, and what it is worth. This chapter is organized around these three central themes: (1) historical ratio analysis, (2) pro-forma forecasting, and (3) valuation. In a perfect world the analysis task would be complete here, but there are a number of other factors to consider that might greatly affect the conclusions reached through these three generalized steps. These include—but are not limited to—understanding firm-specific risks and trends; understanding risks related to macroeconomic factors; identifying accounting measurement issues; and assessing corporate governance, management skill, and expertise. The final subsections of this chapter further summarize these points. Throughout the chapter Home Depot, Inc., one of the most successful retail operations in the world, is used as an illustrative example.[2]

Part I: Historical Ratio Analysis

The objective of historical ratio analysis is to quantify certain financial relationships, with an end goal of understanding past performance and current financial condition. It would naturally be quite difficult to project what might happen in the future, a necessity in firm valuation, without some clear understanding of what has happened in the past. Described in this section are detailed techniques that will help set you on that path.

Common-Size and Percentage Change Analysis

A first step with ratio analysis typically entails recasting the components of a company's balance sheets, income statements, and statements of cash flow in a common historical perspective. Two complementary techniques are recommended: (1) analyzing the proportion of an account relative to other accounts, and (2) analyzing the growth in an account across periods. Common-size statements and percentage change statements, respectively, are the labels given to these tools. View them for what they are—recasting dollar amounts contained in the original financial statements into an easier-to-interpret, more enlightened, and more comparable set of financial ratios. All accounts are either a proportion or a growth variable. Both of these perspectives together help highlight key financial activity, particularly the often subtle but important shifts in asset, liability, and/or cost mix.

Exhibit 10.1 illustrates the percentage change income statement for Home Depot for the years 2003–2006.[3] The change in revenue or top-line growth is the natural starting point. Note that Home Depot net revenues grew 11.4 percent from 2005 to 2006, but not as fast as in 2004 when net revenues grew 12.8 percent.[4] How to interpret these growth rates depends on many things, but, in general, it is often easier for a small company to grow than a big one. Home Depot, with $91 billion of revenue, is obviously a large company, and a growth rate three times that of gross domestic product (GDP) growth is nothing short of admirable. The fact that the growth rate in 2006 was less than that of 2004 would be cause for some concern, and the astute analyst would be looking for other signs that growth might be indeed slowing. When studying financial results like this, it is not just the level of the parameter, 11.4 percent net revenue growth in this case, but any significant change in that parameter, such as from 12.8 percent to 11.5 percent to 11.4 percent, that should be the focus.

Exhibit 10.1   Percentage Change Income Statements

	2006	2005	2004	2003
Net revenues	11.4	11.5	12.8	11.3
Cost of sales	12.7	11.4	10.0	10.2
Gross margin	9.0	11.8	18.7	13.7
Selling, general, and administrative	11.3	8.1	20.0	11.8
Depreciation and amortization	19.7	17.9	22.2	13.1
Operating income	3.3	18.1	15.8	17.4
Interest and investment income	(56.5)	10.7	(5.1)	(25.3)
Interest expense	174.1	104.3	12.9	67.6
Earnings before taxes	0.3	17.3	15.6	16.5
Income taxes	3.0	18.3	14.7	15.0
Net income	(1.3)	16.7	16.2	17.5
Diluted earnings per share	2.6	20.4	20.2	20.5

In 2006, Home Depot's 11.4 percent revenue growth resulted in a slight decline in net income—the bottom line—and a 2.6 percent increase in earnings per share (EPS), in sharp contrast to the previous year when an 11.5 percent increase in revenue produced a 16.7 percent increase in net income and a 20.4 percent increase in EPS. How did this happen? To answer this question, the analysis must switch from revenue growth to profitability analysis.

Review carefully both the percentage change statement in Exhibit 10.1 and the common-size statement offered in Exhibit 10.2. The common-size statement in the vertical format expresses each significant line in the income statement in terms of percentage of sales.[5] Regarding the question of how Home Depot had slower EPS growth, one begins by noting that the 2006 cost of sales percentage increased, leading to a smaller gross margin percentage. Depreciation and amortization increased, but from a small base. There was not much effect due to taxes; the decrease in income taxes as a percentage of net revenue was due to the decrease in earnings before taxes. In sum, the profit story at Home Depot for 2006 was that it turned 11.4 percent revenue growth into a slight decline in net income due to a decline in margins. Looking at all five years of data, one will observe strong growth in sales and steady improvement in gross margins, operating profits, and net income until 2006. As an interesting side note, although not apparent from Exhibit 10.1, the reason a 1.3 percent decline in net income translates into a 2.6 percent increase in EPS is that the company bought back some of its own common stock. This transaction reduces the number of shares outstanding, thereby increasing the EPS metric.

A review of the balance sheets of Home Depot over the same periods, with these same formats, comes next. Exhibit 10.3 shows the balance sheet changes over four of the same five years. For instance, note that total assets grew by $22.2 billion (68 percent), while revenues grew by 56 percent, and net income by 57 percent. Comparisons such as these speak to the company's "asset efficiency."[6] As we move deeper into the analysis, there will be more precise ways of gauging asset efficiency.

Exhibit 10.2   Common-Size Vertical Income Statements

	2006	2005	2004	2003	2002
Net revenues	1.000	1.000	1.000	1.000	1.000
Cost of sales	0.672	0.665	0.666	0.682	0.689
Gross margin	0.328	0.335	0.334	0.318	0.311
Selling, general, and administrative	0.202	0.202	0.209	0.196	0.195
Depreciation and amortization	0.019	0.018	0.017	0.016	0.016
Operating income	0.106	0.115	0.108	0.106	0.100
Interest and investment income	0.000	0.001	0.001	0.001	0.001
Interest expense	0.004	0.002	0.001	0.001	0.001
Earnings before taxes	0.102	0.114	0.108	0.106	0.101
Income taxes	0.039	0.042	0.040	0.039	0.038
Net income	0.063	0.072	0.068	0.066	0.063

Exhibit 10.3   Percentage Change Balance Sheets

	2006	2005	2004	2003
Assets				
Cash and marketable securities	−23.9	−62.7	−24.1	26.6
Receivables	34.5	59.8	36.6	2.3
Inventories	12.5	13.2	11.0	8.9
Other current assets	101.7	24.8	75.9	19.3
Property, plant, and equipment, net	6.8	9.6	13.3	16.9
Goodwill	71.4	160.9	69.5	44.9
Other assets	143.9	−9.5	185.9	−39.3
Total assets	17.7	13.8	13.3	14.7
Liabilities and Equity				
Accounts payable	21.9	4.6	11.8	13.1
Accrued expenses	−60.9	11.4	22.3	8.3
Deferred revenue	−7.0	13.6	20.7	28.4
Other current liabilities	46.9	947.1	−74.9	192.3
Noncurrent long-term debt	335.7	24.4	150.9	−35.2
Other long-term liabilities	54.4	−14.9	39.4	89.9
Common stock	8.7	9.4	7.4	5.5
Retained earnings	14.2	20.8	21.8	23.2
Treasury stock	68.7	45.1	86.4	79.5
Total liabilities and equity	17.7	13.8	13.3	14.7

Copyright © 2010 by Eades et al. To download this form for your personal use, please visit www.wiley.com/go/portablemba5e.

The common-size vertical format statement in Exhibit 10.4 is an easy way to examine changes in the composition of assets over the five-year period. Note that the base for this format is total assets, which is the same as total liabilities and equity. All in all, the proportions changed somewhat on both sides of the balance sheet. The biggest assets were inventories and property, plant, and equipment (PPE), which together were 85 percent of total assets in 2002 and 76 percent in 2006. That should be no surprise. A big-box retailer like Home Depot would expect to have significant inventories and a large portion of PPE.

There were some important changes in Home Depot's mix of assets. Acquisition activity increased intangibles as a proportion of assets from 2 percent in 2002 to 12 percent in 2006. There was also an increase in trade receivables from 4 percent of total assets to 6 percent over that same period. Many retailers operate primarily on a cash basis, but Home Depot must grant credit to some customers, as its revenues from credit sales have been increasing. Focusing on cash and marketable securities, the two items together were $2.2 billion in 2002, increased slightly the following year, and dropped to $614 million by the end of 2006. Cash and marketable securities balances change frequently in many companies. One can think of cash as an idle asset—that is, funds not invested in stores, inventory, and affiliates. It would appear that Home Depot management has made a decision after fiscal year 2004 to operate with substantially lower levels of cash.

Exhibit 10.4   Common-Size Vertical Balance Sheets

	2006	2005	2004	2003	2002
Assets					
Cash and marketable securities	0.01	0.02	0.06	0.08	0.08
Receivables	0.06	0.05	0.04	0.03	0.04
Inventories	0.25	0.26	0.26	0.26	0.28
Other current assets	0.03	0.01	0.01	0.01	0.01
Property, plant, and equipment, net	0.51	0.56	0.58	0.58	0.57
Goodwill	0.12	0.08	0.04	0.02	0.02
Other assets	0.03	0.01	0.02	0.01	0.01
Total assets	1.00	1.00	1.00	1.00	1.00
Liabilities and Equity					
Accounts payable	0.14	0.14	0.15	0.15	0.15
Accrued expenses	0.02	0.07	0.08	0.07	0.07
Deferred revenue	0.03	0.04	0.04	0.04	0.03
Other current liabilities	0.05	0.04	0.00	0.02	0.01
Noncurrent long-term debt	0.22	0.06	0.06	0.02	0.04
Other long-term liabilities	0.06	0.04	0.06	0.05	0.03
Common stock	0.15	0.17	0.17	0.18	0.20
Retained earnings	0.63	0.65	0.61	0.57	0.53
Treasury stock	−0.31	−0.22	−0.17	−0.10	−0.07
Total liabilities and equity	1.00	1.00	1.00	1.00	1.00

On the other part of the balance sheet, total equity increased 24 percent from 2002 to 2006, but decreased from 66 percent to 47 percent as a percentage of total liabilities and shareholders' equity. Long-term debt and other long-term liabilities increased dramatically (by $12.6 billion) during this five-year period, the majority of it during the most recent period. Thus, as the assets increased, it seems that debt has increased faster than equity. It is notable, however, that the biggest balance sheet change was in treasury stock, which has the mechanical effect of decreasing total equity. Treasury stock (common stock bought back from shareholders) increased from $2.0 billion to $16.4 billion over the five-year period with annual buybacks continuing through 2006. One cannot help noticing that in 2006, a flat year for earnings growth, Home Depot repurchased $6.7 billion of its common shares and increased noncurrent long-term debt by $9.0 billion. Was the company borrowing to buy back shares to help raise EPS? We can also think of share repurchases as returning a large portion of net income to shareholders rather than increasing the dividend. Perhaps Home Depot was spending proportionally less in building new stores and was returning cash to its stockholders—a sign that the company is reaching the mature stage of its life cycle.

Attention next turns to the statements of cash flow (SCFs) and to the percentage changes in these statements. Cash flow from operations (CFO) is the first item most analysts will review on these statements. Over this period, net income increased

57 percent and CFO grew by 60 percent, which is a positive outcome and is expected for a strong, growing firm. There was one unusual item of note in the CFO section. Ordinarily, accounts payable should have increased along with the increase in inventories. In Exhibit 10.5 and Appendix A, we see that accounts payable increased from 2003 through 2005, but at a decreasing rate. The SCF adjustments for inventory and receivables reflect *changes* in the level of those assets, so the changes shown in Exhibit 10.5 are changes in the rate of change. The year 2005 was the most extreme. In that year, inventories increased $971 million, while accounts payable increased only $148 million. It is unusual that accounts payable did not increase about as much as inventories. That alone could have meant an $800 million plus change in CFO, bringing it more in line with net income. In 2006, it *reversed*. What we are observing is probably just an anomaly, a one-year unexplained change. In firms like Home Depot, changes in accounts payable tend to track closely with changes in inventories. If this situation had persisted in 2006, it would be a serious and significant event, but it did not.

Exhibit 10.5 Percentage Change Statements of Cash Flow

	2006	2005	2004	2003
Net revenues	11.4	11.5	12.8	11.3
Cash flow provided by operating activity				
Net income (loss)	−1.3	16.7	16.2	17.5
Depreciation/amortization	19.4	19.7	22.6	19.2
(Increase) decrease, in inventory	−42.0	14.4	22.5	−56.5
Increase (decrease) in accounts payable	258.8	−77.1	−18.4	−43.3
Other operating activities	−141.8	−114.0	−26.2	146.7
Net cash provided (used) by operations	18.2	−6.1	5.5	36.3
Cash flow provided by investing activity				
Capital expenditures	−8.7	−1.7	12.5	27.6
(Acq.) disp. of subs., business	67.6	250.2	238.1	0.9
(Purchase) sale of investments	−98.5	1,577.0	66.7	−177.9
Other investing activities	−15.9	70.8	−128.8	−417.1
Net cash provided (used) by investing	66.7	2.4	12.1	36.2
Cash flow provided by financing activity				
Proceeds from common stock sale	−8.0	45.3	25.6	−30.4
Repurchases on common stock	119.9	−2.1	99.9	−22.3
Proceeds from borrowing	371.5	90.5	—	−100.0
Repayments of debt	5,770.8	−95.3	5,566.7	—
Dividends, other distribution	62.8	19.2	20.8	20.9
Other financing activities	−77.2	−150.0	—	—
Net cash provided (used) by financing	−88.4	−37.2	44.1	−10.8
Change in cash	−226.0	−141.9	−157.9	−308.1

In the "cash flow provided by investing activity" section of the SCF, purchases of fixed assets, mostly retail stores for Home Depot, increased slowly in absolute terms from 2002 to 2004 ($2.7 billion to $3.9 billion), but declined the following two years. Exhibit 10.5 indicates that capital expenditures decreased in 2005 by almost 2 percent and by 9 percent in 2006. Apparently, expenditures for new stores have not been keeping up with the growth in revenues and net income. In contrast, depreciation expense was up substantially over the same period. This suggests that either aggregate average depreciation lives have been shortened or a greater percentage of new stores are being financed through capital leases with shorter amortization periods.

Another significant change in the SCF is the increasing amount of acquisitions. These were only a small percentage of net income in 2003, but then became significant in 2004 and beyond. Reference to other corporate documents reveals that Home Depot had changed its strategy from one of building stores to one of acquiring existing store chains and distribution centers. And as we observed earlier, long-term debt increased significantly in the two most recent years, and treasury stock purchases in the past four years represented a significant and increasing percentage of net income.

Other Key Financial Ratios

The common-size and percentage change ratios helped spot key trends in Home Depot's financial statement line items. A series of core financial ratios should also be examined to round out the historical perspective of the company's liquidity and solvency, working capital, and profitability. A summary of these ratios is provided in Exhibit 10.6. Each category contains a set of ratios evaluated by virtually all analysts, and each is discussed in turn. Formulas for these ratios are summarized in Appendix B.

Liquidity refers to how much cash the company has generated, including what can be converted to cash in short order. Solvency, in contrast, refers to the company's ability to meet its obligations. The liquidity ratios for Home Depot reflect two trends. The first ratio tells us that the proportions of current assets and liabilities have remained more or less constant; however, the second depicts a significant downward trend. Current liabilities increased faster than cash and accounts receivable. The solvency ratios for Home Depot tell a different story. Home Depot did not carry much long-term debt until 2006, so any liquidity issues do not yield immediate concerns over long-term solvency. CFO to total liabilities shows a downward trend. Clearly, from this we can conclude that while long-term solvency is not an issue, Home Depot has become less liquid in 2006 than it was in 2003. But should this really be of concern? Efficiency ratios can help provide the answer.

The turnover ratios and the days ratios have opposite interpretations. For example, an inventory turnover of 5.04 is equivalent to the entire inventory being purchased and then completely sold five times per year. This is equivalent to 72.41 days inventory outstanding, which means, on average, the inventory was on the shelf 72.41 days before being sold. The inventory and accounts payable ratios are unsurprising and consistent over the four-year period. The accounts receivable ratios depict a mostly cash-based firm, which has begun selling on credit to relatively few customers.

Perhaps the most interesting metric in Exhibit 10.6 is "net days financing required." Using the 2006 data, one can conclude that Home Depot purchased inventory and held it on the shelf for 40 days before it had to pay for the inventory in cash. Then it was another 32 days (72 less 40) before it was sold. After that, it was 11 more days before those sales

Exhibit 10.6 Summary of Other Key Financial Ratios

	2006	2005	2004	2003
Liquidity Ratios				
Current ratio	1.39	1.18	1.37	1.40
Quick ratio	0.30	0.25	0.35	0.41
Solvency Ratios				
Long-term debt to equity	0.47	0.10	0.09	0.04
Liabilities to assets	0.53	0.39	0.38	0.35
CFO to liabilities	0.28	0.37	0.46	0.54
CFO to capex	2.16	1.67	1.75	1.87
Interest coverage	24.74	65.91	114.03	111.37
Efficiency Ratios				
Accounts receivable turnover	32.33	41.85	56.31	59.77
Inventory turnover	5.04	5.05	5.08	5.08
Accounts payable turnover	9.12	9.19	8.91	9.10
Asset turn over	1.88	1.95	1.99	2.01
Days receivables outstanding	11.29	8.72	6.48	6.11
Days inventory outstanding	72.41	72.33	71.82	71.84
Days payable outstanding	40.02	39.73	40.97	40.10
Net days financing required	43.68	41.32	37.33	37.85
Profitability Ratios				
Return on assets (%)	12.45	14.22	13.74	13.48
Return on equity (%)	22.43	23.04	21.54	20.33
Profit margin (%)	6.34	7.16	6.84	6.64
Financial leverage	1.88	1.65	1.58	1.52

were collected in cash, which means the total financing required for a selling cycle was 32 plus 11 equals 43 days. Some firms, like Dell Computer, historically had *positive* net days financing in excess of 20 days, because their inventories were only about 6 days, the receivables (from individual consumers as well as corporate customers) averaged about 15 days, and payables were about 45 days. Dell's selling cycle was cash positive. In the case of Home Depot, we can only say that the company's selling cycle is 43 days cash negative and, as the proportion of sales on credit increases, so will net days of required financing increase.

Anyone critically evaluating a company is arguably most concerned with whether that company has earned a profit. The interpretation of the size of that profit, however, depends on the amount of capital that management had at its disposal to earn that return. Home Depot has, on average, been generating solid returns as measured by these profitability metrics. For example, in 2006, Home Depot leveraged a 6.3 percent return on sales (ROS) into a 12.4 percent return on assets (ROA), because its net revenues were 1.88 times its average total assets. This asset turnover ratio is sometimes called the asset efficiency ratio, because it is interpretable as follows: Home Depot generated almost

Exhibit 10.7   Averages of Key Profitability Ratios

Industry	Profit Margin (%)	Asset Turnover	ROA (%)	Financial Leverage	ROE (%)
Aerospace and defense	5.9	1.0	5.9	3.6	21.5
Beverages	6.6	0.7	4.4	4.1	18.0
Chemical	6.6	1.0	6.6	3.2	20.9
Commercial banks	16.2	0.1	1.4	10.9	15.3
Computers and office equipment	6.5	1.1	7.4	2.5	18.5
Energy	2.6	1.1	2.9	5.1	14.9
Foodstores and drugstores	2.6	2.3	6.0	2.6	15.4
General merchandisers	3.3	2.3	7.5	2.3	17.0
Home builders	7.1	0.8	6.0	3.2	19.1
Internet services and retailing	10.5	0.5	5.4	1.7	9.3
Mining and oil production	26.6	0.3	8.2	2.7	21.8
Motor vehicles and parts	−1.4	1.4	−1.9	−6.6	12.6
Network and other comm. equipment	14.0	0.8	11.2	2.0	22.3
Pharmaceuticals	19.6	0.5	9.9	2.4	24.2
Railroads	13.1	0.4	5.5	2.7	15.0
Specialty retailers	3.6	2.2	7.8	2.5	19.4
Telecommunications	6.2	0.4	2.7	2.4	6.4
Utilities	6.8	0.4	2.8	3.8	10.6

Source: Fortune, April 30, 2007.

two dollars of revenue for each dollar of total assets. A higher ratio means the company was more efficient in using its assets to generate sales.

When multiplied times the financial leverage ratio, the ROA becomes return on equity (ROE). Home Depot's financial leverage ratio of 1.88 is moderate, meaning less leverage and a more cautious approach to financing. For comparison purposes, Exhibit 10.7 summarizes the averages of key profitability ratios for various industries around roughly the same time period as the data presented for Home Depot. Financially stronger firms usually outperform these averages.

Part II: Forecasting Financial Statements

Financial statement analysis encompasses the tools and techniques used to understand a business through its financial reports. Annual reports in general and financial statements in particular are prepared by management with the investors' needs in mind. Every investor has the objective of predicting future performance. Part I of this chapter illustrated how analysts make assessments of past profitability and risk. Using an array of ratios, the need to examine the historical performance through ratio analysis was highlighted. A critical objective of these assessments is to help project a set of financial statements, often called pro-forma financial statements. Pro-forma financial statements serve as a starting point for valuation, and a complete set of forecasted financial statements yields all possible inputs into all types of valuation models. An added advantage of pro-forma financial statements is that they necessitate consideration of all possible *financial* aspects of the business. Examples include required capital structure, cash-generating ability, solvency risk assessments, and sources of growth.

There are many approaches one might take to constructing a forecasted set of financials, but next we highlight five sequential steps that preclude the final valuation of the firm. A more detailed description of each follows again using Home Depot as an illustration.

Forecasting Steps for the Conventional Financial Statement

1. Project sales growth.
2. Project operating costs before depreciation, amortization, and interest.
3. Project the balance sheet.
4. Project depreciation, amortization, and interest.
5. Project the statement of cash flows.

Each step in the preparation of pro-forma financial statements requires an understanding of what drives the change in an account. The first two steps involve forecasting the income statement before interest, depreciation, amortization, and taxes. The process begins with projected sales, because future asset growth from operations, such as non-capital contributions or debt-financing sources, and expected costs derive directly from the revenue activities of a firm. For Home Depot, note that actual sales have grown by compounded annual growth rates of 11.5 percent, 11.9 percent, and 11.7 percent over the past two-, three-, and four-year periods, respectively. This modest acceleration can be attributed to a combination of store openings, acquisitions, and an improving U.S. economy up to 2006. The analyst should naturally question whether this sales growth will persist. Items to consider would be company-specific factors, such as the rate of new store openings and competition, and economic factors, such as inflation, housing demand, and expected consumer spending. While a thorough review of these factors is beyond the scope of this chapter, the critical importance of the sales forecast cannot be overemphasized. For simplicity, a 10 percent sales growth rate for the company is assumed over the next three years in Exhibit 10.8.

Exhibit 10.8 Forecasted Operating Income for 2007 through 2009

		2007	2008	2009
Net revenues	Growth assumed at 10%	$99,921	$109,913	$120,904
Cost of sales	Two-year average at 66.85% of sales	66,795	73,474	80,822
Gross margin		$33,126	$ 36,438	$ 40,082
SG&A	Two-year average at 22.08% of sales	20,196	22,215	24,437
EBITDA		$12,930	$ 14,223	$ 15,646

Copyright © 2010 by Eades et al. To download this form for your personal use, please visit www.wiley.com/go/portablemba5e.

A number of income statement costs follow directly from the sales activity forecasted. Recurring costs—such as cost of sales and selling, general, and administrative expenses (SG&A)—are viewed as directly related to generating sales, and thus are typically some reasonable function of predicted sales. A fixed-cost component may or may not be estimated for each operating expense component. One typically estimates fixed costs if expenses move in a predictable manner to revenue or if there is some known capacity constraint. For Home Depot, cost of sales and SG&A expense averaged 67 percent and 22 percent of sales, respectively, during 2006 and 2005. These percentages were relatively stable despite the 12 percent sales growth the company experienced. In the forecast, therefore, these costs are predicted to vary at these two-year average rates. Exhibit 10.8 summarizes the forecast of these items as the critical and often used subtotal of earnings before interest, taxes, depreciation, and amortization (EBITDA).

The remaining costs on the income statement—interest, depreciation, and amortization—could be estimated at this stage, but a more practical approach is to tie these values to their respective long-term asset and liability accounts. These latter expenses are thus estimated *after* the balance sheet is forecasted. Therefore the third step in the pro-forma financial statement is a forecast of the balance sheet.

In forecasting Home Depot's pro-forma balance sheets, key relationships with revenue are assumed. Absent information to the contrary, a simple starting assumption is that there are no changes in capital structure, such as additional borrowings or stock issuances. For a retailer like Home Depot, analysts will commonly assume growth rates in asset components that are consistent with predicted growth in sales. Historical turnover rates (i.e., sales divided by an asset account) serve as a starting point. For instance, Exhibit 10.6 shows that inventory averaged five times turnover over the past few years. Thus, using this base relationship, to generate any $5 of forecasted cost of sales, the company must have $1 of forecasted inventory in place. Similar relationships can be derived for receivables, fixed assets, and other operating asset and liability accounts, as indicated in Exhibit 10.9.

After Home Depot's pro-forma balance sheets are completed and capital structure forecasts are in place, bottom-line earnings and EPS can now be estimated (see Exhibit 10.10). Note again that the income statement could have been completed earlier. Waiting until this stage, however, is recommended because capital structure variables will impact the level of interest expense and asset levels affect the depreciation estimate, for example. For Home Depot, interest expense can be computed using the prior-year interest rate of 5.5 percent times the projected debt balance.[7] The depreciation expense can be estimated as the historical depreciation rate of 4.8 percent times the new forecasted fixed-asset base.

At this stage, the analyst has successfully forecasted a series of balance sheets, income statements, and earnings estimates. The final pro-forma step involves preparing the forecasted statements of cash flow as a direct output from the forecasted balance sheets and income statements (see Exhibit 10.11). There are two direct benefits that result from this final forecasting step. First, the projected sources and uses of cash help with the assessments of future liquidity, solvency, investing, and financing issues that Home Depot's management might be facing. Second, estimates of the future stream of nominal cash flows realized by the company can be recast in terms of free cash flows, forming what later becomes the basis for Home Depot's valuation. Conventional discounted cash flow (DCF) valuation techniques are described in the next section.

Exhibit 10.9   Forecasted Balance Sheets for 2007 through 2009

		2007	2008	2009
Assets				
Cash and mkt. sec.	Balance of retained cash + mkt. sec.	$ 5,111	$ 6,929	$ 11,096
Receivables	2-year average turnover (37.1)	2,694	2,963	3,259
Inventories	2-year average turnover (5.0)	13,243	14,568	16,024
Other current assets	2-year average turnover (113.3)	882	970	1,067
PPE, net	2-year average turnover (3.5)	28,754	31,629	34,792
Goodwill	Constant	6,314	6,314	6,314
Other assets	Constant	1,344	1,344	1,344
Total assets		$ 58,341	$ 64,717	$ 73,897
Liabilities and Equity				
Accounts payable	2-year average turnover (9.4)	$ 6,986	$ 7,684	$ 10,334
Accrued expenses	2-year average turnover (7.2)	3,056	3,362	3,698
Deferred revenue	Constant	1,634	1,634	1,634
Other current liabilities	Constant	2,646	2,646	2,646
Noncurrent LT debt	Constant	11,643	11,643	11,643
Other LT liabilities	Constant	2,969	2,969	2,969
Common stock	Constant	8,051	8,051	8,051
Retained earnings	Function of earnings and dividends	37,739	43,110	49,305
Treasury stock	Constant	(16,383)	(16,383)	(16,383)
Total liab. and equity		$ 58,341	$ 64,717	$ 73,897

Exhibit 10.10   Forecasted Income Statements for 2007 through 2009

		2007	2008	2009
EBITDA		$12,930	$14,223	$15,646
Depreciation and amortization	2-year avg. depr./PPE (6.5%)	1,966	2,163	2,266
Interest and investment increase	Constant	27	27	27
Interest expense	Prior-year debt rate (5.5%)	638	638	638
Earnings before taxes		$10,354	$11,450	$12,770
Income taxes	2-year average tax rate (37.6%)	3,894	4,306	4,802
Net income		$ 6,460	$ 7,144	$ 7,967

Exhibit 10.11   Forecasted Statements of Cash Flow for 2007 through 2009

	2007	2008	2009
Cash from Operations			
Net income (loss)	$ 6,460	$ 7,144	$ 7,967
Depreciation/amortization	1,966	2,163	2,266
(Income) decrease, in operating accounts	1,958	(678)	1,135
Net cash provided (used) by operations	$10,384	$ 8,629	$11,368
Cash from Investing			
Capital expenditures	$(4,115)	$(5,038)	$(5,428)
Other investing activities	—	—	—
Net cash provided (used) by investing	$(4,115)	$(5,038)	$(5,428)
Cash from Financing			
Net proceeds from stock transactions	—	—	—
Net proceeds from debt	—	—	—
Dividends, other distribution	$(1,773)	$(1,773)	$(1,773)
Net cash provided (used) by financing	$(1,773)	$(1,773)	$(1,773)
Change in cash	$ 4,497	$ 1,818	$ 4,167

Copyright © 2010 by Eades et al. To download this form for your personal use, please visit www.wiley.com/go/portablemba5e.

Part III: Firm Valuation

The value of any investment depends on two critical factors: (1) the future nominal dollar returns the investment will generate, and (2) the required percentage return demanded by the investor for the use of capital (i.e., the firm's cost of capital). For instance, as an investor a bank would be willing to provide a mortgage—an investment in the borrower—only with the expectation that interest and principal (the dollar returns) will be repaid at the prevailing loan rate (the rate of return). Valuing a security such as Home Depot's stock is essentially no different. At most, investors are willing to pay a price for Home Depot's stock equivalent to the expected future dollar returns they expect the company can generate that in turn result in a rate of return that compensates investors for the riskiness of their investment. The questions then arise: How does one estimate future dollar returns? And how does one measure the required rate of return (cost of capital)? Volumes have been written on those two questions alone, but what follows are the basic input mechanics used in the most popular of valuation models—discounted cash flow.

Review of DCF Basics

The DCF approach attempts to determine the *enterprise value*, or value of the company, by computing the present value of cash flows over the life of the company. To estimate the enterprise value requires that free cash flows (FCF) be estimated and then discounted by the weighted average cost of capital (WACC).[8] The analysis is broken into two parts: a forecast period and a terminal value.

In the *forecast period*, explicit forecasts of free cash flow that incorporate the economic costs and benefits of the transaction must be developed. Ideally, the forecast period should comprise the interval over which the firm is in a transitional state, as when enjoying a temporary competitive advantage (i.e., the circumstances where expected returns exceed required returns). In most circumstances, a forecast period of five or 10 years is used, although it can be much shorter.

The *terminal value* of the company, derived from free cash flows occurring after the forecast period, is estimated in the last year of the forecast period and capitalizes the present value of all future cash flows beyond the forecast period. To estimate the terminal value, cash flows are projected under a steady-state assumption that the firm enjoys no opportunities for abnormal growth or that expected returns equal required returns following the forecast period. Once a schedule of free cash flows is developed for the enterprise, the weighted average cost of capital is used to discount those cash flows to determine the present value. The sum of the present values of the forecast period and the terminal-value cash flows provides an estimate of enterprise value.

A brief review is in order for the calculations of free cash flows, terminal value, and the WACC. It is important to realize that these fundamental concepts work equally well when valuing an investment project (see Chapter 5 on financial management) as they do in the firm valuation setting described here.

Free Cash Flows

Free cash flow is equivalent to the sum of net operating profits after taxes (NOPAT), plus depreciation and noncash charges, less capital investment and less investment in working capital. NOPAT captures the earnings after taxes that are available to all providers of capital. That is, NOPAT has no deductions for financing costs. Moreover, because the tax deductibility of interest payments is accounted for in the WACC, such financing tax effects are also excluded from the free cash flow, which is expressed in Equation 10.1:

$$\text{FCF} = \text{NOPAT} + \text{Depreciation} - \text{Capex} - \Delta \text{NWC} \qquad (10.1)$$

where:

NOPAT = EBIT $(1 - t)$ where t is the appropriate marginal (not average) cash tax rate, which should be inclusive of federal, state, local, and foreign jurisdictional taxes

Depreciation = noncash operating charges, including depreciation, depletion, and amortization recognized for tax purposes

Capex = capital expenditures for fixed assets

ΔNWC = the increase in net working capital defined as current assets less the non-interest-bearing current liabilities[9]

The cash flow forecast should be grounded in a thorough industry and company forecast. Care should be taken to ensure that the forecast reflects consistency with firm strategy as well as with macroeconomic and industry trends and competitive pressure.

The forecast period is normally the years during which the analyst estimates free cash flows that are consistent with creating value. A convenient way to think about value creation is whenever the return on net assets (RONA)[10] exceeds the WACC.[11] RONA can be divided into an income statement component and a balance sheet component:

$$\text{RONA} = \frac{\text{NOPAT}}{\text{Net Assets}}$$
$$= \frac{\text{NOPAT}}{\text{Sales}} \times \frac{\text{Sales}}{\text{Net Assets}}$$

In this context, value is created whenever earnings power increases (NOPAT/Sales) or when asset efficiency is improved (Sales/Net Assets). In other words, analysts are assuming value creation whenever they allow the profit margin to improve on the income statement and whenever they allow sales to improve relative to the level of assets on the balance sheet.

Terminal Value

A terminal value (TV) in the final year of the forecast period is added to reflect the present value of all cash flows occurring thereafter. Because it capitalizes all future cash flows beyond the final year, the terminal value can be a large component of the value of a company, and therefore deserves careful attention. This can be of particular importance when cash flows over the forecast period are close to zero (or even negative) as the result of aggressive investment for growth.

A standard estimator of the terminal value in the final year of the cash flow forecast is the constant growth valuation formula (Equation 10.2). This formula assumes that the cash flows to the company will occur forever (i.e., an infinite time horizon). Although the assumption of infinity is clearly unrealistic, it is mathematically convenient and produces results very similar to an assumption of a 20-year horizon, for example,

$$\text{Terminal Value} = \frac{\text{FCF}^{\text{Steady State}}}{(\text{WACC} - g)} \qquad (10.2)$$

where:

$\text{FCF}^{\text{Steady State}} =$ the steady-state expected free cash flow for the year after the final year of the cash flow forecast

$\text{WACC} =$ the weighted average cost of capital

$g =$ the expected steady-state growth rate of $\text{FCF}^{\text{Steady State}}$ in perpetuity

The free cash flow value used in the constant growth valuation formula should reflect the steady-state cash flow for the year after the forecast period. The assumption of the formula is that in steady state, this cash flow will grow in perpetuity at the steady-state growth rate. A convenient approach is to assume that RONA remains constant in perpetuity; that is, both profit margin and asset turnover remain constant in perpetuity. Under this assumption, the analyst grows all financial statement line items (i.e., revenue, costs, assets) at the expected steady-state growth rate. In perpetuity, this assumption makes logical sense because if a firm is truly in steady state, the financial statements should be growing at the same rate.

Discount Rate (WACC)

The discount rate should reflect the weighted average of investors' opportunity cost (WACC) on comparable investments. The WACC matches the business risk, expected inflation, and currency of the cash flows to be discounted. In order to avoid penalizing the investment opportunity, the WACC also must incorporate the appropriate target weights of financing going forward. Recall that the appropriate rate is a blend of the required rates of return on debt and equity, weighted by the proportion of the firm's market value they make up (Equation 10.3).

$$\text{WACC} = W_D K_D (1 - t) + W_E K_E \qquad (10.3)$$

where:

K_D = the required yield on new debt: yield to maturity

K_E = the cost of equity capital

W_D, W_E = target percentages of debt and equity (using market values of debt and equity)[12]

t = the marginal tax rate

The costs of debt and equity should be going-forward market rates of return. For debt securities, this is often the yield to maturity that would be demanded on new instruments of the same credit rating and maturity. The cost of equity can be obtained from the capital asset pricing model (CAPM). See Equation 10.4.

$$K_E = R_f + \beta(MRP) \tag{10.4}$$

where:

R_f = the expected return on risk-free securities over a time horizon consistent with the investment horizon. Most firm valuations are best served by using a long-maturity government bond yield.

MRP = the expected market risk premium. This value is commonly estimated as the average historical difference between the returns on common stocks and long-term government bonds. For example, Ibbotson Associates estimated that the geometric mean return between 1926 and 2007 for large-capitalization U.S. equities between 1926 and 2007 was 10.4 percent. The geometric mean return on long-term government bonds was 5.5 percent. The difference between the two implies a historical market risk premium of about 5 percent. In practice one observes estimates of the market risk premium that commonly range from 5 percent to 8 percent.

β or beta = a measure of the systematic risk of a firm's common stock. The beta of common stock includes compensation for business and financial risk.

Application of DCF to Home Depot

Exhibit 10.12 illustrates four DCF steps in the valuation of Home Depot:

1. Forecasted free cash flow (FCF) over an assumed three-year horizon.

2. Forecasted aggregate FCF for the years beyond the three-year horizon (i.e., the terminal value).

3. Discount all future cash flows using the appropriate WACC.

4. Subtract any nonoperating liabilities to yield total equity value. Dividing by shares yields share price.

The value of Home Depot is directly dependent on the amount of cash it can generate above what must be retained to keep the company operating and growing. This free cash flow can be directly computed from the company's forecasted financial statements, and it is interpretable as the presumed dollar return that is expected to be generated from Home Depot's operating assets. Exhibit 10.12 illustrates this calculation. For the years 2007 to 2009, these amounts total $6.7 billion, $4.0 billion, and $6.3 billion.

Practically speaking, it is unreasonable to continue to forecast FCF indefinitely and the terminal value assumptions just described must be implemented. For simplicity, in

Exhibit 10.12   Example Discounted Cash Flow Valuation

		2007	2008	2009
NOPAT		$6,858	$7,542	$8,365
Add: depreciation and amortization expense		1,966	2,163	2,266
Less: capital expenditures		(4,115)	(5,038)	(5,428)
Less: change in working capital		1,958	(678)	1,135
Free cash flow		$6,667	$3,989	$6,338
			Terminal value —>	$106,322
Present values under assumed WACC		$6,138	$3,382	$87,934
Enterprise value	$97,455			
Less: market value of debt	11,643			
Market value of equity	$85,812			
Shares outstanding	1,970			
Estimated share price	$ 43.56			
Terminal growth assumed:	2.50%			
WACC estimated:	8.61%			

this illustration a steady-state expected FCF is assumed after three years. The estimated terminal value is approximately $106.3 billion.

Discounted cash flow theory next requires that *future* dollar returns be recast into *current* cash equivalents. As described earlier, the WACC is the average of two returns, those for long-term debt and those for stock equity. The intuition behind the rate is that FCFs are generated by the asset contributions of both lenders and stockholders, and the demanded return for FCFs earned by assets should be a weighted average of those returns. For Home Depot we use the following inputs to estimate WACC:

R_f = 4.56% (10-year U.S. Treasury yield December 2006)

MRP = 5.0%

β = 0.95 (beta estimate from Value Line)

K_E = 9.31% = 4.56% + 0.95 × 5.0%

K_D = 6.22% (Baa corporate debt yield, December 2006)

t = 37.6% (previous two-year average tax rate)

W_D = 13% = debt value/(debt + equity value) = 11,643/(11.643 + 78,800)[13]

W_E = 87% = equity value/(debt + equity value) = 78,800/(11.643 + 78,800)

$WACC = W_D K_D (1 - t) + W_E K_E$ = 17% × (1 − .376) + 87% × 9.31% = 8.61%

Using the estimated WACC to discount the FCF obtained under steps 1 and 2 yields a total enterprise value of $97.5 billion.

Because our computed enterprise value equates to the market value of Home Depot's net operating assets, the final step requires that we subtract the financing liabilities that are embedded in this value. This amount is relatively small, given the low financial leverage the company enjoys. Dividing by total shares outstanding (1.97 billion) yields an estimated share price of $43.56, which compares quite favorably to the actual market price of $40 per share.

Using Multiples

A frequently used valuation technique is to use a market value–based financial ratio to value a firm. A typical approach is for analysts to collect data on competitors to Home Depot such as Lowe's and compare how the market values those competitors relative to Home Depot. The theory is that the market should value the primary drivers of value similarly across companies in the same industry. For example, we can compute the ratio of a company's enterprise value to EBITDA. EBITDA is a measure of a company's earning potential that is close to free cash flow because it includes the cash flow effect of depreciation and amortization. Therefore, the relationship of a company's enterprise value (debt plus market value of equity) to EBITDA should be similar for Lowe's and Home Depot.

To illustrate the use of the multiple, assume for the moment that Lowe's has an EBITDA multiple of 8.1. This says that the capital market values every dollar of Lowe's' EBITDA with 8.1 dollars of market value. To compare Lowe's' multiple with Home Depot's, we can divide Home Depot's enterprise value in 2006 by its 2006 EBITDA:

$$\text{Enterprise Value} = \text{Debt} + \text{Equity} = \$11{,}643 + \$40 \times 1{,}970 = \$90{,}443 \text{ million}$$
$$\text{EBITDA} = \text{EBIT} + \text{Depreciation and Amortization} = \$9{,}673 + \$1{,}762$$
$$= \$11{,}435 \text{ million}$$
$$\text{Enterprise Value}/\text{EBITDA} = \$90{,}443/\$11{,}435 = 7.9$$

Thus, Home Depot's multiple is slightly lower than Lowe's: 7.9 for Home Depot and 8.1 for Lowe's. One could conclude that Home Depot is selling for a small discount in the market, but these multiples are very close and well within the bounds of normal variability across competitors. Thus, the prudent analyst would likely conclude that Home Depot and Lowe's have very similar market valuations and neither appears to be incorrectly priced.

Part IV: Other Critical Considerations in Financial Analysis

The discussion thus far has intentionally focused on summarizing the mechanical aspects of financial analysis: ratio analysis, pro-forma forecasting, and valuation. This basic framework can be applied to virtually any company. Paramount to an effective evaluation of the firm, however, is to look beyond mechanical modeling. Many label these factors as "nonfinancial" performance and valuation drivers. They are not readily captured or observable on the financial statements themselves. These include but are not limited to: (1) a review of textual disclosures that help one understand risks and trends, including macroeconomic factors; (2) evaluating material accounting measurement concerns; (3) assessing corporate governance and management skill at implementing a defined strategy; and (4) gathering and evaluating additional data not on the financial statements but disclosed elsewhere about the firm. Brief summaries of each are discussed in turn.

Management Discussion and Analysis

The degree of rigor one can use in financial analysis is constrained by the level of transparency extending beyond the financial statements. In a speech on the state of corporate disclosure, U.S. Securities and Exchange Commissioner Cynthia Glassman highlighted the importance (and benefits) of transparency for financial analysis.[14] Companies are obligated to communicate to outsiders the financial conditions and results of operations beyond just the mere application of generally accepted accounting principles (GAAP) and the preparation of financial statements. She emphasized that management discussion and analysis (MD&A) is one critical medium where that must happen. The MD&A must be more than just a recitation of what is contained in the financial statements, and should provide management an opportunity to disclose known trends and uncertainties in its business, to present detailed analyses of important year-to-year changes that are material to operations, and to clarify and provide context to the company's operation that are not readily apparent through reference to the financial statements (Reg S–K, Item 303). Home Depot's MD&A clearly satisfies this objective. For instance, the company provides additional guidance on how to interpret the aforementioned 11.5 percent sales growth:

> In the face of a slowdown in the housing market, our retail comparable store sales declined 2.8% in fiscal 2006 driven by a decline in comparable store customer transactions. This was partially offset by an increase in our average ticket of 1.6% in fiscal 2006 to $58.90, including increases in 8 of 10 departments.

As further examples, Home Depot's MD&A also indicates that during fiscal 2006:

- $3.5 billion of capital expenditures was for new-store construction, store modernization, and technology.
- Fully 125 new stores were added, including 12 acquired in China. These new stores cannibalized 13.5 percent of sales from existing stores.
- The increase in SG&A expense as a percentage of sales can be attributed to added associate labor costs, increased spending on store maintenance, executive severance, and the now-required expensing of stock options.
- The company is evaluating strategic alternatives for its supply segment that would enhance shareholder value, including a sale or spin-off.

Consider how valuable these disclosures are to placing a context around interpreting the levels and trends in Home Depot's financial statement data outlined earlier. No financial analysis could be complete without a thorough reading of this required part of the annual report.

Financial Statement Footnotes

The MD&A can be distinguished from the footnotes to the financial statement in that the latter: (1) provides additional detail about items reported in the financial statements, (2) summarizes the method of measurement of critical accounts, and/or (3) provides the value of an account under an alternative accounting method. Footnote disclosures are required under GAAP in most instances. As with the MD&A, a careful read of these notes is critical to understanding and interpreting historical ratios, and a necessary part of developing accurate financial forecasts.

**Exhibit 10.13 Example Interest Expense Forecast
(Dollar Amounts in Millions)**

	Rate	Amount	2006 Month Issue	Partial Year	Full Year
Redeemed	5.375	500	April	$(20)	$(27)
Issued	Floating*	750	December	3	39
Issued	5.2	1,000	March	43	52
Issued	5.4	3,000	March	135	162
Issued	5.25	1,250	December	5	66
Issued	5.875	3,000	December	15	176
				$181	$468

*Assumed as 5.2% to start.

Home Depot's annual report included 13 footnotes with much useful information, including this serious fact that the company recognized a $227 million "unrecorded expense" in 2006 for errors relating to stock option grant dates, although there was "no intentional wrongdoing by any current member" of the management team or the board. It did go on to say the Securities and Exchange Commission (SEC) and a U.S. attorney were investigating.

And surprisingly, the company began booking "breakage" for revenue-gift card balances not expected to be used: $52 million in 2005, the first year of the new policy, and $33 million in 2006.

The two most significant footnotes reported on long-term debt and business segments. During 2006, long-term debt increased $8,971 million or 335 percent. As shown in the Exhibit 10.13, the new debt issues, less the one debt issue retired, increased net interest expense by $181 million in 2006. The full-year effect can be forecasted to be $468 million in subsequent years.

Management and Corporate Governance Considerations

The earnings, cash flows, and other metrics outlined in the preceding sections are simply a quantitative summary of a number of management decisions that influence performance. The most critical of assessments in financial analysis, therefore, pertains to management quality and its effectiveness at implementing a firm's strategy. There can be no precise recipe for such an assessment, but attempts should be made nevertheless. And unfortunately, even in the long run a well-managed firm often cannot overcome negative economic forces and weak demand. A poorly managed firm, however, will rarely extract significant performance and returns in the long run.

During the years 2002 to 2006, Home Depot struggled mightily with negative perceptions of executive management. The much maligned CEO during that time, Bob Nardelli (later CEO of beleaguered Chrysler), was hired after a long, distinguished career at General Electric. In the move to Home Depot, Nardelli brought with him many former GE managers, but they were ill prepared to adapt to the home improvement retailing market. He resigned his post under shareholder and board pressure in early 2007. During his appointment, the company's financial performance was relatively strong, but its stock price lagged. Commentators cited a number of factors for this divergence.[15] The following are short examples of how particular management decisions at Home Depot had alienated each of the company's main stakeholders.

- *Analysts:* Home Depot ceased releasing same-store sales figures. Analysts, Nardelli argued, needlessly focused on this "misleading" retail metric.
- *Employees:* After 2001, there was massive turnover in upper management, with over 98 percent of the top 170 managers new to their positions, and 56 percent of those from outside the company. Full-time store workers were replaced with part-time workers in an effort to drive up gross margins.
- *Customers:* The cuts in store staffing led to a marked reduction in customer satisfaction, previously the hallmark of the Home Depot experience. By 2005, the company had slipped to dead last in one very influential consumer satisfaction survey.
- *Shareholders:* Although the company's stock price had significantly underperformed, Nardelli earned over $38 million in compensation in 2005. At the 2006 annual shareholders' meeting, no members of the board of directors were present to face investors' angry questions, and Nardelli himself left immediately following a brief summary of the company's financial performance.

Frank Blake, Home Depot's new CEO, had the task of restoring the confidence of each of those stakeholder groups.

Other Financial Metrics

Financial analysis must include an examination of other financial metrics relevant to a company that, in combination with reported financial statement data, enhance both the understanding of past performance and the accuracy of financial projections. For example, airlines commonly disclose revenue per available seat-mile, hotels disclose available rooms and revenues per available room, and utilities disclose available megawatts capacity. For retailers such as Home Depot, alternative financial metrics include but are not limited to:

- Number, locations, and square footage of stores.
- Number of new stores opened.
- Comparable same-store sales.
- Weighted average sales per square foot.
- Number and average dollar amount of transactions.
- Number of employees.

Home Depot discloses each of these metrics annually for the immediate prior 10 years. A more complete analysis of how knowledge of these metrics would influence projections is beyond the scope of this chapter, but suffice it to say that taken together they help analysts understand critical items, such as the components of growth (i.e., organic store growth versus store expansion), geographic expansion efforts, customers, and other trends. No analysis would be complete without considering alternative disclosed financial metrics.

MBA Concepts in Action

Firm valuation is a critical skill for investment bankers and equity analysts. Equity analysts compare their estimates of a company's stock price to the actual market price in order to recommend whether the stock is undervalued, overvalued, or correctly valued. Investment bankers value companies in a variety of situations, but most prominently during a merger or acquisition transaction. When a company seeks to acquire another, the price offered is critical to getting the target shareholders to accept the offer, and it is also critical to avoid overpaying for the target company.

Increasingly, however, there is another arena in which firm valuation plays a critical role: bankruptcy court. When a firm enters a Chapter 11 bankruptcy, the management is charged with the responsibility of formulating a plan of reorganization (POR). The POR details a new capital structure for the company that management feels will be conducive to the long-term survival of the company. Typically this means that a large amount of debt on the company's books is converted to equity in order to reduce the interest burden on the company. When a company's earnings fail to cover interest expenses, some sort of capital restructuring is necessary to keep the company afloat. Without the protection of the bankruptcy court, it is often impossible to gain agreement from the many different lenders and other providers of capital because no party wants to voluntarily take a loss on its investment.

Delphi Corporation

Delphi Corporation operated as a separate business sector within General Motors for almost eight years, before it was spun off in 1999 as an independent company. Delphi became one of the largest global suppliers of vehicle electronics, transportation components, integrated systems and modules, and other electronic technology. Though GM continued to be Delphi's key customer, Delphi developed relationships with every major global automotive original equipment manufacturer (OEM), including Ford Motor Company, DaimlerChrysler Corporation, Volkswagen Group, Hyundai, and Renault/Nissan Motor Company. In 2005, Delphi was number 63 on the Fortune 500 list of the largest corporations in the United States.

Delphi was profitable in the first two years after separation from GM, but it incurred substantial losses afterward. By 2005 Delphi was having difficulty making its interest payments. After discussions with GM and its major unions failed to result in a restructuring of its U.S. operations, Delphi filed voluntary petitions under Chapter 11 of the Bankruptcy Code in October 2005. The objective of the filing was to take advantage of the protection offered by the bankruptcy court to allow the development of a sustainable financial reorganization and thereby preserve value for its stakeholders. The filing listed Delphi's consolidated global assets and liabilities as of August 31, 2005, as $17.1 billion and $22.2 billion, respectively.

In year-end 2007, after more than two years in bankruptcy, Delphi management had a plan of reorganization that would pay some stakeholders 100 percent while others would take substantial losses (see Exhibit 10.14).

For Delphi to emerge from bankruptcy would require the acceptance of the POR. Each claimant class had a vote, which was deemed favorable if two-thirds of those within the class voted to accept and if those votes represented at least 50 percent of the value of the class. The viability of the plan to the claimants, however, depended on the value of

Exhibit 10.14 Summary of Delphi Plan of Reorganization

Claimant Class	Amount Due ($ millions)	Proposed Plan	Recovery
Debtor in possession lenders	3,427	To be paid in full	100%
Administrative expense allowed by Bankruptcy Code	520	To be paid in full	100%
Claim of taxes by government	50	To be paid in full	100%
Secured claims	25	To be paid in full	100%
General unsecured claims	3,872	Impaired by plan	(a) New common stock for 78.4% of claim value. (b) Discount rights to buy equity at 35.6% discount to plan value of $59.61 for balance 21.6% of claim.
General Motors' claim	2,573	Impaired by plan	(a) $1.073 billion in junior preferred securities. (b) $1.5 billion in a combination of at least $750 million in cash and the balance in second lien note.
Section 510(b) note claims, equity claims, and ERISA claims	552	Impaired by plan	(a) New common stock for 77.3% of claim value. (b) Discount rights to buy equity at 35.6% discount to plan value of $59.61 for balance 22.7% of claim.
Existing common stock of Delphi Corporation		Impaired by plan	(a) 461,552 shares of new stock. (b) Par value rights exercisable at the plan equity value. (c) Seven-year warrants exercisable at a 20.7% premium to the plan equity value. (d) Six-month warrants exercisable at a 9.0% premium to the plan equity value. (e) Ten-year warrants exercisable at plan equity value.

the new securities offered them by the POR. For example, the general unsecured claims amounted to $3,872 million of loans to Delphi. In exchange for these loans the POR offered shares of stock in the post-bankruptcy Delphi Corporation. No one knew for certain, however, what the value of the new shares would be, so the claimants' decision had to be based on an assessment of firm value. Delphi management used an investment bank's valuation of the company that utilized a discounted cash flow model to estimate the projected price per share of the recapitalized Delphi Corporation.

The investment bank's valuation model projected free cash flows for the company and discounted those cash flows at the company's WACC to get an estimate of the enterprise value. To arrive at the new equity value, the amount of new debt was subtracted. The price per share equaled the equity value divided by the number of shares to be issued to all the different claimants. Therefore, if the assumptions of the model were accurate, the claimant classes could judge the extent to which the new Delphi shares they were to receive would repay their claim.

The POR was approved in part because claimants were comfortable with the valuation of Delphi. At the last minute, however, the new funding for Delphi fell apart and the reorganization plan had to be abandoned. The value of the new shares was premised upon the amount of new debt that would be raised to pay in full the unimpaired classes such as the secured creditors. Without the new debt, the plan was not implementable.

Delphi was forced to remain in Chapter 11 until it emerged on October 6, 2009.

Financial Analysis and Firm Valuation in MBA Curricula

Financial analysis and firm valuation are popular electives in MBA programs. Sometimes the topics are combined into a single elective, but often they are taught across several courses in the accounting and finance areas. Students interested in investment banking will seek out such courses, which often appear as a mergers and acquisitions elective or as a securities valuation course.

Appendix A: Home Depot Financial Statements

Home Depot Income Statements

Fiscal Year	2006	2005	2004	2003	2002
Net revenues	$90,837	$81,511	$73,094	$64,816	$58,247
Cost of sales	61,054	54,191	48,664	44,236	40,139
Gross margin	$29,783	$27,320	$24,430	$20,580	$18,108
Selling, general, and administrative	18,348	16,485	15,256	12,713	11,375
Depreciation and amortization	1,762	1,472	1,248	1,021	903
Operating income	$ 9,673	$ 9,363	$ 7,926	$ 6,846	$ 5,830
Interest and investment income	27	62	56	59	79
Interest expense	392	143	70	62	37
Earnings before taxes	$ 9,308	$ 9,282	$ 7,912	$ 6,843	$ 5,872
Income taxes	3,547	3,444	2,911	2,539	2,208
Net income	$ 5,761	$ 5,838	$ 5,001	$ 4,304	$ 3,664
Diluted earnings per share	2.79	2.72	2.26	1.88	1.56

Home Depot Balance Sheets

Fiscal Year	2006	2005	2004	2003	2002
Assets					
Cash and marketable securities	$ 614	$ 807	$ 2,165	$ 2,852	$ 2,253
Receivables	3,223	2,396	1,499	1,097	1,072
Inventories	12,822	11,401	10,076	9,076	8,338
Other current assets	1,341	665	533	303	254
Property, plant, and equipment, net	26,605	24,901	22,726	20,063	17,168
Goodwill	6,314	3,684	1,412	833	575
Other assets	1,344	551	609	213	351
Total assets	$52,263	$44,405	$39,020	$34,437	$30,011
Liabilities and Equity					
Accounts payable	$ 7,356	$ 6,032	$ 5,766	$ 5,159	$ 4,560
Accrued expenses	1,295	3,311	2,971	2,430	2,243
Deferred revenue	1,634	1,757	1,546	1,281	998
Other current liabilities	2,646	1,801	172	684	234
Noncurrent long-term debt	11,643	2,672	2,148	856	1,321
Other long-term liabilities	2,969	2,194	2,378	1,634	708
Common stock	8,051	7,407	6,769	6,303	5,976
Retained earnings	33,052	28,943	23,962	19,680	15,971
Treasury stock	(16,383)	(9,712)	(6,692)	(3,590)	(2,000)
Total liabilities and equity	$52,263	$44,405	$39,020	$34,437	$30,011

Home Depot Statements of Cash Flow

Fiscal Year	2006	2005	2004	2003	2002
Cash Flow Provided by Operating Activity					
Net income (loss)	$ 5,761	$ 5,838	$ 5,001	$ 4,304	$ 3,664
Depreciation/amortization	1,886	1,579	1,319	1,076	903
(Increase) decrease in inventory	(563)	(971)	(849)	(693)	(1,592)
Increase (decrease) in accounts payable	531	148	645	790	1,394
Other operating activities	46	(110)	788	1,068	433
Net cash provided (used) by operations	$ 7,661	$ 6,484	$ 6,904	$ 6,545	$ 4,802

Home Depot Statements of Cash Flow

Fiscal Year	2006	2005	2004	2003	2002
Cash Flow Provided by Investing Activity					
Capital expenditures	$(3,542)	$(3,881)	$(3,948)	$(3,508)	$(2,749)
(Acq.) disp. of subs., business	(4,268)	(2,546)	(727)	(215)	(213)
(Purchase) sale of investments	25	1,677	100	60	(77)
Other investing activities	138	164	96	(333)	105
Net cash provided (used) by investing	$(7,647)	$(4,586)	$(4,479)	$(3,996)	$(2,934)
Cash Flow Provided by Financing Activity					
Proceeds from common stock sale	$ 381	$ 414	$ 285	$ 227	$ 326
Repurchases of common stock	(6,684)	(3,040)	(3,106)	(1,554)	(2,000)
Proceeds from borrowing	8,935	1,895	995		1
Repayments of debt	(1,409)	(24)	(510)	(9)	—
Dividends, other distribution	(1,395)	(857)	(719)	(595)	(492)
Other financing activities	(31)	(136)	272	—	—
Net cash provided (used) by financing	$ (203)	$(1,748)	$(2,783)	$(1,931)	$(2,165)
Change in cash	$ (189)	$ 150	$ (358)	$ 618	$ (297)

Appendix B: Ratio Formulas

Liquidity Ratios

$$\text{Current Ratio} = \frac{\text{Current Assets}}{\text{Current Liabilities}}$$

$$\text{Quick Ratio} = \frac{\text{Cash} + \text{Marketable Securities} + \text{Receivables}}{\text{Current Liabilities}}$$

$$\text{CFO/CL} = \frac{\text{CFO}}{\text{Current Liabilities}}$$

Solvency Ratios

Long-Term Debt to Equity $= \dfrac{\text{Long-Term Debt}}{\text{Shareholders' Equity}}$

Liabilities to Assets $= \dfrac{\text{Total Liabilities}}{\text{Total Assets}}$

CFO to Liabilities $= \dfrac{\text{Cash from Operations}}{\text{Current Liabilities}}$

CFO to Capex $= \dfrac{\text{Cash from Operations}}{\text{Capital Expenditures}}$

Interest Coverage $= \dfrac{\text{Net Income} + \text{Taxes} + \text{Interest Expense}}{\text{Interest Expense}}$

Efficiency Ratios

Accounts Receivable (AR) Turnover $= \dfrac{\text{Net Revenue}}{\text{Average AR}}$

Inventory Turnover $= \dfrac{\text{Cost of Goods Sold}}{\text{Average Inventory}}$

Accounts Payable (AP) Turnover $= \dfrac{\text{Cost of Goods Sold}}{\text{Average AP}}$

Asset Turnover $= \dfrac{\text{Net Revenue}}{\text{Average Assets}}$

Days Sales Outstanding (DSO) $= \dfrac{365}{\text{AR Turnover}}$

Days Inventory Outstanding (DIO) $= \dfrac{365}{\text{Inventory Turnover}}$

Days Payables Outstanding (DPO) $= \dfrac{365}{\text{AP Turnover}}$

Net Days Financing Required $= \text{DSO} + \text{DIO} - \text{DPO}$

Profitability Ratios

Profit Margin $= \dfrac{\text{Net Income}}{\text{Net Revenue}}$

Return on Assets (ROA) $= \dfrac{\text{Net Income} + \text{Interest}(1 - t)}{\text{Average Total Assets}}$

Financial Leverage $= \dfrac{\text{Average Total Assets}}{\text{Average Equity}}$

Return on Equity (ROE) $= \dfrac{\text{Net Income}}{\text{Average Equity}}$

Notes

1. This chapter draws heavily on two technical notes from the Darden School of Business: "An Overview of Financial Statement Analysis: The Mechanics" (UVA-C-2255) and "Methods of Valuation for Mergers and Acquisitions" (UVA-F-1274).

2. For simplicity we use the data as reported in the company's 2006 annual report, a time period that immediately preceded the atypical circumstances accompanying the financial and economic crisis of 2008–2009.

3. Home Depot is a retailer, and like most retailers, it runs on a weekly accounting cycle. For Home Depot, its fiscal years close on the Sunday nearest to the last day of January.

4. Net revenue is total sales or revenue less estimated sales discounts, returns, and other allowances.

5. Common-size statements and percentage change statements usually include only the most important line items on the income statement. In this case, Home Depot interest and investment income and interest expense have been ignored, because the amounts are small. Although not shown in Exhibit 10.2, we can also arrange a common-size statement in a horizontal format. This format begins with the oldest data (2002 in this case) and then shows the percentage changes in each line item from that base year. The percentage change statement and the vertical and horizontal format statements show three different perspectives on this same set of results.

6. See Appendix A for the three financial statements from which these 2002 to 2006 percentage changes were derived.

7. If current interest rates are noticeably different from historical rates, the interest expense should be updated to reflect the differential cost for the new borrowing.

8. This chapter focuses on valuing the company as a whole (i.e., the enterprise value). An estimate of equity value can be derived under this approach by subtracting the value of the interest-bearing debt from the enterprise value. An alternative method is to value the equity directly using residual cash flows, which are computed as net of interest payments and debt repayments plus debt issuances and then discounted at the cost of equity.

9. The net working capital should include the expected cash, receivables, inventory, and payables levels required for the operation of the business. If the firm currently has excess cash (more than is needed to sustain operations), for example, the cash forecast should be reduced to the level of cash required for operations. Excess cash should be valued separately by adding it to the enterprise value.

10. In this context, we define net assets as total assets less non-interest-bearing current liabilities, or equivalently as net working capital plus net fixed assets. A similar relationship can be expressed using return on capital (ROC). Because the uses of capital (working capital and fixed assets) equal the sources of capital (debt and equity), it follows that RONA (return on net assets) equals ROC, and therefore $ROC = NOPAT/(Debt + Equity)$.

11. WACC is discussed in Chapter 5, Financial Management, and reviewed later in this chapter as the appropriate discount rate used for the free cash flows.

12. Debt for purposes of the WACC should include all permanent interest-bearing debt. If the market value of debt is not available, the book value of debt is often assumed as a reasonable proxy. The shorter the maturity of the debt and the closer the

correspondence between the coupon rate and required return on the debt, the more accurate the approximation. Equity is the price per share times shares outstanding; it is also called the company's market capitalization or market cap.

13. The debt amount represents the long-term debt on Home Depot's balance sheet, and the equity represents Home Depot's market cap (i.e., the price per share times number of shares outstanding). The market price was $40 per share and there were 1,970 million shares outstanding, implying a total market value of equity of $78.8 billion.

14. The full text of Commissioner Glassman's speech can be found at www.sec.gov/news/speech/spch041003cag.htm.

15. "Out at Home Depot," *BusinessWeek*, January 15, 2007.

Downloadable Resources for this chapter available at www.wiley.com/go/portablemba5e

Financial Ratio Template (Home Depot Example)

Exhibit 10.1: Percentage Change Income Statements

Exhibit 10.2: Common-Size Vertical Income Statements

Exhibit 10.3: Percentage Change Balance Sheets

Exhibit 10.4: Common-Size Vertical Balance Sheets

Exhibit 10.5: Percentage Change Statements of Cash Flow

Exhibit 10.6: Summary of Other Key Financial Ratios

Exhibits 10.8–10.12: Forecasts and Firm Valuation Estimation

Consumer Behavior

11

Successful firms do well at many aspects of business practice, from finance to marketing to accounting to human resources. If you ask managers at successful firms about the key to their success, they often answer that the single most important component of their business is external to the firm: their customers. As Peter Drucker said, "There is only one valid definition of business purpose: to create a customer."[1]

Because firms try to provide value to consumers, understanding their consumers is essential. Business strategy requires a definition of what customers the firm should serve and how it should serve them. Positioning against competition in the marketplace, designing valued products and brands, and communicating their value all require knowledge of what customers think and do. Ideally, a firm should have a fine-grained understanding of how its final customers make purchase decisions. There are many influences on purchase decisions, from internal attitudes and knowledge held by each individual customer to external social groups that surround a customer and may have a stake in the final purchase decision. Understanding what consumers do and why they do it involves answering many types of questions using many different methods and disciplines.

Exhibit 11.1 shows a simplified overview of the forces that affect consumer decision making. For any given decision, a consumer can be influenced by a variety of internal and external factors, which may operate singly or in combination. The exhibit gives an overview of cultural, environmental, and psychological processes in individual decisions, along with examples of each general kind of influence. Of course the levels of influence are not wholly separate—a consumer's age can affect what family members are influential and which subcultures are open for membership, for example. But the diagram gives an overview as a starting point for discussing consumer behavior.

Culture

At the broadest level, consumer behavior is influenced by the consumer's culture. *Culture* refers to customs, beliefs, and values held within a society; for understanding consumers there is special interest in the power of culture to shape approved or acceptable ways to behave. Consumer judgments ranging from what and when to eat dinner to how to evaluate product quality to who is included in a decision-making unit can depend heavily on culture. Culture's influence on consumer behavior is pervasive, and cultural influences are not normally experienced consciously (that is, until they are violated or contravened). Culture is also assumed to be learned, rather than genetically determined. Following this definition, culture can cover almost anything except physical drives, such as hunger or thirst (but culture does influence when and how these drives are satisfied).

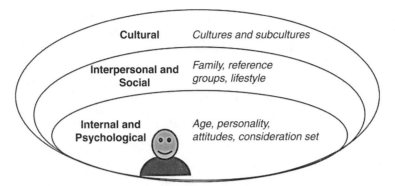

Exhibit 11.1   Forces Affecting Consumer Decision Making

One major cultural difference is a continuum of individualism-collectivism. Consumers in individualistic cultures, such as that of the United States, conceive of the individual as being separate from others, and value self-reliance, self-interest, and self-esteem. In contrast, consumers from collectivist cultures, such as much of China, conceive of individuals as being inherently part of groups, and value group goals and collective harmony and success. Individualists see value in individual action, sometimes even if it goes against the prevailing group norm; an English saying that expresses this sentiment is "The squeaky wheel gets the oil." Collectivists find success of a group goal preferable to individual success, especially if the individual is at odds with the group; an East Asian saying is "The nail that stands out gets pounded down."

Individualistic and collectivistic cultural differences account for broad-ranging differences in consumer self-concepts, goals, and habits. But these cultural differences can also be seen in day-to-day behaviors and reactions. For instance, individualistic (American) and collectivist (Korean) consumers react differently to advertising slogans, even for ad copy where only the slogan differs. American consumers had more positive attitudes about a chewing gum brand after seeing it advertised with the slogan "Treat yourself to a breath-freshening experience" than the slogan "Share this breath-freshening experience," while Korean consumers preferred the latter slogan. Slogans with individualistic themes, such as "[This product] isn't for everybody—but then again, you're not everybody" or "Make your way through the crowd" appeal most strongly to individualistic consumers. Collectivistic consumers, in contrast, react most positively to slogans that emphasize how the advertised product harmonizes with group goals, such as "7 out of 10 people are using [this product]" or "We have a way of bringing people closer together."[2]

Cultural differences can also lead consumers to categorize products and consumption experiences differently. For instance, many consumers in China and Japan think of McDonald's hamburgers as snack food, rather than an entrée of a meal. The custom of having rice at a meal is so ingrained in the culture that the absence of rice excludes McDonald's food from consideration as a full meal. Interestingly, this perception of what food qualifies as a snack seems to carry over to consumers' assessment of the food. In one survey, 55 percent of consumers who ate at McDonald's said that the food did not make them feel full.[3]

A subculture is a subgroup that shares many of the beliefs, values, and customs of the larger culture, but also has distinctive characteristics of its own. For example, subcultures could be based on nationality, social class, religion, political affiliation, and so on. Identifying subcultures can give a firm valuable insights into its consumers. For example, first- and second-generation Americans tend to follow newspapers and radio broadcasts in their native languages, and to patronize merchants with ethnic ties. Hispanic Americans often set aside some of their food budget to shop at bodegas, or small stores, even if a large supermarket has better prices.

Another set of subcultures can be derived from social class, or a division of society based on social status. Status is determined by factors such as wealth, power, and prestige; occupation (correlated to income) and education are the most frequently used measures of these factors. Sometimes consumers engage in status consumption, when they try to raise their social status through purchase and consumption decisions. For example, consumers might try to increase their social status through purchase decisions that they believe will signal membership in a higher status group: upscale magazine purchases, vacation spot selection, paying for a private elementary school, and so on. Conversely, it is also important for a firm to understand if consumers avoid a product because they perceive it would reduce their social class: selection of generic clothes, down-market brands and media, and so on.

Consumer decisions that act as status markers can filter from one part of the social status hierarchy toward either end. A trickle-down effect describes lower classes imitating behavior or trends begun within higher classes, such as what types of formal education are best. A "status float" effect describes a trend or style that moves upward through the status hierarchy; the classic example is the adoption of blue jeans by lower- and mid-status teens in the 1950s that eventually spread to all levels of social status.

Social Groups

Consumers also belong to smaller groups that can have an impact on their purchase and consumption behavior. Groups to which a consumer belongs are called membership groups. Perhaps the most influential membership group is the consumer's family.

For some types of purchases, the family or household unit is the most relevant unit of analysis, rather than any individual within the household. Together, members of a family comprise a decision-making unit (DMU), with different roles in purchase decision and consumption that are played by different family members. Potential roles within a family or household include:

- *Gatekeeper*—the person who gathers and manages what information is relevant to the decision. For example, parents may control information seeking about expensive gifts for children, or one family member may be in charge of researching vacation options.
- *Influencer*—a person who attempts to sway the decision in a particular direction. For instance, children are generally not shy about expressing their preferences in food and entertainment purchases.
- *Decider*—a person who makes the final choice. Most men's underwear, for instance, is not chosen by the men who wear it but by their wives or girlfriends.

- *Buyer*—a family member who pays and/or physically acquires the purchase. If a five-year-old is allowed to choose her favorite cereal, the parents actually pay for the product.
- *User*—a consumer who uses (consumes) the product.

It should be clear that these five roles are not necessarily carried out by different people for every decision—sometimes consumers play multiple roles, and sometimes there are multiple consumers playing any given role. Firms try to understand complex DMUs such as families in order to know how to plan marketing efforts, especially including targeting and positioning, product design, communications, and distribution. If the gatekeeper and user are not the same person as the decider, for example, then the firm faces the task of convincing both the gatekeeper/user and the decider that its product has unique value. For example, studios that market children's movies have an easy time capturing children's attention with movie promotions. But parents may be reluctant to spend the time and money on a movie unless they can be reassured that they will enjoy the movie as well. Often children's movie promotions include nostalgic references likely to have meaning only to parents, or a joke that adults but not children will understand.

The DMU roles for families and households closely mirror the complexities of DMUs in business-to-business relationships. The same basic roles are taken by people within a purchasing firm, and the selling firm must understand each person in each significant role. As with households, the more expensive or risky the purchase, the more people are involved in the decision (or the higher up in the firm's hierarchy they are).

MBA Concepts in Action: Complex Decision-Making Units

A firm introduced a new high-tech shower system to the household market. The system included an advanced showerhead with a separate heated water tank to be installed just behind the shower wall, and a digital control so that shower takers could preselect an exact water temperature. Mostly because of the water heater and tank, the system required a plumber to install it. The system was more expensive than a regular showerhead, but consumers stood to save money over the long run from less wasted hot water traveling through the house's pipes as the shower warmed up. Homeowners liked the product and believed it represented a significant advance over regular showers.

When initial sales failed to mirror the interest expressed by consumers in showrooms, the firm conducted some market research. They found that plumbers were not enthusiastic about spending extra time on a job to install the system's heated tank. In essence, they were talking consumers out of their preference for the firm's new product and changing the purchase decision at the last minute.

Who plays what roles in the DMU in this scenario? How can the firm enlist the help of plumbers, or at least ease their disincentive to install the system?

(See Youngme Moon and Kerry Herman, "Aqualisa Quartz: Simply a Better Shower," Harvard Business School, Prod. #: 502030-PDF-ENG.)

Another important type of group for understanding consumers is a reference group. A consumer may not belong to a reference group, but it nonetheless forms a point of comparison for the consumer. Reference groups, especially those to which consumers aspire to belong, can influence a consumer's attitudes, and can expose consumers to new products and behaviors. Unlike membership groups, reference groups do not necessarily have any direct contact with a consumer. Reference groups can be formed of celebrities whom the consumer will never meet or friends whom the consumer sees every day.

In some cases, a firm-centered membership group or reference group develops around a particular brand: a brand community. For example, some committed owners of Harley-Davidson motorcycles get together each year for a planned cross-country HOG (Harley Owners' Group) ride. Harley executives ride along with customers, and the group develops complex bonds with other consumers and with the brand itself. On occasion, firms create product offerings designed to foster brand-related membership groups. For example, some cell phone services encourage users to establish a small network of frequently called consumers who share the company's service.

Firms pay particular attention to opinion leaders for a group or product category, or consumers to whom other consumers turn for purchase and consumption advice. Opinion leaders hold an especially strong sway over other consumers through expertise or a strong or attractive personality. For instance, celebrities who endorse a product or a behavior (e.g., messages about avoiding drug use or appeals to vote) may or may not have expertise material to their appeal. The celebrities may be effective because consumers want to imitate their behavior or affiliate with them. Opinion leaders can be very effective in spreading consumer information and inducing trial or purchase (or in turning consumers away from an undesired product or brand). When firms try to identify opinion leaders, they search for consumers with deep knowledge of the category, exposure to special-interest media on the category, and social attributes such as willingness to communicate freely with others and openness to innovation.

Sometimes opinion leaders are influential in determining how an innovative new product, service, or idea spreads through a population. Firms try to understand how they can influence diffusion of innovation through their own communications efforts to key social groups. New products are not adopted by all members of a population at the same time; some consumers seek out new innovations as they enter the market, and other consumers may wait years to adopt the same innovation. Exhibit 11.2 shows the diffusion process through an ordering of groups of consumers who will eventually adopt a given innovation. Innovators, representing about 2 percent of the total group of adopters, are the first to try new innovations. They tend to communicate frequently with other innovators, and they don't mind the social and financial risk associated with first-generation innovations; in fact, they may even embrace these risks. Early adopters, who make up about 13 percent of eventual adopters, are generally responsible for translating an innovation for later adoption by other groups. The early adopter group contains most of the category's opinion leaders, who freely communicate their experiences and advice to the first large group of adopters.

The early majority, about 35 percent of the group, are next to adopt and can be responsible for pushing a new product into the growth phase of the product life cycle (see Chapter 4 on marketing). Consumers in the early majority tend to be a bit more risk-averse than consumers in the early adopter and innovator categories, and will deliberate before adopting a new innovation (opening the door for influence by the opinion leaders

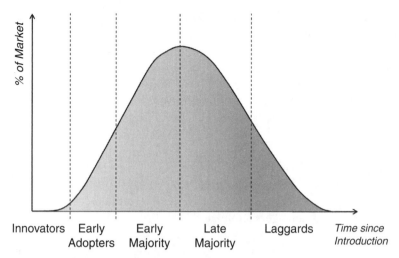

% of Market

Innovators | Early Adopters | Early Majority | Late Majority | Laggards | *Time since Introduction*

Exhibit 11.2   The Adoption of Innovations

Source: Adapted from Everett M. Rogers, *Diffusion of Innovations*, 5th ed. (New York: Simon & Schuster, 2003).

among the early adopters). The late majority, about 35 percent of all adopters, are characterized by their skepticism toward a given innovation, or toward innovation in general. Consumers in this group adopt later generations of a new technology, and may be responsive to price and peer pressure in the adoption decision. Finally, consumers in the laggards group, about 15 percent of the total, are the last to adopt. They may resist adopting an innovation relative other adopter groups, because they see little value in the innovation, because they hold a traditional view that would be challenged by the innovation, and so on.

Consumers who are innovators in one product category may be laggards in another; there is no fixed cross-product standing implied by the groups. In addition, not all innovations diffuse through the population at the same rate. Firms work to understand how to best communicate value and influence adoption of their products for all adoption groups, and they also try to understand what characteristics of their product will affect the rate of diffusion through the population of adopters. Five general characteristics of products are most commonly examined in determining rate of diffusion: relative advantage, compatibility, observability, trialability, and complexity.

Relative advantage refers to how much better a new product appears to consumers than the product it is intended to replace. Relative advantage is the main way that consumers initially perceive the value to them of a new product. Note also that the advantage is to the consumers, not the firm: An innovation that only helps the firm, or an advantage that is appreciated by the firm's product designers but is not valued by consumers, will not influence adoption. Other product characteristics relate to how easy it is for consumers to learn and take advantage of the innovation's benefits.

Compatibility refers to a match between the innovation and consumers' prior behavior and values. New versions of men's razors, for example, do not require consumers to learn a new shaving technique; the new razors are said to be high in compatibility. However, suppose that a new razor was found to have a wasteful or highly polluting manufacturing process—this fact would reduce the product's compatibility for environmentally conscious consumers by conflicting with their values.

Observability is a measure of how easily the innovation's value can be described to consumers or imagined by them. New clothing has relatively high observability; the performance of a new mattress is relatively low. Products with low observability present the firm with a special challenge in communicating value to consumers. One mattress firm includes in its advertisements explicit appeals to consumers to talk with other consumers of the product, either face-to-face or through social networking. A related product characteristic, *trialability*, is the degree to which consumers can try an innovation provisionally in advance of full adoption. Some firms increase trial by giving away samples of a new product. When Pert shampoo was introduced to the market, for example, consumers didn't believe that a product could function simultaneously as a shampoo and conditioner. Pert brand managers stimulated trial through free samples of the product. At the other end of the trialability scale, there is no way to try out a plastic surgery procedure before making a permanent change. Trialability is especially important at the beginning of the product life cycle, and for innovators and early adopters.

Finally, *complexity* refers to consumer's anticipation of difficulty in understanding or using the innovation—in short, how difficult consumers think it will be to extract value in using the innovation. For instance, despite strong advantages over film cameras, digital cameras were slow to diffuse because of perceived complexity of use. Some products, such as certain brands of microwavable lunches, position themselves strongly on simplicity of preparation, with advertisements that demonstrate how easy product use will be for consumers.

The Decision-Making Process

Consumer decisions are driven by many types of influences, as outlined in the preceding section, from cultures and subcultures to reference groups to product characteristics. Firms can also seek to understand more fine-grained aspects of consumer decision making, such as the steps in a single purchase or consumption decision. Exhibit 11.3 presents a simplified scheme of the consumer decision-making process for an individual purchase.

Each stage of the process involves specific marketing tasks. In the first stage, problem recognition, the task is to remind consumers of a need they currently have that the firm's offering can satisfy better, or to alert them to a new need. For example,

Exhibit 11.3   Stages of the Purchase Decision Process

Stage of Decision	Role of the Firm
Problem recognition	Remind consumers of a current need; introduce a solution to a new need.
Information search	Increase chances of consideration for purchase.
Evaluation of alternatives	Match type of information provided with consumers' basis
Choice strategies	of purchase decision.
Postpurchase behavior	Gauge and enhance consumer satisfaction; improve disposal after end use.

high-definition television (HDTV) was initially advertised as a way to get even better picture quality for programming that consumers already watch. Or consider how cosmetics companies offer skin care products for men, often accompanied by advertising and point-of-purchase materials suggesting that men's current skin care is inadequate. The point is to trigger consumers' recognition of a problem, after which consumers may search for more information before making a purchase.

The second stage of the process is information search. Consumers search for information in very different ways depending on a number of internal factors. If the purchase being considered is expensive or has high social risk, such as a new car or a greeting card for a close friend, then consumers will spend more time and effort searching for detailed information. In contrast, some purchase decisions are made on the spur of the moment, and the firm's task is to get product information to consumers at the right time. For instance, the decision to order pizza for delivery is often made shortly after consumers arrive at home from work. Mailed coupons are thought to be effective: As consumers arrive home, they check their mail and may be influenced by a coupon as they make a purchase decision. For some brands and products, such as long-established market leaders, consumers will not actively search for information; the firm's task is to remind them of the brand to ensure top-of-mind awareness.

When consumers evaluate alternatives in the third stage, they are trying to assess their options and narrow down the range of alternatives to a final few. The criteria that consumers use for these evaluations are important to understand. For some decisions, consumers use attribute-based criteria. For instance, the presence of antilock brakes on a car may be an important attribute for safety-conscious consumers. In other cases, consumers use more emotion-based criteria. As an example, consider the purchase of a wedding gown. Often the consumer (the bride-to-be) is expecting to rely on a spontaneous emotional reaction to a wedding gown, and that reaction will help guide the purchase decision. Evaluation of alternatives can be strongly influenced by the composition of the consideration set (for further examples, see Chapter 4 on Marketing Management).

Consumers employ various choice strategies when making a final decision. When following a compensatory strategy, for instance, consumers make a decision based on the ratio of positive to negative features in a product. In a noncompensatory strategy, consumers have a threshold for some negative features of a product; these negative features could be enough to eliminate a product from the choice set altogether. Knowing the cutoff point for negative features of a product is clearly important in product design and positioning.

MBA Concepts in Action: Prospect Theory

When price information enters into a consumer's choice process, the perception of price can be just as important as how the price compares to a budget. From the perspective of the firm, successful pricing should reflect customers' reactions to prices, and not just the internal concerns of the firm. Several influential notions about consumer price perception arise from prospect theory, which is depicted

(continued)

(Continued)

in the S-shaped curve in Exhibit 11.4. The assumption is that customers translate exchanges, like purchases, into gains or losses relative to some standard or reference point. Two significant ideas in the theory have significant implications for price perception. First, the subjective value (happiness or unhappiness) of gains and losses decreases marginally. In other words, an initial gain of x \$ confers some level of happiness to consumers, but a second gain of the same amount confers a smaller increase in happiness. In Exhibit 11.4, following a gain of x \$ on the horizontal axis to the S-curve and then to the vertical axis shows the boost to subjective utility from the x \$ gained. The next gain of x \$, however, does not result in an equivalent gain in happiness.

Second, the curve describing the subjective utility of losses falls away more steeply than does the curve for gains. In other words, losses loom larger than gains—losing x \$ is more aversive than gaining x \$ is pleasurable. One implication of these ideas is that it is better to frame a purchase in terms of discounts rather than surcharges. For example, customers would rather purchase gasoline from a station that prices a gallon at \$4 with a 50-cent discount for cash than from a station selling a gallon for \$3.50 with an extra 50-cent charge for credit cards, even though the gasoline at the two stations is identical.

Purchases and their associated prices can often be thought of as combinations of multiple losses or gains. Following the implications of the S-curve, two distinct gains of x \$ are better than one gain of $2x$ \$, and two distinct losses are worse than one big loss. In general, the marketing implication is to separate gains and bundle losses. For example, accessories to larger purchases should be easier to sell—the price should cause less unhappiness, so to speak—if the purchases can be made all at once, rather than separated. In addition, there is greater utility for customers through separating a small gain from a large loss. For example, cash back on a car purchase helps offset the displeasure of a larger loss with a small gain, and the net amount of displeasure will be less than if the sticker price of the car were simply reduced by the cash-back amount.

Postpurchase behavior includes further evaluation of the purchased product or service. Satisfaction over time with a purchase predicts repeat purchase behavior, and may build brand loyalty. Assessment of postpurchase behavior becomes more complicated as the DMU complexity increases, especially as the number of users increases and as the amount of time increases between purchase and use. For example, a large durable good such as a dishwasher may last for a decade or more before consumers assess its performance with a new purchase in mind. Consumers may dispose of the product by selling it, throwing it out, or passing it along to someone else, all of which can be important for marketers. For instance, magazines that are passed on to friends or neighbors mean greater exposure for the ads in the magazine, and possibly to new market segments. At this point in the decision process, the cycle returns to the problem recognition stage.

An important caveat is that these decision-making steps best describe decisions where consumers are motivated to think carefully about their choice and to expend some time

Subjective Value

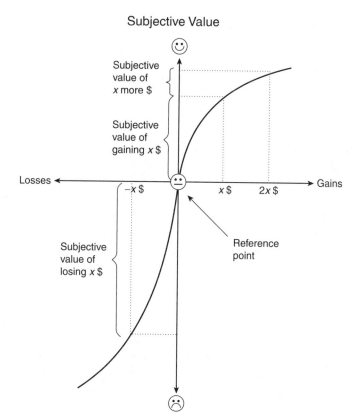

Exhibit 11.4   Prospect Theory Curve and the Asymmetric Subjective Value of Gains and Losses

and effort processing the relevant information. If you are deciding on a laptop to buy with your own money, or deciding on which MBA program to attend, you will likely go through all the steps as described. However, when consumers are not motivated to examine their choice, they may skip steps altogether. For example, a habitual purchase such as a favorite soda may involve only product recognition and a final choice, without a search for additional information or evaluation of alternatives.

Exhibit 11.5   Consumer Behavior in MBA Curricula

Business School	Elective Course Name with Close Overlap to Chapter
University of Pennsylvania (Wharton)	Consumer Behavior
University of Chicago (Booth)	Consumer Behavior
	Current Topics in Behavioral Science
Columbia University	Behavioral Economics and Decision Making
Northwestern University (Kellogg)	Understanding Consumers
Harvard University	Consumer Marketing
University of Virginia (Darden)	Consumer Behavior

Consumer Behavior in MBA Curricula

The topics of consumer behavior are normally offered as elective courses, often in the second year of an MBA program. Most of these courses are listed in the marketing area. Exhibit 11.5 lists example courses from six leading MBA programs.

Notes

1. Peter F. Drucker, *The Essential Drucker: The Best of Sixty Years of Peter Drucker's Essential Writings on Management* (New York: Harper Paperbacks, 2009), 20.
2. S.-P. Han and S. Shavitt, "Persuasion and Culture: Advertising Appeals in Individualistic and Collectivistic Societies," *Journal of Experimental Social Psychology* 30 (1994): 326–350.
3. Yunxiang Yan, "McDonald's in Beijing," in *Golden Arches East*, ed. James L. Watson (Stanford, CA: Stanford University Press, 2006).

For Further Reading

Ariely, D., *Predictably Irrational: The Hidden Forces That Shape Our Decisions* (New York: HarperCollins, 2009).

Gladwell, M., *The Tipping Point: How Little Things Can Make a Big Difference* (New York: Back Bay Books, 2002).

Haugtvedt, C., P. Herr, and F. Kardes, eds., *Handbook of Consumer Psychology* (New York: Taylor & Francis, 2008).

Hoyer, W., and D. MacInnis, *Consumer Behavior*, 4th ed. (Boston: Houghton Mifflin, 2007).

Schiffman, L., and L. Kanuk, *Consumer Behavior*, 9th ed. (Upper Saddle River, NJ: Pearson Education, 2007).

Sunderland, P. L., and R. M. Denny, *Doing Anthropology in Consumer Research* (Walnut Creek, CA: Left Coast Press, 2007).

Underhill, P., *Why We Buy: The Science of Shopping* (New York: Touchstone, 2000).

Wilcox, R. T., *Whatever Happened to Thrift?: Why Americans Don't Save and What to Do about It* (New Haven, CT: Yale University Press, 2009).

Zaltman, G., *How Customers Think: Essential Insights into the Mind of the Market* (Boston: Harvard Business School Press, 2003).

Downloadable Resources for this chapter available at www.wiley.com/go/portablemba5e

Stages of the Purchase Decision Process

12

New Product Creation

While entrepreneurs face the uniquely daunting task of building entirely new businesses, all companies must continuously renew their portfolios of products and services to survive. This does not mean that every company must be a technology leader; but no company will remain a going concern in a free market economy without new products or services. Entrepreneurs often operate on a shoestring pursuing a passion with constant adjustments in response to new information, challenges, and constraints. In a corporate environment, however, new product creation demands strong process leadership and clear linkages to corporate strategy. MBA students with an entrepreneurial bias for creating new concepts but who are comfortable operating with the corporate-mandated budgets, milestones, and deadlines can experience the rewards of product creation without the risk—and frankly the ongoing funding distractions—experienced by the typical start-up entrepreneur.

Successful corporate product creation delivers products or services that customers will buy at a price that exceeds cost. Though simple to describe, that objective proves hard to achieve in the real world. The vast majority of new products and services fail to meet predefined financial objectives. To improve those odds, a company needs to explicitly manage three distinct portfolios in a systematic, thoughtful way: new product creation projects, advanced technology capabilities, and the product portfolio offered in the market. As shown in Exhibit 12.1, the integration of the three portfolios occurs within a context framed by corporate goals, market dynamics, and consumer needs and connected to strategic plans and budget constraints.

As noted by Harvard professor Clayton Christensen, maintaining a competitive product portfolio through new products and services proves particularly challenging to existing companies due to the nature of disruptive technologies. Christensen researched a number of industries ranging from steam shovels to computers and uncovered a pattern of failure based on prior success. Industry leaders tend to focus on existing customers and continually refine products to meet those customers' expanding needs, often ignoring marginal competitors and market segments. For example, during the early part of the twentieth century steam shovel manufacturers built equipment with ever-larger buckets to allow mine operators to collect more material with each scoop. They ignored the new entrants offering smaller gasoline- and diesel-powered excavating equipment. More critically, the established players also ignored the transition to hydraulic technology starting after World War II. Prone to leaks and lacking the lifting power of a cable-driven machine, hydraulic technology was correctly viewed as inferior by the cable-actuated steam shovel companies. But over time, hydraulics became more reliable and producers like Caterpillar and Komatsu developed larger equipment that could compete with

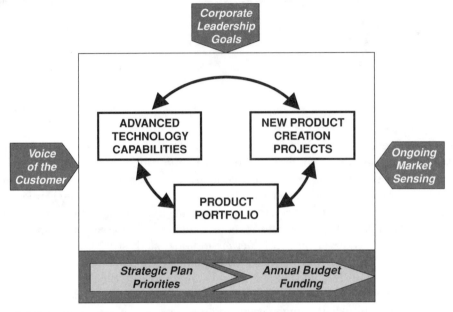

Exhibit 12.1   Corporate Product Creation Framework

Source: Ronald L. Kerber and Timothy M. Laseter, *Strategic Product Creation*
(New York: McGraw-Hill, 2007).

smaller cable-driven shovels. The traditional leaders in excavation equipment continued to migrate to the high-end applications where cable-driven technology maintained
its advantage and never embraced the lower-cost disruptive technology of hydraulics.
Ultimately, even the high-end applications fell prey to hydraulics, leaving the previous
industry leaders bankrupt.

To succeed over the long term, companies need to serve their existing customers
and acquire new ones through ongoing product creation leveraging both sustaining
technologies and disruptive ones. The following principles help achieve that goal.

Principle 1: Start with the voice of the customer and end with customer needs.

Given the innovation challenges, corporate leaders must seek new ideas broadly to
maintain a competitive product portfolio. Specifically, companies need to look for new
concept ideas by firsthand observation of existing and potential customers, by constant
monitoring of actions by current and potential competitors, by selective investment in
advanced technology capabilities, and through partnerships with others.

Many companies still rely too heavily on traditional market research to drive new
product and service creation. Existing customers inevitably express a desire for expanded
functionality at the same or lower cost. Rarely can they articulate the unmet needs that
trigger a true innovation. Focus groups rave over new product concepts but then fail to
"vote with their pocketbooks" when the product reaches the market.

Accordingly, leading companies such as Mars Corporation have turned to firsthand
observation of customers to identify the true (but often unvocalized) voice of the customer. For example, Mars observed how moms distributed M&M'S to children in small

quantities as rewards for good behavior and identified the need for resealable packaging. Observations of mothers and children in cars led to the introduction of special packaging designed to fit into the cup holders.

Career Profile

1988 MBA

Craig Wynett

Chief Innovation Officer

Procter & Gamble

Education:

BS, Biochemistry, University of Georgia

MBA, Darden Graduate School of Business Administration

Now the senior executive responsible for developing the creative capabilities necessary to create, qualify, and launch game-changing products and services for Procter & Gamble, Mr. Wynett's career spans more than 20 years at P&G. He joined P&G in 1988 in the U.S. health care sector and advanced through increasing levels of responsibility to become the Director of Health Care New Products. In 1994, he was appointed as the founding director of the newly established Corporate New Ventures (CNV) organization. In 1998, he rose to General Manager. Under his leadership, CNV produced many of P&G's most successful new products.

In addition to applying his creative talents to the packaged goods industry, Craig was the inspiration for and co-author with Dr. Mehmet Oz of the "You" series of health books.

Source: http://worldbenefit.case.edu/global-forum/about/speaker.html.

Whirlpool Corporation, the world's leading appliance manufacturer, maps the process flows involving dishwashers, ovens, refrigerators, microwaves, washers, and driers. For example, by observing customers in their homes, Whirlpool product creation staff members have a deeper understanding of the food preparation, kitchen cleanup, and clothes care processes. Observation that many consumers maintained a second refrigerator in their garage led the company to introduce the highly successful Gladiator line, which includes a refrigerator as well as matching cabinets and shelves, with a more industrial-looking design.

Otis, a division of United Technologies Corporation, found observation equally useful outside of the consumer environment. Otis product developers observed the difficulty contractors faced when installing an Otis elevator. The equipment arrived at the job site in a plethora of crates, many of which were too large to fit through a typical doorway, and organized based on manufacturing convenience rather than installation requirements. Therefore, Otis redesigned its product to ease the installation process. Crates were designed to fit on a specially developed dolly and explicitly packed to align with the installers' needs.

Principle 2: Separate invention and execution.

One of the most common causes of failure in corporate product development results from the failure to separate invention and execution. Invention tackles the unknown and inherently faces uncertainty regarding timing and cost—and sometimes even feasibility at any cost or over any time frame. Product creation involves the introduction of new technologies into a product released for consumption and proves profitable only when it meets a market need at a given price and cost. Trying to integrate an unproven technology into a fixed budget on a fixed time line rarely works.

To avoid this primary failure mode, the best companies separate research efforts from new product or service creation projects. Research teams seek breakthrough technology capabilities over a longer time horizon but face ongoing scrutiny over feasibility and market relevance. These teams strive for proof of concept through *advanced technology demonstrators* (ATDs), a form of prototype. Not necessarily a complete product, an ATD can be a module with application over a broader range of products—for example, voice-activated controls for a company making home entertainment systems.

Product creation teams draw from the pool of advanced capabilities but do not allow one that is still in the research phase to become part of the critical path to development of a new product. Using the voice-recognition system example, the team might have identified the desired timing and product model for the introduction of such a technology but would not design it into a product line unless it has already been proven with an advanced technology demonstrator.

Managers use *technology road maps* to keep the research efforts and product creation teams aligned but distinct. As shown in Exhibit 12.2, a technology road map offers a

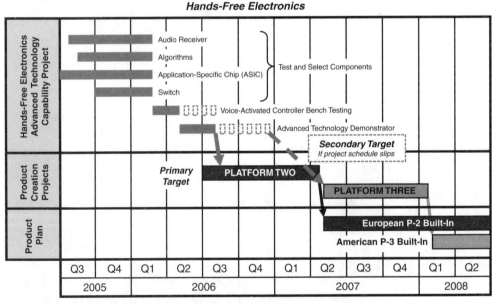

Exhibit 12.2   Technology Road Map Example

Source: Ronald L. Kerber and Timothy M. Laseter, *Strategic Product Creation* (New York: McGraw-Hill, 2007).

tentative plan and shows links to the product portfolio. But it also shows contingency options and indicates cutoff thresholds that ensure the separation of invention and execution.

Large corporations generally separate research from development organizationally as well. This allows the company to attract creative researchers who seek autonomy and the freedom to explore outside-the-box ideas. The development organization tends to employ forward-looking but results-oriented people who want to see a new product come to fruition and are comfortable working against tight time lines and budget constraints.

Classic Teaching Case: Intel Research: Exploring the Future

This case examines a *networked-research* model used at Intel for exploratory research. Intel's off-road map research, inspired by the Defense Advanced Research Projects Agency (DARPA)'s research model, senses the environment to spot emerging areas of focus. Intel then deploys its human and financial resources to build a research program around each emerging area. Features of this model include collaboration with universities to develop Intel-university lablets, corporate venture investments by Intel capital, and strategic research projects run in Intel's own R&D facilities. The case explains how Intel developed and implemented this research model and lists some of its successful projects. It describes in detail the research lablets with universities, and presents a challenge the company was facing with the measurement of the success of these lablets. The lablets aimed for the somewhat amorphous goal of sensing and shaping new technologies that might one day threaten Intel's core business or provide opportunities to build radically new businesses from scratch. However, given the massive resources expended in building the network, the management needed some technique for measuring its performance to ensure ongoing funding.

This case exposes students to the importance of and challenges in staying abreast of the latest technological developments in a fast-evolving competitive industry, while illustrating one of the research models used, describing its process of development and implementation.

Source: Alan McCormack and Kerry Herman, "Intel Research: Exploring the Future," Harvard Business School Case 9-605-051.

Principle 3: Seek disciplined speed through a clear product creation process.

Technology road maps and advanced technology demonstrators offer the key tools for managing research efforts. For product creation projects, however, the best companies employ a clearly defined process of milestones and review hurdles typically described as a *stage-gate process*. Such a process typically involves three to seven stages, depending on

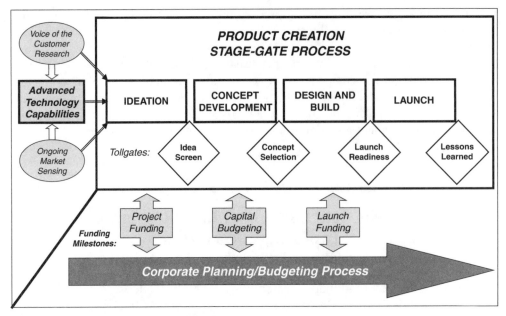

Exhibit 12.3   Product Creation Stage-Gate Process

Source: Ronald L. Kerber and Timothy M. Laseter, *Strategic Product Creation* (New York: McGraw-Hill, 2007).

the complexity of the product or service under development, the length of time required, and the amount of funding necessary.

Managers need to help product creation projects achieve a balance between speed and discipline. Just as in car racing, the goal is consistent speed that pushes the car and driver to the limit...but not beyond. Fast to market can offer a competitive advantage and fast-paced projects consume fewer resources than slow, drawn-out efforts. But rushing ahead too fast can cause the project to careen out of control. The stage-gate process should be designed to meet the needs of the particular business, just as Indy race cars are designed for different needs than a sprint car for dirt track racing.

As an example, Exhibit 12.3 shows a fairly standard process with four stages: *ideation, concept development, design and build, and launch.* Each stage feeds a tollgate where management approves the project to move to the next stage, sends it back for further work, or, if necessary, cancels it. As the chart indicates, the stage-gate process has many points of interface to other company processes. As discussed earlier, advanced research feeds but is distinct from the product creation process. The product creation process also connects to the corporate planning and budgeting process, which provides funding at various stages.

The goal in the *ideation* stage is to develop an idea that has a reasonable chance of producing a positive business opportunity. Accordingly, at the tollgate management seeks to confirm that there is a compelling customer need that will generate sufficient market potential. At this stage the project team need not have a full-blown product concept but merely a rough business model and an idea of the potential for competitive advantage as well as the risks involved.

Classic Teaching Case: The Fate of the *Vasa*

This case examines the development process for the *Vasa*, a Swedish warship that was to be the largest, most powerful, and most expensive vessel ever built for the Swedish navy. Richly decorated with 700 sculptures and armed with 64 massive cannons arrayed on two decks, the *Vasa* cost over 5 percent of the nation's gross domestic product (GDP) but sank on its maiden journey in 1628 after covering barely 1,400 yards. The case describes the three-plus-year development effort and the series of design changes the project went through as the navy's needs evolved during that time. The case also touches upon the inquiry process to investigate the reasons for the ship's failure.

Although this case is based on an incident that took place almost 400 years ago, the lessons it generates remain as relevant today as they were then. Students are encouraged to systematically analyze the project's history, choices made in design, the changes the design underwent, as well as the reasons behind them. The case enables students to gain insight into the management of complex projects in an environment where the value of specific design choices changes over time. Further, it demonstrates that a poorly performing product may be a sign of deeper organizational problems. The case also illustrates the dynamic and uncertain nature of innovation.

Source: Alan McCormack and Richard Mason, "The Fate of the *Vasa*," Harvard Business School Case 9-605-026.

In the *concept development* stage, the team explores a range of possible product or service concepts designed to meet the identified customer need. This stage pushes the financial model further to confirm the likely customer value under various scenarios. If the selected concept passes the tollgate, it will expand into a full-blown development project requiring substantially more resources. Thus, the concept selection tollgate proves to be one of the most critical.

The *design and build* stage shifts the focus of the project into execution. The project team now needs to create a production-ready design, fully tested and ready for market launch. At this stage, the team must make trade-off decisions to keep the project on budget and on time. For example, if some portions of the product appear to be running above the cost target, should features be cut to keep the product on target overall? Projects are rarely canceled at the launch readiness tollgate, but delayed launch dates are unfortunately not uncommon at many companies. Clearly, it is better to be late than to introduce a product or service that is not market ready. (See Exhibit 12.4.)

The *launch* stage involves the actual rollout of the product, typically over some ramp-up period and perhaps regional rollout pattern. During this phase the team is measured against the original commitments: Are customers responding to the product or service

Egg Drop Experiment	Successful Large Egg Solution
This hands-on exercise challenges groups of students to safely drop an egg from a second-story window onto a two-foot target without cracking the egg. Working under time pressure, teams develop a design using a wide selection of materials including balloons, paper cups, rubber bands, straw, and tape. In addition to safely landing on the target, teams are judged on the cost-effectiveness of their solution based on the total time employed and the cost of the various materials. A debriefing compares the teams' results to the dozens of Mars space missions of the past 50 years.	

Comparison of Results across Teams

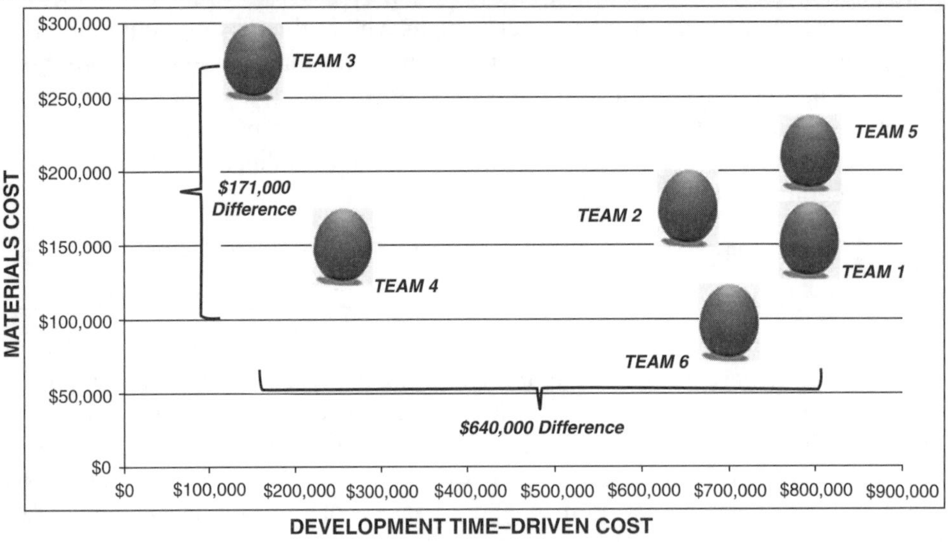

Exhibit 12.4 Egg Drop Experiment

Source: Unpublished Darden School teaching materials.

as expected? Did the product hit desired target quality levels in production and not just the pilot program? Can the plant hit the expected cost targets at full production? Though often ignored by less committed companies, the final tollgate, lessons learned, should be treated as the most critical for building long-term innovation capabilities. By reviewing the entire project from start to finish, the team has the opportunity to learn. This applies to the company as a whole as well if the lessons learned are used to modify the stage-gate product creation process with a mind for continuous improvement.

Simulation Exercise: Global Supply Chain Simulation

This simulation offers a unique opportunity to consider product development and outsourcing together rather than separately. Students act as the management team of a producer of wireless handsets over the course of four years. Each year the students must select the features for the product based on information from a team of expert forecasters. Next, the teams must select a supply base to support the sales of each product, making trade-offs among setup cost, lead times, and unit costs. Once the design decisions for both the product and the supply chain are completed, the students have the opportunity to react to real-time events in managing the firm to maximize profitability. At the end of each year, students see their financial results and meet with a virtual board of directors who cast votes of confidence (or lack thereof) based on the quality of decision making.

Source: Harvard Business School.

Principle 4: Use a well-planned portfolio and product architecture to balance inherent trade-offs.

In the 1924 annual report, Alfred Sloan articulated his vision for General Motors to produce "a car for every purse and purpose." Sloan understood the need to position

Career Profile

1990 MBA

Brian R. Christian

Principal,

DASO Consulting

Education:

BS, Chemical Engineering, University of Michigan

MBA, University of Chicago, Booth School of Business

Prior to launching DASO Consulting, Mr. Christian spent 11 years at Whirlpool Corporation, where his last role was Vice President of Global Product Development for the $1 billion home cleaning category.

Mr. Christian first learned the consulting craft during his five years in Booz Allen & Hamilton's Chicago office. His assignments spanned multiple industries and multiple strategic areas. His work included a complete global procurement strategy for one of the world's largest international oil companies, an organizational restructuring for one of the largest paper products companies in the United States, a manufacturing strategy for a leading casual footwear brand, a new product development process for a prominent U.S. sportswear company, and a sales force effectiveness study for a Canadian publishing company.

Source: DASO Consulting.

products with distinctly different price points, but he also recognized the more subtle point that GM had to leverage its scale to gain an advantage over the smaller competitors. Unless GM could use common parts across products, it would not have a distinctive advantage over a focused competitor serving a single niche. Sloan's insight allowed GM to displace the narrowly focused Ford Motor Company as the leader in the still-nascent automotive industry. Ford's mass production system had propelled the company to an initial leadership, but Henry Ford's disdain for customer-driven variety was captured in his infamous quote regarding the Model T, "Any customer can have a car painted any color that he wants so long as it is black."

Unfortunately, GM lost sight of the balance between variety and commonality in the 1980s. As an executive at the time lamented, "We used to have two dozen cars that looked different on the outside but were the same underneath. Now we have two dozen cars that look the same on the outside but are different underneath!" This executive had observed the transition from his position at Delco-Moraine, at the time GM's captive supplier of brakes and other critical components. His plant was built in the early 1970s to supply two disc brake designs—standard and heavy-duty—which met the needs across the full lineup of General Motors cars for a decade or more. By the early 1990s, when the executive expressed his frustration, that same plant was manufacturing more than 20 different styles of disc brakes.

Companies today continue to struggle with the inherent conflict between offering variety and limiting complexity. The most successful find the balance through a clearly thought-out product architecture employing platforms, modules, and differentiators. The automotive industry, where many models share the same chassis, provides the typical example of product architecture, but the concept can be seen in a wide variety of applications. Mars Corporation applies the platform logic to leverage its proprietary process technology. Its hard-shell candy coating technology has been applied to a wide range of products, from the various types of M&M'S to the growing variety of Skittles. The software industry increasingly seeks to leverage the underlying code across a wide range of applications by applying a clear product architecture.

Platforms define the major groupings of products in a product line. A multibrand company like Whirlpool sells a variety of appliances off of a common platform. For example, at any given time Whirlpool may be producing several different washing machine platforms stretched across a half dozen brands ranging from the eponymous Whirlpool to the recently acquired Maytag to the European regional brand Bauknecht to the private-label Kenmore brands. Though each brand targets a different segment and offers different features, they may draw from a common platform design.

Modules allow companies to mix and match components and subsystems to produce variety with limited complexity. This approach can be readily seen in the personal computer industry. Shop online for a Dell computer and you are offered options to upgrade your PC, including a choice among processors, amount of memory, display quality, hard drive capacity, wireless cards, integrated webcams, sound cards, and of course a host of preloaded software. The modular design of the product allows Dell to offer this range of options with limited increase in the complexity of its business. Suppliers hold most of the inventory and Dell simply snaps together most of the parts in its assembly plants.

Of course, common platforms and modular design can prove disastrous if competitors can mix and match the same components or if consumers see no difference between a company's high-end and mass-market brands. Thus, successful product architecture demands a clear vision for product differentiation. Whirlpool uses the term *green line* to demarcate between logically common parts and key differentiators. Consumers focus on key design elements in front of the green line, like the control panel or the racks in a dishwasher, but pay little attention to the lightbulb and drain, which metaphorically lie behind the green line. Therefore, each Whirlpool brand can focus on a different market segment through a unique design concept while optimizing component standards in areas where consumers care little.

A clear product architecture also enables low-cost upgrades to the existing product. Cost reductions can be aggregated at the module level and phased in by end model as needed. Designed with the product architecture in mind, even new technology capabilities tested in advanced technology demonstrators can be folded into the existing product lineup easily and thereby provide a step-function change from a consumer standpoint but limited change operationally.

Principle 5: Staff right—light—and learn from failures.

Technology road maps, stage-gate processes, and product architecture provide critical tools for managing product creation. But fundamentally innovation requires people, and the people attracted to research and development often have different motivations than the typical employee. The creative types often found in this discipline need to be inspired and guided rather than controlled and managed. Don Goodman, former president of Walt Disney Imagineering, likened the leadership role to that of the business manager of an orchestra. The director guides the performers, who mostly want to make great music. They understand that the symphony needs an audience to pay the bills, but they prefer to ignore the business details and focus on their art. Creating a top-performing product-creation organization requires building the right culture, one that balances individual empowerment versus managerial control, outside-the-box thinking versus pragmatism, and earnest optimism versus experienced judgment.

The appropriate culture must also work for a diverse milieu that encompasses individuals with the wide range of skills necessary to create new products and services. For example, Disney Imagineering, which has responsibility for designing the special attractions at Disney theme parks, employs "cast members" covering over 140 disciplines. Some represent relatively common business functions such as project managers, engineers, scientists, and software developers. But, given Disney's scope, Imagineers also include model makers, musicians, sculptors, and landscapers. Creativity experts highlight the importance of such diversity in developing the kind of breakthroughs Imagineers achieve to make the magic of Disney real for the theme park guests.

Fostering openness provides another critical ingredient in shaping an innovation culture. Product creation and research teams can bury bad news in the wrong environment. Often project teams hide problems out of a sometimes false confidence that they will solve them without senior management attention. Other times, teams share their concerns but bury them in footnotes or technical jargon that obfuscates the issue from management in an attempt to cover the team members just in case the problem crops up later. Managers with a problem-solving mind-set (and competence) naturally encourage openness and will learn about issues before they become critical. Those who focus on assigning blame will inevitably be the last to learn of an issue . . . and often too late.

Canceling a project raises a related issue. Tollgates offer an opportunity to cancel projects as well as reshape them. Companies that never cancel a project before launch likely have a disproportionate percentage of failures—or an inappropriate level of successes. A lack of failures can indicate insufficient risk taking. A robust creative process should create some outside-the-box ideas that should have stayed in the box, because you never know until you try. Accepting failure well requires separating the people from the idea. People can succeed even when ideas fail. Teams need to feel secure that their jobs exist beyond the specific project and accept that canceling a project is good (or at least better than having it fail later).

Classic Teaching Case: IDEO Product Development

This case examines the process of product development at IDEO, the award-winning and world's largest design firm. For two decades IDEO has supported such major clients as Apple Computer, AT&T, Samsung, Philips, Amtrak, and Steelcase in developing new products ranging from the computer mouse to the stand-up toothpaste dispenser. The case touches upon the history of the company as well as its design philosophy and culture. IDEO has an equal emphasis on design and engineering and a culture that promotes innovation and creativity through practices such as no dress code policy and a tradition of encouraging employees to design their own individual workspaces.

The case presents the challenge the firm faced when it was asked to design a handheld computer under an enormously compressed time line. Since IDEO places heavy emphasis on extensive observation and experimentation during the early phases of development, the firm feared that the end product would suffer from the aggressive development schedule. Students must consider the interdependent elements of IDEO's innovation system in grappling with the time line problem. By illustrating IDEO's system of innovation in detail, the case also introduces students to the concepts of experimentation and prototyping in product development and design.

Source: Stefan Thomke and Ashok Nimgade, MD, "IDEO Product Development," Harvard Business School Case 9-600-143.

Principle 6: Avoid the "not invented here" syndrome.

The first principle highlighted the imperative to observe customers and capture their true needs to drive ideation. Researchers and marketers need to look outside to discover the problems that need to be solved. Equally true, companies should look outside to find solutions to the problems. Technologists suffering from the "not invented here" syndrome dismiss any idea that was not generated, gestated, and vetted internally. Inspired by the open source code software like Mozilla's Firefox Web browser, many companies now recognize that innovation can come from anywhere. Craig Wynett, innovation guru at Procter & Gamble, argues that innovation does not necessarily stem from a spark of genius but from systematic efforts to make nonobvious connections among things that don't normally go together. In fact, close examination of one of the most prodigious inventors of modern times, Thomas Edison, reveals that he looked outside for ideas. Edison leveraged his vast array of contacts in the nascent railroad and telegraph industries for existing solutions to the problems he sought to solve: the phonograph, for example, employed existing technologies from the telegraph industry.

Procter & Gamble has adopted an open innovation model seeking ideas from outside parties. Rather than dismissing ideas as "not invented here," open innovation embraces ideas from the outside. The company now posts its needs on its "Connect + Develop" web site and invites inventors to submit their own ideas or, better yet, browse P&G's identified product needs seeking innovative solutions. To date, the "Connect + Develop" strategy has resulted in over a thousand active agreements leveraging innovative ideas of others through P&G but also allowing others to better use intellectual property assets of P&G. Two examples illustrate the flow of ideas. P&G's SpinBrush battery-operated, disposable toothbrush emerged from the inventor-entrepreneur John Osher's spinning lollipop. In an outward flow of technology, P&G auctioned its patented adhesive technology used in Crest Whitestrips. This led to a joint venture with Clorox, the owner of the Glad brand, to produce the Glad Press'n Seal food wrap, which displaced former U.S. market leader Saran wrap, produced by S.C. Johnson.

Leading companies also count on their network of suppliers to provide ongoing innovation. Toyota, for example, relies heavily upon Denso, a formerly captive supplier that it spun off in 1949. A supplier of critical engineered products like radiators and alternators, Denso now serves automotive producers the world over and relies on Toyota for less than half of its sales. Denso's technical leadership results from its deep understanding of Toyota but also its increasingly global scope, which exposes Denso staff to emerging issues across the industry and the world in general. Whirlpool looks for innovative solutions from its component and subassembly suppliers and has even invested in training to help suppliers better understand Whirlpool's customers.

Though looking outside offers greater access to ideas than the not-invented-here syndrome, it does present risks if not managed thoughtfully. Companies need to strategically select outside partners and structure deals that create value, not competitors. Agreements need to have clear guidelines on who owns the intellectual property, including technology and brands. As modeled by P&G, Toyota, and Whirlpool, leveraging others requires investment in capabilities and clear technology road maps. The old adage that "Any road will do, if you don't know where you're going" holds true in leveraging outside partners in innovation. Successful companies know where they want to go and share their road maps with innovation partners.

Classic Teaching Case: Whirlpool Corporation: Supplier Innovation

This case describes a supplier innovation program at Whirlpool aimed at cultivating more actionable ideas from its supplier base and expanding its diversity of thought. Whirlpool sought to instill brand loyalty in its customers to counteract the increasing commoditization of home appliances. Fostering innovation, one of the key components of this new strategy, drove a cultural shift in the organization from simple cost cutting and quality improvement to

(continued)

(Continued)

a customer-oriented, brand-centric mind-set. The supplier innovation training, an extension of innovation efforts to the supply base, aimed to give suppliers an understanding of Whirlpool's target customers and tools with which to create relevant and innovative ideas. The case focuses on the challenge Whirlpool faced rating subsequent supplier idea presentations based on the principles taught in the training program, and highlights the need to design a scorecard and mechanism to rate supplier ideas.

This case illustrates the development of a culture of innovation and customer-focused new product development in an organization, and its further extension into the supply base. It also introduces students to a framework for generating new ideas as well as implementing and testing them. Furthermore, it encourages students to think about the concept of competing on price versus customer/brand loyalty, as well as the importance of creating value for both the customers and the company. Finally, the case also challenges students to consider ways to further improve the training program by adding meaningful and logical extensions.

Source: James Hammer and Tim Laseter, "Whirlpool Corporation: Supplier Innovation," Darden Business School Publishing Case UVA-OM-1192.

Maintaining the Lifeblood

New product creation is the lifeblood of any business. "You can't sell from an empty wagon," explained department store mogul William Dillard in 1938. New ideas abound, even ones that wow the customer. Generating ideas isn't the hard part. The real managerial challenge is to create products and services that customers will buy at a price that exceeds cost. Anything less is a recipe for failure.

The principles for achieving profitable new products highlight the need to listen to customers as well as competitors and even lone inventors to find the best ideas. But the principles also make it clear that management demands structure and discipline in separating invention and execution and providing simultaneous loose/tight controls in managing projects and people. Ultimately, corporate managers need to build and sustain a portfolio of products and services to ensure ongoing business success. The constant change implied by this objective offers a daunting but rewarding career path for MBAs willing to take on the challenge.

New Product Creation in MBA Curricula

While most top business schools do not force students to take a core course in new product creation, most offer at least one elective in the subject (see Exhibit 12.5). The orientation to the subject can vary widely. Some courses provide a practicum or lab approach, which encourages the students to develop business plans and prototypes for new business ideas. Other courses take a more strategic perspective with a focus on the challenges of managing in dynamic, high-tech industries or how to address the "innovator's dilemma,"

Exhibit 12.5   New Product Creation Course Offerings

Business School	Course Name	Type
Carnegie Mellon University (Tepper)	High-Technology Product Innovation	Elective
	New Product Management	Elective
Columbia University	New Product Development	Elective
Dartmouth (Tuck)	Strategic Management of Innovation	Elective
Duke University (Fuqua)	Marketing of Innovation	Elective
Harvard University	Leading Innovative Ventures	Elective
	Managing Innovation	Elective
INSEAD	Strategies for Product and Service Development	Elective
MIT (Sloan)	Product Design and Development	Elective
Northwestern University (Kellogg)	Disruptive Technology and Business Models	Elective
	Innovation Process Management	Elective
NYU (Stern)	New Product Marketing and Design	Elective
	Technology Innovation and New Product Development	Elective
Stanford University	New Product Development	Elective
UC Berkeley (Haas)	Managing the New Product Development Process	Elective
	Innovation in Services and Business Models	Elective
UCLA (Anderson)	New Product Development	Elective
University of North Carolina–Chapel Hill (Kennan-Flagler)	Innovation and Product Development	Elective
University of Michigan (Ross)	Integrated Product Development	Elective
	Innovation and New Product-Service Leadership	Elective
	Service Innovation Management	Elective
University of Navarra (IESE)	Innovation Management	Elective
	Innovation and New Technologies	Elective
	Total Creativity	Elective
University of Toronto (Rotman)	Design Practicum/Business Innovation Lab	Elective
University of Virginia (Darden)	Innovation and Product Development	Elective
	Developing New Products and Services	Elective
Yale University	Innovator's Perspective	Core
	Product Planning and Development	Elective

Source: School web sites, accessed October 2009.

which can occur in any industry. In addition to the courses shown in Exhibit 12.5, most schools offer courses in entrepreneurship. Such courses go beyond the narrow focus of developing new products but would be important to any student seriously interested in pursuing a new business idea.

For Further Reading

Christensen, Clayton M., *The Innovator's Dilemma: When New Technologies Cause Great Firms to Fail* (Boston: Harvard Business School Press, 1997).

Christensen, Clayton M., and Michael E. Raynor, *The Innovator's Solution: Creating and Sustaining Successful Growth* (Boston: Harvard Business School Press, 2003).

Hargadon, Andrew, *How Breakthroughs Happen: The Surprising Truth about How Companies Innovate* (Boston: Harvard Business School Press, 2003).

Kerber, Ronald L., and Timothy M. Laseter, *Strategic Product Creation* (New York: McGraw-Hill, 2007).

Morris, Peter A., Elizabeth O. Teisberg, and A. Lawrence Kolbe, "When Choosing R&D Projects, Go with the Long Shots," *Research-Tech Management*, January–February 1991.

13

Entrepreneurship

Entrepreneurship is about creating a new enterprise with resources that are in your control. Successful entrepreneurs, through their imagination, energy, talent, knowledge, contacts, and activities, create new wealth in societies. They do this either by reducing existing inefficiencies in markets and firms or by bringing to the market new products or processes. When people create new businesses or firms to exploit inefficiencies or create and sell new and innovative products, we call them entrepreneurs and their activities entrepreneurial.[1]

Inefficiencies arise from one of two sources: (1) when it is difficult to remove poorly used resources from where they are currently employed and reapply them in ways that are more useful, and (2) when different people have different information, conjectures, or ideas about the future prospects of resources, products, customer needs and preferences, the value chains of industries, and the broad social, economic, political, and technological trends. These inefficiencies offer enterprising people an enormous pool of opportunities for the creation of a successful new business. Practically every industry has pockets of such inefficiencies, although the scale and scope of such inefficiencies are likely to be much higher in newer industries, where the technologies or customer tastes and habits have had less time to form and mature, than in older ones.

Opportunities to create new products arise because of limits to our current knowledge, but also because we humans are creative and are constantly looking at the world around us in new ways. An example of limits to our knowledge is the limitations in technology to satisfy certain known but unfulfilled market needs. We know that the curse of cancer exists, and the market for a cure is both huge and worthwhile, but we have limited knowledge and means with which to develop a cure to solve the problem. This known inefficiency is obviously a target for aspiring entrepreneurs (in universities, new biotechnology firms, and the large pharmaceutical companies). Every industry faces such technological frontiers—in design, manufacturing, distribution, sales, marketing, logistics, quality, and so on—and is a source of both *known* and sometimes *unanticipated* opportunities.

It is from these major sources, namely *stickiness* of resources, information *asymmetries*, *limited* knowledge, and *creativity*, that new wealth is often created for the enterprising entrepreneur and for society. Many of the great success stories of our times are ones in which ordinary individuals overcame significant odds to create something new and exciting just with commonly available resources. Think of companies like Google, Under Armour, and JetBlue, to name a few. Think of the reinvention of Apple. Think of products such as Facebook, LendingTree, and BET. How did successful entrepreneurs create something from little? What can we learn from them? Is it possible to reduce their experiences to a set of principles that we can use? Let us now turn to these questions.

Entrepreneurial Creation

Entrepreneurial creation is the process of carving out a specific new business idea from the raw material of broad social, economic, technological, and political trends with the help of our commonly held resources—namely, talent, imagination, energy, education, time, and contacts.

Entrepreneurial Leader

An entrepreneurial leader is one who imagines a future business possibility within a framework of macro forces and trends, and acts to bring the future into existence with a sense of urgency, unconstrained by the limited set of means at his or her disposal, with commitment and flexibility during the creation process, in order to profit from the journey.

What Is an Entrepreneurial Opportunity and Where Does It Come From?

Principle 1: Entrepreneurial opportunities are rarely *found*; they have to be *created and earned*.

We have all heard the apocryphal story of the economics professor walking down the street with his student when the student exclaims, "Look, professor, a hundred-dollar bill!" and we have a good laugh when the professor says, "Don't bother picking it up, John—it must be a fake, for if it was real, someone would have picked it up by now."

The economics textbook notion that it is impossible to anticipate and profit from "easily discovered money" appears to run counter to the many examples we find around us. We think of giant technology corporations, such as Microsoft, Cisco, and Dell, built from modest beginnings, with many lucky breaks along the way. We also think of the many successful restaurants, retail stores, and manufacturing companies that were built and run by ordinary individuals, some less talented than we are. While we certainly appreciate their hard work and sacrifice, we realize that given the right breaks and circumstances, we might very well have been in their positions.

In one sense, the professor in our story is indeed correct. Really, how many of us have found hundred-dollar bills lying around—even once? Opportunities rarely lie around—they have to be created and earned through imagination, hard work, and certainly a little bit of good luck. What we loosely call entrepreneurial opportunities are really broad macro forces, such as social trends, demographic shifts, technological breakthroughs and inventions, and political revolutions from which we as individuals have to carve out a specific piece that eventually becomes an opportunity for creating something new.

Entrepreneurial opportunities rarely come in prepackaged forms (like our hundred-dollar bill lying around). They usually have to be created from trends and forces much larger than the ones we directly control. To understand entrepreneurship, then, we have to understand the raw materials of entrepreneurial opportunities—the macro forces. We must understand how entrepreneurs imagine and crystallize specific new business ideas, and the way in which the imagined future is created by embodying human aspirations in concrete products and markets. We must understand the actions and forces that dictate which futures are worthwhile and which are not.

A major source of entrepreneurial opportunities is the emergence of significant changes in social, political, demographic, and economic forces that are largely outside the control of individuals. Economists call these kinds of macro forces *exogenous* changes because they often occur outside the boundaries of the business environment and are rarely influenced by them. On the contrary, these changes have a profound impact on the business world. Of course, sometimes social and political changes are a result of business practices or cultures (such as globalization), but in most cases, individual firms can rarely influence such forces.[2]

These large-scale macro forces give rise to fundamental changes in how we live, where we live, and what we prefer, thus providing numerous opportunities for entrepreneurs to create and market new products and services. Indeed, these changes also provide opportunities to renew and reinvent existing products and services. When existing firms cannot or will not adapt to these changes, opportunities are created for entrepreneurs in new firms. Demographic changes alter the size, average age, structure, composition, employment, educational status, income, and health of the population.

Social, political, and economic changes have the effect of altering the mind-sets and preferences of people. Environmentalism, feminism, globalism, urbanization, democratization, poverty, and a variety of other social, economic, and political movements have fundamentally changed the attitudes of people about what is important and urgent in life. Whether or not facts do indeed change, their meaning and implications do change for us. Sometimes successful products themselves have the effect of ushering in profound changes—some claim that the birth control pill ushered in feminism and all the changes associated with this movement in society. While in the rare instance we have the offerings of an entrepreneur unleashing a profound social or political change,[3] more often than not social and political changes serve as the necessary ingredients from which lucrative business ideas can be hatched.

Because of these demographic, social, political and economic changes, new needs emerge (or can be induced) in a wide variety of areas, including health, education, entertainment, financial security, housing, and travel. These changes also alter the relative size of segments and markets for existing products and services, as once dominant or popular brands and products fade while others emerge to take their place. Thus, demographic, social, political, and economic changes provide the aspiring entrepreneur with the ideal conditions for creating solutions to new, and sometimes even old, problems.

A second source of opportunity is inventions and discoveries that produce new knowledge. Technological developments and breakthroughs in university laboratories and other research institutions, corporate or otherwise, offer excellent prospects for commercial opportunities. Of course, we need not interpret technology narrowly in just scientific terms. The latest developments in science, arts, crafts, and music all present conditions for fashioning entrepreneurial opportunities. These developments may occur in scientific labs as much as in craft shops, garages, studios, and basements.

Almost all technological breakthroughs first begin as scientific or artistic discoveries or inventions. To be useful to society, these discoveries and inventions have to be converted to products and processes of everyday use. It is when knowledge is embodied in products of everyday use that the intellectual property of the artist, the scientist, or the lab becomes a tradable item, and can be produced and exchanged for profit. Whenever and wherever artistic and scientific breakthroughs occur, conditions are created for converting the new knowledge into products and processes either to solve existing problems or to create new needs and markets for these needs. One only has to think of the recent developments in genetic and computing technologies to appreciate the possibilities of converting the science of these technologies to products and services to satisfy the everyday needs of people. This process of converting artistic and scientific knowledge into products and processes that satisfy specific needs and problems is another major source of entrepreneurial opportunity.

A third source of entrepreneurial opportunities is the inefficiencies embedded in a society's existing economic structure. Inefficiencies often manifest themselves in the form of incongruities. An incongruity is a "discrepancy, a dissonance, between what is and what ought to be."[4] Incongruities exist when there are contradictions within the economic realities of an industry (for example, high growth accompanied by low profitability); when the reality of an industry clashes with the assumptions about it (when the things people within the industry know and think about themselves are different from the things people outside know and think about them); when there is a gap between perceived and actual customer needs and expectations; and when there is a gulf between the pace of change in the business processes within an industry and in the world around it. Whenever and wherever these incongruities are large, we are faced with forces to carve out profitable new entrepreneurial opportunities. Thus, incongruities present conditions that are favorable for the creation of something new.

Individuals and Macro Forces and Trends: The Nexus of Opportunity and the Individual

It is one thing to observe and appreciate the unfolding forces and trends, but an entirely different matter to be able to fashion an opportunity out of these trends and forces. How does one fashion a specific opportunity from such macro forces and trends? Norbert Wiener, an eminent scientist, commented that at the beginning stages of a new idea, the effectiveness of the individual is enormous: "Before any new idea can arise in theory and practice, some person or persons must have introduced it in their own minds. . . . The absence of original mind, even though it might not have excluded a certain element of progress in the distant future, may well delay it for fifty years or a century."[5]

The Oxford English Dictionary defines opportunity as "a time, juncture, or condition of things favorable to an end or purpose, or admitting of something being done or effected." Thus, at the minimum, an opportunity involves an end or purpose, and things favorable to the achievement of it. Therefore, for something to be an opportunity there must be an "original mind," as Wiener put it. Further, in the case of an entrepreneurial opportunity, the "things favorable" consist of two categories: (1) beliefs about the future, and (2) actions based on those beliefs. Thus, "before there are products and firms, there is human imagination; and before there are markets, there are human aspirations."[6] To form beliefs and to act on them requires information and a predilection to act on this information.

Where is the inspiration and information that allow one to endow and enrich the abstract and impersonal forces and trends with specific meaning so that the individual is able to imagine a product, a market, and the means to bring them together? It is partly within us and partly outside. The Austrian economist Friedrich von Hayek postulated the concept of dispersed knowledge where no two individuals share the same knowledge or information about the environment. We can distinguish between two types of knowledge: first, the body of scientific knowledge, which is stable and can be best known by suitably chosen experts in their respective fields; second, the dispersed information of particular time and place, whose importance only the individual possessing it can judge.[7] This dispersion has an extremely important implication as far as entrepreneurial opportunities are concerned. Dispersed information is a basic explanation for how an enterprising individual and the unfolding forces and trends combine to crystallize an opportunity to create and exploit new products in existing or new markets.

The key is that this information is diffused in the economy and is not a given or at everyone's disposal. Thus, only a few people know about a particular scarcity, or a new invention, or a particular resource lying fallow. This knowledge is typically idiosyncratic *because it is acquired through each individual's own circumstances, including occupation, on-the-job routines, social relationships, and daily life.* It is this specific information, obtained in a particular "information corridor," that leads to some profit-making insight.

Each and every one of us experiences the grand and impersonal forces and trends both differently and through our everyday activities and experiences. It is useful to separate two main categories of information sources: primary sources of experience and information and secondary sources. Primary sources are those that exist within us: experiences, knowledge, and information that are personal. Secondary sources are experiences of other people and institutions, and often involve deliberate search among sources outside of our own self and experience.

We look within ourselves and use our painful and pleasurable experiences for inspiration. Or it may be our areas of competence or expertise that are the source of inspiration. Perhaps it is the experience of those near and dear to us—the ones that sociologists call "strong ties"—who are the source of inspiration about specific opportunities. Such crystallization of opportunities may occur serendipitously or through deliberate search. Sometimes the unexpected outcome of a deliberate search creates new possibilities. The search for a cure for cancer may well yield some unexpected new solution to an old problem, or even a new idea for which no known need or market exists and for which we may have to create a new market. Some of the best-known names are actually products of such serendipitous creations including "Post it" Notes, developed by 3M, and nylon from DuPont, where the scientists set out to solve one problem but came up with an unrelated new product. The biggest success story of our time, namely Microsoft, got its break during one such failed search by IBM for an operating system to run its proposed personal computer. Correspondingly, the necessary inspiration for ideas may come from the information and experiences of other people or organizations. These encounters have the potential to provide us with specific information that contains the seeds of a new opportunity.

In summary, in the words of Professor Saras Sarasvathy, "entrepreneurship is a function of individuality: who you are, what you know, and who you know."[8] We cannot imagine how certain firms could have come to be aside from the particularity of certain individuals: Disney without Walt Disney, Ford without Henry Ford, General Electric without Thomas Edison, Wal-Mart without Sam Walton, Apple without Steve Jobs. The bottom line is that when we use our individuality and our idiosyncratic means to make specific sense of a changing world of ideas, issues, needs, and preferences around us, and then act upon them to imagine a product-market combination, we are indeed in the presence of an entrepreneurial opportunity. We can say that we have discovered it or created it, but the fact is that it exists very much because of our individuality.

Sometimes the discovery or creation is serendipitous; sometimes it comes without much effort or search. At other times, we may have to expend much creative and physical energy to crystallize it. Some of us may be able to detect it through sheer imagination and analysis, while for others it may come only through the very act of creating a new business.

We have spoken until now about how an individual might arrive at an opportunity. It is one thing to arrive at an entrepreneurial opportunity, but an entirely different matter to act on this opportunity and ride it through to execution and profitability. Let us now turn our attention to the predilection to act on an entrepreneurial opportunity.

Problems in Pursuing an Opportunity with Limited Resources

Entrepreneurial opportunities present us with possibilities for both a gain and a loss. By definition, entrepreneurship requires making investments (time, effort, and money) today without knowing what the distribution of the returns will be tomorrow. Economist Frank Knight pointed out an important quality about entrepreneurial opportunities, namely that there is a fundamental uncertainty about them. He observed that one cannot collect more information or perform more analysis in order to reduce uncertainty. Rather, only the collective actions of competing entrepreneurs, resource suppliers, and customers can reduce uncertainties. There is no meaningful way in which to predict the future prospects of an entrepreneurial opportunity and then act on it. Knight pointed out this important distinction between uncertainty (outcomes that cannot be imagined and are unknowable) and risk (both outcomes and their probabilities can be subjectively assigned). While one can insure against or diversify away risk, one cannot insure against or diversify away an uncertainty.

Bringing new products and markets into existence usually involves an element of downside (partly influenced by risk and partly by uncertainty). Indeed, risk and uncertainty provide the opportunity for profit in the first place. This opportunity for profit attracts many people toward entrepreneurship. Individuals vary in their perception of downside risks and profit opportunities, and in their aptitudes and capacities to deal with and manage them. From past research we know that people have systematic biases and heuristics for dealing with risk and uncertainty. Two biases are relevant for us. These are a *bias toward analysis* and a *bias toward action*.

Sometimes people focus on the risk and uncertainty involved in an entrepreneurial opportunity. Fear of realizing the downside often prevents individuals from acting on such opportunities. Instead, individuals have a great need to search for information in an attempt to reduce the risk and clear the uncertainties. The natural reaction is to analyze the information in order to improve one's chance of success. While such analysis can certainly improve one's chance of success, too much information gathering and analysis can lead to paralysis. More information often has the effect of raising even more questions and doubts about the entrepreneurial opportunity. Recall that such opportunities involve uncertainties that cannot be reduced by more information gathering or analysis. The only way to deal with such uncertainties is to act on them. Thus, we have a conundrum. While more information gathering and analysis may certainly improve our chances of success, analysis begets more analysis and the individual may never act on the opportunity. This leads to our second principle of entrepreneurship: A fear of realizing the downside increases the bias for analysis. A bias for analysis decreases the probability of acting on an entrepreneurial opportunity, even while it improves the odds of success if you do act.

Principle 2: A fear of realizing the downside of creating a new business biases one toward analysis. A bias for analysis significantly decreases the probability of business entry, but increases the probability of success.

Sometimes people focus on the profit potential of an entrepreneurial opportunity. Fear of missing the upside propels individuals to act and act quickly on an entrepreneurial opportunity. In a desire to be first to market or preempt potential competitors, individuals may enter a market with poorly thought-out strategies, faulty products, ill-conceived ideas, and insufficient resources. While the opportunity may be an attractive one, the urgency to act creates many loose ends and increases the number of things that can go wrong with the new venture. While a certain amount of reflection, analysis, and planning might allow the individual to improve the quality of execution, the fear of losing the upside to real or imagined competitors biases the entrepreneur toward action. Again, we have a conundrum. While the urgency to act certainly increases the probability of entering a market with a new product or service, the same urgency increases the probability of failure due to an ill-conceived idea and poor execution. This gives us the third principle of entrepreneurship, which has to do with this bias toward action.

Principle 3: A fear of missing the upside of a good opportunity biases one toward action. A bias for action significantly increases the probability of business entry, but often decreases the probability of success.

How do successful entrepreneurs deal with the tension between a bias for analysis and a bias for action, between the fear of realizing the downside and the fear of losing the upside? Through her research on successful entrepreneurs, Professor Saras Sarasvathy found that such entrepreneurs used what she calls the *affordable loss principle*. Affordable loss is the amount of personal resources that the entrepreneurs feel psychologically comfortable committing to an idea, and, at an extreme, they follow the rule of using zero resources to market. The entrepreneurs that Sarasvathy studied chose strategies and methods that involved generating early revenues with minimum expenditure of resources such as time, effort, and money. The affordable loss principle allows entrepreneurs to act without being paralyzed by the fear of the downside, because they do not stand to lose much if the venture fails. This leads us to the fourth principle of entrepreneurship: adopting the affordable loss principle to resolve the tension between a bias for analysis and a bias for action.

Principle 4: By adopting the affordable loss principle, enterprising individuals are able to resolve the tension between a bias for analysis and a bias for action.

While idiosyncratic insight and the propensity to act on an idea are necessary for successful creation, these same qualities also present entrepreneurs with other problems. In a typical scenario, the enterprising individual does not own or control all the resources required to create the product, develop the market, establish the value-chain infrastructure, and eventually profit from his or her particular knowledge. Most of these resources have to come from other people and institutions. Thus, the entrepreneur has to assemble the resources and the value-chain infrastructure before potential profits can be realized. The process of creating products and markets implies that much of the information required by potential resource suppliers—for example technology, price, quantity, tastes, supplier networks, distributor networks, and strategy—is not reliably available. Relevant information will become available only when the market has been successfully created.[9] Potential stakeholders thus have to rely on the entrepreneur for information, but without the benefit of the entrepreneur's special insight. In almost every project, entrepreneurs have more information about the true qualities of the project and themselves than do any of the other parties. Because of this information asymmetry, neither buyers nor suppliers may be willing to commit the necessary investments in the specialized assets required by the entrepreneur or enter into formal contracts to develop the business. As a result, resources are difficult to assemble at the early phase of a new venture.[10]

Even if suppliers and other resource controllers were willing to overlook the uncertainty or were willing to make specialized investments by charging a risk premium, there remains the ever-present danger of opportunism[11] (where the entrepreneur or the resource supplier may willfully fail to comply with contracts and agreements). Once specialized investments have been committed, the entrepreneur can hold the other party hostage in order to drive bargains that are more favorable.[12] Of course, once an investment has been made, it is not possible to ensure that the entrepreneur's every action (or inaction—also called the problem of *shirking*) is in the best interests of the resource suppliers.[13] In this situation, establishing cooperative relationships is difficult unless the entrepreneur is willing to make significant and irreversible commitments to the business in order to establish his or her credibility. This drives up sunk costs and therefore exposes the entrepreneur to a potential loss.

We thus have a vicious cycle, which brings us to the fifth principle of entrepreneurship.

Principle 5: All creative endeavors involve a vicious cycle: No product implies no customers; no customers implies no revenue; no revenue implies no cash for investment; no investment implies no legitimacy or credibility; no legitimacy implies no resources; no resources implies no product.

While the affordable loss principle allows the entrepreneur to keep the loss exposure low, a strategy of starting with what you already have in order to build the business rapidly is important for breaking out of the vicious cycle. By using their human capital (talent, education, and knowledge); intellectual capital (creativity, resourcefulness, enthusiasm, and optimism); and social capital (contacts with people and their contacts), entrepreneurs are able to *leverage* the necessary resources required to break out of the vicious cycle without increasing their overall exposure to loss from a failed venture. In the entrepreneurship literature, we call the strategy of using commonly available resources to break out of the vicious cycle *bootstrapping*. Bootstrapping starts with the resources that the entrepreneur already has (rather than the idea or product) and allows the entrepreneur to build up the business gradually, customer by customer, product by product, employee by employee (i.e., pulling yourself up by your bootstraps).[14]

Professor Saras Sarasvathy extends the bootstrapping idea one step further by suggesting that many good entrepreneurs do not even start with a specific idea, but develop the business idea during the process of creation. She calls this a strategy of *effectuation*. In the effectuation process, rather than starting out with a specific business idea, the entrepreneur tries to figure out what businesses can feasibly be created with the resources he or she controls. Given *means*, what *ends* can one create? Successful entrepreneurs do not necessarily cling to a specific product or company idea, but are willing to let these ideas emerge and evolve as they use the resources at their command to create a successful business enterprise. This leads us to the sixth principle of entrepreneurial creation: It is out of available resources (intelligence, energy, enthusiasm, education, and contacts) that you have to break the vicious cycle.

Principle 6: Out of commonly available resources (one's own human capital, intellectual capital, and social capital) can one break the vicious cycle.

Bootstrapping involves at least three components. These are using assets parsimoniously, leveraging social assets, and employing resourcefulness. By studying habitual entrepreneurs (people who have started several new businesses), Professor Ian MacMillan and his colleagues highlighted the fact that these entrepreneurs used resources very sparingly.[15] They call the systematic approach to operating with sparse resources *asset parsimony* strategy. Asset parsimony strategy keeps the loss exposure of the entrepreneurs very low, and at the same time allows one to create something with little. As habitual entrepreneur Zenas Block says, the basic tenet of asset parsimony strategy is to *invest your imagination before you spend your money*. The logic of asset parsimony rests on using underutilized resources, thus keeping costs low. With a frugal investment strategy, the entrepreneur can pursue or create opportunities and, if necessary, abandon them with limited exposure. We can illustrate how the logic works with the following rules of thumb.[16]

- Do not buy new what you can buy used.
- Do not buy used what you can lease.
- Do not lease what you can borrow.
- Do not borrow when you can barter.
- Do not barter what you can beg (moral obligation is incurred).
- Do not beg what you can scavenge.
- Do not scavenge what you can get for free.
- Do not take for free what someone will pay you for.
- Do not take payment for something that people will bid for (create an auction).

While one may not be able to practice all of this successfully in an endeavor, the discipline provided by this way of thinking forces the entrepreneur, as Professors McGrath and MacMillan point out, "to find ways of avoiding costly investments and commitments until there are revenue streams to justify them. The philosophy is that assets and fixed costs are earned by the evidence of income."[17]

Where does an entrepreneur pursuing an idea obtain underutilized resources? One major source of such resources is the entrepreneur's social network. The currency of one's social network is friendship and goodwill rather than dollars. Since entrepreneurs have limited resources to invest, they must creatively exchange the goods and services they need for noncash assets at their disposal, such as information, friendship, charm, enthusiasm, obligations, time, and imagination. The bases of these exchanges are emotions and values, rather than logic and reason. In exchanges based on social relationships, entrepreneurs use their social skills and accumulated social capital to obtain the resources necessary to build on their initial ideas much more cost-effectively than by purchasing these resources at open-market prices. Professors Dew, Read, Sarasvathy, and Wiltbank find that expert entrepreneurs are more likely to exhibit these important traits, while novices use a "predictive frame" and tend to "go by the textbook."

Professors Starr and MacMillan have identified five categories of *social capital* that are relevant for entrepreneurship. They are obligation, gratitude, trust, liking, and friendship.[18] Think of these as debts that people owe you because of many favors you have done for them or happy moments you have shared with them over the years. In the course of our lives, we have all accumulated an inventory of social capital and are in a position to deploy these assets at the time and place of our choosing. Building a new business offers aspiring entrepreneurs an opportunity to exchange these social assets for resources of value to the business.

Obligation is a mutually perceived understanding of a debt incurred sometime in the past and a mutual expectation that this debt will be released under suitable circumstances. Thus, obligation is earned and discharged like any other commodity. However, it remains an unstated expectation. The other person may or may not return the favor. *Gratitude* is a more valuable asset than obligation because the emotional ties are stronger. This is a case where there is clear recognition, not just an expectation, that a favor must be repaid in the future and the account will be discharged by the return of the favor. *Trust* is even stronger than gratitude because there is a more formal recognition that favors will be returned, as opposed to mutual but unspoken expectation or perception. In contrast to obligation and gratitude, where there is always an uncertainty that an emotional debt will be repaid, trust reduces the uncertainty that an appropriate repayment will take place in the future. *Liking* takes us further in this spectrum of emotional debt. The feeling for the other individual is more intense and there is a genuine desire to help the person we like. Our happiness and well-being are enhanced when people we like do well, especially when we play a part in their achievements.

Finally, *friendship* evokes the strongest emotional reaction. Friendship's distinctive quality is that it can be used repeatedly without being exhausted, unlike gratitude and obligation, which may be exhausted after past favors or debts are fulfilled. Indeed, the act of helping a friend in need may actually reinforce the friendship. However, friendships are fragile, take a long time to initiate, nurture, and deepen, and are relatively rare. There are very limited opportunities to deliberately construct and use such social assets.

By resourcefully finding and using underutilized assets, an entrepreneur can work his or her way out of the vicious cycle. Using social capital resourcefully to purchase valuable assets is not only less costly but also less risky than acquiring these assets through regular markets. This leads us to the seventh principle of entrepreneurship: bootstrapping to break the vicious cycle.

Principle 7: Bootstrapping is an ideal way to break the vicious cycle at start-up.

A central tenet of entrepreneurship is the refusal to accept a lack of resources as an insurmountable constraint. Indeed, many entrepreneurs claim that you are better off having sparse resources because it lowers risk, forces you to be more creative, and focuses you on generating revenues to build the business—the cheapest form of capital available. While having sparse resources has its advantages, it of course also presents problems. It is well known that failure rates of new businesses are high. While exact statistics are not available, it is fair to say that more than two-thirds of all business start-ups do not make compensatory returns for their founders. The most common reason cited for failure is under-capitalization. That is another way of saying the new firm ran out of cash.

Cash is the most important asset for any start-up because it is the ultimate store of value that can be traded for other valuable assets. While social capital certainly helps, it is not as liquid or as tradable as cash. Further, social capital is most effective at the earliest stages of a creative process. Growth demands a more fungible asset such as cash. The ability to *sustain* the creation process therefore hinges on the availability of cash. As soon as cash dries up in a business, it is susceptible to failure. Important to appreciate is that a business can be profitable and yet go out of business if it runs out of cash.

For example, you could be very successful in selling large volumes of your product, but your customers may not pay you when you make the sale. Instead, the sale may remain locked up in accounts receivable. Thus, even though you have accounting profits, you have not yet collected the cash. If now you have to pay your employees or if a loan outstanding comes due, you do not have the necessary cash to make these payments. While you could certainly sell your accounts receivable at a discount to institutions that are willing to purchase them, not all such assets are as liquid as cash, nor are the markets for these assets as predictable and reliable.

If cash inflows and cash outflows in a business do not match each other, then the probability of running out of cash is quite high. This imbalance arises due to many factors, such as lags between sales and collections, seasonality of business, inability to reliably predict inflows and outflows because the business is too new to be able to do so, and so on. The literature on entrepreneurship calls these problems the *liabilities of newness* and the *liabilities of smallness*.[19] Because your firm is new and small, you face systematic challenges in management, especially cash management.

The worst possible time to raise cash (through debt, fresh equity infusion, speeding up inflows and drying up outflows with more effective management, or through sale of assets such as accounts receivable) is when you need it most. Then you have the lowest bargaining power. The need is greatest at the early stages of a new venture and when you face a crisis. Not only is your bargaining power weak, but the uncertainty surrounding your business is at its highest and your personal credibility is at its lowest when you start out and when you face a crisis. As a result, the cost of capital could become prohibitive. This leads us to the eighth principle of entrepreneurship: Cash is critical, and often most difficult to obtain when it is most needed.

Principle 8: Cash is king—and is most expensive when you need it most.

In addition to the liabilities of newness and smallness, entrepreneurial ventures face what may be called the *liabilities of complexity*. One need not emphasize the point that managing a business venture is a highly complex process. Three specific complexities need special mention. They are management of ideas, management of attention, and management of logistics.

For an entrepreneur, the biggest challenge is to pursue an idea to its conclusion. Indeed, experienced entrepreneurs often claim that there is no such thing as a bad idea, only poor execution. It is generally accepted that entrepreneurs are more action oriented and need to occupy themselves with new problems and challenges. This often tends to promote a short-term problem orientation and a need to demonstrate progress. This has the effect of inducing premature abandonment of ideas because even if problems are not being solved, the appearance of progress requires moving on to the next batch of problems. Thus, because of their inherent impatience, many entrepreneurs often leave behind half-solved problems or premature ideas. Related to this is also the problem of management of attention.

Well established empirically is that most individuals lack the capability to deal with complexity. People have short attention spans. The average person can retain raw data in short-term memory for only a few seconds. Because of this inherent limitation of the human mind, people are most efficient at repetitive tasks—you do not need to concentrate on repetitive tasks once they are mastered. But new business creation is hardly repetitive. There are many details to think about and execute. Each task and each new problem looks different from the earlier one. The entrepreneur has to take on all roles, from the receptionist to the chief strategist. An average person can hold or deal with seven plus or minus two bits of information or issues at any given time. The moment the number of issues exceeds this, people become more subjective, solutions become increasingly error-prone, and rationalization replaces rationality. New business creation often entails dealing with more than seven plus two issues at a time.

Finally, new entrepreneurs have to learn a host of new roles and functions and create new structures and systems for everything—accounting, sales, purchasing, information systems, and payroll, among others. Due to the variety and the number of tasks involved, entrepreneurs have to learn as they go. Thus, errors are common as they learn the new business. These added costs from learning on the job systematically lower the probability of survival of new ventures. This leads us to the ninth principle of entrepreneurship: If cash does not kill you, logistics will!

Principle 9: If cash does not kill you, logistics will.

With so many challenges and so many things that can go wrong, why bother with entrepreneurship? How is it ever possible, especially for first-time entrepreneurs, to ever be successful? Is luck then the only solution to success? In answering these kinds of questions, it is always good to get back to the basics and to keep things simple. As we have emphasized throughout this book, the main business of business is to create value. Entrepreneurship is about discovering or creating a new formula or yet another way to create value. By combining resources in a new and better way or by purchasing resources more cheaply and applying them to more profitable uses, entrepreneurs can create value and keep some of that added value as a reward for the creation. Indeed, "an entrepreneurial discovery (or creation) occurs when someone makes the conjecture that a set of resources is not put to its 'best use' [i.e., the resources are priced too low, given a belief about the price at which the output from their combination could be sold in another location, at another time, or in another form]. If the conjecture is acted upon and is correct, the individual will earn an entrepreneurial profit. If the conjecture is acted upon and is incorrect, the individual will incur an entrepreneurial loss."[20] This is a roundabout way of saying that the essence of entrepreneurship is finding ways to "buy low and sell high"!

The point of this chapter is to make clear that each one of us already possesses the fundamental resources required to create value in the economy. We possess differential information. We have valuable contacts and a social network. We possess human capital: our education and knowledge. We possess intellectual resources: our talent, imagination, and emotional energy. If success in business is all about buying low and selling high, we already start with the cheapest resources at our disposal. The task of entrepreneurship is to creatively endow these resources with value that society will appreciate and for which it will pay dearly. At the end of the day, there are only a few ways to combine resources in order to create value. These few actions influence either the costs of doing business or the sales accruing from them. At the early stages, every business has three to five variables that have the most impact on costs and revenues. The trick is to find these critical factors and focus on them. By focusing the limited time, attention, and intellectual energies on the three to five critical factors that can make or break the creation process, entrepreneurs can have more control over the process. This keeps the complex, uncertain, and risky task of business creation simple and manageable. And this leads us to the final principle of entrepreneurship: Finding and focusing on three to five fundamental drivers eases the task of business creation.

Principle 10: Every new business has three to five fundamental drivers. Find them and focus on them. The task of creation becomes easy.

Entrepreneurship is about finding new formulas or ways to create value. You profit if you can create ways to use resources more cheaply and creatively in order to create products and services that offer new value to customers. In this chapter we have seen some simple rules you can follow to ensure that the probability of success during this discovery and creation process remains high while the potential exposure to loss due to failure is kept at affordable levels.

Entrepreneurship in MBA Curricula

Entrepreneurship and the study of entrepreneurial behavior account for a large number of electives in MBA programs. All of the top 20 general management programs as ranked by *BusinessWeek*'s 2008 poll offer significant numbers of entrepreneurship courses in their curricula. Exhibit 13.1 summarizes the first courses related to entrepreneurship

Exhibit 13.1   Entrepreneurship in MBA Curricula

Business School	First Entrepreneurship Course	Required?	Total Entrepreneurship Electives
Northwestern (Kellogg)	Entrepreneurship and New Venture Formation	No	45
Harvard University	The Entrepreneurial Manager	Yes	26
University of Michigan (Ross)	Introduction to Entrepreneurship	No	17
Stanford University	Entrepreneurship: Formation of New Venture (One Example)	No	21
Duke University (Fuqua)	Entrepreneurial Strategy	No	19

and the total number of courses for five of the full-time MBA programs with the highest-ranked general management specialty in *BusinessWeek*'s poll.

Notes

1. Entrepreneurship can occur within existing firms, or individuals can create new firms to pursue their business ideas.
2. For some compelling arguments of how business practices can influence political and social realities, see Benjamin Barber's *Jihad vs. McWorld* (1995).
3. Indeed, of all the forces that give rise to change, including wars, epidemics, and revolutions, the economist Joseph Schumpeter isolated the unfailing power of innovation in goods and services to bring about changes in the social and political landscape. And the agent of this innovation, he argued, is the entrepreneur. The "fundamental impulse that sets and keeps" in motion such systemic change "comes from the new consumer goods, the new methods of production or transportation, the new markets, and the new forms of industrial organization" (1976). "The history of business is littered with such entrepreneurially introduced innovations. Each succeeding innovation has altered the economic, political and social landscape" (Venkataraman 2002).
4. See Drucker (1985).
5. Wiener (1993, 7).
6. See Venkataraman and Sarasvathy (2001, 652).
7. Hayek (1945). See also Shane (2000).
8. Sarasvathy (2001).
9. See Arrow (1974).
10. Economists refer to this as the adverse selection problem (Akerlof 1970). Overcoming this problem imposes extra costs for revealing credible information, writing in all kinds of contingencies in contracts, and, at an extreme, driving better-quality entrepreneurs and resource suppliers from the market (as in the case of newly emerging market economies such as Russia) unless some other mechanism exists to reduce such costs.
11. See Williamson (1975).
12. Economists call this the hold-up problem (Williamson 1985).
13. Economists refer to this unobservability problem and the incentive to use others opportunistically as the moral hazard problem (Arrow 1971). Overcoming the moral hazard problem also introduces significant postcontract costs, unless some other mechanism exists to reduce such costs.
14. See Amar Bhide (1992) for a nice summary of the bootstrapping process.
15. See Hambrick and MacMillan (1984), Starr and MacMillan (1990), and McGrath and MacMillan (2000).
16. This is a significant elaboration of the principles first put forward by Block and MacMillan (1993).
17. See McGrath and MacMillan (2000, 245).
18. Starr and MacMillan (1990) survey an extensive literature in sociology to come up with their typology. They have captured the essence of the diverse nature of social capital with this typology.
19. See Aldrich and Auster (1984) for an outstanding review of these ideas.
20. See Shane and Venkataraman (2000, 220).

For Further Reading

Barringer, Bruce R., *Preparing Effective Business Plans: An Entrepreneurial Approach* (Upper Saddle River, NJ: Prentice Hall, 2009).

Barringer, Bruce R., and Duane Ireland, *Entrepreneurship: Successfully Launching New Ventures* (Upper Saddle River, NJ: Prentice Hall, 2010).

Bhide, Amar, *The Origin and Evolution of New Businesses* (New York: Oxford University Press, 2000).

Drucker, Peter, *Innovation and Entrepreneurship* (New York: Harper & Row, 1985).

Katz, Jerome A., and Dean A. Shepherd, eds. *Cognitive Approaches to Entrepreneurship Research* (Bingley, UK: Emerald Group Publishing, 2005).

McGrath, Rita, and Ian MacMillan, *The Entrepreneurial Mindset* (Boston: Harvard Business School Press, 2000).

Sahlman, William, Howard Stevenson, Michael Roberts, and Amar Bhide, *The Entrepreneurial Venture*, 2nd ed. (Boston: Harvard Business School Press, 1999).

References

Akerlof, G. A. 1970. "The Market for 'Lemons': Quality Uncertainty and the Market Mechanism." *Quarterly Journal of Economics* 84:488–500.

Aldrich, H., and E. Auster. 1986. "Even Dwarfs Started Small: Liabilities of Age and Size and Their Strategic Implications." In *Research in Organizational Behavior*, vol. 8, ed. L. Cummings and B. Staw, 165–198. Greenwich, CT: JAI Press.

Arrow, K. J. 1971. *Essays in the Theory of Risk Bearing*. Chicago: Markham.

Arrow, K. J. 1974. "Limited Knowledge and Economic Analysis." *American Economic Review* 64 (1): 1–10.

Barber, B. R. 1995. *Jihad vs. McWorld*. New York: Ballantine Books.

Bhide, Amar. 1992. "Bootstrap Finance: The Art of Start-ups." *Harvard Business Review*, November–December.

Block, Zenas, and Ian MacMillan. 1993. *Corporate Venturing: Creating New Business within the Firm*. Cambridge, MA: Harvard University Press.

Dew, Nicholas, Stuart Read, Saras D. Sarasvathy, and Robert Wiltbank. 2009. "Effectual versus Predictive Logics in Entrepreneurial Decision-Making: Differences between Experts and Novices." *Journal of Business Venturing* 24 (July): 287.

Drucker, Peter. 1985. *Innovation and Entrepreneurship*. New York: Harper & Row.

Hambrick, Donald, and Ian MacMillan. 1984. "Asset Parsimony: Managing Assets to Manage Profitability." *Sloan Management Review* 25:67–74.

Hayek, F. A. 1945. "The Use of Knowledge in Society." *American Economic Review* 35 (4): 519–530.

McGrath, Rita, and Ian MacMillan. 2000. *The Entrepreneurial Mindset*. Boston: Harvard Business School Press.

Sarasvathy, S. 2001. "What makes Entrepreneurs Entrepreneurial?" University of Washington working paper series.

Shane, S. 2000. "Prior Knowledge and the Discovery of Entrepreneurial Opportunities." *Organization Science* 11 (4): 448–469.

Shane, Scott, and S. Venkataraman. 2000. "The Promise of Entrepreneurship as a Field of Research." *Academy of Management Review* 25 (1): 217–226.

Starr, J., and I. C. MacMillan. 1990. "Resource Cooptation via Social Contracting: Resource Acquisition Strategies for New Ventures." *Strategic Management Journal* 11 (Summer): 79–92.

Venkataraman, S. 2002. "Stakeholder Value Equilibration and the Entrepreneurial Process." *Special Issue of the Society for Business Ethics*. Ruffin Series No. 3: 45–57.

Venkataraman, S., and S. Sarasvathy. 2000. "Strategy and Entrepreneurship: Outlines of an Untold Story." In *Handbook of Strategic Management*, ed. Michael Hitt, R. Edward Freeman, and Jeff Harrison. New York: Blackwell Publishing.

Wiener, Norbert. 1993. *Invention: The Care and Feeding of Ideas*. Cambridge, MA: MIT Press.

Williamson, O. E. 1975. *Markets and Hierarchies: Analysis and Antitrust Implications*. New York: Basic Books.

Williamson, O. E. 1985. *The Economic Institutions of Capitalism*. New York: Macmillan.

14

Emerging Markets
and Development

The world economy has experienced more profound change in the past 30 years than at any time since the onset of the industrial revolution. For more than a century, since at least the early 1800s, economic development has been virtually synonymous with the United States and Western Europe. The rapidly rising living standards that accompanied growth and development in the West were of a scale never before seen in human history. Growth in the West, which began with a burst in agricultural productivity, led to a surge in material well-being that established the economic primacy of the United States and Europe. Economic supremacy in the West extended through the end of the twentieth century and carried with it the focus of academics in business-related disciplines.

The relative isolation of growth within the Western Hemisphere has changed markedly in the past 60 years and looks to reshape the world economy entirely within the next few decades. This chapter explores the important differences between the economies and commercial environments of developed and emerging markets. High-income developed economies have been the focus of almost every discipline taught in business schools despite the fact that their relevance in the world economy is shrinking. In the pages that follow, we explore the "economic nature" of emerging economies (i.e., countries growing rapidly from a base of low average-income levels). The primary goal of the chapter is to explain the critical elements that enable a country to grow and the challenges faced by firms operating in such an environment. A related goal is to understand the forces and conditions that prevent economies from growing, and which in turn prevent firms from succeeding.

The New World Economy

Beginning slowly after the end of World War II, economic growth began to spread beyond the West to nations like Japan and South Korea. These economies and those of a few others produced growth rates three to four times as high as those in the West. So rapid and so sustained was the growth in Japan that by 1990 it had grown from approximately 25 percent of U.S. gross domestic product (GDP) per person in 1950 to more than 90 percent. By the start of the 1990s, Japan was richer than any major European economy. Other economies like South Korea, Singapore, Taiwan, and Thailand began to post growth rates similar to Japan's and to rapidly converge on the living standards of Western nations. Finally, the secrets of economic modernity and rapidly rising living standards had begun to spread across the world.

The rise of Japan and the so-called Asian Tigers was an important beginning and a genuine signal that wealth and, along with it, new markets for commerce were coming to nations that were once seen as closed or simply unimportant to big business. But the excitement and fascination caused by the rise of Japan and the Asian Tigers masked the broader lack of growth throughout most of the world. While a few nations with mostly small populations had gone from low to high income in a few decades, the vast majority of the world's population resided in stagnant economies. For most of the world, growth, when it came at all, came in short bursts that were followed by substantial reversals. By the beginning of the 1990s and despite the notable economic successes outside the West, the world economy had grown more unequal than at any time in history.

The inequality of the world economy had at least a few key causes, but one of the most important was the ideological view of markets taken in some of the world's most populous nations and regions. With more than a billion citizens each, China and India represented approximately one-third of the world's population. Though politically very different, both nations' economies were heavily directed by the state, with comparatively few similarities to the economic structures that governed Western economies. Similarly, the economy of the Soviet Union was state-directed with virtually no significant commercial enterprise run by private parties. Among others, these three economies were managed in a manner fundamentally different from that followed by nations where economic growth had been the most rapid and sustained. The economic consequences of following these ideologies ultimately led to a broad mandate for change that fundamentally reinvented much of the world economy.

The Rise of the New Giants

It doesn't matter whether a cat is black or white, so long as it catches mice.

—Deng Xiaopeng

Well into the latter half of the twentieth century, the leaders of China, India, and the Soviet Union held to the values that supported their systems of economic management. And each eventually experienced the complete stagnation of economic growth that ultimately led to the abandonment of heavy state-directed approaches. Chinese Premier Deng Xioapeng began the shift toward a market-based economy in 1978. A similar reversal was punctuated with the fall of the Berlin Wall in 1989 and the dissolution of the Soviet Union soon thereafter. By the early 1990s, India, too, had begun a sharp shift toward market-based economic management. Within little more than a decade, 40 percent of the world economy that had previously been closed or suspicious of free markets and private commercial activity was linked to the broader network of markets and economies where market-based approaches dominated. In a very real sense, these changes blew open the doors to the new world economy.

In stark contrast to the comparatively mature and slow-growing Western economies, the new world economy would challenge business to understand markets that were chaotic, evolving rapidly, and driven by new players and unique cultural mind-sets. The opportunities were abundant, and so were the risks and uncertainties. Nevertheless, by the end of the twentieth century, the world economy had taken an entirely new shape. Growth, challenges, and opportunities now exist in all corners of the world for domestic and multinational firms. The newly emerging economic giants, China and India, occupy the headlines, and rightly so; but notable changes and promises of growth can also be found in Latin America, Africa, the Middle East, and Southeast Asia.

The welcome emergence of economic growth and rising living standards where once there was stagnation commands attention and requires that we seek to understand how economic growth emerges, how the process of growth is shaped by formal and informal institutions, and how firms and the actions of managers relate to the process of growth. The remainder of this chapter focuses on these questions and on the ways that the new world economy challenges and complements that of the old one. To begin, we examine a simple accounting method for thinking about growth and the process by which firms relate to growth.

A Simple Accounting of Economic Growth

High among many objectives of nations and cultures is the desire to provide adequate resources for comfortable living and to achieve an increase in material living standards from one generation to the next. Material living standards are not an end in and of themselves, but rather a means by which we can achieve health, security, and freedom from the myriad threats of poverty. Sufficiently high material living standards are essential to sustain any society, and yet they are not always easy to maintain. History abounds with examples of economic failures and of suffering and death as a result of extreme poverty.

The fundamental pursuit of development economics is to understand how growth emerges and, consequently, to understand why it sometimes does not. To begin to explore this question, let's consider a simple framework for thinking about all the forces that can contribute to an economy's success or failure. We start with the economic objective of growing material living standards, and decompose it into three components or buckets. By material living standards we mean the average resources, goods, and/or services available to citizens of a given economy. The distribution of resources across society matters greatly if not critically in the evaluation of any economy's success, but we begin by examining how the overall quantity of resources is generated.

Our metric of material living standards is gross domestic product per person, or GDP per capita. Recall that GDP measures the value of all final goods and services produced in an economy in a year. By simply dividing that value, GDP, by the number of persons in any economy, we have the most basic measure of material living standards, GDP per capita. Equation (14.1) decomposes GDP per person, which is calculated as GDP divided by the population, into three simple terms.

$$\frac{GDP}{Population} = \frac{Output}{Workers} \times \frac{Workers}{Labor\ Force} \times \frac{Labor\ Force}{Population} \tag{14.1}$$

where:

$$GDP = \text{value of total output}$$
$$GDP\ per\ capita = GDP\ per\ person = GDP/population$$

It is easy to see that the three terms on the right-hand side of equation (14.1) equal GDP per capita, since the total value of output in a given year is equal to GDP. Though it seems too simple to be useful, equation (14.1) reveals how key factors, including the actions of firms and managers, contribute to the rise (or lack thereof) in material living standards. To see how equation (14.1) helps us to understand the various relationships between country and firm factors and growth, let's discuss a few examples of how emerging economies tend to differ from mature, high-income markets and how this matters for growth.

Demographics

Anyone who has visited a low-income nation notices social, cultural, and economic differences from high-income economies. One commonly noticed difference is average family size. Average family size is influenced by many factors, but the most important factor is the average number of children born to women. In developing economies, women tend to give birth to twice as many children (or more) as in higher-income nations. Regardless of any attributions one may make about the effects of larger family size on a society, it has important implications for economic growth.

The reason is that an economy with larger numbers of children per mother on average will typically have a higher ratio of children under 16 to adults between the ages of 16 and 65. Since the labor force, meaning those in an economy suited to take full-time jobs, is comprised of those between 16 and 65, the ratio of the labor force to the whole of the population is smaller in low-income than in high-income nations. This means that there are fewer people to do the work of producing society's resources relative to consumers of those resources. And this, in turn, means that even if those in the labor force were equally productive across economies, GDP per capita will be lower in an economy with a low ratio of labor force to population than in one with a high ratio of labor force to population. Even if they were otherwise identical, GDP per capita will be lower in nations with a demographic skewed toward young children, who are not typically in the labor force.

Demographics skewed to those outside the labor force can also be a challenge for nations with small numbers of children per mother. Consider economies like Japan, Italy, and Russia where the population is actually falling. Population growth in these nations is said to be below replacement rate because of the small average number of children per birth-age female. These are aging nations where there are more people exiting the labor force due to retirement than there are entering the labor force as they become adults. Though the causes are quite different, the effects on GDP per capita are the same. As the ratio of the labor force to the population falls, there are fewer working in society to create resources relative to those who are consuming them, and as a result, GDP per capita is pulled downward. All other things being equal, this demographic trend works to lower GDP per capita.

The third term on the right-hand side of equation (14.1) gives us insight into why countries with a low ratio of labor force to population, regardless of the cause, might struggle to grow and seek policies to alleviate the demographic drag on growth. For example, countries where the population skews toward young children outside the labor force may face extreme distributional issues even as it adds jobs in highly productive industries. Likewise, countries that are aging toward a lower ratio of labor force to population may grow more open to immigration to provide tax revenues and the production that a society needs. Thus, demographics matter for economic development and can help explain the thin labor markets, low relative tax base, and persistence of poverty in the midst of positive economic development.

The Employment Rate (1 Minus the Unemployment Rate)

Like the ratio of labor force to population, the second term on the right-hand side of equation (14.1) illustrates how key features of the economy contribute to economic growth. This term is merely the employment rate, which is 1 minus the unemployment rate. The ratio of workers, meaning those in the labor force who have jobs, to the overall labor force reflects the efficiency of an economy to put its labor force to work. The logic behind the importance of the employment rate is straightforward. Having a proportionately high labor force is a benefit because it enables a high producer-to-consumer ratio in a country. But someone is a producer only if they have employment. Here we should think of gainful full-time employment, including self-employment. The more members of the labor force who have jobs, the greater is the number of producers of resources in an economy. In turn, this implies a higher producer-to-consumer ratio and the possibility of higher GDP per capita.

As with the third term, low and high values of the second term lead to lower or higher values of GDP per capita irrespective of the values of the other terms. And policies and/or cultural characteristics that lead to higher or lower employment rates directly affect GDP per capita. If an economy had a high ratio of labor force to population but could not generate jobs for those in the labor force, it could still be poor. An unstable macroeconomy and policies that discourage firms from adding jobs are common contributors to a low employment rate.

The variance in this term can be quite broad and explains a notable portion of the differences in GDP per capita across countries. Using a common definition of employment, the rate of unemployment has typically been 3 percent to 4 percent higher in continental Europe than in the United States, where 5 percent is considered a healthy, normal level. The unemployment rate in Japan is usually much lower than in the United States at approximately 3 percent. But in South Africa the unemployment rate has been as high as 40 percent in recent years. It is not uncommon to measure unemployment at over 10 percent in emerging economies or for unemployment to surge markedly in the aftermath of an economic crisis.

The large range of unemployment levels and hence of employment rates across countries matters greatly in the determination of GDP per capita. Relatively low employment rates are symptomatic of emerging economies, which are typically challenged by a host of issues, from weak institutions and an unstable political environment to macroeconomic mismanagement. The obvious results of low employment are less production and fewer resources for society to consume and lower wages. Emerging economies often struggle the most around low employment rates both because they directly lead to lower material living standards and because they often foment political instability, which can in turn keep employment levels low.

Taken together, the second and third terms on the right-hand side of equation (14.1) suggest key differences between low-income economies and mature, developed ones. In low-income economies employment levels are relatively low and the labor force can be small relative to the overall population. These two factors represent challenges that may exist irrespective of the actual skills available in the workforce. Indeed, the workforce may be talented and driven compared to those of other countries, and yet income may be kept low by demographic challenges and the inability to create jobs to put the labor force to work.

Average Worker Productivity

Finally, consider the first term on the right-hand side of equation (14.1), $\frac{Output}{Workers}$. This term reflects the average productivity of all the workers in any economy and is the most important term in equation (14.1). It is important to note that this figure reflects the value of total output from all workers, not just workers in certain industries or in export sectors. Rather, this term acknowledges that all labor inputs go toward producing the output that society can consume or export to other economies. The ratio of this total output to the actual number of workers is, by definition, average worker productivity. The average level of productivity of the workforce is a very good metric for overall income levels in the economy since workers are paid from the value of the output that they create. Owners of capital receive the portion that does not go to workers, which tends to be about 30 percent of total output in the United States.

Variation in average worker productivity explains most of the difference between high- and low-income nations around the world. The typical emerging market, which begins as a low-income nation, is one where workers on average produce lower-valued output than those in higher-income nations. In large part, the process of growing from a low-income to a high-income nation is the process of raising the productivity of the workforce.

Think of all the ways that average worker productivity could be raised. One obvious way that matters to emerging markets is by raising the human capital of the workforce. Better-educated and better-trained workers are more capable of adding value to goods and services through their work than are workers who are less well educated and trained. Thus, economic policies aimed at increasing the number of children who complete secondary or tertiary education benefit society in part by raising the average productivity of the workforce. Similarly, firms that invest in training their employees benefit society through their effects on the productivity of their workers.

Increasing human capital has rather obvious benefits for individuals and society through increased productivity. Increasing physical and technological capital offers the same benefits to worker productivity, but without necessarily raising the skills or capabilities of the workers themselves. Rather, the environment in which they work supports more productivity by providing workers with greater tools of productivity. Perhaps the most easily appreciated link between physical capital and average worker productivity is found in infrastructure. A high-quality, efficient network of roads, bridges, ports, and airports lowers the time and expense of trading and transporting goods and thereby raises the value of output a worker can produce in a given hour. Similarly, a broadly available and efficient telecommunications/broadband network facilitates communication and information sharing, thereby making workers more productive. Thus, increases in human or physical capital raise worker productivity and material well-being.

The path to productivity and higher living standards through increments to capital, or capital deepening, seems straightforward, but not all countries can take that path. The basic reason this simple path to growth may not be possible is that it takes resources to create physical and human capital. Emerging economies frequently struggle to generate the resources necessary to provide ample education to their citizens or to build and maintain a high-quality physical infrastructure. Moreover, in emerging economies building physical infrastructure and funding education often has to compete with immediate poverty alleviation, the payments of salaries to government workers, and the paying of internal and external debts so as to ensure macroeconomic stability. Without the ability, and will, to use enough scarce resources to invest in human and physical capital, low-income economies may never grow.

One option for augmenting capital without making all the sacrifices internally is to attract funding for capital from foreigners, including foreign firms. If firms are willing to take a risk on investing in a given economy, they can contribute to rises in average worker productivity through their investments in plants, technology, and even physical infrastructure. Similarly, using management practices that efficiently and effectively run firms raises average worker productivity. This is true whether the firm is a domestic or foreign firm, though the most productive practices are often found in firms based in high-income nations.

The links between the activities of firms and societal well-being flow largely though average worker productivity in the ways just described. But it is also easy to see how the dynamics of competition in free markets also flows through this concept. The simple logic of free markets states that the most efficient and productive firms will displace less efficient and productive firms. Thus, an economy's resources are drawn toward those firms that use them most efficiently. Another way to state this is that for an economy to make the highest material value use of its resources, more efficient and productive firms must gain market share from less efficient firms. This implies that competition be present and that the rules of competition be widely applied. When firms compete for market share, they contribute to average worker productivity even if they are not the most efficient firm in the marketplace. By spurring innovation and providing the necessary pressure to manage efficiently, competition can and usually does raise average worker productivity.

As the preceding paragraphs explain, firms, domestic or foreign, can and often do contribute to rising living standards through their influence on average worker productivity and employment, though most of the influence of firms occurs through their direct and indirect influence on productivity. Firms do contribute to material well-being when they add to employment, but most of the effect is typically through the type of employment they offer relative to existing alternatives. If the new jobs create higher value added than the old jobs, this contributes to GDP per capita. Labor markets tend to clear—that is, to equate supply with demand—through adjustments to the wages, so most foreign firms do not typically have a real or significant effect on employment rates when they enter an economy. The third demographic term on the right-hand side of equation (14.1) is almost completely outside the influence of firms except for instances in which firms seek to import workers, such as expatriate managers from abroad. Even then, the effect is trivial and so the effects of firms on well-being and on the speed with which low-income nations begin to emerge come mostly through their effects on productivity.

An Example: Dell Tries Brazil

At the peak of the tech boom of the 1990s, leading firms were flush with cash and looking for ways to expand their growing empires.[1] Few companies had fared as well as Dell, which had revolutionized the PC market with its lean, build-to-order, direct-to-consumer model. With a stock price that had risen more than 5× in the previous five years, Dell was poised for global expansion and had started with successful manufacturing facilities in Ireland and China. With presence in Europe and East Asia established, South America seemed a logical choice for expansion and Brazil was the largest market in the region. PC usage in Brazil was high for an emerging economy with its income level, but most PCs were sold by small producers that often avoided many of the country's high business taxes and import tariffs. In 1999, the year of Dell's entry into Brazil, these gray market producers held a bit more than 50 percent of the market. Dell, which typically held the highest market share everywhere it operated, kept to its strategy and brought its best-in-class management practices to Brazil.

Despite its historic successes everywhere it had operated, Dell struggled in Brazil, but not against its traditional competitors. By the end of 2004, Dell was the market leader in Brazil, but held only 4 percent of the market share. While Dell had gained ground against the likes of Compaq and IBM, the horde of very small informal firms had steadily gained market share. The share of the market held by gray market firms had grown from 50 percent in 1999 to more than 70 percent by November 2004. What had gone wrong? How had one of the world's best PC producers failed to beat, and even lost market share to, small firms? Why was one of the most productive PC manufacturers in the world, possibly the most productive one, unable to gain market share in Brazil?

At least one reason for Dell's failure to win early in Brazil were the high tariffs and taxes in Brazil coupled with the fact that gray market producers often didn't pay them. By successfully avoiding payment of relatively high business and labor taxes and tariffs, gray market firms had a built-in cost advantage that derived from their ability to avoid legal penalties. Dell did pay the taxes and high tariffs. Moreover, gray market firms often sold their PCs with pirated software. Since software represented 10 percent or more of the total PC cost, this additional breach of the law added to the already substantial cost cushion of gray market firms. In essence, because they avoided many legally required costs and operated under a different set of rules than could Dell, gray market firms held onto and gained market share even against a more productive rival.

It is straightforward to conclude that the growth in market share by informal firms should lower average worker productivity in the PC market. And, according to the framework that follows from equation (14.1), this represents a drag on GDP per capita over what would be possible if more productive firms held this market share. The more difficult questions to answer relate to why more productive firms couldn't win market share and whether this alone really reflects a drag on GDP per capita.

Institutions and Emerging Economies

> *The key problem is to find out why that sector of society of the past, which I would not hesitate to call capitalist, should have lived as if in a bell jar, cut off from the rest; why was it not able to expand and conquer the whole of society? . . . [Why was it that] a significant rate of capital formation was possible only in certain sectors and not in the whole market economy of the time?*
>
> —*Fernand Braudel, as quoted in Hernando de Soto,* The Mystery of Capital: Why Capitalism Triumphs in the West and Fails Everywhere Else *(New York: Basic Books, 2000), 66–67.*

The pains of poverty compel nations to seek the recipe for growth and better living standards. But growth and emergence of an economy are not readily produced by copying the experiences of successful economies. We still wonder, as did the French historian Fernand Braudel, why remarkable economic success was produced in some countries and never developed in others. Put plainly in the terms of our organizing equation of GDP per capita, what is it that makes average worker productivity so much higher in some countries than in others? We have already explored how human, physical, and technological capital raises average worker productivity, but why do some countries generate and attract so much more capital than others?

Capital can be scarce for many reasons, but one of the leading causes of insufficient capital is the institutional environment of the country itself. Country-level institutions include the legal system, financial system, political system, and also less formal and discrete entities such as the business culture, social norms, and the pervasiveness of corruption. Institutions are, broadly, the rules of the game in a given country. Institutions shape how business is conducted and how society is organized. For our purposes, we focus on how institutions affect capital formation, the environment of business, and which businesses flourish and why.

The key to understanding how institutions matter for business is to consider why capital is formed in a free market system. Quite simply, capital is formed because those who invest in capital can reap the benefits of that investment. To form capital, whether it be physical or the type we carry around in our heads and hands, requires investment and the sacrifice of time and other resources. Risk accompanies any investment, so those who invest in capital must expect to be compensated for the sacrifice of resources and the risks they take. In nicely functioning markets, these investors in capital receive the benefits of their investments through, for example, the higher wages that accompany education and skill acquisition, increased sales and profits, or increases in the value of the capital itself. In short, capital is formed where those who form it receive sufficiently high returns.

Even if capital is scarce, useful, and sorely needed in a country, it won't likely be formed if individual investors don't expect to benefit as a result. Even a benevolent government may find it challenging to invest in capital if its benefits cannot be garnered or put toward its intended uses. Here is where institutions come into the picture. Institutions determine incentives. Legal and financial systems largely determine who receives the benefits of financial investments and how much they receive. Social norms and the culture of ethical behavior or the prevalence of corruption play a heavy role as well. Wherever the rewards for investment are more predictable and directly tied to productive investments, capital is more likely to form and productivity will follow. Good institutions make productivity profitable. Moreover, they make other activities, like corruption, cheating, and preying on others' efforts, costly and far less profitable than productive activities.

Examples: Corruption and Bureaucratic Inefficiency

Let's consider a few examples to clarify the role of institutions in the development of emerging economies. Recall from our discussion that the path toward higher living standards flows largely through increases in average worker productivity. In turn, the path to productivity requires that good firms (i.e., more productive firms) gain market share from bad or inefficient firms. In free and fair markets this process is largely automatic as rational buyers select the firms that offer the best value. But buyers—individuals, firms, or governments—can be motivated by much more than value.

Corruption

At least one motivation is personal gain that often contradicts official duties of managers or the rights of others. Bribes, kickbacks, and other forms of illegal quid pro quo often influence or determine the choices buyers make. Where corruption holds sway, it channels resources away from the most productive, efficient, and innovative firms. It can and sometimes does fully subvert the process by which free markets deliver innovation and development. As a result, managers who seek success may quickly learn that investments in capital, in better products, services, or lower costs, are less valuable than expenditures on bribes and cozy relationships with key buyers and politicians. Corruption can thereby pervert competition among firms from one that incentivizes socially valuable objectives like efficiency and innovation to one that spurs cronyism and socially damaging relationships.

As with firms, corruption perverts incentives for individuals considering investments in human capital. Individuals have strong incentives to invest in education and skill acquisition where jobs and salaries are awarded to the most capable and skilled. But where corruption is prevalent, jobs and top salaries are themselves a form of currency used in exchange for favors and decisions that are not based on value creation. Where individuals are not rewarded for their investments in education, they make fewer of those investments. Where firms are not rewarded for their investments in efficiency, they worry less about it. Where corruption is pervasive, capital formation is relatively low, and, almost always, so is development.

Exhibit 14.1 presents the Corruption Perceptions Index (CPI) as measured by the group Transparency International, which ranks countries according to their level of corruption. Since corruption is by nature intended to be secret, direct and measurable observation of corruption is rare and very difficult to achieve across a broad set of countries. As a rough proxy for corruption, Transparency International aggregates data from polls that measure how widespread corruption is perceived to be across a set of more than 180 countries. As the data show, corruption perceptions are negatively correlated with income levels and measures of economic development. This does not clarify whether corruption causes or results from low-income levels, or both. What is clear is that corruption makes emerging toward higher income levels tougher.

Efforts to remove country and cultural biases in the measurement of the CPI have revealed notable stability in the raw index over time and across cultures. Despite its weaknesses, the CPI seems to offer a reasonable approximation of the true perceived level of corruption. And, while a measure of actual corruption would be ideal, perceptions are critical in decision-making. Thus, even if perceived and actual corruption levels were substantially different, the perceived level of corruption would greatly matter. Corruption is a formidable barrier to development and an institutional characteristic of economies that struggle to develop. Corruption deters investment by both local and foreign firms whose efforts are required to elevate living standards. It also challenges managers of firms that seek to hold to high ethical and legal standards. The challenges can be sufficiently high that such firms avoid a corrupt economy altogether.

Exhibit 14.1 Transparency International's Corruption Perceptions Index

Rank	Country/Territory	Score	Rank	Country/Territory	Score
1	Denmark	9.3	41	Mauritius	5.5
1	New Zealand	9.3	41	Oman	5.5
1	Sweden	9.3	43	Bahrain	5.4
4	Singapore	9.2	43	Macao	85
5	Finland	9.0	45	Bhutan	5.2
5	Switzerland	9.0	45	Czech Republic	5.2
7	Iceland	8.9	47	Cape Verde	5.1
7	Netherlands	8.9	47	Costa Rica	5.1
9	Australia	8.7	47	Hungary	5.1
9	Canada	8.7	47	Jordan	5.1
11	Luxembourg	8.3	47	Malaysia	5.1
12	Austria	8.1	52	Latvia	5.0
12	Hong Kong	8.1	52	Slovakia	5.0
14	Germany	7.9	54	South Africa	4.9
14	Norway	7.9	55	Italy	4.8
16	Ireland	7.7	55	Seychelles	4.8
16	United Kingdom	7.7	57	Greece	4.7
18	Belgium	7.3	58	Lithuania	4.6
18	Japan	7.3	58	Poland	4.6
18	United States	7.3	58	Turkey	4.6
21	Saint Lucia	7.1	61	Namibia	4.5
22	Barbados	7.0	62	Croatia	4.4
23	Chile	6.9	62	Samoa	4.4
23	France	6.9	62	Tunisia	4.4
23	Uruguay	6.9	65	Cuba	4.3
26	Slovenia	6.7	65	Kuwait	4.3
27	Estonia	6.6	67	El Salvador	3.9
28	Qatar	6.5	67	Georgia	3.9
28	St. Vincent & Grenadines	6.5	67	Ghana	3.9
28	Spain	6.5	70	Colombia	3.8
31	Cyprus	6.4	70	Romania	3.8
32	Portugal	6.1	72	Bulgaria	3.6
33	Dominica	6.0	72	China	3.6
33	Israel	6.0	72	FYR Macedonia	3.6
35	United Arab Emirates	5.9	72	Mexico	3.6
36	Botswana	5.8	72	Peru	3.6
36	Malta	5.8	72	Suriname	3.6
36	Puerto Rico	5.8	72	Swaziland	3.6
39	Taiwan	5.7	72	Trinidad and Tobago	3.6
40	South Korea	5.6	80	Brazil	3.5
			80	Burkina Faso	3.5
			80	Morocco	3.5

(continued)

Exhibit 14.1 *(Continued)*

Rank	Country/Territory	Score	Rank	Country/Territory	Score
80	Saudi Arabia	3.5	121	Sao Tome and Príncipe	2.7
80	Thailand	3.5	121	Togo	2.7
85	Albania	3.4	121	Vietnam	2.7
85	India	3.4	126	Eritrea	2.6
85	Madagascar	3.4	126	Ethiopia	2.6
85	Montenegro	3.4	126	Guyana	2.6
85	Panama	3.4	126	Honduras	2.6
85	Senegal	3.4	126	Indonesia	2.6
85	Serbia	3.4	126	Libya	2.6
92	Algeria	3.2	126	Mozambique	2.6
92	Bosnia and Herzegovina	3.2	126	Uganda	2.6
92	Lesotho	3.2	134	Comoros	2.5
92	Sri Lanka	3.2	134	Nicaragua	2.5
96	Benin	3.1	134	Pakistan	2.5
96	Gabon	3.1	134	Ukraine	2.5
96	Guatemala	3.1	138	Liberia	2.4
96	Jamaica	3.1	138	Paraguay	2.4
96	Kiribati	3.1	138	Tonga	2.4
96	Mali	3.1	141	Cameroon	2.3
102	Bolivia	3.0	141	Iran	2.3
102	Djibouti	3.0	141	Philippines	2.3
102	Dominican Republic	3.0	141	Yemen	2.3
102	Lebanon	3.0	145	Kazakhstan	2.2
102	Mongolia	3.0	145	Timor-Leste	2.2
102	Rwanda	3.0	147	Bangladesh	2.1
102	Tanzania	3.0	147	Kenya	2.1
109	Argentina	2.9	147	Russia	2.1
109	Armenia	2.9	147	Syria	2.1
109	Belize	2.9	151	Belarus	2.0
109	Moldova	2.9	151	Central African Rep.	2.0
109	Solomon Islands	2.9	151	Côte d'Ivoire	2.0
109	Vanuatu	2.9	151	Ecuador	2.0
115	Egypt	2.8	151	Laos	2.0
115	Malawi	2.8	151	Papua New Guinea	2.0
115	Maldives	2.8	151	Tajikistan	2.0
115	Mauritania	2.8	158	Angola	1.9
115	Niger	2.8	158	Azerbaijan	1.9
115	Zambia	2.8	158	Burundi	1.9
121	Nepal	2.7	158	Congo, Republic	1.9
121	Nigeria	2.7	158	Gambia	1.9

Exhibit 14.1   (*Continued*)

Rank	Country/ Territory	Score	Rank	Country/ Territory	Score
158	Guinea-Bissau	1.9	171	Equatorial Guinea	1.7
158	Sierra Leone	1.9	173	Chad	1.6
158	Venezuela	1.9	173	Guinea	1.6
166	Cambodia	1.8	173	Sudan	1.6
166	Kyrgyzstan	1.8	176	Afghanistan	1.5
166	Turkmenistan	1.8	177	Haiti	1.4
166	Uzbekistan	1.8	178	Iraq	1.3
166	Zimbabwe	1.8	178	Myanmar	1.3
171	Congo, Democratic	1.7	180	Somalia	1.0

Source: Transparency International, 2009 (www.transparency.org).

Bureaucratic Inefficiency

Corruption incentivizes behavior that disconnects productive business activities from profitable business activities. In a similar fashion, some economies struggle to emerge because of institutions that make business difficult. In particular, they make it difficult to operate according to the law, to utilize formal systems of finance and trade, and to grow more efficient through scale. These economies struggle due to bureaucratic inefficiencies that hold back all business and make starting new businesses virtually impossible.

Hard as it may be to believe, it can take 200 to 300 days and more than a year's average annual income just to start a company in some countries. In a famous set of experiments, Peruvian economist Hernando de Soto started new companies in a wide set of sectors all the while diligently documenting the time, number of steps, and costs involved in the process. De Soto's team found that starting a one-person garment shop took 289 days. To build a house on state land took nearly seven years and took 728 bureaucratic steps.[2] The list goes on and on, and the findings are very similar in countries like the Philippines, Haiti, and Egypt.

By making the path toward operation with the formal legal market system overly costly and difficult to navigate, countries discourage new company formation. Moreover, such burdensome bureaucratic inefficiency encourages company formation outside purview of state records and formal commercial systems. As such, firms operate in the gray markets where they have little to no access to formal banking systems, legal dispute resolution through the courts, and other resources that help small businesses grow into large businesses. Without such support, new firms cannot readily challenge incumbents for market share or win customers through innovation. Rather, their resources are used to compensate for the loss of the supportive resources of the formal economy. And, without ready access to large-scale credit and financial services, these firms tend to stay small. Thus, the virtuous connection between new firm formation, innovation, entrepreneurship, competition, and productivity is broken.

Exhibit 14.2 presents the World Bank's Ease of Doing Business Index for 2009. Following directly on de Soto's experiments, the World Bank documents the many challenges to business that follow from weak or inefficient institutions. The World Bank's

Exhibit 14.2   The World Bank's Ease of Doing Business Ranking, 2009

Economy	Rank	Economy	Rank	Economy	Rank
Singapore	1	Kyrgyz Republic	41	Trinidad and	
New Zealand	2	Slovak Republic	42	Tobago	81
Hong Kong	3	Armenia	43	Albania	82
United States	4	Bulgaria	44	Dominica	83
United		Botswana	45	El Salvador	84
Kingdom	5	Taiwan	46	Pakistan	85
Denmark	6	Hungary	47	Dominican	
Ireland	7	Portugal	48	Republic	86
Canada	8	Chile	49	Maldives	87
Australia	9	Antigua and		Serbia	88
Norway	10	Barbuda	50	China	89
Georgia	11	Mexico	51	Zambia	90
Thailand	12	Tonga	52	Grenada	91
Saudi Arabia	13	Slovenia	53	Ghana	92
Iceland	14	Fiji	54	Vietnam	93
Japan	15	Romania	55	Moldova	94
Finland	16	Peru	56	Kenya	95
Mauritius	17	Samoa	57	Brunei	
Sweden	18	Belarus	58	Darussalam	96
South Korea	19	Vanuatu	59	Palau	97
Bahrain	20	Mongolia	60	Marshall Islands	98
Switzerland	21	Kuwait	61	Yemen, Rep.	99
Belgium	22	Spain	62	Jordan	100
Malaysia	23	Kazakhstan	63	Guyana	101
Estonia	24	Luxembourg	64	Papua New	
Germany	25	Oman	65	Guinea	102
Lithuania	26	Namibia	66	Croatia	103
Latvia	27	Rwanda	67	Solomon Islands	104
Austria	28	Bahamas	68	Sri Lanka	105
Israel	29	Tunisia	69	Egypt, Arab	
Netherlands	30	St. Vincent &		Rep.	106
France	31	Grenadines	70	Ethiopia	107
Macedonia,		Montenegro	71	Lebanon	108
FYR	32	Poland	72	Greece	109
United Arab		Turkey	73	Guatemala	110
Emirates	33	Czech Republic	74	Seychelles	111
South Africa	34	Jamaica	75	Uganda	112
Puerto Rico	35	St. Kitts and		Kosovo	113
St. Lucia	36	Nevis	76	Uruguay	114
Colombia	37	Panama	77	Swaziland	115
Azerbaijan	38	Italy	78	Bosnia and	
Qatar	39	Kiribati	79	Herzegovina	116
Cyprus	40	Belize	80	Nicaragua	117

Exhibit 14.2 (*Continued*)

Economy	Rank	Economy	Rank	Economy	Rank
Argentina	118	Gambia	140	Timor-Leste	164
Bangladesh	119	Honduras	141	Togo	165
Russian		Ukraine	142	Mauritania	166
Federation	120	Syrian Arab		Lao PDR	167
Costa Rica	121	Republic	143	Côte d'Ivoire	168
Indonesia	122	Philippines	144	Angola	169
Nepal	123	Cambodia	145	Equatorial	
Paraguay	124	Cape Verde	146	Guinea	170
Nigeria	125	Burkina Faso	147	Cameroon	171
Bhutan	126	Sierra Leone	148	Benin	172
Micronesia, Fed.		Liberia	149	Guinea	173
Sts.	127	Uzbekistan	150	Niger	174
Morocco	128	Haiti	151	Eritrea	175
Brazil	129	Tajikistan	152	Burundi	176
Lesotho	130	Iraq	153	Venezuela, R.B.	177
Tanzania	131	Sudan	154	Chad	178
Malawi	132	Suriname	155	Congo, Rep.	179
India	133	Mali	156	Sao Tome and	
Madagascar	134	Senegal	157	Principe	180
Mozambique	135	Gabon	158	Guinea-Bissau	181
Algeria	136	Zimbabwe	159	Congo, Dem.	
Iran, Islamic Rep.	137	Afghanistan	160	Rep.	182
Ecuador	138	Bolivia	161	Central African	
West Bank and		Comoros	162	Republic	183
Gaza	139	Djibouti	163		

Doing Business web site (www.doingbusiness.org) offers a wealth of information on the challenges of starting a business, dealing with construction permits, employing workers, getting credit, paying taxes, enforcing contracts, and more. It is the best source available for measures of the business-related institutional quality of economies around the world. A comparison of Exhibits 14.1 and 14.2 reveals the notable correlation between corruption and the challenges of doing business across the world. Such are the challenges of emerging markets and the firms that operate in them while they pursue development.

Some Guiding Principles for Emerging Markets

Having developed a framework and explored the process and challenges that face economies that seek to emerge toward higher living standards and incomes, we can now briefly present a few principles for firms and managers that seek to work with and in emerging markets.

Principle 1: If rapid, steady growth was easy, every country would have it.

Some firms and managers, particularly those from high-income nations, attribute successes in their home markets to their own innovativeness, efficiency, and managerial prowess. To some extent this confidence is deserved, as competition is typically fierce in high-income nations, where capital is abundant and markets are largely open to competition. But these managers are typically taking the institutional environment as given and presuming that their strategies will work in any institutional environment. This simply isn't the case. Almost all strategies are state contingent, meaning that they are adapted to survive in an environment where the government, local norms, and cultural characteristics provide the resources in which the firm prospers. It's a bit like a fish taking the water for granted. Moving to an emerging market where the institutional environment is typically less munificent and certainly different can scuttle even the best firms and strategies. As the Dell example earlier in the chapter emphasized, some markets are better suited to the Davids than the Goliaths of the commercial world. And humility is important for the would-be entrant into the latest emerging markets. It is folly to equate low-income nations with a lack of creativity, drive, or talent in the management pool. Emerging markets are filled with firms and managers that are perfectly suited to their harsh environments. Competing with them often means learning their ways more than importing your own.

Principle 2: Look for countries where productivity is profitable, or becoming more so.

In a sense, the recipe for economic growth is easy to understand, but hard to follow. Free and open competitive markets are incredibly powerful tools for incentivizing innovation, risk taking, and productivity. These are the keys to economic growth, but they unlock growth only when market participants can benefit through them. For this to be true, the institutional infrastructure of the economy must be sufficiently sound and fair so as to reward firms that deliver more value for less year over year. To return to the logic of our simple growth accounting framework, countries raise material living standards when efficient firms gain market share from inefficient ones. Where corruption is high, markets are closed, courts are ineffective, and cronyism is rampant, being the best isn't a guarantee of winning. But, beyond winning, countries don't grow when profits and markets go to economic predators rather than economic producers. The art and science of discerning which economies emerge and which won't is largely driven by the sum of the set of incentives facing individuals and firms and how they are changing.

Principle 3: Bring what's rare; use what's common.

Despite all the challenges to success in emerging markets, they represent the future of the global economy. And the greatest economic gains have come in markets that once were poor and have made the long, amazing journey to higher living standards. Along the journey, emerging markets have become formidable competitors with firms from high-income nations and the manufacturers of many of the world's most important goods and services. In large part, they did this through combinations of the resources they have in abundance—low cost and at least semiskilled labor—with those things that are rare—financial capital, advanced technologies, recognized brands, and management systems and practices. From our analysis of growth earlier in the chapter, we can see that capital of all sorts is typically scarce in emerging markets. Bringing capital in the form of financial resources, brands, and efficient managerial systems to nations where these are scarce offers the greatest potential for success. Local institutions may make exporting capital risky, but the upside can be extraordinary when combined with the abundant resources of emerging markets.

Principle 4: The world is "flat" in some places, lumpy in others, and challenging everywhere.

Not so long ago the idea of trading goods and services with China and Russia was largely theoretical, but no more. The world has opened up to trade and commerce at a remarkable pace in the past three decades. Moreover, through technology, imports of services can be delivered via satellites and technologies that genuinely render distance an afterthought. But the ease of outsourcing and offshoring via Internet technologies and trading goods and services via trade agreements has not rendered the world "flat." For some goods and services geography is dead and a fierce worldwide competition has resulted. By decomposing work into tasks that can be reassembled virtually, some sectors of the world economy have unified at a breakneck pace. But in so many others, the world remains very lumpy. Vastly different institutional environments and cultures, still challenging geographies, and ever-present political tensions remain and keep much of the world economy separate and uniquely challenging. One size won't fit all, and neither will one location for a very long time. Plan accordingly.

Principle 5: Firms and their managers can and should be part of the answers that emerging economies require.

Firms can succeed by dispassionately selecting among emerging economies for the optimal trade-off between risk and reward. When the match is right between firm resources and the economy's needs, profits will follow and so will some contributions to economic growth. But firms can and should consider doing much more than serving as passive participants. Through their influence over jobs, resources, and economic health,

Exhibit 14.3   MBA Courses on Development and International Business

Business School	Course
University of Chicago	No required courses on international business. Elective courses on international commercial and financial policy.
University of Virginia (Darden)	No required courses on international business. Core first-year course on global macroeconomics. Electives on economic development and international business and entrepreneurship in emerging economies.
University of Michigan (Ross)	Strategy course: The World Economy—Theories and Concepts Critical to Globalization.
Northwestern University (Kellogg)	International Business Strategy—Second Year (SY) elective. Global Initiatives in Management (GIM) International Study Course.
University of Pennsylvania (Wharton)	Global Strategic Management—Second Year (SY) Elective on Multinational Corporations (MNCs). Elective on international development strategy.
Harvard University	Managing International Trade and Investment—Second Year (SY) elective.
Dartmouth University (Tuck)	Countries and Companies in the International Economy—Second Year (SY) elective. Country Risk, Development and Exchange Rates.

firms and their managers often operate at the front lines of globalization. They are heavily influenced by the institutional environments that can deter capital formation and growth. And they bear the risks of macroeconomic mismanagement. They are witnesses to the possibilities and the challenges of emerging markets. As a result, they can positively influence the drive toward institutional efficiency and, through smart management, contribute to economic stability and the utilization of slack or underutilized resources. Managers can and should promote ethical behavior through their example and mobilize efforts for fair and open competition. When properly run and ethically directed, firms and their managers can play a vital and substantial role in the development of emerging economies.

Courses on Development and International Business

Business schools offer a substantial and growing range of courses that focus on the specific challenges of doing business across borders, on a global scale, and in high-growth emerging markets. Most top schools do not require a course in international business, though all of them offer elective courses on the subject. Most top schools also offer students the opportunity to integrate their studies in international business with travel outside the school's home country. Most international business courses draw heavily from the field of strategic management, though some draw heavily on development economics and finance. Some offer certification for students who adopt a course concentration in globalization or international business.

Notes

1. Based on the case study by Peter L. Rodriguez and Natalie Casey, "Dell Computadores do Brasil, LTDA," UVA-BP-0482, 2005.
2. Hernando de Soto, *The Mystery of Capital: Why Capitalism Triumphs in the West and Fails Everywhere Else* (New York: Basic Books, 2000).

Downloadable Resources for this chapter available at www.wiley.com/go/portablemba5e

See GDP per capita over time at www.gapminder.org.

See World Bank site at www.doingbusiness.org.

See history of economic growth at www.visualizingeconomics.com/category/angus maddison/page/2/.

Enterprise Risk Management

15

Prediction is very difficult, especially about the future.

—Neils Bohr

Every organization faces a number of uncertainties that can both create and destroy value. On a daily basis, the marketplace produces and assimilates information that becomes either good or bad news for companies. Such risk is inescapable and, in fact, represents a key reason for why organizations exist. Starting a company to create, manufacture, and sell a new product is a commitment to face a series of risks, any one of which can lead to pathbreaking success or outright failure. Skilled managers sort out opportunities from threats when presented with these risks and thereby create value for corporate stakeholders. This risk management is important to investors, who must similarly factor all composite risks facing a company when deciding whether the upside potential overshadows the downside when putting capital to work. The stock market rewards lower risk with higher stock prices, as long as the cost of managing that risk does not exceed the value gained.

Risk management has taken on a new level of importance with the recent subprime mortgage crisis. The degree to which incorrect risk assessment played a role in the credit crisis is debatable, but it was unarguably a key factor. At the heart of the mortgage problem was the presumption that mortgage defaults would occur independently. The models assumed that individuals could experience circumstances that would lead to an occasional default on a mortgage. These same models did not, however, allow for the chance that global unemployment would subsequently spike and most asset prices would systematically fall, causing widespread defaults and sharp declines in the values of most mortgage-related securities. Suddenly, individuals, banks, and companies were all in financial difficulty and, moreover, the crisis had spread to points all around the globe.

Ironically, many banks and other financial institutions had been employing prudent risk management policies with respect to their investments in mortgage-backed securities. The credit default swap (CDS) market developed as a way to insure an investor's exposure to investments such as mortgage-backed bonds. The owner of a credit default swap would receive payments if the underlying bond defaulted on its interest or principal payments. Therefore, if an investment bank bought $200 million of mortgage-backed bonds, it could also buy credit default swaps on those bonds to insure against default. This tactic is a sound strategy as long as the issuer of the CDS is itself a sound company. As the financial meltdown progressed in 2008, it became clear that the unregulated CDS market was dominated by relatively few sellers, such as American International Group (AIG), and they were not likely to be able to make payments on the swaps if a widespread default event occurred. AIG was overexposed as a seller of credit default swaps, which forced the company to accept emergency financial support from the U.S. government to remain afloat.

How could these risk management errors occur by the very industry that marketed and sold so many risk management products? The financial industry was the birthplace of a host of hedging instruments such as forwards, futures, and options. Finance practitioners have long used the risk theories put forward by academicians, such as portfolio theory and option pricing, to successfully manage risk exposures. Despite all this experience and knowledge, the events observed during the 2008 financial crisis remind us that risk management strategies are only as good as the assumptions used in the underlying models. Important to understand is that despite the failure of certain risk management tools during the financial crisis, there remain macro principles of risk management that prudent managers should comprehend and practice. If anything, the events of the crisis remind us of the importance of implementing a sound risk management strategy.

We begin this chapter with a discussion of enterprise risk management (ERM), the holistic management of the key risks facing an organization. Enterprise risk management has emerged as a best practice example of how to manage the many different risks facing an organization. Because of its importance in managing financial risks, the second half of this chapter is devoted to explaining the use of financial contracts such as futures and options as a means of eliminating those risks with financial hedges.

What Is Enterprise Risk Management?

Risk impacts all the stakeholders of the enterprise, but not always in the same manner or magnitude. At one extreme is a negative event that brings about the collapse of the company. Only the attorneys stand to benefit from such disasters. Shareholders lose their investments; employees lose their livelihoods; managers lose their jobs and their control of the enterprise; the supply chain loses a customer; and the community loses a valued member and part of its tax base. All stakeholders have a vested interest in avoiding significant downside events, a clear argument for the value of corporate risk management.

The range of risk categories cuts across all aspects of a business and includes issues such as damage from the weather, injury to workers, product liability, competitors' actions, operating cost management, exposure to foreign currencies, exposure to interest rates, and exposure to commodity prices. Enterprise risk management is a process by which the organization views and manages all of its risks collectively. The process is by definition integrated and coordinated across the entire organization. The key concept is that risks should be identified and managed from an overall corporate perspective, because no single action is suitable for every risk, nor can any particular function within the organization be effective managing the diverse set of exposures typically faced. Prior to ERM, risks tended to be managed within functional silos; risk management was too often ad hoc and narrowly focused. Effective risk management should have a top-down perspective with the senior leadership taking an enterprise-wide view that keeps the management of risks aligned with the company's strategic objectives.

Enterprise risk management is a process with three primary steps:

1. Identification of risks.
2. Assessment/ranking of risks.
3. Contingency planning.

To make the process effective requires ownership by all parts of the organization. Most large corporations have found it effective to appoint a Chief Risk Officer (CRO) to facilitate and coordinate the risk management efforts throughout the firm. Other organizations use the internal auditing group or those charged with developing internal controls to take the lead on creating and implementing ERM.

Creating the CRO position is particularly advantageous, as it makes a statement about the importance of risk management within the organization and encourages a risk management culture. This starts with a well-defined ERM process, but also requires that attention be paid to communicating relevant information across the organization and a strong governance process to ensure proper implementation of risk responses. An effective internal control system likewise has as a major element the identification and analysis of relevant risks within the organization, and is a natural place for ERM processes to begin. Internal control risks are focused on those related to the effectiveness and efficiency of operations, the reliability of financial reporting, and compliance with laws and regulations, and thus encompass many if not all of the critical risk factors facing an organization.[1]

Identification of Risks

The ERM process begins with top-level management identifying appropriate risk categories. This might start by sending all managers a list of potential events that would affect the ability of the organization to meet its strategic objectives. For example, most companies would include being economically strong (i.e., creating value) as a primary objective in their mission statements. This can be measured in a number of ways, including profits, cash flow, stock price, and other metrics. Risks to these measures include such events as price pressure from other competitors, changes in cost structure, regulatory changes, a compromise to the brand, political unrest in a third world country, supply chain disruption, or loss of key personnel. Some managers might add employee safety or a shift in information technology to the list. The treasurer's office might add events such as a downgrading of the debt rating, a change in exchange rates, or an increase in interest rates.

This first stage is critical for two reasons. First, compiling a comprehensive list is necessary to provide the opportunity to ultimately have an action plan when it is most needed. Risk cannot be managed unless it has been raised in the consciousness of management. Most organizations have a strong functional focus such that line managers have a very different view of risks relative to what the finance or accounting or marketing managers might think. All perspectives should be fully represented in this discovery stage to give ERM the best chance of producing a positive outcome for the organization. A second reason for all managers being involved in identifying risks is that the communication necessary for compiling the list is central to creating a risk management culture. The interaction between functional areas across all levels of management contributes to having a culture that understands risks and the importance of sharing information about risks.

A risk vocabulary gives management a common ground on which they can work together to achieve the common goal of minimizing the occurrence and the impact of negative events.

Assessment of Risks

Once risk events have been compiled, they must be ranked. To do this, management assigns a rating as to the likelihood of occurrence and the severity of each. Only those events that are of a reasonable probability or carry significant consequences should be kept on the final list. This assessment can be done either quantitatively or qualitatively.

A quantitative approach would be for management to assign a mathematical probability to each event. The likelihood of price competition might be 25 percent over the next two years, whereas the probability of a brand-compromising event might be only 5 percent. The severity of price competition, however, might be assessed as a loss of $1 per share of the company's stock price compared to a $10 per share drop for a brand event. Thus, the overall assessment for price competition risk would be $0.25 per share (0.25 × $1.00 = $0.25) and the assessment for a brand event would be $0.50 per share (0.05 × $10.00 = $0.50).[2]

A similar ranking can be achieved with a qualitative approach of assigning risks to likelihood categories and severity categories. The likelihood categories could be structured from "Highly Unlikely" to "Almost Certain." The severity categories for earnings per share might include the following four impact levels: minimal, newsworthy, major, and catastrophic. Those events falling in the "High Risk" part of the matrix (at the right) as shown in Exhibit 15.1 should receive the most attention.

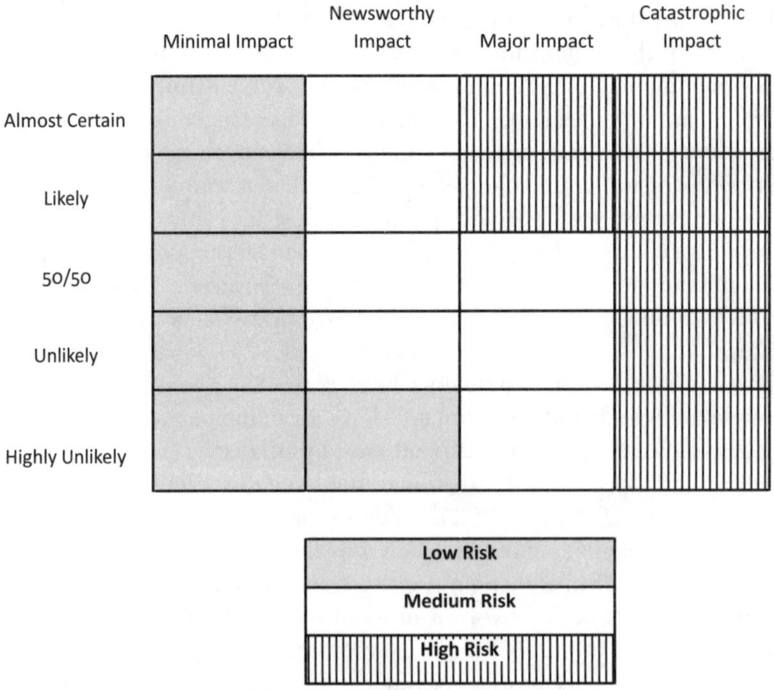

Exhibit 15.1   Risk Assessment Matrix

For a large global corporation, the risk assessment matrix could contain 10 to 20 categorized risk events. Examples could range from human resource events related to changes in demographics and work/life priorities to the death of the CEO. Operating events would include such events as the loss of electrical power and a resulting compromise to computer capabilities, as well as natural disasters such as fires or floods. All firms should also consider the impact of government regulation or intervention both domestically and in non-U.S. locations. Regulated industries face a constant risk of unfavorable regulatory changes, but even a company in a nonregulated industry should include the risk of becoming subject to government regulation or control.

A recent driver of ERM has been the expense and difficulties related to being in compliance with the mandates of the Sarbanes-Oxley Act (SOX) of 2002. SOX was passed by Congress in reaction to a number of accounting scandals that had shaken the confidence of investors in U.S. public companies. Many large corporations such as Enron, Tyco, Adelphia, and WorldCom cost investors billions of dollars of capital when accounting irregularities were exposed and stock prices plummeted. SOX significantly changed governance standards and put in place harsh penalties for board members of companies found guilty of any such misreporting. Senior executives of public companies were required to assume individual responsibility for the accuracy and completeness of corporate financial reports. Penalties for white-collar crime were toughened. And financial disclosure requirements were increased, particularly with respect to off-balance-sheet transactions where some companies had been able to disguise or hide debt.

The enhanced controls and compliance features required by SOX were much costlier and more difficult to accomplish than originally estimated by Congress. The increased effort devoted to compliance efforts, however, also prompted firms to broaden their perspectives beyond mere noncompliance risk and take a comprehensive enterprise-wide risk management approach that increased transparency and added value to the enterprise. Much data had been collected that became a valuable source of understanding and quantifying risks to the company. Thus, the beginning of ERM was an interesting but unintended by-product of SOX.

Not all risks are the same. Most financial risks are relatively easy to identify and measure. The pricing of financial instruments used to hedge risks (i.e., foreign exchange, interest rates, and commodities) is readily available from public markets. The cost of standard insurance contracts is available with a single phone call. However, more strategic risks such as brand reputation, supply chain continuity, technology innovations, consumer tastes, sovereign risk and actions of competitors are not easily quantifiable and do not have straightforward inputs and solutions. For example, Microsoft uses a simulation model to assess the "expected economic value" of particular scenarios. This Monte Carlo technique allowed Microsoft to estimate the impact of a global flu pandemic that would sicken a high percentage of its software developers and delay a project for a client. The costs created by the pandemic would include extra payroll expenses for temporary workers and penalty payments for missing the contracted deadline. Thus, it may be useful to use a blend of quantitative and qualitative assessment approaches, depending on the type of risk.

Regardless of how it is accomplished, it is imperative to produce a comprehensive ranking of the most pertinent set of risks for the organization. At the end of this phase, management should be able to reference a clear profile of risks and their relative importance as a guide for determining the amount of resources for managing each risk.

Contingency Planning

The third step in an ERM process is to explicitly design responses to the various risk scenarios. Low-risk events might require midlevel management attention and response. For example, if business units are profit centers, the managers can be empowered to make pricing decisions to respond quickly to changing market conditions. A brand event, however, might push the company into bankruptcy if not handled promptly and effectively. With such high stakes, the senior management team should be the key decision makers. An example of a brand event is a major lawsuit about the safety of the company's primary product. In anticipation of such an occurrence, ERM should specify an immediate set of actions, such as a definitive statement from the CEO about the safety record of the product and the proactive measures taken in development of the product to ensure its safety; temporary withdrawal of the product from all retail outlets pending further tests by the company's scientific staff; and quick communication with all employees, major stockholders, and other stakeholders as to the company's strategy to handle the emergency.

A risk matrix can also serve as input to a variety of strategic decisions for the company. For example, capital investment proposals should include a discussion related to how the investment affects the company's risks. Maintenance expenditures might do little to increase profits, but at the same time could prove effective in managing employee safety. If capital is constrained, management may want to give preference to projects that address risk objectives most effectively even if those projects have less attractive economics.[3]

Hedging

The financial risk components under ERM are very often managed with the use of financial contracts such as futures, options, and insurance policies.[4] For example, if an organization identified interest rates, foreign exchange rates, or commodity prices (fuel, precious metals, agriculture products, etc.), a straightforward remedy for the risk would be to hedge using futures and/or options. If risks included loss of property value or loss of life, the financial consequences of those risks can be protected with property/casualty insurance. Such hedging strategies are purely financial. That is, they do not address the underlying causes of the risks, but rather provide for an offsetting cash flow to compensate for the monetary losses suffered.

The science of financial hedging has become increasingly sophisticated and more quantitative over the years. Understanding how to use financial instruments for hedging therefore requires some study of statistics as well as a close look at the instruments themselves. Even though the objective of hedging might appear straightforward, it was inadequate risk management during the subprime mortgage crisis that ultimately spelled ruin for financial institutions such as Bear Stearns and Lehman Brothers. In these cases the principles of hedging were not flawed, but rather it was the implementation and the underlying assumptions of the risk models that were flawed. Despite these extreme examples, the financial industry and the use of derivatives and financial hedging will continue to be a mainstay of financial strategies in the future. Like the broader topic of enterprise risk management, hedging also has a certain vocabulary that facilitates thinking about risk and whether it should be hedged, and if so, how it should be hedged. With this in mind, the remainder of the chapter is organized as follows:

- Risk and statistical analysis.
- Futures and options contracts.
- The hedging decision.

Risk and Statistical Analysis

We start the study of financial hedging with a quick review of how a statistician would describe risk. When asked, most people would define risk as the possibility that something bad will happen in the future. For the study of risk, however, we need to find a more useful and usable definition. Because statistics are a means of quantifying uncertainty as a measure of risk, business managers must think about risk within this framework. Statistics incorporate the study of probabilities within which we can define risk as the uncertainty, both upside and downside, around an expected value. For example, if a business analyst was making a forecast of company sales for next year, the analyst's best guess would be the expected value around some distribution, as illustrated in Exhibit 15.2.

The expected value is the midpoint of the potential outcomes; that is, it represents the value for which it is equally likely that the realized value will be either higher or lower than the forecast. If the firm performs better than expected, the realized value will fall to the right of the expected value in the "good news" part of the distribution. If the firm performs worse than expected, the realized value will fall to the left of the expected value in the "bad news" half of the distribution.

A normal distribution is a representation of how uncertainty is resolved. There is a distribution of outcomes that tend to cluster around the expected value (the mean) with fairly high likelihood, and there are larger variations farther away from the mean that occur much less often, but with equal chance above and below the mean. In other words,

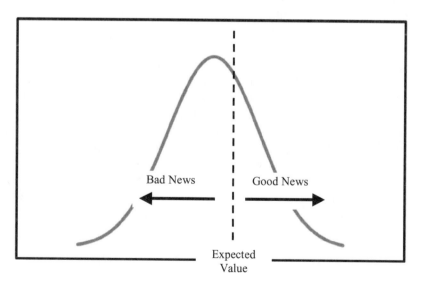

Exhibit 15.2   The Normal Distribution

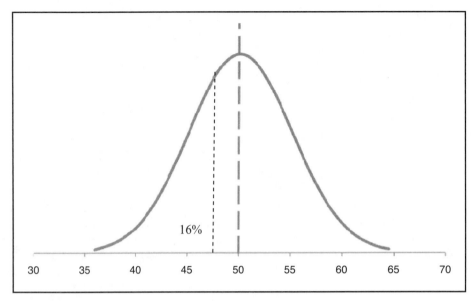

Exhibit 15.3 High-Risk Event

the normal distribution is symmetrical. We get good news just as often as we get bad news and with just as much surprise; that is, the degree of good news (distance above the mean) is the same on average as the degree of bad news, and it occurs with the same frequency.

While we know that the normal distribution is not exactly correct for many types of variables, we do know that it is a good approximation for most events. When considering risk, a statistician also thinks about the degree of uncertainty of an event in terms of how tight the distribution is. If an analyst is not very confident in the forecasted estimate, then the statistician will say that it is a high-risk event; higher deviations from the mean are expected relative to a low-risk event. Exhibits 15.3 and 15.4 illustrate the difference between high-risk and low-risk events.

The high-risk event in Exhibit 15.3 has the same mean of 50 as the low-risk event in Exhibit 15.4. Therefore, on average, the two events will give the same outcome, but there is a much higher likelihood that a realized outcome for the high-risk event will be farther away from the mean than a realization for the low-risk event. We can measure the degree of dispersion by computing the standard deviation. For example, you might want to know the risk associated with your company's sales per week to Germany, so you collect sales data about weekly unit sales over the past 52 weeks to get the average units sold (μ) and the standard deviation (σ) of unit sales using the following equations:

$$\text{Average} = \mu = (\text{units}_1 + \text{units}_2 + \text{units}_3 + \cdots + \text{units}_{52})/52$$
$$\text{Variance} = \sigma^2 = [(\text{units}_1 - \mu)^2 + (\text{units}_2 - \mu)^2 + (\text{units}_3 - \mu)^2$$
$$+ \cdots + (\text{units}_{52} - \mu)^2]/51$$
$$\text{Standard deviation} = \sigma = \sqrt{\sigma^2}$$

Exhibit 15.3 shows that the high-risk event has a standard deviation of 5.0 whereas Exhibit 15.4 shows the low-risk event has a standard deviation of 2.5. Knowing the

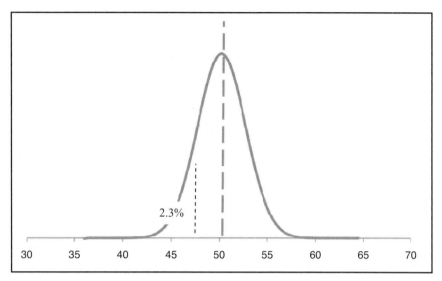

Exhibit 15.4   Low-Risk Event

standard deviation allows us to express the probability of a certain event occurring if it has a normal distribution. Exhibit 15.3 shows that the chance of getting 45 or lower is about 16 percent, whereas the chance of getting 45 or below in Exhibit 15.4 is only 2.3 percent. Of course, it is also true that the high-risk event has a higher likelihood for every good outcome. Therefore, risk should be viewed as a double-edged sword: high risk/high standard deviation describes the chance of getting both positive and negative news.

The use of statistics plays an important role in decision making under uncertainty. If managers knew with certainty what would happen in the future, it would be an easy task to take the appropriate action today that will give the best possible result in the future. Statistical distributions, however, recognize that the best one can do is characterize the future as a picture of possibilities. A picture of the distribution does not tell us what will happen, but it does help us think about the range of possibilities and the probability of observing an outcome above or below a certain level. Managers can then decide how much effort and cost they want to expend to avoid the possibility of the undesirable events. The hedging decision keys upon these likelihoods in conjunction with the overall impact on the firm of the event.

Value at Risk

An excellent example of risk measurement and risk management is the technique called *value at risk* (VaR). VaR relies on statistics to quantify risk and is commonly used within the financial industry. The technique relies on estimating the shape of the distribution of outcomes for an event. For example, a portfolio manager might want to know the likelihood of the portfolio losing more than 20 percent over the next year. Within the world of statistics it is often more convenient to answer the question by assessing the maximum the manager should expect to lose with 95 percent confidence over the next year. This is equivalent to asking what percentage loss (or greater) translates to a 5 percent chance of occurrence over the next year.

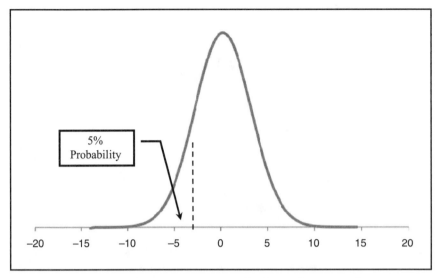

Exhibit 15.5   Portfolio Return Example for Value at Risk

The answer lies in how one estimates the normal distribution for the event. Exhibits 15.3 and 15.4 show a high-risk and low-risk event. If the portfolio manager has high-risk investments, the VaR answer might be: "With 95 percent confidence, we expect that our worst annual loss will not exceed 30 percent." If the manager holds low-risk investments, the VaR answer might be: "With 95 percent confidence, we expect that our worst annual loss will not exceed 5 percent." Both responses rely on the analyst's assessment of the distribution of possible returns. Modest returns are more likely than either high gains or high losses; that is, the tails of the distribution represent the low-probability events. For the portfolio examples, the 95 percent confidence level translates into a percent loss at the 1.65 standard deviations below the mean.

Exhibit 15.5 shows the low-risk portfolio analysis. A loss of 5 percent or more is expected to occur only 5 percent of the time over the next year. This assessment would likely have been made using historical return data for portfolios with similar investments. Since the likelihood of the loss is 5 percent, the risk manager can state that she is 95 percent confident of not losing more than 5 percent next year.

Most financial institutions compute VaR on a daily basis—for example, "We are 95 percent confident that losses will not exceed 10 percent on any given day of trading." In retrospect with regard to the recent financial crisis, the VaR assessments were woefully conservative, as banks and hedge funds experienced losses far in excess of historical experiences. In other words, the actual distribution was much wider than anticipated or, equivalently, the distribution was not normal and instead had very fat tails; that is, extreme events were much more likely than suggested by the normal distribution of returns.

Futures and Options Contracts

Futures and options contracts are the building blocks of financial hedging. Over the past few decades, a wide range of these contracts have evolved and are actively traded on public exchanges around the world. There is a long list of these contracts that span a host of different economic variables.[5] To give an idea of the abundance of the supply of futures and options, Exhibit 15.6 lists many of these types of contracts, which include futures for

Exhibit 15.6   Futures and Options Contracts Examples, July 2009

Exchange	Futures Contract	Options
Eurex		
Germany/Switzerland	Emissions Trading	
	EU Emission Allowances (EUR)	Yes
	Certified Emission Reductions (CERs)	Yes
	Energy	
	Power	Yes
	Natural Gas	Yes
	Exchange-Traded Funds	
	DAX EX	Yes
	Dow Jones EURO STOXX 50 EX	Yes
	iShares Dow Jones EURO STOXX 50 EX	Yes
	XMTCH on SMI	Yes
	Metals	
	Gold	Yes
	Silver	Yes
Chicago Board		
Options Exchange	Commodities	
United States	Soybeans	Yes
	Corn	Yes
	Oats	Yes
	Wheat	Yes
	Rice	Yes
	Coffee	Yes
	Cocoa	Yes
	Sugar	Yes
	Cotton	Yes
	Orange Juice	Yes
	Lumber	Yes
	Financials	
	U.S. Treasury	Yes
	Euro Dollar	Yes
	Metals	
	Gold	Yes
	Silver	Yes
	Meats	
	Live Cattle	Yes
	Feeder Cattle	Yes
	Pork Bellies	Yes
	Lean Hogs	Yes

(continued)

Exhibit 15.6 (*Continued*)

Exchange	Futures Contract	Options
New York Mercantile		
Exchange	Energy	
United States	Crude Oil	Yes
	Heating Oil	Yes
	Natural Gas	Yes
	Uranium	
	Diesel	
	Propane	Yes
	Electricity	Yes
	Gasoline	Yes
	Metal	
	Aluminum	Yes
	Copper	Yes
	Gold	Yes
	Palladium	Yes
	Silver	Yes
	HRC Steel	
	Platinum	Yes
	Weather	
	Temperatures	Yes
	Hurricane	Yes
	Frost	Yes
	Snowfall	Yes

such items as metals, oil products, food products, interest and foreign exchange rates, U.S. Treasury bonds, and the S&P 500 index. As a commodity or financial index becomes more important to businesses and bankers, a futures contract will eventually be created to meet the demand for managing its risk. This is particularly true for high-risk variables (high σ) because they have a greater chance of producing a negative impact on a business.

A futures contract is an agreement by two parties to transact at some point in the future at an agreed-upon price.[6] Commodity futures markets had their beginnings long before there were formalized exchanges. For example, consider the grain markets. Futures markets developed for this product due to the self-interest of the participants in the production of grain. Now consider a farmer who had purchased corn seed in the spring. As he enters into the new harvest year, he faces a large amount of uncertainty as to (1) how well the seed will grow to produce corn and (2) the price of corn that the miller will pay him at the time of harvest. The miller is also worrying about how much demand he will have for the flour he will make as well as the price he will have to pay for the corn to make the flour. Both the farmer and the miller can reduce some of their uncertainty by entering into a corn *forward contract*. The forward contract would specify the amount of corn to be delivered by the farmer on a certain date and the price to be paid by the miller on that date. Thus, a high-risk variable such as the future price of corn could be changed to a certainty event (i.e., $\sigma = 0$) with the use of a forward contract.

Over time, forward contracts became standardized and were traded on exchanges, at which time they were renamed as *futures contracts*. Note that any futures commodity can be purchased immediately in the *spot market* (i.e., at the going price today). The futures price, however, can be higher or lower than the spot price for a number of reasons. The easiest way to interpret a futures price is that it reflects the market's best guess of what the spot price will be at that date in the future. If corn is selling at $3.50 per bushel today, the futures price for 12 months later might be $4.00 per bushel due to the expected effect of inflation and the impact of increased demand. Or the futures price might be $3.00 per bushel if forecasters are expecting a bumper crop in corn next year. In any case, regardless of the expected value of the distribution of future prices (μ), there is always uncertainty (σ) surrounding the actual price that will be observed.

On any given day we can see quotes for the current cost of corn as well as the futures contracts for many months in the future. All sorts of traders are involved in buying and selling futures, including speculators who try to find inconsistencies between the spot price and a futures price. This constant activity ensures that these markets contain the collective wisdom of all market participants and therefore the best possible forecast of the future spot price and the best possible price to use for hedging purposes.

Here is an example of how a futures contract works for both the buyer and the seller and how it could be used by a miller to hedge his exposure to the price of corn. Exhibit 15.7 shows that futures contracts are available to buy or sell No. 2 yellow corn for delivery over three years in the future. If a miller wants to buy corn immediately on July

Exhibit 15.7   Corn Futures Prices, Chicago Board of Trade, July 13, 2009

Spot Price = $3.48	
Expiration Month	Price per Bushel
Sep '09	$3.28
Dec '09	$3.37
Mar '10	$3.50
May '10	$3.56
Jul '10	$3.66
Sep '10	$3.72
Dec '10	$3.82
Mar '11	$3.95
May '11	$3.95
Jul '11	$4.07
Sep '11	$4.05
Dec '11	$3.95
Jul '12	$4.21
Dec '12	$4.05

Corn futures are traded on the Chicago Board of Trade. Each contract provides for the delivery of 5,000 bushels of No. 2 yellow corn on the last business day prior to the 15th calendar day of the contract month. The contract months are March, May, July, September, and December.
Source: Wall Street Journal, July 14, 2009.

13, 2009, it would cost $3.48 per bushel. However, if he wants to buy corn for delivery in September 2009, he has a couple of choices. He can either take his chances by waiting to buy the corn when September rolls around or he can enter into the September futures contract today, which commits him to buy the corn at $3.28 per bushel. Since the miller is agreeing to buy the corn, he takes a long position. The person who agrees to sell the corn on the other side of the contract is taking a short position.

Note that in this example the futures price is lower than the spot price by 20 cents. This is likely true because the market expects an increase in supply that will push the price of corn down over the next two months. Of course, no one knows how far the price will drop or if it will drop at all, which is why the miller might want to lock in the price he will pay in September by using the futures contract.

To illustrate how the futures contract works as a hedge, consider the following example. Assume that in two months there are three possible corn prices with equal likelihood: $2.98, $3.28, and $3.58. In truth, there is a wide range of possible corn prices, both higher and lower than the expected price of $3.28. The miller takes a long position in the September 2009 contract, which matures in two months. The beauty of using a futures contract is that when the contract matures, the miller does not need to actually enforce the contract to buy the corn he wants. Instead, he can simply settle the contract by either making or accepting a cash payment and then he can simultaneously buy the corn at the going price on the market.[7] As the example in Exhibit 15.8 shows, the miller will end up paying exactly $3.28 after netting the gains or losses of the futures against the actual price he ends up paying. Conversely, the person with a short position will be guaranteed to receive exactly $3.28 for the corn he sells, regardless of what the actual price of corn turns out to be in September. Since both the buyer and seller of a futures contract have equal probabilities of winning or losing, there is no cost of entering the contract.

An *option contract* is a bit more complicated than a futures contract and is best explained with another example. Recall that the September 2009 corn futures contract is trading at $3.28, and consider the $3.35 call option on the September corn futures. The $3.35 is called the *strike price* and is a key attribute of an option. Buying a $3.35 September call option gives the owner the right to enter into a $3.35 September futures contract on or before the expiration date. This is very different from the futures contract for which the two parties are *obligated* to either buy or sell at the futures price upon expiration. The owner of the option has the choice, but not the obligation, to enter into the futures contract during the last few days of the futures contract's life. You will choose to enter into a futures contract only if its price has moved in a way that gives you an instant profit. For a call option, this will be true if the futures price is above the strike price at expiration. However, if the futures price turns out to be equal to or lower than the strike price, the owner of the call will do nothing and simply let the option expire worthless.

Now consider the value of the $3.35 call option for different scenarios. If the price of the September futures should happen to stay constant at $3.28 until the option expires, the owner of the call will be facing of choice of exercising the option to receive a September futures with a price of $3.35 or letting the option expire. In this case, there is no incentive for using the call option to get a $3.35 futures because the owner can get a $3.28 futures on the open market. Why enter a contract to buy corn for $3.35 when you can get into a contract for $3.28 on the open market? If, however, the futures price happens to increase during the life of the option such that it is $3.50 at maturity, the option owner would

Exhibit 15.8 Corn Futures Hedging Example

- Assume a miller buys a September corn futures with a futures price of $3.28 per bushel.
- The miller enters the September contract in July, two months before it matures.
- The miller is long the futures contract, which means he has agreed to buy the corn on the maturity date, or, equivalently, he has agreed to pay the difference between the market price and $3.28 to the seller (and the seller has made the same commitment) to ensure the seller will receive $3.28 regardless of the prevailing market price.
- Upon maturity there are three possible corn prices: $2.98, $3.28, and $3.58.

Probability	$1/3$	$1/3$	$1/3$
Price of corn Sept.	$2.98	$3.28	$3.58
Futures payoff	($0.30)	$0.00	$0.30
Net price to miller	$3.28	$3.28	$3.28

Probability weighed cost to miller $= 1/3 \times \$3.28 + 1/3 \times \$3.28 + 1/3 \times \$3.28 = \$3.28$

- When the price turns out to be $2.98, the miller is happy to see the price of corn so low, but he must pay $0.30 to the short side of the futures contract, leaving him with an all-in cost of $3.28.
- When the price turns out to be $3.58, the miller is disappointed to see the price of corn having risen so high, but he receives $0.30 from the short side of the futures contract, leaving him with an all-in cost of $3.28.
- When the price turns out to be $3.28, the market expectation was exactly correct and neither side of the contract owes anything, so the miller's all-in cost is $3.28.

exercise the option because he would receive a $3.35 September futures, which would allow him to buy corn 15 cents per bushel cheaper than the going rate.

A *call* option gives the owner the perfect payoff: all upside and no downside! The only catch is that everybody in the market sees the lopsided payoff and they bid on an option according to how much value they expect it to give them. Therefore, unlike a futures contract, which has no up-front cost for the buyer or seller, options always carry a price, which is called a *premium*. Exhibit 15.9 lists call and put premiums for the September 2009 futures contract. The $3.20 call sells for the highest premium because it has the lowest strike price of all the options listed, which also makes it the most likely to be exercised. A *put* option gives the owner the right to enter the short side of the futures contract. Therefore, the put premiums are reversed from the call premiums: The $3.20 put sells for the lowest price because it is the least likely to be exercised for a put option. Exhibit 15.9 only lists options for the September 2009 futures. Options for longer-maturity futures will tend to have higher premiums for both calls and puts because the longer maturity gives the owners more time for the corn prices to hit the strike prices.

How could the miller use an option to hedge his exposure to the price of corn in September? There are as many ways to hedge as there are call options listed on the exchange. The calls differ only by their strike price and the price necessary to buy them. Lower strike prices command higher premiums, but lower strike prices also give the

Exhibit 15.9 Options for the September 2009 Corn Futures

	September Futures = $3.28	
Strike Price	**Call Option Premium**	**Put Option Premium**
$3.20	$0.110	$0.043
$3.25	$0.100	$0.085
$3.30	$0.095	$0.090
$3.35	$0.076	$0.144
$3.40	$0.053	$0.176
$3.45	$0.030	$0.214

- A call option gives the buyer the right to enter the long side of a September futures contract at a given strike price. A lower strike price makes a call option more valuable. For example, the $3.20 call is $0.08 in-the-money, whereas the $3.45 call is $0.17 out-of-the-money.
- A put option gives the buyer the right to enter the short side of a September futures contract at a given strike price. A higher strike price makes a call option more valuable. For example, the $3.20 put is $0.08 out-of-the-money whereas the $3.45 call is $0.17 in-the-money.

highest chance of paying at maturity for the owner. Therefore, it is the trade-off for the miller is that he can get better protection by buying a call option that has a lower strike price, but he will have to pay a higher premium to buy the call. Exhibit 15.10 shows an example of how the miller could use the $3.35 call option as a hedge. The net cost to the miller differs from using the futures as a hedge, because the call premium raises his all-in cost across the board. However, if the price of corn is low enough, the miller's all-in cost is lower than it would be for a futures hedge.

Exhibit 15.11 represents the price distribution for the September 2009 corn futures. The futures contract is priced at $3.28 per bushel, which is the mean of the distribution with an equal number of prices below and above the mean that could occur.

Exhibit 15.12 shows the impact on the price distribution when using a futures contract. The hedge results in only *one* possible outcome: $3.28 per bushel.

Exhibit 15.13 shows the impact of a call option hedge upon the price distribution that the hedger would see. The first effect is that all the prices above the strike price of $3.35 have been removed. The second effect, however, is that all the *net prices* are higher due to the premium paid for the call option, which is $0.076 per bushel. Thus, the option premium is the price paid to eliminate the prices above the strike price.

Role of the Exchange

Exchanges like the Chicago Board of Trade (CBOT) serve an important role for futures by creating an environment that facilitates a high volume of trading. For example, when traders want to buy corn futures, they know the contracts are traded on the CBOT and that they are standardized with respect to maturity dates and size (5,000 bushels). The standardization removes the time-consuming process of negotiating these terms. In addition, the trader does not need to spend the time and effort of finding a counterparty.

Exhibit 15.10   Call Option Hedging Example

- Assume a miller buys the $3.35 September call option for $0.076 per bushel.
- At expiration of the call the miller buys corn at the current market price and exercises the option if the futures price exceeds the call's strike price.
- Upon maturity there are three possible corn futures prices: $2.98, $3.28, and $3.58.

Probability	$1/3$	$1/3$	$1/3$
Price of Sept. corn futures	$2.98	$3.28	$3.58
Call option payoff	$0.00	$0.00	$0.23
Call option premium	($0.076)	($0.076)	($0.076)
Net price to miller	$3.056	$3.356	$3.426

Probability weighed cost to miller $= 1/3 \times \$3.056 + 1/3 \times \$3.356 + 1/3 \times \$3.426 = \$3.28$

- When the price turns out to be $2.98, the call is out-of-the-money and the miller allows it to expire without exercising it. He buys corn at the market price, but because of the $0.076 premium paid for the call, his all-in cost is $3.056.
- When the price turns out to be $3.58, the miller is disappointed to see the price of corn having risen so high, but he receives $0.23 from exercising the in-the-money call ($4.50 − $3.35), which when netted against the $0.076 premium paid for the call gives an all-in cost of $3.426.
- When the price turns out to be $3.28, the call is out-of-the-money and the miller allows it to expire without exercising it. He buys corn at the market price, but because of the $0.076 premium paid for the call, his all-in cost is $3.356.

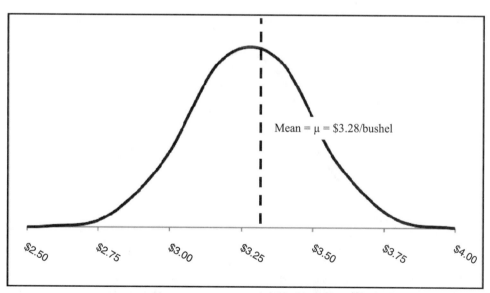

Mean = μ = $3.28/bushel

$2.50 $2.75 $3.00 $3.25 $3.50 $3.75 $4.00

Exhibit 15.11   September 2009 Corn Futures Price Distribution

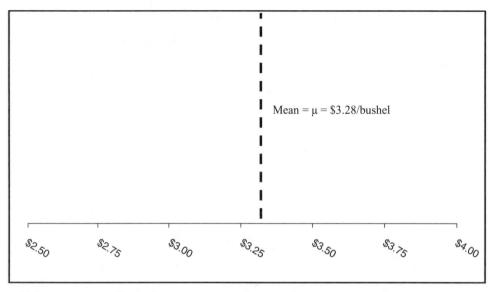

Exhibit 15.12   Effect of a Futures Hedge on the Price Distribution

The exchange stands between the longs and shorts and acts as the counterparty to all trades. This means that the exchange takes on the collective credit risk of the market participants such that as long as the exchange operates smoothly and remains solvent, the futures markets will flourish.

The exchange manages the credit risk by requiring a *margin account* from each trader. A margin account on a futures exchange simply means that the buyer and the seller of a futures contract must deposit a certain amount of cash up front to be used as collateral. In addition to requiring a margin, the exchange settles the contracts with a mark-to-market transaction every trading day. At the end of each trading day the accounts for

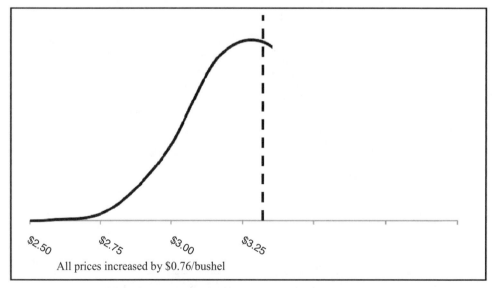

Exhibit 15.13   Effect of an Options Hedge on the Price Distribution (Strike Price = $3.35)

every futures contract are settled by moving money either from the seller's account to the buyer's account or from the buyer's account to the seller's account. If the futures price went up during the day, the buyer receives funds corresponding to the amount of the price increase. If the futures price fell during the day, the seller receives funds corresponding to the amount of the price decrease. Therefore, the exchange is limited to facing no more than a single day of credit risk, and each buyer or seller cannot lose more than one day's worth of price change.

Buying a derivative on an exchange is very different from buying a contract from a bank or insurance company. If either side goes bankrupt, the other side stands to be left with nothing, which completely negates the hedge. In effect, this is what happened during the credit crisis of 2008–2009. Banks were buying credit default swaps as a hedge against their investments in bonds and in particular subprime mortgage-backed securities. There was no exchange for CDS contracts and, as it happens, AIG was a large seller of these contracts. This meant that the banks were highly exposed to AIG's creditworthiness and that AIG was highly exposed to the performance of the CDS contracts. When the subprime mortgages hit the wall, so did AIG, forcing the U.S. government to come to the rescue by injecting $85 billion to keep AIG afloat. Note that the purchase of financial contracts as a hedge was a reasonable strategy by the banks, but it was not reasonable for the banks or for AIG to expose themselves to such high counterparty risk with contracts that were not traded on an exchange or otherwise regulated. Going forward, such derivatives will likely be regulated under President Obama's financial reform.

The Hedging Decision

The hedging decision is complex, as it requires a set of both fundamental and detailed questions to be answered:

- Why hedge?
- Is the exposure significant?
- Can the risk be hedged?
- How should the hedge be structured?

Why Hedge?

The first question management should ask is whether any risk should be hedged. Froot, Scharfstein, and Stein[8] provide an intuitive framework for thinking about risk management and the decision whether to hedge. They take the shareholders' perspective and argue that reducing risk does not by itself increase shareholders' value. The first rule of investment is to hold a well-diversified portfolio of stocks. This eliminates a wide range of risks for the investor because price changes within the portfolio can be offsetting. For example, if an investor owns shares of an oil company plus shares of a railroad, the oil company's stock price will rise with the price of oil, whereas the railroad's stock price will fall in anticipation of a rise in the price of diesel fuel, a primary cost element for a railroad. Thus, the diversified portfolio provides an excellent hedge for the investor.

Looking at risk from the lens of how it affects the overall portfolio value of an investor tells us, however, that shareholders may not want management to hedge. In fact, if the oil company began to hedge against oil price shocks, its shareholders would lose their portfolio hedge and would suddenly be exposed to oil prices. Thus, it would appear that the best solution for the shareholders in this example for this particular risk is for the railroad and the oil company to do nothing about their exposures to oil prices.

Froot et al. point out that a well-diversified portfolio does not mean that management should never hedge. If we change our focus to thinking about how a company creates value, it could make sense to hedge. Few people would argue that a railroad's primary means of creating value is by expending resources to hedge diesel fuel prices. Rather, the real source of value creation is by delivering freight in the most cost-effective manner for as many customers as possible. When the economy is in high gear, management can increase the value of the railroad by buying more locomotives and cars to move more freight. Railroads are highly capital intensive; that is, they require significant investment dollars to add new assets and to maintain current assets. The amount of funds available for investment in such assets, therefore, becomes a key variable for a successful business model. The real risk to the company occurs when profits are unexpectedly reduced and the railroad is short of the necessary cash flow to fund its investment needs. If profits are down, the company has to either reduce its capital spending or make up the shortfall by borrowing money or selling shares.

Raising funds from the debt or equity market is a costly process. Not only does it add new financing costs, but it is also a cumbersome process that involves investment banking fees and considerable time and effort on the part of management. This is particularly true for issuing new equity, which for most firms is a rare event. By far the most prevalent way of raising new equity is by retaining profits: The profits not paid as dividends represent equity dollars reinvested in the company. With all these frictions working against raising funds externally, the most likely solution to a shortfall in profits is for a company to defer capital investments. On the flip side, when cash flows are unexpectedly higher, capital spending is maintained and the profits and cash flow that result are eventually returned to shareholders via a dividend or share repurchase.

The link between cash flow uncertainty and capital spending creates an economic rationale for shareholders to favor risk management practices and hedging. Note, however, that different firms will see risks differently. The management of the railroad will see the price of oil as a significant risk due to its correlation with the price of diesel fuel, a significant cost component for a railroad. Shareholders should reward management for hedging fuel price risk, because oil and fuel prices are likely to rise when the economy is hot and railroads need investment dollars to expand their capacity. The management of an oil company, however, sees a very different problem. First, the price of oil is a risk to the top line of an oil company because it affects revenues, not costs as for the railroad. Therefore, the oil company sees the risk as occurring when oil prices drop (i.e., when the economy experiences a slowdown). When oil prices are low, however, the value of oil exploration is reduced and oil companies need fewer dollars for investment. Thus, changes in oil prices do not compromise an oil company's business model. Therefore, there is no need to hedge against oil price movements, because the company's cash flow needs are correlated with the price of oil: High oil prices create high cash flows for investment, and low oil prices create low cash flows for investment.

Is the Exposure Significant?

This step is the same as explained for the enterprise risk management process and involves the combination of probabilities and costs. For example, if a risk is identified but the range of possible outcomes is limited, then it is a low-risk event such as shown in Exhibit 15.4. Unless the cost to the company is very high for this event, it is not likely to merit the efforts required to hedge. This might be the risk of a change in power costs for a plant, which rarely change by more than inflation. Unless the production process is highly dependent upon electricity, the total cost impact will not be material for the company. If, however, the risk has a profile as shown in Exhibit 15.3 (high σ event), even moderate costs could result in significant cash flow swings for the company. The risks with the highest economic consequences should receive the closest attention for hedging.

As explained in the early part of this chapter, the level of exposure should be evaluated at the level of the corporation. Enterprise risk management is an effective process for identifying risks as well as for discovering if risks are offsetting within the organization. For example, one business unit may supply another and use market-based pricing. Both the buying business unit and the selling business unit see the price of the good as a risk, but one unit sees it as a revenue risk whereas the other unit sees it as a cost risk. From a corporate perspective, however, the two risks cancel out and the two units should not devote resources to hedge it. At the same time, pay bonuses for the unit managers should not be influenced by how much the price variation affects their profits.

Can the Risk Be Hedged?

Not all risks can be hedged. Consider the risk faced by a soft drink bottler. One of the bottler's major cost risks is the cost of aluminum cans. Aluminum is an actively traded commodity on the futures market. The bottler, however, is not exposed directly to aluminum, but rather to the *price of aluminum cans*. Over the long term the price of aluminum cans moves with the price of aluminum, but over the short term the prices can move in different directions. The problem for the bottler is that it faces the risk of the price of aluminum plus the risk of the profit margin of the aluminum can manufacturers.

The aluminum can manufacturers compete to sell their products, which means that when inventories are high, the price of cans falls along with the can manufacturers' profit margins. If the manufacturers happen to have a high inventory of cans when demand for raw aluminum is rising, the aluminum futures will rise to reflect the increased demand, but the price charged for an aluminum can could drop due to the excess supply. This makes the aluminum futures a poor hedging instrument for the bottler, but a good hedging instrument for the can manufacturers. In fact, attempting to hedge the aluminum can price with the aluminum futures could increase the volatility of the bottler's profits.

How Should the Hedge Be Structured?

As a manager, the best possible hedging choice is the one that eliminates the downside risk while keeping the upside *and* is costless. Based on the hedging examples given earlier, however, we see that we cannot get this utopian solution. The hedge always costs us something. Using a futures contract for the hedge means forfeiting the upside potential to eliminate the downside risk. Using an option for the hedge eliminates the downside while keeping the upside potential, but it also requires an up-front payment to buy the option.

So, which hedging strategy is best? If the futures and options are frequently traded on an exchange, they will be efficiently priced. An efficiently priced security is one that carries a price that is fair to the buyer and to the seller. This means that the expected costs of different hedging alternatives should be approximately the same. The futures hedge is costless, but in an efficient market the value of buying the call option for the option hedge will be offset by the expected upside gains. Therefore, neither strategy dominates on an economic basis. A hedge has a zero net present value (NPV): Value is neither destroyed nor created based on the price of the instruments; thus the choice between strategies becomes one of managerial preference.

More important than the particular hedge strategy is how the strategy will be evaluated in hindsight. From a simplistic view, every hedge will turn out to look like the work of either a financial genius or a financial neophyte. If a futures contract is used to hedge, it has to be that the futures will have either a positive payoff or a negative payoff. There is a natural tendency to second-guess the decision to use the contract when it has the negative payoff, because the company would have been better served to have not hedged. But how can you judge the outcome of the hedge after the fact with perfect hindsight when the hedge was implemented because of the lack of knowledge about the outcome? Hedging is an important decision and must have senior management support. Part of that support is the up-front acknowledgment that the objective of the hedge is to reduce risk, and to achieve the risk reduction always requires some sort of explicit or implicit cost. The hedge should only be judged as to how well it worked to reduce the risk afterward, not whether the futures happen to create a positive or negative cash flow. Hedging strategies will not survive unless they are fully understood by senior management and are judged after the fact with the appropriate view.

MBA Concepts in Action

The role of enterprise risk management has risen dramatically in its importance for corporations over the years. Most large corporations have risk management positions with duties that intersect all the different segments of the organization. For example, Fred O. Pachón is Select Staffing Inc.'s Vice President of Risk Management and Insurance and was named the 2009 Risk Manager of the Year by *Business Insurance* magazine.[9]

Select Staffing Inc.

Select Staffing, a Santa Barbara, California–based company, provides "workforce management services, including recruiting and screening professional job candidates, payroll and time attendance management, on-site supervision, proactive safety programs, and specialty staffing solutions, to a wide variety of client companies, including manufacturing, industrial, clerical, administrative, accounting, finance, information technology, and professional services."

Following the 9/11 terrorist attack, the company was struggling to remain profitable in the wake of the rise in cost of workers' compensation insurance that was increasing every month. However, due in part to the competitive advantage of having world-class risk management programs put in place by Fred Pachón, who joined the company in 2001, Select has shown strong growth both internally and through an aggressive acquisition strategy. Although the company remains privately owned, by 2009 it had grown to annual revenue level of $1.6 billion.

Pachón focused his energies on managing the workers' compensation costs for Select. At times this meant saying no to clients who represented higher than normal likelihood of incurring claims. In total, Pachón programs resulted in the removal of $31 million of accounts that he identified as being responsible for generating too many liability losses. The salespeople were often frustrated with these sorts of controls, but the reduced risk of Select's client base prompted insurance underwriters to lower their quotes for the company's insurance programs. Ultimately the cost of the average claim was reduced by 75 percent, which resulted in a savings for the company in excess of $100 million.

Such cost savings fueled profit growth for Select and also gave the company a competitive advantage in its acquisition program. Over the past seven years Select has purchased 39 different companies, a major contributor to the company's growth strategy. With the in-house ability to reduce workers' compensation costs, Select Staffing Inc. targets acquisitions with high workers' compensation costs and then reduces those costs after acquiring the company. The millions of dollars in cost savings add substantial value to Select, as well as giving the company a clear advantage in the price it can offer to buy a company. As Select grows in size, it also gains bargaining power with the underwriters, which also adds value to the company. In addition, as is true for most acquisitions, Select was able to eliminate redundant labor costs and office space to generate further cost savings.

Risk Management in MBA Curricula

Risk management courses are not specifically offered in every MBA curriculum, and when they are offered they are typically electives and not part of the required curriculum. However, every MBA program provides the principles of risk management across a variety of courses within their curricula. For example, corporate finance and investments rely heavily on portfolio theory for cost of capital measurement and asset management strategies. The accounting principles for hedging are often included in the financial accounting course, as hedging is a common corporate practice and it can have a significant impact on reported earnings. Microeconomics and international finance study the effect of currency risk on firm value. Financial hedging is often taught as a method to manage currency exposure within an efficient market where interest rate parity holds. Finance courses also teach the financial instruments that form the building blocks of hedging: futures, forwards, options, and other derivative securities.

Exhibit 15.14 lists examples of risk management courses offered by some of the top 20 full-time MBA programs.

Exhibit 15.14 Risk Management in MBA Curricula

Business School	Course
University of Chicago (Booth)	Financial Engineering: Cases in Financial Risk Management—required
University of Michigan (Ross)	Risk Management in Banks and Financial Institutions—not required
Northwestern University (Kellogg)	International Operations and Risk Management—not required
	Risk-Bearing Markets and Insurance—not required
University of Pennsylvania (Wharton)	Risk Management—required
	Risk Analysis and Environmental Management—required
	Risk and Crisis Management—required
	Risk Management and Treatment—required
University of California–Berkley (Haas)	Risk Management—not required
	Risk Management via Optimization and Simulation—not required
Columbia University	Risk Management—not required

Notes

1. See Chapter 1 for principles of accounting.
2. We explore probabilities more formally later in the chapter when we discuss financial hedging.
3. See Chapter 5 for a discussion of evaluating capital investment projects using net present value to measure value added.
4. Insurance policies are in reality a special application of options. Although beyond the scope of this book, we can model insurance as the purchase of a put option from the insurance company.
5. For more detail on derivative contracts and financial hedging, see Charles Smithson, *Managing Financial Risk* (New York: McGraw-Hill, 1998).
6. Futures contracts exist for many things, including physical goods, like corn, copper, and oil, as well as for foreign currencies, a U.S. Treasury bond, and so on. Most often futures contracts are cash settled; that is, there is no actual delivery, but rather the parties settle by paying cash to satisfy the contract.
7. It is convenient to assume that no cash changes hands until the end of the contract for the sake of this example. Strictly speaking, however, a futures contract is settled every day along the way, rather than completely on its maturity date. Please see the section on the role of the exchange and mark-to-market to better understand how the futures markets operate.
8. See Froot, Scharfstein, and Stein, "A Framework for Risk Management," HBR Reprint 94604.
9. See www.selectstaffing.com/SelectStaffing/main.cfm?nlvl1=1.

For Further Reading

Allen, Steven, *Financial Risk Management* (Hoboken, NJ: John Wiley & Sons, 2003).

Barton, Thomas L., William G. Shenkir, and Paul L. Walker, *Making Enterprise Risk Management Pay Off: How Leading Companies Implement Risk Management* (Upper Saddle River, NJ: Prentice Hall Books, 2002).

Bernstein, Peter L., *Against the Gods: The Remarkable Story of Risk* (New York: John Wiley & Sons, 1996).

Cox, Louis A., "What's Wrong with Risk Matrices?" *Risk Analysis* 28, no. 2 (2008): 497–512.

Froot, K. A., D. S. Scharfstein, and J. C. Stein, "A Framework for Risk Management," *Harvard Business Review* 72, no. 6 (1994), 91–102 (*HBR* Reprint 94604).

Hull, John, *Options, Futures, and Other Derivatives*, 7th ed. (Upper Saddle River, NJ: Prentice Hall, 2008).

Lowenstein, Roger, *When Genius Failed: The Rise and Fall of Long-Term Capital Management* (New York: Random House, 2001).

Smithson, Charles, *Managing Financial Risk: A Guide to Derivative Products, Financial Engineering, and Value Maximization* (New York: McGraw-Hill, 1998).

Taleb, Nassim N., *Fooled by Randomness: The Hidden Role of Chance in Life and in the Markets* (New York: Random House, 2007).

16

Leading from the Middle

"Who wants to be a middle manager?"

—*Article by Stephanie Armour,* USA Today, *August 13, 2007*

Not many people do. That was the conclusion of this article in *USA Today* a few years ago. The article cited high levels of dissatisfaction among middle managers, perhaps linked to lack of flexibility (and expectations of 24/7 access and response), more work (cutbacks have folded several jobs into one), limited promotional avenues, and general distrust of those above (due to increased layoffs). For someone just starting out with an MBA in hand, these views may seem sobering and disconcerting since the reality of organizations is that someone with an MBA has a greater probability of being in a middle management position than in the C suite. While this might seem like an unsatisfactory or undesirable outcome, it is not.

A fresh look at middle management focuses attention on the important leadership role of a middle manager today. Middle managers these days are not the *Man in the Gray Flannel Suit* icon from the 1950s who follow directions blindly, nor are they generally akin to the bumbling, clueless, or incompetent managers featured in the television series *The Office*. Middle managers today can be strong managers who realize the leadership power they have by harnessing new skills and abilities. Many are revitalizing both their companies and themselves.

Consider the Harris Corporation in Melbourne, Florida, an international communications and information technology company serving government and commercial markets worldwide. Harris's top management, driven by its chief executive officer, Howard Lance, realized that their future lay in growing organically, in other words trying to create new markets and products by thinking creatively about current technologies and expertise. So the company turned to and invested in its *middle managers* to figure out just how such change could occur.

The Harris story exemplifies the new leadership role of middle managers, as leaders of change from the middle. That new role puts middle managers in the position of translation and integration. They take often ill-formed or general directions and make sense of them in light of the business realities. Howard Lance and his team set the strategic direction and overall vision of the company. As the formulators, they recognized only broadly that the future lay partly in growing organically. How that growth would occur or from where it would originate was neither specified nor outlined, nor necessarily even suspected by those at the top. Yet the top team turned to its managers in the middle to translate that very generic directive (organic growth) into business actions and activities that would

301

achieve results. Along the way the middle managers at Harris began to see the leadership role they possessed. What directions were taken and what opportunities were followed (and what were not) were theirs to create and nurture. How to generate excitement and enthusiasm for those new directions and how to motivate others to get on board were their challenges to master. And master they did. The company soon saw success in business growth and innovative technology. In 2009, the company was honored with a Stevie Award in the category Best Overall Company of the Year—More Than 2,500 Employees.

This chapter discusses the emerging leadership role of a middle manager, as well as the different ways of thinking and acting that a middle manager needs. It also discusses why middle managers can find it difficult to be in the middle. The last part of the chapter is a discussion of some strategies for being a leader in the middle.

Caught in the Middle

Being a manager in the middle is not easy. You feel and experience the weight of the requirements and demands from the top at the same time as you hear and see the reactions and concerns from those below in the organizational hierarchy. The end result is either the compression pressure of being in a vice (literally squeezed together by the top and bottom) or the sensation of being pulled into opposite directions (more graphically, pulled apart). Neither of these necessarily create positions of strength, which may be why middle management is an organizational role that is seldom put in a positive light. Middle managers are often seen as the organizational bloat and excess to be downsized or eliminated or they are the resisters of change and innovation who stand in the way of progress or the managers who merely do what they are told and nothing more, thus failing to keep up with the times and trends. They are rarely the individuals who get attention or are given attention within the organization.[1] The attention goes to the top team or the high-potential employees on the rise. While middle managers were seen as victims and heroes for 30 years, since the 1980s their favor has been significantly declining.[2] That is, until now.

What more and more middle managers realize is that their position is a powerful one. The middle vantage point allows them to see more and understand more about what is going on in the organization than either the top or the bottom does. Through the teams that they manage or oversee, they touch many stakeholders in the company and can feel the pulse of the marketplace. They can see the bigger strategic picture on the horizon and they know what the operational issues are now. This "middleness" places them in a position of integration and synthesis more than ever before.[3]

Out of middleness come opportunities and challenges. The opportunity lies in the changes they can craft; so does the challenge. More often than not, the charge given to a middle manager is simple, yet paradoxical, something like "change but don't change" or "fix it but don't break it."[4] They are responsible for helping their companies change, but at the same time they must meet current business goals and objectives. That mission impossible, as it might seem, can send a middle manager's head spinning. Each manager knows how to deliver results and probably has some ideas about what can be done differently, but they are also keenly aware that orchestrating changes can affect the level of results they deliver. However, different results never come from the same behavior.

At the same time, there are lower-level employees awaiting the operational instructions as to what to do next. Those employees know they need to contribute and want to contribute, yet require an overarching view and meaning. They seek answers to three questions: What does this direction mean to me personally? What will it mean for my job and my ability to carry out my work? In the end, will it be worth it?[5] Those employees desire specificity and direction, not because they are unable to think on their own, but because they want to successfully invest their time and energy in profitable endeavors.

So what's a middle manager to do?

Middle Managers as Translators

The role of translator is a new leadership paradigm for middle managers.[6] It is a role that the middle managers at Harris soon discovered. Being a translator calls upon a different way of thinking and acting than they were trained for as well as a different set of skills. In the process they needed to drop some tools they were using and get some new ones.

So what does it mean to be a translator? Being a translator means *being an interpreter*. Middle managers must interpret or make sense of the vision and direction handed down to them and then turn that vision into operating activities for those below them. There is great power in being a translator, having the ability to interpret a new direction and give it operational life. So, for example, when Harris's top management says to find growth opportunities, it is left to middle managers to figure out what that means and how to frame such opportunities so that others in the organization can be excited and contribute. They are able to bring it to life through their own experience, expertise, and thinking.

Oftentimes when we think of an interpreter, we think of someone who is literally converting a message from one language to another word for word or phrase for phrase. Often a word-for-word translation would result in a nonsensical statement, so the interpreter understands and distills the essence of the message into the language that the listener understands. Middle managers sometimes forget that they have the ability to put their own spin on a top directive. This does not mean ignoring the essence of the directive or changing completely the substance of the message just because they feel like it, however tempting. It does mean putting the message in their own words or terms so that it becomes meaningful to them, not to mention those they work with.

Take the example of two middle managers charged with establishing an R&D center in China for Cisco. The company said essentially, "Get us into China." These two managers, however, had a strong set of beliefs about how such a center should be structured, what it should do, and how the operation should be more than another outsource location. These managers wanted the center to be a positive creator of new intellectual capital and technology for the corporation as well as a training ground for strong global managers. They took the corporate directive (get us to China) and made it their own, growing to more than 300 employees in three years.[7]

In fact, being a translator is a *two-way interaction*. A huge advantage of being a manager in the middle is access to those in the organizational trenches. These are the folks who know what is going on day to day and can tell a middle manager in no uncertain terms whether an idea will fly or whether there is a better way to deploy a strategy. Sometimes those implementers (organizational employees who just get the job done) have great ideas. The famed GE Workout strategy of the 1990s was based on tapping into the knowledge of operating workers to improve efficiencies and literally work out unnecessary practices and procedures. A strong middle manager creates a two-way interaction and interprets the messages from the top in light of the implementation realities of those underneath. Take for example Philipp Justus at eBay Germany.[8] Justus was directed by San Jose to bring the corporate platform into Germany. However, his staff quickly pointed out to him the dangers and difficulties, given the very different customer base and use of credit within the German user base. It fell to Justus, as translator, to work actively between both groups and integrate the concerns with the need to move forward.

Such seamless back-and-forth between top and bottom also means middle managers must be *multilingual*. They need to speak the language of top management as well as that of others lower down in the company. They need to understand strategic thinking and processes as well as the operational languages of the functional disciplines, such as finance, accounting, marketing, operations, or human resources. It is no surprise that many companies send middle managers to executive education programs where they are exposed to various functional disciplines. In part, these managers are learning to be language facile so that they can talk to finance folks as easily as someone in their own engineering department, for example.

To become effective translators, middle managers also need to act in ways different than those implied by traditional models of change. At its core, middle management is a role for change. J. Kotter outlines his eight steps: develop a sense of urgency, build a guiding coalition, develop the vision and strategy, convey the change vision, empower action, find short-term wins, cement gains, and anchor the new change culture.[9] While this model and lots of others contain very sound change principles, the steps rarely unfold in a linear manner. What middle managers want to know is this: what do I do day to day, minute by minute to encourage that we move forward? Being a translator is what positions a middle manager to best answer these questions. This is where the power of being a translator lies—in real time, every day, through decisions and interactions these managers have with their teams.

Furthermore, this real time, everyday focus demands that middle managers consider:

- Thinking like designers.
- Acting like partners.
- Becoming teachers.

Each set of activities presents unique challenges and opportunities for middle managers. Let's explore these a bit more.

Thinking Like Designers

Design is both a noun and a verb. As a noun, it is "the design," the blueprint, for example, of a building or new product that specifies the key elements and their relationship to one another. But design is also a verb, "to design," representing the process of getting from now to some future state (such as old kitchen to new gourmet cooking space). Rarely does any design (noun) spring forth fully formed; it evolves from a process of conversation and exploration—from design thinking, which is one of the newest and hottest ideas today in management.

Design thinking is *"a process of creative and critical thinking that allows information and ideas to be organized, decisions to be made, situations to be improved, and knowledge to be gained."*[10] According to one online synthesis, design thinking is, among other things, interpretive in terms of framing the problem and evaluating possible courses of action, integrative by synthesizing multiple perspectives, and personal because it considers the unique context of each problem and the people involved.[11] These are many of the characteristics associated with middle managers as translators.

So how can middle managers begin to think more like designers and as a result become better translators? Here are four ideas:

1. *Identify and be guided by core design parameters.* There are always key elements that must guide the design and be incorporated into it. For an architect of a house, that house design might require a central kitchen with connected living space, separate bedrooms on the second story, a view of the mountains, and a big front door. These are the design parameters that guide the design. In a translation context, this means identifying the must-haves of the change—those values, attributes, or characteristics that are fundamental building blocks for the future. Is it entrepreneurship, nimbleness, quality, innovation, reliability, or employee creativity, to suggest just a few? For the R&D start-up in China, the guiding parameter was simply ownership, not outsourcing.

2. *Engage in blue-sky thinking.* Designers consider possibilities—lots of them—first and foremost. One of the elements of thinking like a designer is the ability to create multiple possible futures from the same set of must-haves. Usually design thinking starts with "if anything were possible," initially without regard for constraints. For middle managers this means opening up opportunities and being open to new ideas, looking for new solutions (rather than re-creating someone else's best practices), thinking creatively, and above all not applying constraints or using killer phrases too early.

3. *Recognize that an iterative process is essential.* Designers go back and forth as ideas are refined and the problem better understood. Middle managers go back and forth between those at the top and those at the bottom ferrying ideas, gauging interest or resistance, and framing or reframing until messages work. To design means to continually try out sketches of the future, get feedback, and try again. This is not "get the plan and execute the plan."

4. *Reframe and rephrase, not just communicate.* Oftentimes managers will cite the need to be better communicators as an essential middle management translation skill. Communication is absolutely essential. However, it is more than better communication, an often overused term among managers. As one manager mentioned during an interview: "This is a time when middle managers need to reframe and rephrase how they communicate and what they communicate in order to have it understood differently or finally understood at all."[12] This is what middle managers as translators do, finding new and creative ways to deliver the same message.

Never forget that design thinking is highly collaborative. Thus, it is equally important for middle managers to act like partners.

Acting Like a Partner

No agent of change ever works alone. No middle manager accomplishes his or her goals without the assistance of others. Too often, however, this assistance is thought of simply as involvement—getting others drawn in, engaged, and committed. While involvement is necessary, *partnering is more powerful and absolutely essential.*

Here are some partnering hints:

- *Have a partnering mind-set.* Partnering is about building strong relationships that are based on give-and-take and win-win. Trust is the basis, and the outcome is not about power, winning, controlling, or getting only "my way." Too often we encounter others who say they are about partnering but their actions look more like attempts to control. A true partnering mind-set would be composed of a set of expectations that involves mutual gain, collaboration, and trust. One internal auditor once discussed how difficult this mind-set can be to foster but how helpful it had been in his work. He viewed his job as partnering with his internal clients to help them generate the best reports. This mind-set, he reported, allowed him to be a better auditor because his clients did not fear they were under scrutiny or investigation.

- *Focus on what others will get before focusing on what they need to give.* Most often a manager's first thought when involving others is this: "Here is what I need from you and why I need you to do this." But acting like a partner means something different: "Here is what's in it for you to be part of the effort." When one international manager needed to relocate the office, he asked each employee to indicate on a map where they lived. He made every attempt to select an office location that was within an easy commute of the majority of home addresses. That manager understood that the decision to relocate the office was more than just an economic decision or a space consideration. It was a decision that would affect the daily routines of many families. He was acting like a partner when he answered the question on everyone's mind: "What does this new activity mean to me personally?"

- *Build relationships as well as take care of business.* This is a theme echoed in Chapter 7, Managing People. Acting like a partner means spending time building, maintaining, and, when necessary, repairing relationships. It also means having the interpersonal savvy and awareness to connect in a trusting way with others. One manager once reported that a simple e-mail of "Are you okay?" after a series of devastating storms did more to build that relationship than any number of working lunches or chats over beer. Many managers forget that it is important to connect to the whole person, not just the job an employee can perform.

- *Know whose partnership you need today and might need tomorrow.* As middle managers, it is important to recognize whose help and assistance is needed to cultivate to fulfill your change or leadership mission. Strong middle managers think strategically and carefully about whom they need to involve. One manager kept being blocked in carrying out a project until he built a relationship with another manager's assistant. As a result, the assistant better understood the requests for information and time from her boss. When the project got tough, he never failed to get what he needed quickly. This seems quite simple and reasonable, but in the ever moving and changing workplace, the obvious and simply things are easy to forget. Strong relationships can be great assets when times get tough; bad relationships make the tough times even worst.

Be a Teacher

Every day, every minute, middle managers must be teachers. Teaching is very much a translation process. Good teachers are able to take the knowledge that they have and make it understandable to others. Having expertise is one thing, but knowing how to make that expertise accessible to others involves translating sometimes complex ideas into simple components. Middle manager as teacher means:

- *Learn to be a good learner.* While managers in the middle may have knowledge from the top and bottom to draw from, they must also recognize that there are things to learn—either about themselves and how they interact, a new idea or strategy, or a facet of another of which the manager was unaware. No good teacher dismisses the expertise of his or her students. Good teachers understand implicitly that they have something much greater to learn if they are open to being learners.

- *Watch for and leverage the teachable moments.* Teachable moments are times when another is receptive to learning, and they don't announce themselves with signs or placards. But good middle managers learn to identify and utilize the times when another is ready to hear an important message, get feedback about performance, or really listen to the viewpoints of another. Parenting is one continual lesson in watching for and leveraging teachable moments. We use teachable moments almost automatically as parents. Why not be equally as diligent as managers?

- *Have a teachable message.* Teachable moments must be accompanied by teachable messages. If one is a parent, the teachable message might be "Watch for cars as you cross the street" or "The stove is hot." Strong middle managers know what they want others to learn from a teachable moment, and they have that message at the ready. Consider James Scott, a former battalion commander of the Lynchburg Fire Department in Lynchburg, Virginia.[13] He tells the story of a young firefighter who violated protocol on his first fire. Instead of following directions after a small kitchen fire (open windows and set up fans to clear out the smoke), he instead went around to every room in the house removing plants. He did not remove all the plants, just selected ones. He ended up with maybe 25 plants in the driveway.

    When the firefighters returned to the firehouse to review the fire, James Scott asked the firefighter why he took that action instead of following commands. The firefighter replied that when he was not fighting fires he was a horticulturalist. Because he knew that the many rare specimens in the house would not survive the acrid environment after the fire was extinguished, he decided to take the initiative. James Scott could have reprimanded the firefighter for violating orders. Instead, he expressed his appreciation at the initiative the young firefighter displayed in this circumstance. One of Scott's strong messages in building the fire department was for firefighters to take the initiative when appropriate. And here was an opportunity to reiterate that teaching message. Strong middle managers should always know their teachable messages—those concise, precise statements that reflect a value, a way things can be, the way we want them to be.

- *Recognize that the mail gets delivered at different rates.* Individuals learn, make changes, and adapt to new technologies or procedures at very different rates. Some people adapt to new technology or ideas seemingly instantaneously, like a text message that pops up on your phone. Others seem to take a bit longer, perhaps like receiving an e-mail or even getting a letter by next-day delivery or regular mail. Of course in some cases the mail gets lost and needs to be resent. Middle managers recognize that the mail, their message, the task at hand, whatever it is, is being received and processed at different rates for different people. And they create the time for those around them, not to mention themselves, to assimilate the message.

- *Create firehouse time to cement learning and generate new ideas.* When firefighters are not battling a fire, they are in the firehouse, the place where they live while on their shift. It is the place where they relax and recharge, prepare for the next fire, review past fires, update and stay current with firefighting techniques, as well as maintain the equipment and infrastructure. All this so that when the alarm sounds, they are ready. Unfortunately, managers, especially middle managers, report spending most of their time (upwards of 90 percent) on the fire grounds, which is where the fire is burning.

Middle managers need "firehouse time," and so do the people who work for them. Think of firehouse time as time during the working day when a manager takes a moment to think quietly, talk to an employee, read an interesting article, or simply let his or her mind wander. It is a space for reflection and learning. Managers might get ideas on the fire grounds. However, firehouse time is needed to really cement the ideas and learn from them. Successful middle managers *create firehouse time* so that their people can reflect and improve on what they do. These need not be large blocks of time. Firehouse time could be 10 minutes at the beginning of staff meetings to share challenges; 15 minutes during which e-mail, voice mail, and knocks on the door are ignored; a quick walk to talk to a colleague for no reason; or pausing in a stairwell to exchange a hot idea with a colleague. What is important for firehouse time is creating a space in which new ideas can emerge. Fire grounds are about performing, but learning is strengthened in the firehouse.

But what if, after reading the chapter so far, one question might be this: "Okay, I get middle managers as translators. As a middle manager I experience that middleness. I can see how thinking like a designer helps, I recognize the importance of acting like a partner, and I experience every day the need for me to teach. But I don't know where to start."

You may be having difficulty because you need to drop your tools.

Why Tools Aren't Dropped and What to Do about It

Two major forest fires have garnered a great deal of attention and research: One in 1949 in Mann Gulch, Montana, and the other in 1994 in South Canyon, Colorado, at Storm King Mountain.[14] These two wildfires shared similar characteristics. In each, crews were deployed into those canyons to clear out the combustible brush. In the event the fire moved in that direction, it would be stopped for lack of fuel. At Mann Gulch the grass was nearly waist high and very dry. South Canyon was home to many juniper berry bushes, which contain a natural yet highly combustible resin. Nothing on either one of those fateful days indicated that the respective wildfires would move in the direction of those canyons. Yet, unbeknownst to the firefighters, each wildfire exploded in a new and foreseen direction—directly toward them. Fueled by grass and bushes, each fire raced over the ridge and down into the canyon and sent the firefighters scrambling up the steep slope. Between the two fires, 27 firefighters (23 men and 4 women) died, unable to reach the safety of the opposite ridge. Forensic research showed that they might not have died if they had dropped their tools.

Wildfire fighters or smoke jumpers wear all the turnout gear of ordinary firefighters, but in addition carry with them the tools needed to fight remote fires—tools such as a pickax, shovel, chainsaw, and extra gasoline. When the call to drop tools and run was made, 27 firefighters either didn't heed the call or hesitated too long and were overcome by the flames. What does dropping your tools have to do with middle managers and leadership? Everything, actually.

Consider failure to drop your tools as an analogy for not changing, not adapting, or not being flexible. Being a middle manager is more and more calling upon different skills and approaches than ever before. Economic changes and uncertainty, advances in technology, and changes in workplace demographics are just a few of the circumstances that challenge not only the strategies and activities that have worked successfully in the past but the business models we use. To a greater and greater extent the skills and abilities that brought managers to where they are in the middle may not be the tools to help them reach future success. Managers just beginning their careers remember that time (generally when they were in their late twenties) when they realized promotions over time were more related to interpersonal and political skills than to quantitative abilities. To be successful, those managers had to embrace these new tools and learn to put aside strict reliance on those old ones. For current middle managers, the skills that built one's career to date or assist one in doing the job may not be the skills today's environment needs. The job of middle management is changing; that fact is undeniable.[15] What the managers at Harris Corporation soon discovered was that there might be new tools as translators that could help. But first, they needed to drop the tools they currently had.

The research into each of these fires pointed to 10 reasons why tools were not dropped. Each one of the reasons for not dropping tools has implications for all of us in companies, but especially for middle managers. We discuss the reasons and offer key questions for middle managers to consider. Here is what these fires can tell middle managers:

1. *Some firefighters literally did not hear the call to drop.* Wildfires are noisy, and the Mann Gulch and South Canyon fires were no different. The sound of the flames and the updrafts of wind created a deafening roar. When the call to drop was made in the South Canyon fire, some firefighters literally did not hear it. Organizations, too, are noisy places, and middle managers are in the loudest part of the company. Middle managers are constantly bombarded by the noise of every layer of management—rumors, complaints, tensions, questions, concerns, issues, dilemmas, challenges. Sometimes that noise is barely discernible. Sometimes the noise can be heard, but its level is manageable. But at other times the noise is deafeningly loud. *The key questions for middle managers: How can you get your messages (of change, of translation, of leadership) through the corporate noise? Alternatively, how can you put on your noise-reduction headphones in order to keep going, despite the uproar around you?*

2. *There was no rationale given, no justification offered.* When the call came in that the fire was on the move, some firefighters hesitated because the data did not make sense in light of the situation they were currently experiencing. As professional firefighters, they had checked all the relevant indicators that would predict the fire's behavior. There were no visible signals of its movement. And with heads

down in the canyon digging trenches, the firefighters were not focused on the red sky on the horizon. Creating changes when no change seems needed is the hardest change of all. But that is exactly what is being demanded of middle managers. *The key questions for middle managers: How do you ensure that people have the right information so that they can see the importance, the urgency, the threat, and thus the need to act and act now? How do you determine ahead of time just what that best information is yourself?*

3. *There was no or little trust in the messenger.* Some firefighters did not trust the person delivering the "drop tools" message. In the Mann Gulch fire, the foreman, Wagner Dodge, used a protective technique that was unknown to his fellow firefighters and for which there was no protocol. He started a small fire to clear the ground of combustible material, got down on the burned ground, and ordered his men to do the same. Because he was not well known by members of the fire crew, they did not know whether they should trust his suggestion, let alone follow his orders.[16] Some didn't. *The key questions for middle managers: How do you develop trusting relationships so that when you have a message to deliver, people will take you seriously? Who do you need to have relationships with now, as well as potentially build for the future so when you have a message to deliver, it will be heard and acted upon?*

4. *Keeping tools meant success and control.* Some firefighters did not want to lose control by dropping the tools instrumental to their success. Their tools allow firefighters to fight the fire and stave off the ill effects of the fire. For firefighters at South Canyon, retaining their tools gave them the means to clear brush if they needed to erect a fire shelter. Tools gave the Mann Gulch firefighters a way to combat any flames that impeded their exit. Without tools, a firefighter has no actual control over his or her fate—or so it seemed. The habits firefighters had developed and the strength of the cause-effect relationships established (tools = success; no tools = no chance for success) made it particularly difficult. All managers develop habits of working from what has been successful or not. Alec Horniman, a colleague at the Darden School, says that "people don't resist change; their habits resist changing."[17] We do what we do because it has worked in the past, and thus, we believe, those actions have a high probability of working again in the future. *The key questions for middle managers: How can you identify and change the habits so important to your present success but perhaps fatal to your future? What models are you using or assumptions are you making that might no longer be getting you want you want or need?*

5. *Admitting failure was not in a firefighter's lexicon.* No firefighter wants to admit that the fire is beyond his or her ability to combat it. Therefore, admitting failure is not easy for firefighters whose job is to save lives and property. In a newscast surrounding some recent fires in California, one firefighter stated that his hardest job was convincing his fellow firefighters that letting one house burn meant saving a hundred others. The fire seasons the year before the South Canyon and Mann Gulch fires were light. Few fires and smaller fires may have given firefighters a sense they could succeed in any conditions. In a can-do culture such as firefighting, an admission of defeat can be embarrassing in the least.[18] In the can-do cultures of many business organizations, no manager finds it easy to admit he or she doesn't

have the answers or solutions, either. *The key questions for middle managers: How do you know when to ask for help? How do you know when your judgment is clouded by overconfidence or an unwillingness to admit failure?*

6. *We are our tools and our tools are us.* Firefighters become acclimated to having the tools instrumental to success with them at all times. Sometimes they are just not conscious of carrying their tools in the first place nor aware of the packs into which those tools might be stuffed. These tools become part of a firefighter's identity and sense of self. Recall all the times when any one of us goes through airport security and forgets to take the change out of our pockets or the cell phone from the holder clipped to our belt. Those items have become part of who we are, just as firefighters' tools become part of their identity and self-understanding. *The key questions for middle managers: How can you develop a sense of self-awareness that identifies the tools you carry versus who you are? How can you also develop an awareness of which tools are no longer effective?*

7. *There was no skill at tool dropping.* Dropping tools ought to mean simply putting the tools on the ground—any ground, anywhere. However, for firefighters dropping tools was not that easy. The tools firefighters use are expensive, so protecting them becomes instinctive. One firefighter, research showed, hunted five minutes for a place to leave his tools so that they would be safe and could be retrieved once the fire passed. He was successful in that the tools were found untouched by the flames, but those five minutes cost him his life. Karl Weick suggests that middle managers have no skill at tool dropping because they have no skill at dropping their reliance on numbers and trusting their intuitions.[19] Numbers are tools and just may need to be put aside for other models. *The key questions for middle managers: What business models are you holding, and how are they influencing, positively or negatively, your decisions? How can you develop more intuition and less reliance on numbers?*

8. *Finding and using a replacement activity takes practice.* Two firefighters died in the Storm King Mountain fire because they did not properly erect their fire shelters. While the fire shelters were not new technology, the conditions under which the firefighters had to deploy those shelters had not been part of their training. The terrain, the strong wind gusts, and the gases that exploded when released by the indigenous plants created conditions not normally experienced. Firefighters had never practiced erecting fire shelters under these severe conditions. Management is one of the few professions for which there is no practice field. Doctors intern, lawyers clerk, airline pilots fly in simulators and with check airmen. The same practice fields do not exist for managers. Yet the firefighters' story reminds us that we don't perfect new skills the first time they are employed, nor are we necessarily ready for new conditions using skills we already have. Skills development takes practice and time. *The key questions for middle managers: How can you create practice fields for yourself to learn new skills or refresh old skills? And if you need to practice, so do the people working with you—so how can you create practice fields for the people who work for you?*

9. *We take comfort that no one else has dropped their tools.* Visualize a line of firefighters traveling up a steep ridge with safety at the top. Firefighters at the front of the line, almost to the top of the ridge, would have little reason to drop their tools,

as they would be almost out of danger. The firefighters at the bottom of the canyon, most in danger, would probably be looking at the folks in the middle but taking great comfort that no one else had dropped their tools. As a middle manager, you are that firefighter in the middle, one of the ones not dropping tools. While those at the top may have no reason to drop their tools because they are safe, you, as a middle manager, may be endangering those under you who look to you for guidance. If you don't drop your tools, no one else will. In other words, the onus of change, or setting an example, rests with managers in the middle. *The key question for middle managers: Do you have the courage to step out of line and drop your tools?*

10. *Small changes seem trivial.* In both fires it was demonstrated that if firefighters had dropped their tools, each would have traveled an additional eight inches per second. While this seems like an inconsequential and trivial distance, in five minutes every firefighter at Storm King Mountain would have traveled an additional 228 feet, given their existing rate of movement. Safety would have been within reach. Oftentimes managers want to make big changes and have a big impact. However, it is those small, seemingly inconsequential decisions or actions that make an incredible difference over time. As translators, middle managers are making those small steps with every action, every reaction, every inaction. *The key questions for middle managers: What is the equivalent of your eight inches per second? What small changes can be made that over time make a tremendous difference?*

Conclusion

Rather than caught in the middle, middle managers are at the nexus of organizations. They have the ability to connect with the strategic world of those at the top as well as the operational realities of those employees in the trenches. What may seem like pressure is a gift of sorts, the gift of access and potential insight. While the challenges are real, the opportunities are immense. Middle managers are translators who have the ability to create new pathways in our companies. Their central position makes them easy conduits of information flow and activities. No longer is it helpful for middle managers to think of themselves as pressured or pressed. Middle managers can be powerful forces in our companies. When they think like designers, act like partners, and become teachers, they benefit all those around them. When they begin to drop their tools and take on new ones, they create the organizations of the future.

Notes

1. See T. deLong and V. Vijayaraghavan, "Let's Hear It for the B Players," *Harvard Business Review* 81, no. 6 (2003), 96–102.
2. Paul Osterman, *The Truth about Middle Managers: Who They Are, How They Work, Why They Matter* (Boston: Harvard Business Press, 2009).
3. Barry Oshry has written and spoken about middleness. The site at www.executive forum.com/PDFs/oshry_synopsis.pdf accesses a presentation he gave in 2003 in which he discusses middle issues and challenges.

4. This phrase is a classic quote from the Harvard Business School case study, "Peter Browning and Continental White Cap." Copy available at www.whitecapllc.com/ HarvardBusinessReview.pdf.

5. L. A. Isabella, "Managing the Challenges of Trigger Events," *Business Horizons,* September–October 1992. Article available at http://findarticles.com/p/articles/mi_m1038/is_n5_v35/ai_12774369/.

6. I first documented the notion of translator in my doctoral dissertation in 1984. The idea was expanded in a book chapter in 1986. L. A. Isabella, "Culture, Key Events and Corporate Social Responsibility," in *Research in Corporate Social Responsibility and Performance,* ed. J. E. Post (Greenwich, CT: JAI Press, 1986).

7. From a case study, "Cisco Switches in China: The Year of Assurance," Darden Business Publishing.

8. See Harvard Business School case study, "Philipp Justus at eBay Germany (A)," 402007-PDF-ENG, 2002.

9. See J. Kotter, *Leading Change: Why Transformational Efforts Fail* (Boston: Harvard Business School Press, 1996).

10. Quote copied from http://noisebetweenstations.com/personal/weblogs/?page_id=1688.

11. Read more on this topic at http://noisebetweenstations.com/personal/weblogs/?page_id=1688#ixzz0MBlGcFUr.

12. Personal conversation with chapter author.

13. Story told by James Scott when he visited a Darden class at the University of Virginia to discuss the case "James Scott and the Lynchburg Fire Department."

14. This section on dropping tools draws on the work of Karl Weick in 1996. See "Drop Your Tools: An Allegory for Organizational Studies," *Administrative Science Quarterly* (1996): 301–313. This article challenged organizational scholars to examine and drop the research tools they had used for so long. I've adapted the core premises in that article to speak to middle managers and their ability to change and adapt. In addition, I've drawn implications that parallel the experience of middle managers.

15. Osterman, *Truth about Middle Managers.*

16. As referenced in Weick, "Drop Your Tools," 306.

17. Statement used by Professor Alec Horniman, Darden Business School, University of Virginia.

18. Personal communication, Karl Weick, August 23, 2009.

19. Personal communication, Karl Weick, August 23, 2009.

Managing Teams

Keyword: "managing teams":

- Google Scholar, 0.12 seconds, about 6,290 hits.
- Amazon.com, 10 seconds, 155 books on this topic.
- General Web search, 0.43 seconds, upwards of 617,000 sites.

There is no shortage of information about managing teams. There are books and articles, both scholarly and practitioner based, as well as consultants and consultancies ready to lend their expertise to teams and team building. To some extent the proliferation of information on and resources for teams and managing teams stems from the fact that teams are one of the primary business conduits today. Cross-functional teams explore and implement new business strategies, departmental units strive to work as internal teams as opposed to a set of loosely connected individuals, and production floors assemble workers into teams for increased integration and coordination across stations. In recent years especially, virtual teams span time and location, enabling individuals to connect anytime, any place, for any reason. In fact, the very nature of work is changing such that presence in an office is no longer required. An individual can work from home in Virginia but be part of a team in Boston, Massachusetts. Dual teams, one in India and one in the United States, can be charged with working together to develop software. Any individual manager is often both someone on a team and someone in charge of another team.

Threaded through all the disparate advice and ideas available online and in print, there are commonalities, however. Chapter 7, Managing People, provided a few basic principles generally covered as part of an MBA core course in organizational behavior. Chapter 7 discussed how teams evolve over time, the importance of group norms in guiding team behavior, and the roles needed for effective teams. This chapter builds on those principles by looking more in depth at what it takes to create and sustain high-performing teams. To begin, we need to understand what is at the core of any high-performing team—teamwork.

The Essence of Teamwork

Every year since 1980, the Romanian women's eight has received an Olympic medal in rowing, in 2000 and 2004 winning the gold. No doubt these women were all strong individual rowers and competitors, but what it takes to row together with seven other people is a true manifestation of teamwork in action. For those unfamiliar with the sport of rowing, an eight has eight rowers, each with one oar, who sit on sliding seats in a narrow boat, facing backwards. The coxswain (cox) faces the rowers, steering down the course while orchestrating when and how fast the boat needs to move.

Winning boats share some common characteristics. First, every rower on that boat must have a high level of mastery of technique, rowing strongly and well and at a commensurate level of mastery as other team members. Second, each rower must learn to row *with* (not against) her fellow rowers. As a member of the boat, each rower must learn how to follow and lead simultaneously. The rower in the stroke seat is leading the rowers, but following the pace and strategy set by the coxswain. The rower in seven seat just behind stroke "watches the neck in front of her," following stroke's lead, and by so doing simultaneously sets the pace for the rower in six seat and so on down the line. For the boat to travel at maximum speed and efficiency, all rowers must row together, meaning putting their paddles in the water at the same time, taking their paddles out of the water at the same time, and moving up and down the slide in unison.

At its core, the sport of rowing is all about teamwork. The athlete trying to stand out in an eight will only make the boat slower; individual star status does not make a good crew. The crew made up of individuals willing to sacrifice their personal goals for the team will be on the medal stand together. Winning teammates successfully match their desire, talent, and bladework with one another.[1] Put in the context of business, what will make the difference in one team being great and the other team not is how they team with each other. Great individuals create a great team only when they work with each other as partners. Think of *teamwork as a process of partnering with a distinct group of individuals to accomplish an objective meaningful to all.*

This definition has four nuances worth noting:

1. Process implies being dynamic and fluid over time, not static or routine. Just possessing certain attributes or characteristics does not ensure or directly result in good teamwork. Nor does doing something well once connote teamwork. Teamwork is an ongoing evolutionary process of continual interactions that requires attention and effort on the part of all involved.

2. Partnering implies collaborating with, not working against others on the team. Good teamwork cannot exist if members of the team compete with one another for time, attention, resources, or number-one status. Competition is a motivator, but competing internally is not the road to good teamwork. *Partnering with* requires recognized interdependence and collaboration, not independence, dependence, or competition.

3. Good teamwork evolves because individuals know who their team members are. They know each other's strengths and weaknesses and know how to leverage the first and minimize the second. Individuals also understand their role and contribution to the team, both tangible and intangible. They are the right members for this team.

4. The definition of teamwork does not include a one-size-fits-all objective. While a business objective, such as increasing market share by 10 percent, may provide the context for the team's being formed, the team must internalize the goal in a way that is meaningful for them. Not everyone may have the same personal goal, but everyone shares the same overarching and meaningful goal. Everyone on the team is connected with the goal and has made it his or her own.

The Case for Strong Teamwork

There are two important reasons for strong teamwork. One has to do with the business realities faced today. The other has to do with the leadership skills learned through the execution of teamwork.

Business Needs Demand Teamwork

Working in teams is not new to business. That point has been underscored. What is different and new, however, are the conditions making teamwork a competitive business necessity. Most companies can no longer engage the marketplace solo without the support of external or internal partners. Working together with others, whether they be inside the company or outside in the competitive arena, is management of the future. Here's why:

- *Environmental complexity and pace.* The rapid pace and general uncertainty of the business climate require a more complex approach or thinking process. Clearly two heads are better than one, and multiple heads can be even better. Today's companies require that individuals, in order to get the work done, increasingly work together, not alone, and involve others outside their department, function, or area. This often means involving individuals over whom there is no direct authority or responsibility. It is more and more difficult to compartmentalize tasks under the exclusive purview of one company department.

- *Drawing upon multiple sources of information is required for success in today's marketplace.* No one individual has all the information required at a given time. Information may be distributed among a variety of individuals and must be pieced together in real time. Think of firefighters who arrive at a fire with little or no understanding of the nature of the fire except what they see or hear reported over their radios. Some firefighters will have information concerning the roof of the structure, others of the interior upper floors, and still others of the subterranean levels. Without data from all these sources, there cannot be a complete and full fire assessment. Multiple people gathering multiple pieces of information are required for a full evaluation. In addition, the source of the best information is rarely constant. Sometimes firefighters in the kitchen know more than firefighters on the roof; sometimes it is firefighters in the bedroom or attic who have critical data. Sometimes people lower in the company have the best information and should be part of the team. Sometimes top management has less information than anyone in the company.

- *There is an increasing need for varied perspectives and diverse thought.* As businesses move into totally new markets and parts of the world, teams are needed to provide diversity of perspective and vantage point. Consulting cross-functional specialists or tapping into the knowledge of diverse individuals may ensure that a variety of lenses are used to view problem situations and frame solutions. Consider the simple story of the truck that got stuck under a bridge. All the engineers gathered around were unable to figure out how to bump, rock, or cajole the vehicle loose. It was a young boy who finally suggested that the men simply let the air out of the tires, lowering the truck enough to drive it through. When different perspectives are available within them, teams increase the probability that creative solutions will be found.

Teamwork Augments One's Leadership Skill Set

Good teamwork today defines leadership ability tomorrow. There is probably no company today that does not measure or consider the quality of its leadership as dependent on its ability to create and work through high-performing teams. Those who study highfliers, and how to identify them, regard bringing out the best in others (that is, fostering good teamwork) to be at the top of the merits list. High-potential leaders in training have a special ability to pull people together into highly effective teams. They are able to work with a wide variety of people, drawing out the best of them and achieving consensus in the face of disagreement. We have long contended that the skills needed for partnering in external alliances—constituting the capacity to enhance teamwork—are the leadership skills of the future.[2]

The Good, the Bad, and the Ugly Concerning Teams and Teamwork

The business and leadership case for teams and teamwork is compelling. While teams have many benefits, teams also have negatives. It is important to understand both.

On the Positive Side

Teams can make better decisions than individuals can. The perspectives, creativity, and thought processes that can be tapped in teams on average far outweigh the work of any one individual. The power of collective thinking was brought out in the story of the Apollo 13 mission to the moon, documented in the film *Apollo 13*. After a devastating explosion crippled the spacecraft, engineers on the ground had to come up with a way of filtering increasingly lethal levels of carbon dioxide out of the cabin air. Creating a filter for this purpose meant quite literally fitting a square part into a round hole, using only the equipment available onboard the spacecraft. The NASA engineers combined their talents and ideas to accomplish this task.

The quality of team members' solutions will be in direct proportion to the quality of the teamwork they exhibit. Given limited information or a new situation, teams can develop better solutions than any one individual by pooling knowledge and reasoning out the situation. Good teamwork is the product of practice, takes time and effort to develop, and needs a supportive context in which to thrive. While the benefits of teamwork are enormous, teamwork is not without its dark side.

On the Negative Side

Teams do not make decisions quickly. Teams require time: time for team members to understand their individual and collective talents and ways of working; time to understand the problem collectively and to agree on a direction; time to work the process as well as the task; time to achieve simply adequate discussion. If a speedy decision is necessary, teamwork may not provide an advantage. In addition, teams are conflictual. There will be disagreements, dissent, and arguments simply because groups of people rarely agree immediately, see the same situation in exactly the same way, or hold identical expectations for moving forward. By virtue of their very nature, teams place individuals in situations that draw out issues.

What becomes more important than the inevitability of conflict is how poised the team is as a whole and how skilled its individual members are at working with others in a collaborative setting. Egos need not apply in teamwork, and not standing out in a team is one of the hardest management tasks. Good teamwork requires members to voice concerns and disagreement. While there will be conflict and disagreement even in strong teams, the distinguishing factor between good and poor teamwork is the length of time a team spends arguing and the productive nature of these interactions. Conflict that encourages members to think in different or new ways or that brings out critical issues for discussion or that identifies stumbling blocks to success has positive attributes. Conflict that targets individual dysfunctional members, causes the same issues to resurface again and again, or degenerates into personal attacks on individuals is conflict unbecoming of a strong team process.

Different Teams, Same Teamwork Needed

The process of teamwork can take place across many different kinds of teams. Each kind of team presents unique challenges to teamwork and to the team itself. This section highlights some of the teams we see most often in business and the teamwork issues they face.

Management Teams

Management teams consist of executives within a business unit or function who are responsible for that function or unit. Thus, the management of a plant (composed of manufacturing, sales, finance, marketing, etc.) would be considered the management team. The job of management teams is to orchestrate organizational actions in a way that adds value to the company, its shareholders, and its stakeholders. In the least, management teams are responsible for linking the activities of a variety of departments or individuals and moving them toward a desired goal. The top management team refers to the executives at the apex of a company. They comprise the constellation of executive talent reporting to the CEO and responsible for running the company. While these individuals may refer to themselves as a top management team, they are often not a team at all.

The use of the word *team* can be a misnomer. The challenge of teamwork is embedded in the job itself. In managing individual departments or business units, a manager's focus is silo-based. The manager concentrates on the importance of that entity—its goals, its challenges—and less on the goals and challenges of other units or areas, especially when rewards are based on that unit's performance. Working collaboratively with other business units or departments, knowing that helping them might mean less for your department, is a hard pill to swallow. Yet what can make a management team (top or other) a team is the fact that, as a collective unit, it is focused on the strategic direction of the firm as much as its individual management members are focused on their particular slices of the enterprise. Team members understand the impact that decisions made in their function or business unit will or might have on the functions or business units of others in the team.

Task Forces or Project Groups

These types of teams are short-term groups of cross-functional participants brought together because of their specialized expertise to confront a defined organizational issue or challenge. A task force or project group might be formed to develop a new product, design a prototype, research the company's strategic direction, or evaluate its price positioning. In these teams the leader has a defined role as liaison between the organization and the team. Because of the short-term focus, established procedures are needed to ensure efficiency of outcome. The team especially needs to adhere to well-understood and agreed-upon measures concerning information development, data sharing, and decision making.

The downside of task forces is that they become a political microcosm of the company and its politics. Particularly if the task force assignment is politically charged, members may impose their own personal agendas or may be tempted to force a direction beneficial to their business unit. Following an established procedure for collaboration can help the task force be objective.

In today's companies, task forces are able to take advantage of technology to carry out their assignments. Sometimes one or more task force members are physically located in different geographical regions, increasing the need for more effective communication and processes. Generally the business issues tackled by such project teams are so complex that members must interact with outside vendors, customers, internal partners, and peers. No longer is a task force simply a solitary body making a given decision. They are decision makers, researchers, policy advisers, and change agents.

Virtual Teams

Virtual teams are those teams that must accomplish their tasks by working across distance, time, and/or organizational boundaries and by using technology to facilitate communication and collaboration. One feature distinguishing virtual teams from the task forces and project groups mentioned earlier is geographical diversity. Teams are virtual when all members work in different parts of the world and communicate primarily via electronic or other non-face-to-face means. While these teams can come in many forms,[3] their use in today's global companies is increasing. Project innovation can be the result of people working on several continents: Software programming may follow the rising of the sun, as 24-hour programming work travels the time zones.

Understanding the challenges to teamwork when members cannot interact face-to-face is vital to the health and success of a virtual team. That means finding ways to make conversations more personal and to create one-on-one time with individual team members.

Professional Support Teams

These are teams of front-line individuals whose output is tangible and repetitive day after day, such as production teams or customer service representatives. Teams on the production floor may come together to make sausage, assemble a motor or motor component, craft a downhill ski, or produce a pharmaceutical drug. Support teams in customer service may be part of a call center or customer service hotline, taking phone orders, booking airline reservations, or discussing billing disputes or phone service. All members do the same kind of work, which teams them together by task. These individuals often manage to supervise their own quality, schedule their time, maintain equipment, and even in some companies hire and fire their own team members.

While the output of these kinds of teams is not often considered strategically high-level, their good functioning is essential to smooth product production and/or to maintenance of the company's good image with its customers. Creating a team environment suitable for the complexities of their jobs has also proven to increase employee satisfaction and performance.

Action (or Performance) Teams

Action or performance teams are those groups of individuals who demonstrate highly specialized and collective skills in a time-limited, intensive fashion. Team members are skilled, highly trained professionals who come together for a designated performance event. Teams that fit this category would include surgical teams, cockpit crews, athletic teams, firefighter or rescue teams, or professional musicians and theatrical performers. These teams combine established routines and training with improvisations dictated by the environment. For example, a surgical team may be executing a routine operation, following established procedures. Yet, if an anomaly should present itself, the team must react quickly, decisively, collaboratively, and sometimes uniquely. Each team member must know what the other members have been doing and can expect to be doing at all times. Because of this, performance team members often train for years to reach a level of individual expertise and collaborative ability. That is why, for example, surgeons in the United States are apprenticed for up to eight years before they can receive certification as lead surgeons.

A high degree of coordination and readiness is essential in such teams. Emphasis on these teams is on every individual performing his or her task expertly and flawlessly at precisely the right moment. No orchestra can deliver a pleasing symphonic performance unless each musician plays masterfully and in concert with the musical score, the direction of the conductor, and the other performers.

The Platform for Strong Teams and Teamwork

If teams come in so many different forms (i.e., management teams, task forces, and project groups) and have such a diversity of objectives, are there fundamentals of teamwork or effective teams that transcend the type of team? How can you ensure that the team and teamwork your company creates harnesses more of the good than the bad? Consider a biological analogy: the genus mammals. Many different animals fall into the classification of mammals. Humans are mammals, but so are whales, horses, pigs, deer, and bears, for example. Obviously these mammals do not look the same. However, to be classified as a mammal, any species must display four characteristics: They (1) are warm-blooded, (2) give live birth to their young, (3) suckle their young, and (4) have hair. Even though mammals can come in very different shapes and sizes, they must share the same four characteristics.

The same is true of teams with strong teamwork. There are a number of characteristics that strong teams have in common, independent of the type of team. While there is not one way of organizing that defines or distinguishes good teamwork, there are characteristics that must be present for strong teams and teamwork to evolve:[4]

- *Goal compatibility.* Strong teamwork is based on the individuals on the team having compatible goals. This does not mean the same goals, by any means. It just means that the goals each individual has must complement or be compatible with the goals of others or of the group as a unit. In an orchestra, everyone has the common goal of a good performance, even though musicians may have individualized goals depending on their instrument and their training. Thus, for example, one musician might be more interested in mastering a complex musical score, while another is interested in the challenge of the live performance. Each individual goal can be accomplished within the context of the team's goal—give an outstanding concert. In addition, the team, in this case orchestra, accepts the multiple interpretations of the goals that team members will strive for.

- *Trust and commitment.* Strong teamwork is based on a sense of commitment to the group and a sense of trust in the individuals on the team. *Trust* is a word that is used quite liberally. While easily spoken about, trust is difficult to earn and can be lost very easily. Trust takes time to develop; it does not pop up in a group fully formed. The more closely individuals work together, the greater the need for trust. Groups of firefighters need to trust their fellow firefighters, as they are responsible for each other's lives on the fire grounds. Surgeons need to have trust in their operating room staff as the patient's life is literally in their hands. While not as dramatic, teams in business with strong levels of trust in each other's competence, intentions, and commitment to each other have a performance edge.

- *Interdependence.* Strong teamwork is characterized by high levels of interdependence. What one individual does (or what one department does) affects the rest of the organization. Teams with strong teamwork understand the integration of their activities and decisions. Management teams need to understand that marketing decisions may affect production and engineering. Being strongly interdependent also connotes that decisions that optimize one's own area may not be best for the corporation. A recognized sense of interdependence puts the burden on the higher goal. It is more about the enterprise than any individual unit within that enterprise.

- *Open communication.* Good teamwork means that individuals on those teams have open, honest, and relatively codeless conversations with one another. This does not mean that folks tell all without tact. It does mean that people on the team can speak honestly and openly about what is on their minds without fear of retribution or attack. This is not implying that good teamwork does not involve conflict and disagreements. It often does. However, good teamwork at its core helps to dissipate conflict constructively before it explodes into a serious conflagration.

- *High levels of coordination.* Members understand that the work they do affects and is affected by one another. Not only is there interdependence, but there is a realization that work must be coordinated. Strong teams check in with each other. They realize that their completion or work on a task affects others in the teams. They work in a way that acknowledges their responsibility to the team, such as doing something for the team before attending to something personal.

- *Similar team mind-set.* A team can have all the other characteristics, but if deep down there are any individuals who don't believe in the value of teams or collaboration or who feel that the effort and energy put into teamwork fail to maximize their personal goals or who want star status, this group of individuals does not share a similar team mind-set. Mind-set is important because it is the cognitive structure that frames how individuals on the team interpret what happens and decide what to do. If the mind-set is one of individuals first, then those individuals will act in ways that promote self and not team. In teamwork and collaboration there are no egos and no stars.

Setting the Record Straight about Team Myths

Even with a strong platform for teamwork, myths about teams and teamwork can persist. Acknowledging and refuting those myths brings into focus the true reality of teams—realities that pose natural and inherent yet not insurmountable challenges.

Myths about Teams and Teamwork

There are many myths about teams and teamwork.[5]

Myth #1: Working together lessens the importance of individual contribution. Not true. As stated before, unless an individual's contribution adds value, the team will not progress. Teamwork does not mean the end to individual contribution or to individual mastery. Folks still need to know how to do their best and practice their techniques.

Myth #2: High-performing individuals equal (and ensure) high-performing teams. This is simply not the case, as has been pointed out earlier. Taking talented and strong individuals and assuming that they will create a strong team is a disaster in the making. Oftentimes, high-performing individuals do not have a team mind-set at all, making their working in a team difficult.

Myth #3: Teams can avoid conflict. A fact of life is that teamwork means conflict—at just about any stage. What is more important is that the conflict be acknowledged, planned for, and worked through. A good analogy is to consider that teams have natural "fault lines."[6] When the pressure builds up, the ground has to shake to release that pressure. This is the conflict that often rocks a team. All those little tremors have their place in preventing the pressure from exploding. To hold a view that "Once we get through this conflict everything will be fine" is denying the reality of what collaboration is all about.

Myth #4: Teams should make decisions by consensus. Teams should have a decision-making strategy that makes sense for the team and for the task in which they are engaged. Therefore, if one individual has the expertise and the authority, why shouldn't that individual have the final say on that decision? Teams work best when everyone is appreciated for their value-added contribution to the team, even when the contribution of each may be quite different. In real terms this means that a group must acknowledge that contributions to the softer side of team development are as important as the actual work being done on the team.

Myth #5: Accountability in teams means that everyone is responsible for everything. This, of course, leaves no one accountable for anything. Responsibility in a team lies first with the individual members to do their part to uphold the norms of the team and second with the team to police itself. Accountability lies with each individual.

Myth #6: A good team needs *a* leader. Teams just don't need *the same* leader all of the time. Teams do need leading and they do need leaders. But in high-performing teams, leadership is shared by all team members, even if one individual on the team is the designated leader. Effective team members know when to lead and when to step aside. Everyone must be prepared to step into a leadership role.

The Reality of Teams and Teamwork

When all is said and done, teamwork requires coming to grips with several conflicting tensions that are paradoxical in nature. How these paradoxes are understood, interpreted, and balanced within the team are manifestations of the teamwork in which the team engages.[7]

Paradox 1: Embrace individual differences *and* collective identity and goals. Strong teams need to be about both the individual and the team. When focusing on individual members, there is concern for individual priorities, skills, demands, expectations, needs, and desires. While each individual may have different individual personal goals and characteristics, the team needs to have a collective identity. Everyone wants to be part of something bigger than themselves,[8] which is how teams can be both about the individual and about the team.

Paradox 2: Foster support *and* confrontation among members. Team members need to be supportive of each other, understand the pressures each individual may be under, and encourage in good times and bad. However, members need to hold each other accountable for commitments and interactions that work against the team rather than for the team.

Paradox 3: Focus on performance *and* learning and development. Strong teams can't just be about getting the job done or the task accomplished. They need to be also about laboratories for learning and reflecting. Performing and learning are opposite sides of the same coin. The kind of environment we need in order to learn is different from the environment that maximizes performances. Teams need to leverage both.

Paradox 4: Balance managerial authority *and* team member autonomy. Many teams have designated leadership who are responsible for the team's output. The chairperson of the task force or the manager of a business unit often set the agenda of their teams. However, team members also need to experience a sense of autonomy and discretion. Results may be required, but there is discretion in how those results are achieved by each member.

Paradox 5: Attend to the team's place in the company. No team exists in a vacuum. As a result, teams must consider simultaneously individual team members, the team itself, the manager, *and* the company/context in which the team operates. Each of these dimensions has an effect on the team and the team's ability to work together.

Teams versus Groups

Is it a team or a group, or does it really matter? Most recently, differences have been drawn between work groups and high-performing teams.[9] The premise is that teams are better than working groups. The distinction between a working group and a team appears to be relatively clear-cut. Either one has the characteristics of a working group or a true team. The problem is that teams or work groups are dynamic entities that change and develop over time. Work groups have some team elements, though those elements might be shallow or underdeveloped. Managers can spend considerable time diagnosing, arguing, and worrying about whether they have a group or a team. This focus may be misplaced. The distinction between a working group and a team is less important than the strength of teamwork taking place on the team and the degree to which the team and the quality of teamwork are congruent. Knowing how to distinguish great teamwork from not so great teamwork is a first step.

Great Teamwork or Not

Think of a bell curve of teamwork. Some teams exhibit teamwork at its best, while other teams could not be more opposite. Most teams, however, end up somewhere in the middle with a significant opportunity to become even better.

Teamwork at Its Best

Strong teamwork combines learning and partnering for the team and for its members. This level of teamwork, while difficult to achieve, is the level that can produce the most outstanding results and create the highest level of internal satisfaction and personal growth of team members. Members recognize and accommodate the different learning styles and working styles of teammates. Members know what to expect from each individual and how to integrate individual strengths toward goal accomplishment. The team stays focused by maintaining flexibility and drive, by accommodating each other's needs, and by constantly growing and evolving goals and expectations. There are open discussions of team process and honest self-assessments on the parts of team members as to their contributions. Members have an ability to manage and resolve conflict successfully. In fact, conflict is viewed as a signal of opportunity, rather than a sign that the team is in trouble. Rest assured there is conflict, but members take care of each other, as both friends and team members. There is a high degree of camaraderie and friendship among members. They support one another through the ups and downs of everyday life and business. Many times, members are strong friends and definitely more than just professional colleagues.

Teamwork at Its Worst

All of us have been on teams that come nowhere near having the characteristics of strong teamwork. As a whole, the group does not understand or practice any aspects of sound team process. In fact, the members may believe that time spent on team process is wasted time. Members exhibit little or no support or encouragement for other members. Emphasis is on "You do your job and I'll do my job and we'll be done."

There is no shared destiny, meaning that individuals do not connect their work in the group with anything that might happen to themselves or the group. What each does in time 1 is believed to have little or no relationship to what another does or will have to do in time 2. There is virtually no socializing. Members barely get through their required interactions as part of the group meetings. Rarely, if at all, do they engage with one another on a social or friendship basis. Meetings end and folks disappear quickly.

Members feel little personal joy in working with others. It's just a job to do.

The Middle Ground

Most often teams are somewhere in the middle. The teamwork is not a disaster, but it certainly is not ideal. There is uneven commitment to the team and to each other. Members are more committed to the task than to each other's well-being and may identify with selected members more than the team. Members feel at least some degree of trust of one another's abilities and desire to contribute to the team, but that trust may not be uniformly held by all. There are attempts at social interaction, but these attempts are not appreciated by all team members. The team allows some process conversation, but these are never more than five minutes long. The team engages in some process conversations, but most often they are precipitated by one or more dissatisfied team members. There are established systems for who will take a leadership role and when. Some team members feel the team could be better; others feel it is just fine as it is. Team members see the blind spots, but don't know how to work effectively to counter them. The team is having more and more conversations facilitated by a team member. Members are able to leverage internal expertise, but do not become overreliant on it. Social interaction occurs, but for the sole reason of having fun, not necessarily to understand one another better.

Should the Level of Teamwork Be Higher?

That depends. Ideally the highest teamwork achieves maximum benefit for both the individual and the team. However, such teamwork takes time and effort on the part of team members, members who ultimately find what to do to improve how the team operates. Three interrelated criteria for assessing the effectiveness of the level of teamwork deserve consideration.[10]

1. *Does the team's output (e.g., its decisions, products, or services) meet the standards of those who have to use it?* That the team is pleased or that the output achieves some objective performance standard is not enough. If the team's output is unacceptable to those who have to use it, it is hard to argue that the team is as effective as it could be. Moreover, the various constituencies who rely on the team's output may focus on different performance standards (e.g., quantity, quality, innovativeness, timeliness).

2. *Does the team experience contribute to the personal well-being and development of the team members?* Some teams operate in ways that frustrate the personal satisfaction of team members and thwart their development. Other teams provide their members with multiple opportunities to satisfy individual needs. If team members do not feel satisfied with their personal connection to the team, teamwork levels might need to change.

3. *Does the team experience enhance the capability of members to work and learn together in the future?* If the team functions in ways that lead members to distrust one another, the team will find it difficult to work together on future initiatives. For instance, if members feel that there were hidden agendas or unnecessary internal competition, these same members will be reluctant to engage in new projects. If members feel the need to revitalize themselves, correct these processes, or just create new ones, the level of teamwork could be changed.

If the answer to any of these questions is a definitive no or "We are not sure," the level of teamwork might need to be improved.

Improving Teamwork

Improving the level of teamwork is contingent on three critical factors. The first is trust; the second is communication in the team; and the third is the process through which conflict is managed.

Get to Know Team Members as People

The basis of strong teamwork is trust. Find ways to get to know team members. Teams often do self-assessment instruments, such as the Myers-Briggs Type Indicator (MBTI) or Belbin team roles (both mentioned in Chapter 7), to increase their understanding of the contributions and strengths of individual members. Teams often participate together in team-building exercises and outdoor challenge experiences. Teams can enjoy meals together, socialize over happy hour, or merely spend time discussing topics other than business.

Communicating in a Team

As stated earlier, open communication is a critical requirement for any team. Many people would support the importance of communication. However, very few people can articulate precisely what makes good team communications. Here are some requirements:

- *Involve everyone.* First of all, good team communication starts with the involvement of *every* team member. When only a few team members dominate the interactions, vital perspectives and potential information are lost or unavailable. Each team member must ensure that all members of a team are equally and actively involved. Simply asking for the views of more silent members is one strategy. Another strategy is for more vocal team members to recognize the amount of time they dominate the conversation (precluding others from speaking) and be quiet. If you are spending more time talking than listening in a team, you might want to focus on changing your own behaviors first.

- *Avoid assuming understanding.* Words and meanings are not always similar. For example, consider when executives from U.S. Airways arrived in London to meet with executives from British Airways. It was not very long before the team focused on a difficult issue. Everyone agreed "to table" the issue. As a result, the executives from British Airways began discussing the issue, while the American executives shook their heads with surprise. In the United States, to table means to end the conversation; in Britain, however, to table means to begin discussion. Both were tabling but neither was communicating. The lesson: Always test understanding.

- *Stick to one language.* All of us are most comfortable when things are familiar. Therefore, speaking our own language is preferred. It is therefore tempting to lapse into our home language, especially if there is at least one other team member who speaks that language. While this makes us comfortable, it may make others feel alienated or dismissed. There is nothing more frustrating than to sit in a team and listen to several members discuss an issue in their language. The normal human reaction is to assume that they are exchanging secret information. While they most likely are not, the damage to trust in the group may already be done.

- *Whatever the language, understand that not all members may speak it well.* More and more international teams communicate in a language foreign to some members, or conversely, in a second language, such as English, that is nonnative to all team members. When we use our own native language, we can express our thoughts fully, use words and phrasing that optimize what we want to say, and in general achieve the level of expression and emotion we want. When communicating in a new language, however, our communication ability may be limited. It is easy to think that some team members are less smart, less knowledgeable, or less valuable to the team because they may not be as articulate as a native speaker. Making this assumption is dangerous to communication.

- *Avoid misuses of technology.* With all the technology available, more and more teams can rely on electronic exchanges. These are not substitutes, however, for face–to-face interactions. Take the time to communicate face-to-face. Build social interactions for team building. Trust cannot be turbocharged, nor can it be fully built without getting to know a person face-to-face.

- *Balancing advocacy with inquiry.*[11] Most of us are much better at telling than we are at listening. In team communications, there needs to be a balance between making one's point (advocacy) and listening to the thoughts of others (inquiry). Inquiry means taking team time to actively explore the opinions and views of others and, more importantly, to understanding their assumptions and rationales. Advocacy means spending time debating and discussing. Teams make better decisions, we believe, when there is more inquiry than advocacy.

Managing Conflict in the Team

Teams experience conflict, and conflict is not bad. Conflict usually signals to a team that something is not right. Issues may not be addressed to the satisfaction of all, goals might be clashing, and individuals might disagree on approaches. It is not conflict that is bad; it is how conflict is handled that can make the difference in the level of teamwork a team can achieve. Handled well, conflict can unleash creative energy otherwise tied up in disagreements and arguments.

Conflict in a team can exist between individuals on the team or within the team itself. When handling conflict between individuals, five strategies have been identified: collaborating, competing, compromising, accommodating, and avoiding:[12]

1. *Collaborating* emphasizes finding an integrative solution that incorporates the concerns of all who are in conflict.

2. *Competing* emphasizes fighting for a preferred option by arguing for it and by finding weaknesses in the other's propositions. The goal is winning.

3. *Compromising* means adjusting one's stance to another's. In turn it is expected that at some point in the future others will act similarly.

4. *Accommodating* means understanding the importance of the conflict to others and letting them have it their way.

5. *Avoiding* means just that: not engaging in the conflict or ignoring that there is a dispute.

In interpersonal relationships, any of these strategies are reasonable, depending on the relationship, its importance, and the time involved.

When handling conflict at the team level, however, strategies that create a win-lose outcome, such as competing or avoiding, are less favorable. Strategies such as accommodating, compromising, and collaborating tend to produce more successful resolutions, in part because each is based on concern for others, as opposed to primarily concern for self.

Sometimes a team needs a structured methodology to deal with its disagreements and tensions. In those cases, a process advocated for teams within a strategic alliance context can prove helpful. This process is called the "no-blame review."[13] Such a process places the emphasis on surfacing and discussing important areas of disagreement, but without blame, recrimination, or judgment. For those with military backgrounds, the after-action review is quite similar. During such a conversation, the team would discuss its goals, objectives, successes, and shortcomings, as well as how each team member feels about the experience. Finger-pointing or accusations are verboten; communication is based on what is needed for the team to succeed, rather than what any one individual is doing incorrectly. Sometimes teams benefit from considering practices or interactions they wish to continue, those they want to stop, and those they want to change. Overall, addressing conflict at the level of the team places the conflict within the greater context of the team's goals.

Summary

This chapter has introduced the importance of teams and the foundations of successful teamwork. Some of the different kinds of teams that are seen in business settings have been described and the core characteristics that make for effective teamwork across those types of teams identified. Some attributes to assess the level of teamwork have been laid out and strategies have been presented for increasing that level through better communication and conflict management. Although increasing in prominence, teams can be difficult to manage, not to mention belong to, in part because of the paradoxes they contain. However, when there is strong teamwork in a strong team, in rowing parlance "you can hear the boat sing!"

MBA Concepts in Action

Someone wise once said, "A job worth doing is worth doing together." Yet why is it so difficult to work together as a team? The ability to function as an effective team member and/or team leader is a must-have for today's managers, yet, as shown in the following example, it requires a deep understanding of the paradoxes of teamwork. Not only are there issues about how teams function well or not and how to intervene on a dysfunctional team, but there are also implications of poor teamwork on other individuals in the company.

Project Teams at Tireworks AG

As part of an internal management development program designed for high-potential managers, teams of three or four people were created to work on issues of strategic importance to Tireworks AG, a German company. The intent was to challenge those individuals with strategic projects of importance to the corporation and to observe how they handled themselves and the project itself. Sponsored and guided by a senior line manager (the mentor) with a burning strategic problem or question (the project), participants worked in cross-functional and cross-national teams to provide answers and advice. For many participants, the program provided their first business cross-cultural experience—Germans with non-Germans and vice versa; an opportunity to work in English (the corporate business language, but the native language for only a few participants); and a platform for broader general management skills and corporate exposure.

Participants were carefully selected and screened from nominations by their bosses and human resources staff. Being chosen to participate was a great honor. The program had been in existence long enough to produce a string of success stories. One past participant now sat on the *Vorständ*, the German equivalent of the board of directors, and quite a few former participants, because of their senior management status, now mentored projects themselves. For those participants who rose to the challenge, the program and the project could be their ticket into higher management. There had never been a failure example from this program.

The software team was one of six project teams. The title of their project, as crafted by the mentors, was "Software: Product or Service." The project mentors, two senior managers in the automotive systems side of the business, had in mind a project that explored this notion: Was the pricing of the software embedded in brake systems possibly an independent stand-alone product, or was it essentially a service that went with the hardware? This was a challenging question indeed. As automobiles and automotive systems became more complex, electronics, which were governed by software, played an increasingly important role. What the customer saw as a brake system was much more than the metal hardware. Sophisticated software was integral to brake system operation. Industry estimates suggested that by 2020, 40 percent of the car would be electronics, and software would be the integrating core.

Literally from the very first meeting when teams were put together and matched to mentors and projects, the members of the software team project were in complete disagreement about almost every aspect of the project and its development. A 38-year-old German PhD engineer, a 32-year-old German attorney, and an American-born 28-year-old accountant got off to a rocky start. They disagreed on what the mentor wanted them to accomplish and how they might begin to approach answering the key questions. Furthermore, even though there were some personal interest overlaps, the styles of team members mixed like oil and water. The program director suspected that this team would be challenged by its membership, but believed the team members had the ability to figure out their dynamics. However, despite repeated conversations and interventions to help the team gain momentum, the team floundered and its work languished. It was painfully obvious that the team had made very little progress in seven months, and they were slated in just four weeks to give a presentation to an audience of over 100 Tireworks AG top-level executives and managers, including the CEO, and four members of the *Vorständ*.

The program director had to decide what to do. On the one hand, the director could do nothing, letting the team continue as is and letting the results be the results, embarrassing as that would be. Even though it was common knowledge to most in the program that the team was having problems, if the team went ahead and presented the poor project, the program director's credibility could be negatively affected and the desirability of the program itself might be in question. Alternatively, the director could pull the project now. Ending the project would mean that the senior line manager who had paid a significant amount of money for the investigation had wasted his time and money. A third possibility was to intervene with the team. But since former attempts to get this team on the right track had not been close to successful over many months, just what might be done to encourage different results was a challenging question.

While this situation might represent the worst of the worst, it does highlight important team and teamwork issues. The program director needed to weigh the cost of the team's dysfunction on the organization, the program, and the director herself against the probability that the team would pull off a decent project and presentation. In addition, if the director chose to intervene, what series of actions would encourage the team to change their poor teamwork behavior, get down to the task, and create something minimal enough to survive the presentation? No matter which option was selected, the director also knew that a full review needed to happen to understand just why this team was so dysfunctional. This was a teamwork nightmare and a teamwork opportunity for sure.

Managing Teams in MBA Curricula

Courses in teams and teamwork are generally offered as electives in MBA programs, as Exhibit 17.1 summarizes. Given the heavy use of teams in the workplace, many students desire to increase their conceptual knowledge of working collaboratively with others. Many of these electives provide in-depth understanding of group principles, often requiring students to be part of team throughout the course in order to experience teams evolution firsthand. At the Darden School, University of Virginia, the Managing Teams course is unique in that students act as mentors to the first-year learning teams. By observing team case discussions and building relationships with team members and the team itself, the mentors get the opportunity to watch a team evolve and help out as needed. Students get just-in-time delivery of concepts as they experience a safe practice field for team learning and intervention.

In addition, however, to an actual course in teams or managing teams, all MBA students work in teams during most of their MBA journey. These activities provide another significant learning laboratory for team learning. Starting in the first year of a traditional two-year MBA program, students can be placed into learning teams or study groups during their first year of study. These teams or groups provide a learning laboratory for students to work with diverse individuals in high-pressure situations in preparing for

Exhibit 17.1   Managing Teams in MBA Curricula

Business School	Course Offered
University of Michigan (Ross)	Developing and Managing High-Performing Teams—not required
	Leadership Coaching Practicum—not required
Northwestern University (Kellogg)	Leading and Managing Teams—not required
	Creating and Managing Strategic Alliances—not required
Harvard Business School	Leading Teams—not required
MIT (Sloan)	Building and Leading Effective Teams—not required
Stanford Graduate School of Business	Managing Groups and Teams—required
University of Virginia (Darden)	Managing Teams—not required

class and supporting each other during the learning experience. Throughout their second year, students have multiple group projects associated with courses, all of which force them to learn to work together on graded deliverables.

Notes

1. Excerpted from 11 insights into rowing that appear on the web site of the U.S. Rowing Association. (See www.usrowing.org/NewToRowing/ElevenInsightstothe SportofRowing/index.aspx.)
2. For a full discussion of the leadership skills of the future, see L. Isabella and R. Spekman, "Alliance Leadership: Template for the Future," in *Advances in Global Leadership*, vol. II, ed. W. Mobley and M. McCall (JAI/Elsevier Press, 2001).
3. For a more complete discussion of all facets of virtual teams, see http://en.wikipedia. org/wiki/Virtual_team#Basic_types_of_virtual_teams.
4. These characteristics mirror arguments made by Spekman and Isabella in their book on alliance competence. See R. Spekman and L. Isabella, *Alliance Competence: Maximizing the Value of Your Partnerships* (New York: John Wiley & Sons, 2000).
5. These myths have been adapted from J. Beck, "Moving Beyond Team Myths," *Training and Development* 50 (3): 51–56.
6. D. Lau and K. Murninghan, "Demographic Diversity and Faultlines: The Compositional Dynamics of Organizational Groups," *Academy of Management Review* 22, no. 2 (1998): 325–340.
7. Linda Hill, "Managing Your Team," technical note 9-494-081 (Boston: Harvard Business School Press, 1994). See also K. Smith and D. Berg, *Paradoxes of Group Life: Understanding Conflict, Paralysis and Movement in Group Dynamics* (San Francisco: Jossey-Bass, 1987).
8. Drawn from the eight secrets of inspirational leadership proposed by Dan Lyons (www.teamconceptsinc.com).
9. J. Katzenbach and D. Smith, "The Discipline of Teams," *Harvard Business Review*, March–April 1993, 111–121.
10. These questions and their descriptions have been adapted from Linda Hill's technical note, "Managing Your Team," 9-494-081.
11. For a full discussion of these concepts, see P. Senge, *The Fifth Discipline* (New York: Doubleday, 1994).
12. T. Kilman, "The Conflict Handling Modes: Toward More Precise Theory," *Management Communication Quarterly* 1 (1988): 430–436.
13. L. Isabella, "Managing an Alliance Is Nothing like Business as Usual," *Organizational Dynamics* 31, no. 1 (2002): 47–59.

Downloadable Resources for this chapter available at www.wiley.com/go/portablemba5e

Teamwork Paradoxes

18

Starting Your New Career with an MBA

Some people believe an MBA degree is the ticket to the senior ranks of corporate America. Most MBA programs impart the necessary core knowledge—accounting, operations, economics, marketing, strategy, and finance. Many programs help sharpen key leadership skills like communication, judgment, and vision. Yet an MBA education is not complete without the knowledge and skills needed to navigate one's career and, specifically, to land that first MBA job. Embarking on an MBA career requires a carefully planned, precisely executed job search. Key steps in the process include:

- Self-assessment.
- Defining a career objective.
- Researching the market.
- Preparing marketing materials.
- Going to market.
- Tracking and evaluating.
- Landing the job.
- Getting started.

Success requires thoughtful consideration of each step—skipping a step risks delay and rework.

Self-Assessment

The plethora of career options available to MBAs can make defining a career objective a difficult process. In order to be successful in the job and to advance in a career, the job must be a good match or fit with the person applying. A career must fit a person's life in the same way that a glove fits a hand. A perfect glove fit requires detailed knowledge of the hand—the length of the fingers, the size of the palm. Similarly, successful career fit requires thorough self-knowledge. Most top MBA programs build self-assessment into their career development curricula. One common approach is the use of CareerLeader, a Web-based career assessment tool (www.careerleader.com) that measures a person's interests, abilities, and motivations regarding their work. Another approach, Career Next Step (www.careernextstep.com), is based on a course taught for over 30 years at Harvard

Business School and the Darden Graduate School of Business at the University of Virginia. The site employs multiple self-assessments and a proven methodology to help students create a personal profile of their unique interests, values, and ambitions, and then uses this knowledge to identify a career that best matches the student's personal profile. Whatever the methodology, the goal of this phase is a thorough understanding of oneself in order to determine the best career match.

Defining a Career Objective

The next step in the process is to clearly articulate a career objective, based on what was learned in the self-assessment phase and on information gathered in the research phase. A useful career objective starts with a desired function and industry. The function is the type of work (like marketing, finance, or operations); the industry is the setting of the work (financial services, health care, or energy, for example). Most career objectives will have a single function, but may have multiple industries.

Beyond function and industry, a comprehensive career objective will also contain:

- Geographic preference or constraint.
- Size of company.
- Company culture.
- Company position in industry.
- Company approach to development.

Researching the Market

A key enabler of writing a good career objective is a thorough understanding of the MBA marketplace. Research includes gaining a thorough understanding of key MBA functions, industries, and companies. The leading sources for company research are Vault Guides (www.vault.com) and Wetfeet Guides (www.wetfeet.com). Once an objective begins to form, the key deliverable of this stage is a target list of companies that reflects the career objective.

A point should be made that the first three stages—self-assessment, defining an objective, and researching the market—are iterative and circular. As one researches, one discovers more information that clarifies one's career objective and spawns more research. Again, outcomes of these three phases are a comprehensive career objective based on self-assessment and research and a target list of companies.

Preparing Marketing Materials

Once a career objective is clear and a target list of companies is identified, then a candidate creates marketing materials for the job search. The most common materials, of course, are resumes and cover letters, but also needed are networking e-mails, networking profiles, and occasionally references. The core component of each of these marketing pieces is a candidate's story, sometimes called positioning or even the personal brand. The story is a clear, compelling articulation of a candidate's relevance to the target company (sometimes called the buyer's needs) and point(s) of difference versus other candidates for the job. The story is reflected in all marketing materials.

The resume is the most visible marketing piece. Usually one or two pages, the resume is targeted to a particular company (or type of company), is accomplishment oriented, emphasizes a candidate's point(s) of difference, and communicates other transferable skills. Transferable skills are those that a company needs and a candidate possesses. A resume is not a comprehensive work profile or job history, but a selling document that puts a candidate's best foot forward.

Cover letters and networking e-mails amplify the most significant points of a resume and tell the candidate's story in prose form. Critical to the success of a cover letter is its ability to connect the dots, or help the reader understand why a person has done what he or she has done and why the company would want to hire this candidate at this time.

Many professional agencies offer resume writing and cover letter writing services. Writing resumes is not an easy skill; if a person has little experience, then seeking professional help or, at a minimum, getting friendly assistance is advised.

Going to Market

Armed with powerful marketing materials, candidates are ready to go to market—that is, to make themselves known in the marketplace. The most effective means of doing this is networking. Some sources say that 80 percent of jobs are never posted—they are, in fact, found only through networking. Networking by definition is building relationships, particularly in one's area of interest. Networking is not cold calling and asking for a job; it is about making it known that one is seeking a position in a given professional space.

Networking is also about identifying hiring managers and creating interview opportunities. Once hiring managers are identified, a networking conversation may turn into an evaluative interview. Candidates may or may not realize that they are being evaluated. Many times a formal interview will be set up at a later date.

Another important, but sometimes overemphasized, way of going to market is through searching job postings via the Internet. Companies post open positions on their own web sites, and many professional sites exist for mass job postings. A few common ones for MBA jobs include:

- CareerShift (for external job postings).
- CareerSearch (a good company directory).
- MBA Focus (job postings).
- Indeed (job postings).
- RiteSite (executive-level postings).
- MBAinteract (professional network).
- Simply Hired (job postings).

The desired outcome of networking or dropping a resume for open positions is an interview. Interviewing for MBA jobs requires substantial preparation, especially along two fronts: understanding what skills the company is seeking in the hire and determining what the candidate can do for the company (how the candidate's transferable skills might be applied). A candidate should seek a job description before interviewing, so that he or she is clear about what is being sought. Many times a candidate should create a matrix of answers to be thoroughly prepared for all types of questions, like the one shown here:

Hiring Criteria	My Transferable Skills	Best Story That Illustrates This Skill

The second part of interview preparation requires that a candidate thoroughly research the company and the businesses with which it competes. A company's web site is an excellent source of information, especially the "investor relations" section of the site. Many times this will contain the latest analysts' reports and CEO presentations to analysts of the company's strategy. Beyond just reading about the company, the best candidates can clearly articulate the ways in which they can have the greatest impact on the company.

The interview itself can take many forms. The most common is the behavioral interview. This type of interview seeks to identify past behaviors that demonstrate competency of needed skills. Technical interviews dig into a person's mastery of the needed technical competencies for a job, like finance, accounting, or researching skills. Case interviews, most commonly used by management consulting interviewers, present a business problem for the candidate to solve on the spot. Case interviewing is quite rigorous, and, like behavioral interviewing, requires significant practice.

Tracking and Evaluating

Job searching requires attention to detail. Many contacts lead to dead ends, while many lead to other contacts. Calls require follow-up or other actions. Keeping up with the various details can seem endless. Critical to a successful outcome is detailed and accurate tracking. A candidate should keep detailed notes of each conversation, so that a point from a prior conversation can be referenced or a referral can be remembered. Sources for future leads are easily lost in a conversation if not immediately captured. For each call, a minimum of the following should be recorded: name and contact information, names and companies discussed, action steps agreed upon, highlights of conversation, date of next step, and follow-up.

Similarly, like every good action plan, a good job search should be evaluated at regular intervals. In general, an MBA job search will take a minimum of six months. Every month, the candidate should evaluate each element of the search. Has the objective changed? Has the market changed such that the marketing materials need reworking? Have the outreach efforts yielded interviews? Have the interviews resulted in further discussions? In the final analysis, have the actions led to job offers that meet the original objective and constraints?

Landing the Job

Many times the entire evaluation process is quite lengthy. A phone screen interview may lead to an on-site interview, then a series of meetings, then perhaps some form of skills or psychological evaluation, then perhaps more interviews. Throughout the process a candidate should:

- Prepare for every interview as if it's the first one.
- Take notes after the interview on what was discussed.
- Send an e-mail note of thanks and continued interest after each step.

Eventually, the pot of gold at the end of the rainbow—the job offer—arrives, sometimes by phone, sometimes by mail, occasionally in person. Congratulations, but the work is not finished; there are four more steps. Now you need to:

- Thank them.
- Set up a time to discuss all components of the offer.
- Negotiate (if necessary) based on the market and your needs.
- Accept graciously.

A point on negotiation: While negotiating compensation is acceptable and often needed, many MBA hirers have fixed salaries/bonuses that are standard across schools and are not negotiable. When negotiating, consider total compensation, not just salary. Consider components like stock options, paid leave, relocation, and spousal assistance as possible ways to sweeten the deal. In addition, approach negotiation as a problem-solving exercise, not a confrontational one. Work with the company to meet needs, then be prepared to say yes. Consider the fact that the person with whom one is negotiating is likely to be highly involved in future decisions affecting one's career, so a positive process is critical.

Getting Started

Once many of the details of the job offer have been negotiated, the final item on which to settle is the start date. Sometimes the candidate who is the most flexible and the most available is the one who gets the position. Ideally, a job seeker will be able to negotiate a start date at least a few weeks into the future, so that the person can prepare to get off to a fast start in the new job.

First, and not to be underestimated, a person should take a vacation of some sort to prepare his or her mind for the upcoming new position. A thorough job search is exhausting, and, since a new job requires a substantial emotional and intellectual investment, the employee should make sure he or she is mentally rested and prepared.

Second, the first day of work should not be the first day one begins thinking about the new assignment. Much literature exists on how to prepare for the first day. At a minimum, a new employee should research the market and understand the situation being entered. A new employee should have a tentative action plan on what should be accomplished in the first 90 days. Of course, this plan needs to be vetted with a new manager the first week, but the act of thinking through a plan will help a person be mentally prepared for the new challenges.

Finally, a successful job search is self-rewarding given its outcome, but the skills discussed in this chapter should be continually employed, even after one starts a job. In today's business climate, everyone must constantly be proactively managing one's career.

This does not mean that you should be constantly job changing or even job seeking, but it does mean that you should be prepared for unexpected events, both internally and externally. The same skills needed for an external search are also useful for internal advancement. Internally, a senior position may become available. The employee who has been clear about his career objective with his manager and who has networked within the company and made himself known is the one who will be considered first when an opening becomes available. Thus, management of one's own career is a critical learned skill, and it all begins with self-assessment. Good luck!

Index